Austin Dobson

A Paladin of Philanthropy and other Papers

Austin Dobson

A Paladin of Philanthropy and other Papers

ISBN/EAN: 9783743331426

Manufactured in Europe, USA, Canada, Australia, Japa

Cover: Foto ©ninafisch / pixelio.de

Manufactured and distributed by brebook publishing software (www.brebook.com)

Austin Dobson

A Paladin of Philanthropy and other Papers

*Uniform with the present volume, crown 8vo,
blue buckram, 6s. each.*

EIGHTEENTH CENTURY VIGNETTES.

FIRST, SECOND, AND THIRD SERIES.

By AUSTIN DOBSON.

'The characteristic of Mr. Dobson appears to be a singular power of perception and appreciation. It would be difficult to name another contemporary critic with such nicety of observation, and with such a happy faculty of discovering and pointing out the peculiar merits of works well known to all, but in which Mr. Dobson is able to point out some fresh beauties or a new charm of thought or expression.'—*Athenæum*.

'It presents the most exact series of pictures of a certain past society which has ever been given to us.'—*Speaker*.

'These papers breathe the spirit of the philosophic century; they speak its language; they know where to find poetry and humanity beneath the powder and the patch; but, most of all, they know its books and literary people, and write of them with a tender sympathy which to many readers will make these books and literary people more interesting than they would be in themselves.'—*Scotsman*.

'Mr. Austin Dobson has written a book instinct with vitality, abounding in delicate observation, its details artistically selected, its learning most pleasantly disguised.'—*Tablet*.

'Mr. Dobson calls these charming studies "Eighteenth Century Vignettes." Each essay is a mosaic of minutiæ, gathered from every quarter, and exquisitely pieced together so as to form a little picture. Not merely the literature, but the topography and iconography, of the period are at Mr. Dobson's finger-ends.'—*Daily Chronicle*.

'The good qualities which distinguished the first series of Mr. Austin Dobson's "Eighteenth Century Vignettes" distinguish the second. There is the same admirable mastery of facts, minute and complete. There is the same pleasant sympathy with the subject, and the same easy and sufficient power of exposition. . . . An admirable chronicler—in fact, admirable with the knowledge of an expert and the spirit of a scholar.'—*Pall Mall Gazette*.

'. . . The other papers are not less delight-giving; but, after all, the book is not so much one to be written about as one to be bought and read and lent—though only to impecunious book-lovers—and, when it returns to its shelf, to be read again.'—*Westminster Gazette*.

'Pleasant is only too mild and general a word for the contents of a book which, for all its singular unpretentiousness, is very nearly unique at the present day.'—*Manchester Guardian*.

'Mr. Dobson's fresh group of "Eighteenth Century Vignettes" will not disappoint those who felt the spell of its predecessor. The love of letters is in the book. The atmosphere of the age of Swift and Richardson, Hogarth and Johnson, is in these choice and delicately-wrought pages, together with subtle insight, swift appreciation, and lightly-handled but real knowledge. . . . The tender grace of a day that is

A

gone is in this imaginative outlook, as well as much sly humour, an urbane spirit, and a literary judgment which is seldom at fault.'—*Leeds Mercury.*

'There is no one who excels Mr. Austin Dobson in the art of bringing out the permanent interest still surviving in . . . bygone men and things. His Third Series of "Eighteenth Century Vignettes" displays the same nicety of observation, and the same happy power of preserving what is valuable for us in the people and literature and places of his period, that characterize his previous volumes. . . . Needless to say that half the charm . . . comes from Mr. Dobson's own manner, than which nothing could be more adapted for the perfect setting of the material with which he deals—a combination of rare knowledge, an exquisitely light and humorous touch, and absolute sympathy.'—*Academy.*

'The characteristic ingredients of the papers are as good as ever—a little gossip, a little bibliography, a little research (just the tit-bits picked for us out of long-hidden labours), a little criticism, a few telling circumstances of the age, and all mixed plentifully with quiet humour. Arduous work was never given so delightfully frivolous an air. Mr. Dobson hides the pains of his learning and offers us the sweets.'—*Sketch.*

'A Third Series of Mr. Austin Dobson's "Eighteenth Century Vignettes" is very welcome. We hope he may live to complete a baker's dozen of them, and that in his ripe old age he may throw them all together, rearrange the studies in chronological order, and so raise a durable monument to his knowledge, taste, and industry. . . . The preface to the present volume is a copy of octosyllabics that Gay or Parnell might have been very glad to sign. . . . We believe we exaggerate nothing when we say that Mr. Dobson alone of living scholars has the requisite eighteenth-century knowledge for such a work of sustained, minute erudition.'—*Saturday Review.*

'This Third Series of "Eighteenth Century Vignettes" will be very welcome to that circle who during the last twenty years have learned to take so much interest in the life of the eighteenth century, and to find in Mr. Austin Dobson one of the most charming and trustworthy of its historians.'—*Times.*

'The author . . . has enriched our shelves with a book for which no greeting is too warm. Modesty and brilliancy make a capital blend. Before closing this notice we feel it imperative to remark upon the telling manner in which Mr. Dobson occasionally allows a sly humour to escape from him. These sudden freshets of wit are as welcome as cuckoos in March.'—*Literary World.*

'Mr. Dobson has a happy knack of discovering out-of-the-way records long ago forgotten and of shaping them into literary sketches, pleasantly illustrative of a bygone age. . . . The whole book may be read and re-read with pleasure, and Mr. Dobson may be encouraged to further research in the literary mine he has made peculiarly his own.'—*Morning Post.*

'Adequate praise of it [the Third Series] is to say that it is as delectable reading, as bright and informing as any of its predecessors.'—*Illustrated London News.*

'The book, like its predecessors, is full of curious knowledge; and we need hardly add that it is delightfully written. All intelligent readers will hope that Mr. Austin Dobson's eighteenth-century mine is not yet worked out.'—*Spectator.*

LONDON: CHATTO & WINDUS, 111, ST. MARTIN'S LANE, W.C.

A PALADIN OF PHILANTHROPY,
ETC.

GENERAL OGLETHORPE.

FROM AN ETCHING BY SAMUEL IRELAND.

A PALADIN OF PHILANTHROPY

AND OTHER PAPERS

BY

AUSTIN DOBSON

Ipsa varietate tentamus efficere, ut alia aliis, quædam fortasse omnibus, placeant

LONDON
CHATTO & WINDUS
1899

TO
EDMUND GOSSE.

My dear Gosse,

'*Labuntur anni!*'—which reminds me that I have never dedicated a volume of my papers to you. And yet it must be nearly a quarter of a century since we first began to interchange ideas:—a long time to have watched '*les étoiles qui filent*'! Will you accept these Miscellanies in memory of those detached and delightful hours (between Ambition and Despair!) when we have sometimes loved Books for their own sakes, careless alike of those who wrote and those who write about them?

Sincerely yours,

Austin Dobson.

PREFATORY NOTE.

THE majority of the papers in this volume are reprinted, by permission, from the 'Contemporary Review,' the 'National Review,' the 'Church Quarterly Review,' 'Longman's,' and the 'English Illustrated Magazine.' Others are reproduced with the consent of Messrs. Dent, and of Messrs. Kegan Paul, Trench, Trübner and Co. All have been revised or extended; and I hope they will be found sufficiently diversified in subject to justify the motto I have borrowed from Pliny, who, by the way, seems to have been in agreement with the later—

'Wer Vieles bringt, wird manchem Etwas bringen;
Und jeder geht zufrieden aus dem Haus—'

of the Prologue to 'Faust.'

AUSTIN DOBSON.

† March, 1899.

ILLUSTRATIONS.

GENERAL OGLETHORPE . . . *Frontispiece*

OLD WHITEHALL. From Fisher's Plan of 1680

to face page 194

CONTENTS.

	PAGE
A PALADIN OF PHILANTHROPY	1
GOLDSMITH'S POEMS AND PLAYS	33
ANGELO'S 'REMINISCENCES'	61
THE LATEST LIFE OF STEELE	85
THE AUTHOR OF 'MONSIEUR TONSON'	115
BOSWELL'S PREDECESSORS AND EDITORS	137
AN ENGLISH ENGRAVER IN PARIS	173
OLD WHITEHALL	194
LUTTRELL'S 'LETTERS TO JULIA'	216
CHANGES AT CHARING CROSS	233
JOHN GAY	253
THE GRUB STREET OF THE ARTS	293
MARTEILHE'S 'MEMOIRS'	315
APPENDIX ('THE BURNING OF WHITEHALL')	335
INDEX	337

A PALADIN OF PHILANTHROPY.

IN February, 1785, when the books of the 'late learned Samuel Johnson, Esq; LL.D. Deceased,' were being sold by Mr. Christie at his Great Room in Pall Mall, one of the persons present was the poet, Samuel Rogers, then a youth of two-and-twenty. He recalls his attendance at this particular sale in order to chronicle the fact that he there met a very old gentleman,—so old that the flesh of his face looked like parchment,—who entertained the younger generation of Mr. Christie's clients by discoursing of the changes that had taken place in London within a memory which, to his auditors, seemed to rival that of the Count de St. Germain. He himself who spoke, he asserted, had 'shot snipes in Conduit-Street,' when Conduit Street was an open mead; and it may be added that he had a friend, Mr. Carew Hervey

Mildmay, who had done likewise.¹ Concerning his age, beyond these indications, he was reticent; and he was popularly supposed to be what he appeared to be—at least a hundred. Oddly enough, the only well-known portrait of him was taken by Samuel Ireland at just this time and place. It exhibits a very ancient personage indeed, lean as a grasshopper, with a profile not unlike that of Fielding in Hogarth's posthumous sketch. He wears a military-looking hat, and a caped coat with deep cuffs and ruffles. His sword hilt projects between his skirts; and in his right hand, which is propped upon a stout walking-cane, he holds a book which has been knocked down to him, and which he is reading attentively without the aid of spectacles.

The cadet of a Jacobite family in the West Riding of Yorkshire, with an English father and an Irish mother, General JAMES EDWARD OGLETHORPE—for such was the name of Ireland's sitter—was not so old as he looked, and perhaps wished to be thought. When in July, 1785, he died,

---

[1] Mr. Mildmay died in 1780, being then ninety-six. Fifty years ago people were wont to boast of shooting snipe—it is always snipe!—on the marshy site of Belgravia (the Five Fields); now they speak of Battersea and Bedford Park.

contemporary prints vaguely stated his age at one hundred and two,[1] and his epitaph in Cranham Church—an incontinent production by Capel Lofft which rivals the performances of Pope's Dr. Freind—is silent as to the date of his birth. His fullest biographer, Mr. Wright, and his latest biographer, Mr. Bruce, concur in fixing this as June 1, 1689. But shortly after Mr. Wright's book appeared in 1867, an indefatigable amateur of the parish register, the late Col. J. L. Chester, pointed out in 'Notes and Queries' that the date of the General's birth was plainly recorded at St. Martin's-in-the-Fields, being there given as December 22, 1696—a date which (as regards day and month) is practically confirmed by the fact that, in the colony of Georgia, which he founded, the 21st December was long kept as his birthday. The seven years thus deducted from his lifetime make legend of many of the facts related of his youth. Even if he were really, as his epitaph avers, a 'Captain-Lieutenant' of the Queen's Guards in 1714 (at eighteen), it is very

---

[1] 'ONE HUNDRED Two! Methusalem in age,
A vigorous soldier, and a virtuous sage:
He founded GEORGIA, gave it laws and trade;
He saw it flourish, and he saw it fade!'
Gentleman's Magazine, lv. 573.

improbable that he could have been the 'Adjutant-General Oglethorpe' who, in the same year, travelled from Lyons to Turin with Dr. Berkeley. But it is pretty clear that in 1714 he matriculated at Corpus, where he was a Gentleman Commoner. In 1715, either upon the recommendation of Marlborough or Argyll, he took service under Prince Eugene, and assisted at the siege of Belgrade by the Austrians. For this we have his own authority. 'Pray, General,' said Johnson to him in 1772, 'give us an account of the siege of Belgrade' (Boswell, by a slip of the pen, says Bender). Whereupon the old warrior, across the walnuts, and with the aid of some of the wine, described that military exploit. *Hac ibat Simois; hic est Sigeia tellus.* 'Here we were, here were the Turks,' etc., etc., to all of which the Doctor ' listened with the closest attention.' It is from Boswell again, and indeed upon the same occasion, that we get the only other authentic anecdote of Oglethorpe's youth. *À propos* of duelling, Boswell tells the following story, as the General told it. Sitting once at table, under Eugene, with a certain Prince of Wurtemberg, the latter, by fillipping the surface of his wine, made some of it fly over the young volunteer, who was thus placed in the awkward dilemma of having to choose between accepting or resenting a gratuitous affront. Oglethorpe's resolution was quickly taken. Saying with a smile, 'That's a good joke, but we do it much better in England!' he raised his glass, and flung the contents in His Serenity's face. Whereupon an old General present pacifically observed, '*Il a bien fait, mon Prince, vous l'avez commencé,*' and the affair passed off in good humour.

With the peace of Passarowitz in 1718, hostilities between the Sultan and Charles VI. were brought to a close, and with those hostilities ended Oglethorpe's experiences as a Continental volunteer. A year or two later, by the death of his second brother, Sir Theophilus Oglethorpe, he succeeded to the family estate of Westbrook, near Godalming, which included a mansion where the Pretender was reported to have lain in hiding; and in October, 1722, like his father and brother before him, he took his seat in Parliament for Haslemere. As a senator, he was conspicuous for a frank speech and a benevolent motive. Colonization, commerce, free trade, and the silk manufacture in England were things which interested him; and he had a knack of homely illustration which was by no means ineffective in debate. But he was a working rather than a talking politician, and his most valuable Parliamentary efforts were in connection with the Committee of 1729-30 into the state of the debtors' prisons in London—a Committee which, indeed, had originated with himself. A friend of his own, one Robert Castell, an amiable amateur architect, who, under guise of an introduction to Vitruvius, had prepared, and dedicated to Richard, Earl of Burlington, a stately subscription *folio* on the Villas of the Ancients, subsequently—and perhaps consequently—fell into grave pecuniary difficulties. He was thrown into the Fleet, at that time farmed by a wretch named Thomas Bambridge, who, in his capacity of Warden, cleared some five thousand pounds a year by fleecing and oppressing the unfortunate debtors under his charge. As long as Castell could contrive to pay heavily for the privilege of residing in one of the four or five shabby streets which then constituted the Rules or Liberties, he was permitted to do so. But when he became unable to satisfy the Warden's immoderate demands for 'presents' (as they were called), he was mercilessly transferred to one of the three spunging houses[1] attached to the prison, a

[1] Johnson (whose knowledge was experimental) accurately defined these establishments in the 'Dictionary' as

crowded and loathsome den in which, moreover, the small-pox was then raging. He had never (as he protested) had that distemper; was extremely apprehensive of it; caught it almost immediately; and died in a few days, declaring, with his last breath, that he had been murdered by Bambridge. Oglethorpe promptly brought his friend's deplorable fate to the notice of the House of Commons; and a Select Committee to inquire into the state of the Gaols of the Kingdom was forthwith appointed, of which he was nominated Chairman. Its three Reports on the Fleet and the King's Bench prisons, still to be read in volume eight of Cobbett's 'Parliamentary History,' disclose the most sickening story of barbarity, extortion, and insanitation. The good and the bad, the sick and the hale, were found to be herded together in filthy dungeons; deaths, often from sheer starvation, were of daily occurrence; iron collars, thumb-screws, and the heaviest fetters were freely used for the refractory; and an unfortunate prisoner might be subjected to all this for the paltry debt of a shilling, which became the nucleus of endless gratuities and 'considera-

⸙ houses ' to which debtors are taken before commitment to prison, where *the bailiffs sponge upon them, and riot at their cost.*'

tions,' and the pretext for perpetual confinement. As a result of the labours of Oglethorpe's committee some of the more crying of these abuses were remedied; but many yet remained, thirty years later, to arouse the pious horror of John Howard. The 'garnish' money of the 'Beggar's Opera' and the 'begging box' of the 'Citizen of the World' still swelled the profits of the Deputy-Marshal and his myrmidons; the terrible gaol-fever continued to claim its tribute of victims; and the prison interiors of Goldsmith's 'Vicar' and Fielding's 'Amelia' can scarcely be regarded as evidences of an attained ideal. One of the most interesting mementos of Oglethorpe's endeavours—which, by the way, were not restricted to his Parliamentary labours—is Hogarth's picture, now in the National Portrait Gallery, of Bambridge under examination. It was painted for Sir Archibald Grant of Monymusk, Knight of the Shire for Aberdeen, and a member of the Committee.[1] Horace Walpole, who had the original oil-sketch, is loud in appreciation of the rendering of the inhuman gaoler. 'It is the very figure that Salvator Rosa would have drawn for Iago in the moment of detection. Villainy, fear,

[1] Sir James Thornhill, the painter, who probably got Hogarth the commission, was also on the Committee.

and conscience are mixed in yellow and livid on
his countenance, his lips are contracted by tremor,
his face advances as eager to lie, his legs step
back as thinking to make his escape; one hand
is thrust precipitately into his bosom, the fingers
of the other are catching uncertainly at his
button-holes. If this was a portrait [and it was],
it is the most speaking that ever was drawn; if
it was not, it is still finer.'

The Committee of Enquiry into the state of
the Gaols was not Oglethorpe's first philanthropic
essay. In 1728 he had published anonymously a
little pamphlet entitled 'The Sailor's Advocate,'
in which he exposed the abuses of the cruel
method of impressment countenanced by the
Admiralty of his day, and, indeed, of many a
day to follow. But the insight he had gained
into the horrors of prison discipline had now
turned his thoughts definitely in fresh directions;
and he began to cast about to find employment
and a future for those hapless beings who, from
no unpardonable fault of their own, were most
liable to fall into the clutches of Bambridge and
his kind. After prolonged and anxious consideration, he was led to believe that the true solution
of the question must be sought in assisted emigra-
tion—a conclusion in which he was fortified (he

says) by the successful settlement of Derry (under James I.) by the Corporation of London. The district he selected for his field of operation was one which had already attracted the projector. It lay on the east coast of North America, beyond and below the Savannah River, and to the north of the Spanish territory of Florida. The Spaniards, who claimed all America, threatened it periodically from the south; bands of desperate runaway blacks infested it from the Carolinas; and to the west were dense and trackless woods, filled with Cherokees, Chickasaws, and other hostile and predatory Indian tribes. But Oglethorpe, nothing daunted, put forward his scheme. With twenty other trustees, he petitioned the Throne for an Act of Incorporation, and in June, 1732, obtained a charter for settling and establishing a new colony, to be called Georgia, in honour of George II. In a couple of pamphlets, published in the same year, and entitled respectively 'An Essay on Plantations,' and 'A New and Accurate Account of the Provinces of South Carolina and Georgia,' he developed his ideas, which he affirmed to be 'the result of various readings and conversations in many years.' His appeal was warmly responded to by the public, and Parliament handed over to the trustees a sum of £10,000, the residue of a grant voted but not paid to Berkeley for his frustrate college in the Bermudas. The trustees, who were themselves large contributors to the scheme, were, by their Charter, restrained from receiving any salary, fee, perquisite or profit whatsoever, nor could they hold any land; conditions entirely honourable to themselves, and not subsequently discredited. Slavery, which prevailed in the Carolinas, was also strictly prohibited, eventually by special Statute. After careful inquiries, thirty-five families, comprising representatives of many trades, and numbering in all one hundred and twenty persons, were chosen for the first settlers; and on the 16th of November, 1732, they set sail from Gravesend in the 'Anne' (Captain Thomas). They were accompanied by Oglethorpe himself; by a chaplain, the Rev. Henry Herbert, and by a Piedmontese named Amatis, whose function it was to instruct the new colonists in the art of rearing silkworms and winding silk. Oglethorpe who was empowered to act as a Colonial Governor, was at this date six-and-thirty, and notwithstanding an undeniable touch of romance in his character, still unmarried. He had already shown energy and tenacity of purpose; he was now to exhibit, in fuller measure, his gifts as an organizer and administrator. He is described as tall, manly, and very handsome; as dignified, but not austere; and if it be added to these things that, as a country gentleman, he had an ample fortune, which he freely employed in the furtherance of his charitable designs, may fairly claim to be written, like Abou Ben Adhem, 'as one that loved his fellow-men.'

On January 13, 1733, after a prosperous voyage of some sixty days, the 'Anne' dropped anchor outside Charleston Bar in South Carolina, and Oglethorpe proceeded to select the site of the new settlement. The spot he fixed upon was a flat bluff or headland on the right (or south) bank of the Savannah, where, about ten miles from the mouth, it bends eastward to the Atlantic. This site extended from five to six miles into the country, with a river frontage of a mile. Forthwith the clearing of the ground began, and streets and squares were marked out. By the middle of March five houses were built or building, and a crane and magazines had been erected. The settlers had been solemnly warned against the dangers of drunkenness; and friendly relations were already in progress with the nearest body of Indians, a branch of the Creek tribe, barely half a mile off, at Yamacraw. Oglethorpe's management of the Indians deserves the highest praise, and he speedily inspired them with a confidence which they never lost. They are 'desirous,' he wrote to the trustees, 'to be subjects to his Majesty, King George, to have lands given them among us, and to breed their children at our schools. Their chief, and his beloved man, who is the second man in the nation, desire to be instructed in the Christian religion.' A month or two later a formal convention was concluded with the Indians, under which the country between the Savannah and the Altamaha (Goldsmith's 'wild Altama' in 'The Deserted Village'), as far as the tide waters flowed, and including most of the islands, was ceded to the trustees; and, by a subsequent treaty, the Creeks engaged to have no dealings with the Spaniards or the French. As a protection against the former, Oglethorpe erected a strong outpost on the Ogechee river, which he christened (in honour of his patron) Fort Argyll; and this was followed, not long after, by the creation, on St. Simon's Island, at the mouth of the Altamaha, of the settlement and military station of Frederica. Meanwhile new emigrants continued to reach Savannah. A large body of these were Protestants, from Salzburg, whose expulsion from their native land, by episcopal edict, had excited considerable sympathy in England.[1] Oglethorpe and his trustees invited them to Georgia, where, in March, 1734, they arrived, to be welcomed warmly by the English colonists, and regaled, *inter alia*, with 'very fine, wholesome English beer.'[2] They took up their abode in a locality chosen for them by Oglethorpe's aid, which they named 'Ebenezer.' As soon as they were established there, Oglethorpe, leaving his new colony in the charge of a bailiff or storekeeper, named Causton, set sail for England in H.M.S. 'Aldborough,' taking with him his now firm friend, the old Creek chief or Mico, Tomo-Chichi, his wife, Senauki, his boy-nephew and successor, Tooanahowi, and Hillispilli, his war-captain.[3] Oglethorpe's politic object in choosing these

---

[1] The Exodus of the Salzburgers has been made the subject of a picture by the German artist, Menzel.

[2] This very minor detail is mentioned for the sake or showing that Oglethorpe's objection to alcohol stopped at 'fire-water.' He would have been thoroughly in sympathy with the respective lessons of Hogarth's 'Beer Street' and 'Gin Lane.'

[3] Tomo-Chichi in his furs, and Tooanahowi holding a live eagle, were painted in London by William Verelst. It was a different Verelst who, in 1710, had painted the Four Iroquois Indian Kings of the 'Spectator.'

travelling companions was to impress his Indian allies with the resources of Great Britain, and the importance of her institutions.

Tomo-Chichi and his suite had certainly a flattering reception in London. The war-captain having been with difficulty restrained from appearing in his 'native nothingness' of paint and feathers, the party were taken to Kensington in three coaches to interview George II., who received them very graciously, and allowed them £20 a week during their four months' stay in town. They subsequently visited the venerable Archbishop of Canterbury (Dr. William Wake) at Lambeth, and were made acquainted with whatever was 'curious and worthy Observation in and about the Cities of *London* and *Westminster.*' They received some £400 worth of presents, including a gold watch which was presented to Tooanahowi, with a pious admonition, by the youthful Duke of Cumberland. In return, they seem to have greatly (or gratefully) admired His Royal Highness's 'Exercise of riding the manag'd Horse', and to have been specially impressed by the magnificence of the Life Guards and the glories of the Thames on Lord Mayor's Day. After their return to Georgia in October, some of the tribe sent an elaborate letter of thanks to

Tomo-Chichi's English entertainers, but scarcely in a shape adapted for preservation in an autograph book. It consisted of the dressed skin of a young buffalo, painted by a Cherokee chief with red and black hieroglyphics; and in this form it long ornamented the Georgia Office in Old Palace Yard. Oglethorpe himself was also naturally the object of much attention, and he received many testimonies to the popularity of his enterprise. Some of these took peculiar forms. At the end of 1735 a certain eccentric Mr. Robert North, of Scarborough, offered prizes in the 'Gentleman's Magazine' for the four best poems entitled 'The Christian Hero' (the name, it will be remembered, of an early devotional manual by Captain Richard Steele of the Guards). The first prize was to be a gold medal with Oglethorpe's head on one side, and that of Lady Elizabeth Hastings (Steele's 'Aspasia') on the other. Lady Elizabeth's effigy was, however, withheld at her own request, and that of Oglethorpe did not prove complimentary as a portrait. As for the poems—well, the poems may still be read in Sylvanus Urban his sixth volume. But the metrical utterance that really handed down Oglethorpe's name to posterity made its appearance a year later (1737). The couplet—

' One, driv'n by strong Benevolence of Soul,
Shall fly, like *Oglethorp*, from Pole to Pole—

in ALEXANDER POPE'S epistle to Colonel Cotterell, has done more to preserve the memory of the founder of Georgia than all the records of the Office at Westminster.

During Oglethorpe's stay in England he had been actively promoting the interests of the new province, but beyond the fact that, from his seat in the House, he had warmly supported two Acts prohibiting the introduction into the settlement of spirits and slavery, his doings have not been particularly recorded. In December, 1735, he set out on his return voyage with two vessels, the 'Symond' and the 'London Merchant,' having on board two hundred and twenty chosen settlers, and a fresh consignment of Salzburgers. He was accompanied, as missionaries, by John Wesley, at this time two-and-thirty, and his younger brother Charles, who was twenty-six. After a passage of many vexations and delays (like Fielding later, they were detained several weeks at the Isle of Wight by contrary winds), they reached their destination. Of course there were disappointments. Tybee Island, at the river-mouth, which should have been lighted, was still dark. But Savannah itself had greatly prospered in its founder's absence. Where, three years before, there had been only the 'matted woods' of Goldsmith, now rose some two hundred comfortable dwellings with garden- and orchard-plots, and pasture lands filled with grazing cattle. There were even public recreation grounds, delightfully situated by the river side, where flourished orange trees and tulip-laurels, and white mulberries for the silk-worms, and tropical plants—coffee and cotton and *palma Christi*—which had been sent from the West Indies by Sir Hans Sloane. Savannah, however, was no longer to be Oglethorpe's chief care. The Spaniards, who had a stronghold at St. Augustine, in Florida, had begun to demonstrate uneasily along the Altamaha, and he turned his energies for the future mainly to the protection of the southern frontier. A body of Gaelic Highlanders from Inverness were already installed at Darien, about twelve miles up the Altamaha; and after adjusting some difficulties of the Salzburgers, who were dissatisfied with the site of Ebenezer, he hastened southward to St. Simon's Island, at the river mouth. Here in brief space he established, and stocked with emigrants, the fort of Frederica, for many years to come the main bulwark against Spanish aggression in North America; and it is with this fort on

St. Simon's Island that, during the remainder of his stay in Georgia, he was chiefly connected.

It has already been mentioned that Oglethorpe was accompanied on his return from England by the Wesley brothers. Their subsequent history is one of the difficult passages of the Georgia chronicle. Charles, the younger, who, besides being chaplain, was to be Oglethorpe's secretary, appears to have speedily wearied of his lay duties, added to which, during Oglethorpe's absence from Frederica, he became involved in a tangle of misunderstandings with the settlers—misunderstandings embittered by jealousies and complicated by feminine tittle-tattle. In a very few weeks he found Frederica too hot for him ('I was overjoyed at my deliverance out of this furnace'), and not long afterwards resigned his post, parting kindly with Oglethorpe, who, in spite of his impetuosity, never bore malice. Meanwhile his elder brother, whom Oglethorpe liked less, was not prospering at Savannah. He had come out to convert the Indians, but he never learned their language. On the other hand, he seems to have contrived to make himself exceedingly distasteful to the colonists. At this stage of his career—as he himself admitted later—he was a bigoted High Churchman. His exhortations, rigorous in doctrine and personal in tone, were angrily resented by the very mixed community of the new settlement. He is, moreover, alleged to have 'interfered in family quarrels and the broils of social life.' Finally came the *affaire du cœur* which has been so frequently related. Always susceptible to feminine charm, he became attached to the storekeeper's niece, a designing coquette, who had nursed him through a fever, and deliberately laid herself out to attract him. Whether he actually made known his sentiments is obscure, but the Salzburg elders were certainly consulted privately as to the expediency of his marrying. They reported unfavourably, and the lady promptly consoled herself with a rival admirer. When afterwards, for some levity of behaviour as a married woman, Wesley declined to admit her to the Communion Table, her uncle and husband indicted him for defamation. The suit failed, but Savannah thenceforth became impossible for John Wesley, and he returned to England in December, 1737, as Whitefield was setting out to join him. Whitefield, in other ways, was equally ineffectual; and he, also, made no long stay in Georgia. In no case does there seem to have been any actual rupture with Oglethorpe. But from a letter he wrote later, *à propos* of the excellent 'Practice of Christianity' which the good Manx Bishop, Dr. Wilson, had drawn up at his request, 'towards an Instruction for the Indians,' he was manifestly of opinion that the teaching of 'our Methodists' (by which he must be understood to mean the brothers and their successor) had not proved to be adapted to the spiritual requirements of the colony. Probably he would personally have preferred more loving-kindness and a little less formality.

The Wesleys, however, are but an episode in Georgian history; and during their residence in the settlement can scarcely have had any prolonged intercourse with Oglethorpe, whose life henceforward reads like a realization of the old stage direction, 'excursions and alarms.' Actually or indirectly he was continuously occupied in watching or checkmating the aggressive movements of the Spaniards; and his resources, offensive and defensive, were uncertain and inadequate. The Indians, his best friends, were excitable, and not always to be controlled by civilization; the Carolinians, besides being committed to slave-labour, were self-seeking and obstructive; while the Salzburgers, though inoffensive enough in their 'petrified Sabbath' at Ebenezer, declined to fight, even for hearth and home, and ultimately had to 'fold their tents' altogether. After nine months of defending Georgia against its different dangers, Oglethorpe took advantage of a temporary lull to sail again for England, and beat up recruits. He was received with renewed enthusiasm, not a little heightened by the fact that the Court of Madrid, while privately strengthening St. Augustine, had the audacity to demand that neither Oglethorpe nor his levies should be allowed to go back. Nevertheless, with the approval of Government, his regiment of 600 men was raised; and in the following September (1738), he once more reached St. Simon's with the title of commander-in-chief of all his Majesty's forces in Georgia and South Carolina. Some further time was occupied in procuring and concluding fresh treaties with the Indians; and then came the long deferred Declaration of War with Spain, one of the first results of which was that Oglethorpe was ordered to reduce St. Augustine. This, a few months later, he prepared to do, but not with his usual good fortune. He had a fair equipment of regulars, Carolina militia, and Indians, and this land force, numbering some two thousand men, was intended to be supported from the sea by English men-of-war. But the Indians proved unmanageable; the colonial militia, besides being inefficient, deserted freely ; and the fleet failed to render the aid expected. Sickness and disaffection complicated matters, and after investing St. Augustine (which was found to be strongly garrisoned and well defended) for five weeks, Oglethorpe had no option but to withdraw ingloriously, to the great prejudice of his prestige both abroad and at home, where his old patron, the Duke of Argyll, had to explain in the House of Lords (what was indeed the truth) that the enterprise had miscarried 'only for want of supplies necessary to a possibility of success.'

Fortunately, for nearly two years after the siege of St. Augustine, Spain remained comparatively quiet. Then, in the spring of 1742, came Oglethorpe's opportunity. Before he had been the attacker, now he was to be the attacked, and the story, on a smaller scale, has a dash of the Elizabethan days. With Castilian deliberation the Spaniards of Florida and the Havana fitted out a pompous armada of forty or fifty ships, snows, galleys, and periaguas, the purpose of which was to sweep the heretics, summarily and for ever, from the North American settlements. The key of Georgia was St. Simon's Island, and St. Simon's Island, the defences of which had been recently strengthened, could not be neglected by an invader. Into St. Simon's Island Oglethorpe accordingly threw himself with a rapidly organized band of followers. When, after an unsuccessful attack on Fort William (in Cumberland Island), the Spaniards arrived in St. Simon's Sound, he allowed them to land, spiked the guns of a smaller fort to the south, and retired upon Frederica, which was flanked by a dense oak forest, and approached by a morass. Here, under cover of the wood, and excellently served by his Indian scouts, he attacked the enemy in detail, a course which subjected them to much the same fate as that which befell Braddock's ill-starred expedition, fourteen years later, against Fort Duquesne. Notwithstanding their superiority, numbers of them, including several officers of distinction, were killed by sallies and ambuscades, and Oglethorpe himself, as a leader, seems to have shown not only extraordinary resource and decision, but also marked personal gallantry, taking two Spaniards prisoner, on one occasion, with his own hand. Finally, by a fortunate stratagem, he contrived, through the medium of a French spy, to persuade his foes that an English fleet was on its way to his relief—a statement which was opportunely supported by the chance appearance of some vessels off the coast. After about a week of this desultory and disastrous warfare, the discomfited Spanish forces re-embarked, with Oglethorpe at their heels. They made a renewed but fruitless attack upon Fort William, which was bravely defended by Ensign Stuart. In a few days more they had faded away in the direction of St. Augustine, and Oglethorpe was able to order a thanksgiving for the end of the invasion. Seven or eight hundred men had put to flight more than five thousand; and Whitefield might well write (as he did) that 'the deliverance of Georgia from the Spaniards is such as cannot be paralleled but by some instances out of the Old Testament.'

During the remainder of his stay in Georgia, Oglethorpe continued to 'harass the Spaniard' by all the means at his command. But he was ill-supported from home both with money and men; and what was worse, his military operations had involved him personally in financial difficulties which sooner or later must have necessitated his return to England. The proximate cause of that return, however, was apparently to meet certain charges which had been preferred against him by one of his subordinates, Lieut.-Colonel Cook. In June, 1744, these were declared by a Board of General Officers to be 'false, malicious, and without foundation,' and Cook was summarily dismissed the service. A month or two later (September 15) the 'Gentleman's Magazine' records the marriage of 'Gen. *Oglethorpe*,—to the only Daughter of the late Sir *Nathan Wright*, Bt., of *Cranham Hall, Essex*.' The lady, who was thirty-five, brought him a fresh fortune (Georgia must by this time have absorbed his own), and a pleasant Jacobean country-house with an old-fashioned garden. One of Mr. Urban's poets seems to have expected that Mrs. Oglethorpe would henceforth share her husband's 'fatigues, and conduct in the field.' But Oglethorpe never again went back to Georgia, which was thenceforth left to go its own gait, and adopt slave labour. In the Forty-Five, he was appointed to a command under that corpulent rival of Eugene and Marlborough, 'Billy the Butcher,' who subsequently accused him of 'lingering on the road' with his rangers in pursuit of the rebels. 'Lingering' was not a fault of Oglethorpe, who was promptly acquitted by court-martial—the King confirming the verdict. But though he was later made a Lieutenant-General, this incident, coupled with some distrust of his Jacobite antecedents, practically closed his career as a soldier. For several years he continued to speak ably and

earnestly in the House of Commons on matters
military and philanthropic. Then, in 1754, two
years after the trustees had finally washed their
hands of Georgia, he lost the seat which he had
held through seven Parliaments; and in 1765,
two years after Florida was transferred to England
at the Treaty of Paris, he became a full General,
soon to be the oldest in the British army. But
it was twenty years more before he finally quitted
the scene, living past the American Revolution
and the famous Declaration which made Georgia
independent, to die at last in his Essex home, not
as one might suppose, of old age, but of a violent
fever which would have killed him at any time.
He is buried in the little church at Cranham,
where his widow was ultimately laid beside him.

There are many references to Oglethorpe in
the memoirs of his day, through which he flits fit-
fully for half a century, vigorous, bright-eyed, and
too eager of speech to complete his sentences. He
was familiar, of course, with Boswell, to which
eminent 'Authour,' after the publication of
the 'Tour in Corsica,' he introduced himself in
a particularly gratifying manner. 'My name, Sir,
is Oglethorpe, and I wish to be acquainted with
you.' He bade him not marry till he had
first put the Corsicans in a proper situation.

'You may make a fortune in the doing of it,' said he; 'or, if you do not, you will have acquired such a character as will entitle you to make a fortune '—words which, if correctly reported, have a curious odd suggestion of his own experience. He was also known to Johnson, whose 'London' he had been one of the earliest to praise 'in all companies,' and there can be no doubt that such lines as those in that poem which speak of 'peaceful deserts, yet unclaimed by Spain', which might afford an asylum to the oppressed, must have found a responsive echo in Oglethorpe's heart. Both the Doctor and Boswell seem to have proposed to write their friend's life, but neither did; and we are left to explain their neglect either by indolence, or that absence of effective biographical material and predominance of minor detail which have proved such a stumbling block to Oglethorpe's biographers. Another contemporary whom he knew was Goldsmith, to whom he offered Cranham as an asylum from the *fumum strepitumque Romæ*. He sends him five pounds for a charitable purpose, and adds—'if a farm and a mere country scene will be a little refreshment from the smoke of London, we shall be glad of the happiness of seeing you at Cranham Hall.' Whether Goldsmith went (he was familiar with another Essex house, Lord Clare's at Gosfield), is not related; but it was when Oglethorpe was calling upon him with Topham Beauclerk that he was insulted by Pilkington's historical pound—no, quarter-of-a-pound—of tea; and it was at Oglethorpe's, in April, 1773, that he sang Tony Lumpkin's 'Three Jolly Pigeons' and that other ditty, to the tune of the 'Humours of Balmagairy' ('Ah, me! when shall I marry me!'), which was left out of 'She Stoops' because the 'Miss Hardcastle' of the play was no vocalist. But the last, and perhaps the most picturesque accounts of Oglethorpe are given by Horace Walpole and Hannah More. 'I have got a new admirer,' writes that lively lady from Mrs. Garrick's in 1784. 'We flirt together prodigiously; it is the famous General Oglethorpe, perhaps the most remarkable man of his time . . . the finest figure you ever saw. He perfectly realises all my ideas of Nestor. His literature is great [he knew some of Miss More's poetry by heart], his knowledge of the world extensive, and his faculties as bright as ever; he is one of the three persons still living who were mentioned by Pope; Lord Mansfield and Lord Marchmont are the other two . . . He is quite a *preux chevalier*, heroic, romantic, and full of the old gallantry.' Walpole, who was feebler, and frailer, and crippled with rheumatism, is hardly as enthusiastic as 'St. Hannah,' which was his own pet-name for Miss More. But his report is fully confirmatory of Oglethorpe's young old age. 'General Oglethorpe, who sometimes visits me . . . has the activity of youth when compared with me. His eyes, ears, articulation, limbs, and memory would suit a boy, if a boy could recollect a century backwards. His teeth are gone; he is a shadow, and a wrinkled one; but his spirits and his spirit are in full bloom; two years and a half ago, he challenged a neighbouring gentleman for trespassing on his manor. "*I* could carry a cannon as easily as let off a pistol."' And this was written in April, 1785, a month or two before Oglethorpe's death.

Hannah More's conventional '*preux chevalier*' strikes the final note of Oglethorpe better than her lightly-penned laudation. When he recommends her to study the old romances because it is the only way to acquire 'noble sentiments,' we are reminded not a little of his own kinship to Don Quixote; when we read of his restless and impulsive energy, we recall (and the parallel was drawn in his own day) the ubiquitous exploits of Swift's Peterborough :

> 'Mordanto gallops on alone,
> The roads are with his followers strown,
> This breaks a girth and that a bone;
>
> 'His body active as his mind,
> Returning sound in limb and wind,
> Except some leather left behind.'

He prosecuted Philanthropy in the spirit of a Paladin, rejoicing in the obstacles, the encounters, the nights *sub Jove frigido;* and it is easy to imagine him declaiming to Johnson and Goldsmith of the dangers of luxury, or quoting the admirable precepts of Mr. Addison's 'Cato.' His method, with all its advantages, had demonstrable drawbacks; and it is quite possible that, reasoning with his heart rather than his head, he was occasionally mistaken both in the means he employed and the agents he chose. It is possible, also, that in the presence of timidity or obstruction, he was sometimes imperious as well as impatient. *Nescit cedere* was the motto of his family. But he was a good man, disinterested, genuinely self-denying, sincerely religious after his fashion,—a fashion perhaps not altogether that of the Wesleys and Whitefields. In the matter of spirits and slave labour he was plainly in advance of his age; and if he was not exactly (as Warton claimed), 'at once a great hero and a great legislator,' there can be no doubt as to his ' Benevolence of Soul,' and his unfeigned sympathy with the oppressed. ' His undertaking will succeed,' said the Governor of South Carolina, ' for he nobly devotes all his powers to serve the poor and rescue them from their wretchedness.' ' He has taken care of us to the utmost of his ability,' wrote the pastor of the grateful Salzburgers. ' Others would not in many years have accomplished what he has brought about in one.' And when, long after, the Spaniards sought to prejudice an Indian chief against his English friend, he answered, 'We love him. It is true he does not give us silver; but he gives us everything we want that he has. He has given me the coat off his back and the blanket from under him.'

GOLDSMITH'S POEMS AND PLAYS.

THIRTY years of taking-in; fifteen years of giving-out;—that, in brief, is Oliver Goldsmith's story. When, in 1758, his failure to pass at Surgeons' Hall finally threw him on letters for a living, the thirty years were finished, and the fifteen years had been begun. What was to come he knew not; but, from his bare-walled lodging in Green-Arbour-Court, he could at least look back upon a sufficiently diversified past. He had been an idle, orchard-robbing schoolboy; a tuneful but intractable sizar of Trinity; a lounging, loitering, fair-haunting, flute-playing Irish 'buckeen.' He had knocked at the doors of both Law and Divinity, and crossed the threshold of neither. He had set out for London and stopped at Dublin; he had started for America and arrived at Cork. He had been many things: a medical student, a strolling musician, an apothecary, a corrector of the press, an usher at a Peckham 'academy.' Judged by ordinary standards, he had wantonly wasted his time.

And yet, as things fell out, it is doubtful whether his parti-coloured experiences were not of more service to him than any he could have obtained if his progress had been less erratic. Had he fulfilled the modest expectations of his family, he would probably have remained a simple curate in Westmeath, eking out his 'forty pounds a year' by farming a field or two, migrating contentedly at the fitting season from the 'blue bed to the brown,' and (it may be) subsisting vaguely as a local poet upon the tradition of some youthful couplets to a pretty cousin, who had married a richer man. As it was, if he could not be said to have 'seen life steadily, and seen it whole,' he had, at all events, inspected it pretty closely in parts; and, at a time when he was most impressible, had preserved the impress of many things, which, in his turn, he was to re-impress upon his writings. 'No man'—says one of his biographers [1]—'ever put so much of himself into his books as Goldsmith.' To his last hour he was drawing upon the thoughts and reviving the memories of that 'unhallowed time' when, to all appearance, he was hopelessly squandering his opportunities. To do as Goldsmith did would scarcely enable a man

---

[1] Forster's 'Life,' Bk. ii. ch. vi.

to write a 'Vicar of Wakefield' or a 'Deserted Village,'—certainly his practice cannot be preached with safety 'to those that eddy round and round.' But viewing his entire career, it is difficult not to see how one part seems to have been an indispensable preparation for the other, and to marvel once more (with the philosopher Square) at 'the eternal Fitness of Things.'

The events of Goldsmith's life have been too often narrated to need repetition, and we shall not resort to the well-worn device of repeating them in order to say so. But the progress of time, advancing some things and effacing others, lends a fresh aspect even to masterpieces; for which reason it is always possible to speak of a writer's work. In this instance we shall restrict ourselves to Goldsmith's Poems and Plays. And, with regard to both, what strikes one first is the extreme tardiness of that late blossoming upon which Johnson commented. When a man succeeds as Goldsmith succeeded, friends and critics speedily discover that he had shown signs of excellence even from his boyish years. But setting aside those half-mythical ballads for the Dublin street-singers, and some doubtful verses for Jane Contarine, there is no definite evidence that, from a doggerel couplet in his childhood to an epigram not much better than doggerel composed when he was five and twenty, he had written a line of verse of the slightest importance; and even five years later, although he refers to himself in a private letter as a 'poet,' it must have been solely upon the strength of the unpublished fragment of 'The Traveller,' which, in the interval, he had sent to his brother Henry from abroad. It is even more remarkable that—although so skilful a correspondent should have been fully sensible of his gifts—until, under the pressure of circumstances, he drifted into literature, the craft of letters seems never to have been his ambition. He thinks of turning lawyer, physician, clergyman—anything but author; and when at last he engages in that profession, it is to free himself from a scholastic slavery which he seems to have always regarded with peculiar bitterness, yet to which, after a first unsatisfactory trial of what was to be his true vocation, he unhesitatingly returned. If he went back anew to the pen, however, it was only to enable him to escape from it more effectually, and he was prepared to go as far as Coromandel. But Literature, '*toute entière à sa proie attachée*,' refused to relinquish him; and, although he continued to make spasmodic efforts to extricate himself from the toils, detained him relentlessly to the day of his death.

If there is no evidence that he had written much when he entered upon what has been called his second period, he had not the less formed his opinions on many literary questions. Much of the matter of the 'Polite Learning' is plainly manufactured *ad hoc;* but in its references to authorship and criticism, there is an individual note which is absent elsewhere; and when he speaks of the tyranny of publishers, the petty standards of criticism, and the forlorn and precarious existence of the hapless writer for bread, he is evidently reproducing a condition of things with which he had become familiar during his brief bondage on the 'Monthly Review.' As to his personal views on poetry in particular, it is easy to collect them from this and later utterances. Against blank verse he objects from the first, as suited only to the sublimest themes—which is a polite way of shelving it altogether; while in favour of rhyme be alleges—perhaps borrowing his illustration from Montaigne—that the very restriction stimulates the fancy, as a fountain plays highest when the aperture is diminished. Blank verse, too (he asserts), imports into poetry a 'disgusting solemnity of manner' which is fatal to 'agreeable trifling,'—an objection intimately connected with the feeling which afterwards made him the champion on the stage of character and humour. Among the poets who were his contemporaries and immediate predecessors, his likes and dislikes were strong. He fretted at the fashion which Gray's 'Elegy' set in poetry; he considered it a fine poem, but 'overloaded with epithet;' and he deplored the remoteness and want of emotion which distinguished the Pindaric Odes. Yet from many indications in his own writings he seems to have genuinely appreciated the work of Collins. Churchill, and Churchill's satire, he detested. With Young he had some personal acquaintance, and had evidently read his 'Night Thoughts' with attention. Of the poets of the last age, he admired Dryden, Pope, and Gay, but more than any of these, if imitation is to be regarded as the surest proof of sympathy, Prior, Addison, and Swift. By his inclinations and his training, indeed, he belonged to this school. But he was in advance of it in thinking that poetry, however didactic after the fashion of his own day, should be simple in its utterance and directed at the many rather than at the few. This is what he meant when, from the critical elevation of Griffiths' back parlour, he recommended Gray to take the advice of Isocrates, and 'study the people.' If, with these ideas, he had been able to divest himself of the 'warbling groves' and 'finny deeps' of the Popesque vocabulary (of much of the more 'mechanic art' of that supreme artificer he *did* successfully divest himself), it would have needed but little to make him a prominent pioneer of the new school which was coming with Cowper. As it is, his poetical attitude is a little that intermediate one of Longfellow's maiden,—

> 'Standing, with reluctant feet,
> Where the brook and river meet.'

Most of his minor and earlier pieces are imitative. In 'A New Simile,' and 'The Logicians Refuted' (if that be his), Swift is his acknowledged model; in 'The Double Transformation' it is Prior, modified by certain theories personal to himself. He was evidently well acquainted with collections such as the 'Ménagiana,' and with the French minor poets of the eighteenth century, many of which latter were among his books at his death. These he had carefully studied, probably during his continental wanderings, and from them he derives, like Prior, something of his grace and metrical buoyancy. The

'Elegy on the Death of a Mad Dog,' and 'Madam Blaize,' are both more or less constructed on the old French popular song of the hero of Pavia, Jacques de Chabannes, Seigneur de la Palice (sometimes Galisse), with, in the case of the former, a tag from an epigram by Voltaire, the original of which is in the Greek Anthology, though Voltaire simply 'conveyed' his version from an anonymous French predecessor. Similarly the lively stanzas 'To Iris in Bow Street,' the lines to Myra, the quatrain called 'A South American Ode,' and that 'On a Beautiful Youth struck blind with Lightning,' are all confessed or unconfessed translations. If Goldsmith had lived to collect his own works, it is possible that he would have announced the source of his inspiration in these instances as well as in one or two other cases,—the epitaph on Ned Purdon, for example,—where it has been reserved to his editors to discover his obligations. On the other hand, he might have contended, with perfect justice, that whatever the source of his ideas, he had made them his own when he got them; and certainly in lilt and lightness, the lines 'To Iris' are infinitely superior to those of La Monnoye on which they are based. But even a fervent admirer may admit that, dwelling as he did in this very vitreous palace of Gallic adaptation, one does not expect to find him throwing stones at Prior for borrowing from the French, or commenting solemnly in the Life of Parnell upon the heinousness of plagiarism. 'It was the fashion,' he says, 'with the wits of the last age, to conceal the places from whence they took their hints or their subjects. A trifling acknowledgment would have made that lawful prize which may now be considered as plunder.' He might appropriately have added to this latter sentence the quotation which he struck out of the second issue of the 'Polite Learning,'—'*Haud inexpertus loquor.*'

Of his longer pieces, 'The Traveller' was apparently suggested to him by Addison's 'Letter from Italy to Lord Halifax,' a poem to which, in his preliminary notes to the 'Beauties of English Poesy,' he gives significant praise. 'There is in it,' he says, 'a strain of political thinking that was, at that time, new in our country.' He obviously intended that 'The Traveller' should be admired for the same reason; and both in that poem and its successor, 'The Deserted Village,' he lays stress upon the political import of his work. The one, we are told, is to illustrate the position that the happiness of the subject is independent of the goodness of the sovereign; the other, to deplore the increase of luxury, and the miseries of depopulation. But, as a crowd of commentators have pointed out, it is hazardous for a poet to meddle with 'political thinking,' however much, under George the Second, it may have been needful to proclaim a serious purpose. If Goldsmith had depended solely upon the professedly didactic part of his attempt, his work would be as dead as 'Freedom,' or 'Sympathy,' or any other of Dodsley's forgotten *quartos*. Fortunately he did more than this. Sensibly or insensibly, he suffused his work with that philanthropy which is 'not learned by the royal road of tracts and platform speeches and monthly magazines,' but by personal commerce with poverty and sorrow; and he made his appeal to that clinging love of country, of old association, of 'home-bred happiness,' of innocent pleasure, which, with Englishmen, is never made in vain. Employing the couplet of Pope and Johnson, he has added to his measure a suavity that belonged to neither; but the beauty of his humanity and the tender melancholy of his wistful retrospect hold us more strongly and securely than the studious finish of his style.

'*Vingt fois sur le métier remettez votre ouvrage*,'

said the arch-critic whose name, according to Keats, the school of Pope displayed upon their 'decrepit standard.' Even in 'The Traveller' and 'The Deserted Village,' there are indications of over-labour; but in a poem which comes between them—the once famous 'Edwin and Angelina'—Goldsmith certainly carried out Boileau's maxim to the full. The first privately printed version differs considerably from that in the first edition of the 'Vicar;' this again is altered in the fourth; and there are other variations in the piece as printed in the 'Poems for Young Ladies.' 'As to my "Hermit,"' said the poet complacently, 'that poem, Cradock, cannot be amended,'—and undoubtedly it has been skilfully wrought. But it is impossible to look upon it now with the unpurged eyes of those upon whom the 'Reliques of Ancient Poetry' had but recently dawned, still less to endorse the verdict of Sir John Hawkins that 'it is one of the finest poems of the lyric kind that our language has to boast of.' Its over-soft prettiness is too much that of the chromo-lithograph, or the Parian bust (the porcelain, not the marble), and its 'beautiful simplicity' is in parts perilously close upon that inanity which Johnson, whose sturdy good sense not even friendship could silence, declared to be the characteristic of much of Percy's collection. It is instructive as a study of poetical progress to contrast it with a ballad of our own day in the same measure,— the 'Talking Oak' of Tennyson.

The remaining poems of Goldsmith, excluding the 'Captivity,' and the admittedly occasional 'Threnodia Augustalis,' are not open to the charge of fictitious simplicity, or of that hyper-elaboration which, in the words of the poet just mentioned, makes for the 'ripe and rotten.' The gallery of kit-cats in 'Retaliation,' and the delightful *bonhomie* of 'The Haunch of Venison,' need no commendation. In kindly humour and not unkindly satire Goldsmith was at his best, and the imperishable portraits of Burke and Garrick and Reynolds, and the inimitable dinner at which Lord Clare's pasty was *not*, are as well known as any of the stock passages of 'The Deserted Village' or 'The Traveller,' though they have never been babbled '*in extremis vicis*' by successive generations of schoolboys. It is usually said, probably with truth, that in these poems and the delightful 'Letter to Mrs. Bunbury,' Goldsmith's metre was suggested by the cantering anapests of the 'New Bath Guide,' and it is to be observed that 'Little Comedy's'

invitation is to the same favourite tune. But it
is also the fact that a line of the once popular
lyric of 'Ally Croaker,'—

> 'Too dull for a wit, too grave for a joker,'—

has a kind of echo in the—

> 'Too nice for a statesman, too proud for a wit'—

of Burke's portrait in 'Retaliation.' What is
still more remarkable is that Gray's 'Sketch of
his own Character,' the resemblance of which to
Goldsmith has been pointed out by his editors,
begins,—

> 'Too poor for a bribe, and too proud to importune.'

Whether Goldsmith was thinking of Anstey or
'Ally Croaker,' it is at least worthy of passing
notice that an Irish song of no particular literary
merit should have succeeded in haunting the two
foremost poets of their day.[1]

[1] This suggestive performance is mentioned in Act ii.
of 'She Stoops to Conquer,' where Tony Lumpkin is
made to say that he no more troubles his head about 'Ali
Cawn' (the Subah of Bengal) than 'Ally Croaker;' and
Miss Edgeworth quotes the first verse in her 'Belinda,'
ch. v.:

> 'There was a young man in Ballinacrasy,
> Who wanted a wife to make him un*asy*,

Poetry brought Goldsmith fame, but money only indirectly. Those Saturnian days of the subscription-edition, when Pope and Gay and Prior counted their gains by thousands, were over and gone. He had arrived, it has been truly said, too late for the Patron, and too early for the Public. Of his lighter pieces, the best were posthumous; the rest were either paid for at hack prices or not at all. For 'The Deserted Village' Griffin gave him a hundred guineas, a sum so unexampled as to have prompted the pleasant legend that he returned it. For 'The Traveller' the only payment that can be definitely traced is £21. 'I cannot afford to court the draggle-tail muses,' he said laughingly to Lord Lisburn; 'they would let me starve; but by my other labours I can make shift to eat, and drink, and have good clothes.' It was in his 'other labours' that his poems helped him. The book-sellers, who would not or could not remunerate him adequately for delayed production and

> And thus in gentle strains he spoke her,
> Arrah, vill you marry me, my dear Ally Croker?'

The whole, which differs somewhat from this, is given in the 'Universal Magazine' for October, 1753, where it is styled '*A New* Song.' The line 'Too dull for a wit, too grave for a joker' comes in the second stanza.

minute revision, were willing enough to secure the sanction of his name for humbler journey-work. If he was ill-paid for 'The Traveller,' he was not ill-paid for the 'Beauties of English Poesy' or the 'History of Animated Nature.'

Yet notwithstanding his ready pen, and his skill as a compiler, his life was a treadmill. 'While you are nibbling about elegant phrases, I am obliged to write half a volume,' he told his friend Cradock; and it was but natural that he should desire to escape into walks where he might accomplish something 'for his own hand,' by which, at the same time, he might exist. Fiction he had already essayed. Nearly two years before 'The Traveller' appeared, he had written a story about the length of 'Joseph Andrews,' for which he had received little more than a third of the sum paid by Andrew Millar to Fielding for his burlesque of Richardson's 'Pamela.' But obscure circumstances delayed the publication of the 'Vicar of Wakefield' for four years, and when at last it was issued, its first burst of success—a success, as far as can be ascertained, productive of no further profit to its author—was followed by a long period during which the sales were languid and uncertain. There remained the stage, with its two-fold allurement of fame and fortune, both payable at sight, added to which it was always possible that a popular play, in those days when plays were bought to read, might find a brisk market in pamphlet form. The prospect was a tempting one, and it is scarcely surprising that Goldsmith, weary of the 'dry drudgery at the desk's dead wood,' and conscious of better things within him, should engage in that most tantalizing of all enterprises, the pursuit of dramatic success.

For acting and actors he had always shown a decided partiality.[1] Vague stories, based, in all probability, upon the references to strolling players in his writings, hinted that he himself had once worn the comic sock as 'Scrub' in 'The Beaux' Stratagem;' and it is clear that soon after he arrived in England, he had completed a tragedy, for he read it in manuscript to a friend. That he had been besides an acute and observant playgoer is plain from his excellent account in

[1] This is not inconsistent with the splenetic utterances in the letters to Daniel Hodson, first made public in the 'Great Writers' life of Goldsmith, where he speaks of the stage as 'an abominable resource which neither became a man of honour, nor a man of sense.' Those letters were written when the production of 'The Good-Natur'd Man' had supplied him with abundant practical evidence of the vexations and difficulties of theatrical ambition.

'The Bee' of Mademoiselle Clairon, whom he
had seen at Paris, and from his sensible notes in
the same periodical on 'gestic lore' as exhibited
on the English stage. In his 'Polite Learning
in Europe,' he had followed up Ralph's 'Case of
Authors by Profession,' by protesting against the
despotism of managers, and the unenlightened
but economical policy of producing only the
works of deceased playwrights; and he was
equally opposed to the growing tendency on the
part of the public — a tendency dating from
Richardson and the French *comédie larmoyante*—
to substitute sham sensibility and superficial re-
finement for that humourous delineation of
manners which, with all their errors of morality
and taste, had been the chief aim of Congreve and
his contemporaries. To the fact that what was
now known as 'genteel comedy' had almost
wholly supplanted this elder and better manner,
must be attributed his deferred entry upon a field
so obviously adapted to his gifts. But when, in
1766, the 'Clandestine Marriage' of Garrick
and Colman, with its evergreen 'Lord Ogleby,'
seemed to herald a return to the side of laughter
as opposed to that of tears, he took heart of grace,
and, calling to mind something of the old incon-
siderate benevolence which had been the Gold-

smith family-failing, set about his first comedy, 'The Good-Natur'd Man.'

Even without experiment, no one could have known better than Goldsmith upon what a sea of troubles he had embarked. Those obstacles which, more than thirty years before, had been so graphically described in Fielding's 'Pasquin,'—which Goldsmith himself had indicated with equal accuracy in his earliest book,—still lay in the way of all dramatic purpose, and he was to avoid none of them. When he submitted his completed work to Garrick, the all-powerful actor, who liked neither piece nor author, blew hot and cold so long that Goldsmith at last, in despair, transferred it to Colman. But, as if fate was inexorable, Colman, after accepting it effusively, also grew dilatory, and ultimately entered into a tacit league with Garrick not to produce it at Covent Garden until his former rival had brought out at Drury Lane a comedy by Goldsmith's countryman, Hugh Kelly, a sentimentalist of the first water. Upon the heels of the enthusiastic reception which Garrick's administrative tact secured for the superfine entanglements of 'False Delicacy,' came limping 'The Good-Natur'd Man' of Goldsmith, wet-blanketed beforehand by a sombre prologue from Johnson. No first appearance could have been less favourable. Until it was finally saved in the fourth act by the excellent art of Shuter as 'Croaker,' its fate hung trembling in the balance, and even then one of its scenes— not afterwards reckoned the worst—had to be withdrawn in deference to the delicate scruples of an audience which could not suffer such inferior beings as bailiffs to come between the wind and its gentility. Yet, in spite of all these disadvantages, 'The Good-Natur'd Man' obtained a hearing, besides bringing its author about five hundred pounds, a sum far larger than anything he had ever made by poetry or fiction.

That the superior success of 'False Delicacy,' with its mincing morality and jumble of inadequate motives, was wholly temporary and accidental is evident from the fact that, to use a felicitous phrase, it has now to be disinterred in order to be discussed. But, notwithstanding one's instinctive sympathy for Goldsmith in his struggles with the managers, it is not equally clear that, everything considered, 'The Good-Natur'd Man' was unfairly treated by the public. Because Kelly's play was praised too much, it by no means follows that Goldsmith's play was praised too little. With all the advantage of its author's reputation, it has never since passed into the *répertoire*, and, if it had something of the freshness of a first effort, it had also its inexperience. The chief character, Honeywood, —the weak and amiable 'good-natur'd man,'— never stands very firmly on his feet, and the first actor of the part, Garrick's promising young rival, Powell, failed, or disdained to make it a stage success. On the other hand, 'Croaker,' an admitted elaboration of Johnson's sketch of 'Suspirius' in 'The Rambler,' is a first-rate comic creation, and the charlatan 'Lofty,' a sort of 'Beau-Tibbs-above-Stairs,' is almost as good. But, as Garrick's keen eye saw, to have a second male figure of greater importance than the central personage was a serious error of judgment, added to which neither 'Miss Richland' nor 'Mrs. Croaker' ever establishes any hold upon the audience. Last of all, the plot, such as it is, cannot be described as either particularly ingenious or particularly novel. In another way the merit of the piece is, however, incontestable. It is written with all the perspicuous grace of Goldsmith's easy pen, and, in the absence of stagecraft, sparkles with neat and effective epigrams. One of these may be mentioned as illustrating the writer's curious (perhaps unconscious) habit of repeating ideas which had pleased him. He had quoted in his 'Polite Learning' the exquisitely rhythmical close of Sir William Temple's prose essay 'Of Poetry,' and in 'The Bee' it still seems to haunt him. In 'The Good-Natur'd Man' he has absorbed it altogether, for he places it, without inverted commas, in the lips of Croaker.[1]

But if its lack of constructive power and its errors of conception make it impossible to regard 'The Good-Natur'd Man' as a substantial gain to humourous drama, it was undoubtedly a formidable attack upon that 'mawkish drab of spurious breed,' Sentimental Comedy, and its success was amply sufficient to justify a second trial. That Goldsmith did not forthwith make this

[1] In the same way he annexes, both in 'The Hermit' and 'The Citizen of the World,' a quotation from Young. The passage from Temple is as follows: 'When all is done, human life is, at the greatest and the best, but like a froward child, that must be played with and humoured a little to keep it quiet till it falls asleep, and then the care is over.' Lamb uses this to wind up his essay on Shaftesbury and Temple ('The Genteel Style in Writing'); and perhaps there is a memory of it in the

'Pleas'd with this bauble still, as that before;
Till tir'd he sleeps, and Life's poor play is o'er'—

of Pope's 'Essay on Man,' ii. 281-2.

renewed effort must be attributed partly to the recollection of his difficulties in getting his first play produced, partly to the fact that, his dramatic gains exhausted, he was almost immediately involved in a sequence of laborious taskwork. Still, he had never abandoned his ambition to restore humour and character to the stage; and as time went on, the sense of his past discouragements grew fainter, while the success of 'The Deserted Village' increased his importance as an author. Sentimentalism, in the meantime, had still a majority. Kelly, it is true, was now no longer to be feared. His sudden good fortune had swept him into the ranks of the party-writers, with the result that the damning of his next play, 'A Word to the Wise,' had been exaggerated into a political necessity. But the school which he represented had been recruited by a much abler man, Richard Cumberland, and it was probably the favourable reception of Cumberland's 'West Indian' that stimulated Goldsmith into striking one more blow for legitimate comedy. At all events, in the autumn of the year in which 'The West Indian' was produced, he is hard at work in the lanes at Hendon and Edgware, 'studying jests with a most tragical countenance' for a successor to 'The Good-Natur'd Man.'

To the modern spectator of 'She Stoops to Conquer,' with its unflagging humour and bustling action, it must seem almost inconceivable that its stage qualities can ever have been questioned. Yet questioned they undoubtedly were, and Goldsmith was spared none of his former humiliations. Even from the outset all was against him. His difference with Garrick had long been adjusted, and the Drury Lane manager would now probably have accepted a new play from his pen, especially as that astute observer had already detected signs of a reaction in the public taste. But Goldsmith was morally bound to Colman and Covent Garden; and Colman, in whose hands he placed his manuscript, proved even more disheartening and unmanageable than Garrick had been in the past. Before he had come to his decision, the close of 1772 had arrived. Early in the following year, under the irritation of suspense and suggested amendments combined, Goldsmith hastily transferred his proposal to Garrick; but, by Johnson's advice, as hastily withdrew it. Only by the express interposition of Johnson was Colman at last induced to make a distinct promise to bring out the play at a specific date. To believe in it, he could not be persuaded, and his contagious anticipations of its failure passed insensibly to the actors, who, one after another shuffled out of their parts. Even over the epilogue there were vexatious disputes, and when at last, in March, 1773, 'She Stoops to Conquer' was performed, its leading actor had previously held no more exalted position than that of ground-harlequin, while one of its most prominent characters had simply been a post-boy in 'The Good-Natur'd Man.' But once fairly upon the boards neither lukewarm actors nor an adverse manager had any further influence over it, and the doubts of every one vanished in the uninterrupted applause of the audience. When, a few days later, it was printed with a brief and grateful dedication to its best friend, Johnson, the world already knew with certainty that a fresh masterpiece had been added to the roll of English Dramatic Literature, and that 'genteel comedy' had received a decisive blow.

The effect of this blow, it must be admitted, had been aided not a little by the appearance, only a week or two earlier, of Foote's clever puppet-show of 'The Handsome Housemaid; or, Piety in Pattens,' which was openly directed at Kelly and his following. But ridicule by itself, without some sample of a worthier substitute, could not have sufficed to displace a persistent fashion. This timely corrective 'She Stoops to Conquer,' in the most unmistakable way, afforded. From end to end of the piece there is not a sickly or a maudlin word. Even Sheridan, writing 'The Rivals' two years later, thought it politic to insert 'Faulkland' and 'Julia' for the benefit of the sentimentalists. Goldsmith made no such concession, and his wholesome, hearty merriment put to flight the Comedy of Tears,— even as the Coquecigrues vanished before the large-lunged laugh of Pantagruel. If, as Johnson feared, the plot bordered slightly upon farce— and of what good comedy may this not be said? —at least it can be urged that its most farcical incident, the mistaking of a gentleman's house for an inn, had really happened, since it had happened to the writer himself. But the superfine objections of Walpole and his friends are now ancient history—history so ancient that it is scarcely credited, while Goldsmith's manly assertion (after Fielding) of the author's right 'to stoop among the low to copy nature,' has been ratified by successive generations of novelists and playwrights. What is beyond dispute is the healthy atmosphere, the skilful setting, the lasting freshness and fidelity to human nature of the persons of his drama. Not content with the finished portraits of the Hardcastles (a Vicar and Mrs. Primrose promoted to the squirearchy),—not content with the incomparable and unapproachable Tony, the author has managed to make attractive what is too often insipid, his heroines and their lovers. Miss Hardcastle and Miss Neville are not only charming young women, but charming characters, while Marlow and Hastings are much more than stage young men. And let it be remembered—it cannot be too often remembered—that in returning to those Farquhars and Vanbrughs 'of the last age,' who differed so widely from the Kellys and Cumberlands of his own, Goldsmith has brought back no taint of their baser part. Depending solely for its avowed intention to 'make an audience merry,' upon the simple development of its humourous incident, his play (wonderful to relate !) attains its end without resorting to dubious suggestion or equivocal intrigue. Indeed, there is but one married woman in the piece, and she traverses it without a stain upon her character.

'She Stoops to Conquer' is Goldsmith's last dramatic work, for the trifling sketch of 'The Grumbler' had never more than a grateful purpose. When, only a year later, the little funeral procession from 2, Brick Court laid him in his unknown grave in the Temple burying-ground, the new comedy of which he had written so hopefully to Garrick was still non-existent. Would it have been better than its last fortunate predecessor?—would those early reserves of memory and experience have still proved inexhaustible? The question cannot be answered. Through debt, and drudgery, and depression, the writer's genius had still advanced, and these might yet have proved powerless to check his progress. But at least it was given to him to end upon his best, and not to outlive it. For, in that critical sense which estimates the value of a work by its excellence at all points, it can scarcely be contested that 'She Stoops to Conquer' is his best production. In spite of their beauty and humanity, the lasting quality of 'The Traveller' and 'The Deserted Village' is seriously prejudiced by his half-way attitude between the poetry of convention and the poetry of nature —between the gradus epithet of Pope and the direct vocabulary of Wordsworth. With the 'Vicar of Wakefield' again, immortal though it be, it is less his art that holds us than his charm, his humour, and his tenderness, which tempt us to forget his inconsistency and his errors of haste. In 'She Stoops to Conquer,' neither defect of art nor defect of nature forbids us to give unqualified admiration to a work which lapse of time has shown to be still unrivalled in its kind.

ANGELO'S 'REMINISCENCES.'

IN the year 175— (it is not possible to fix the date more precisely), there was what would now be called a public assault of arms at one of the great hotels of pre-revolutionary Paris. Among the amateurs who took part in it—for there were amateurs as well as professionals—was a foreign *protégé* of the Duke de Nivernais, that amiable and courteous nobleman who subsequently visited this country at the close of the Seven Years' War, in the character of Ambassador Extraordinary and Plenipotentiary from his Most Christian Majesty, Louis XV. The stranger, who was in the prime of life, was of graceful figure and address, and his name had been no sooner announced than an English lady, then visiting the French capital, and possessed of great vivacity and considerable personal attractions, stepped forward and presented him with a bunch of roses. He received it with becoming gallantry, fastened it carefully on his left breast, and forthwith declared that he would defend it against all comers. What is more, he kept his promise. He afterwards 'fenced with several of the first masters, not one of whom,' says the narrator of the story, 'could disturb a single leaf of the *bouquet*.' The lady was the celebrated Mrs. Margaret Woffington, then in the height of her fame as a beauty and an actress; the gentleman was an Italian, travelling for his pleasure. He was the son of a well-to-do merchant at Leghorn, and he was called Domenico Angelo Malevolti Tremamondo.

Shortly after the foregoing incident, Signor Domenico Angelo Malevolti Tremamondo ('I love'—says Goldsmith of Miss Carolina Wilelmina Amelia Skeggs — 'to give the whole name!') transported his foil and his good looks to this country. In addition to his proficiency as a fencer, he was ' a master of equitation,' having been a pupil of the then famous scientific horseman, Teillagory [1] the elder. These were accomplishments which speedily procured for him both popularity and patrons in London. He became in a few months *écuyer* to Henry Herbert, tenth Earl of Pembroke, who was not only an accomplished cavalier himself, but was then, or was soon

[1] Here and elsewhere we correct Angelo's spelling.

to be, lieutenant-colonel of Elliot's Light Horse, a crack dragoon regiment, which, by the way, numbered among its corporals the future Astley of the Westminster Bridge Road Amphitheatre. Lord Pembroke had private *manèges* both in the neighbourhood of his house in Whitehall Gardens (part of the present No. 7), and at his family seat of Wilton, near Salisbury. At first his *écuyer* confined himself to teaching riding; but a chance encounter at the Thatched House Tavern with Dr. Keys, a well-known Irish fencer, in which he vanquished his antagonist, determined his choice of the calling of a *maître d'armes*. His first pupil was the Duke of Devonshire. Later he was engaged by the Princess of Wales to instruct the young princes in horsemanship and the use of the small sword, for which purposes premises were provided in Leicester Fields, within two doors from Hogarth's dwelling in the east corner. Before many years were over, Domenico Angelo —for he seems to have discarded first one and then the other of his last two names—set up a riding school of his own in Soho. But previously to all this, and apparently not long after his arrival in London, he had fallen in love with, and taken to wife, the daughter of an English naval officer. Judging from the picture of her which

Reynolds painted in 1766, the bride (who was a minor) must have been as handsome as her husband. The marriage took place in February, 1755, at St. George's, Hanover Square, the register of which duly records the union, by license of the Archbishop of Canterbury, of Domenico Angelo Malevolti, Esq., bachelor, and Elizabeth Johnson, spinster. The pair had a son, the Henry Angelo from whose disorganised and gossiping 'Reminiscences'[1] most of the foregoing particulars are derived.

Harry Angelo, so he was called, is not explicit as to the date of his birth, which probably took place at the end of 1759 or the beginning of 1760. It seems at first to have been intended that he should enter the Navy; and, as a matter of fact, he was actually enrolled by Captain Augustus Hervey (Lady Hervey's second son) on the books of the 'Dragon' man-of-war in the capacity of midshipman, thereby becoming entitled, at an extremely tender age, to some twenty-five guineas prize money. After a short period under Dr. Rose of Chiswick, the translator of Sallust and editor of 'The Monthly Review,'

[1] 'Reminiscences of Henry Angelo, with Memoirs of his late Father and Friends,' 2 vols., London: Colburn and Bentley, 1830.

he went to Eton, where his father taught fencing; and at Eton he remained for some years. Two of his school-fellows were Nathan and Carrington Garrick, the actor's nephews; and young Angelo had pleasant memories of their uncle's visits to Eton, where, being a friend of the elder Angelo, he would regale all three boys sumptuously at the Christopher inn, and amuse them with quips and recitations.[1] Harry Angelo had even the good fortune, while at Eton, to be taken to that solemn tomfoolery, the Stratford Jubilee of 1769, in which his father doubled the part of Mark Antony with that of director of fireworks. Another occasional visitor to the school, magnificently frogged and braided after the fashion of his kind, was the Italian quack Dominicetti, also a family friend, who treated the boys royally. But perhaps the most interesting memories of young Angelo's Eton days are those which recall a holiday spent at Amesbury with his father and mother, as the guest of the Duke and Duchess

---

[1] Apparently Garrick often did this. Once, at Hampton, he read Chaucer's 'Cock and Fox' to the boys after supper, and then, having recited Goldsmith's 'Hermit,' fell asleep in his arm-chair. Thereupon Mrs. Garrick, taking off her lace apron, fondly placed it over his face, and motioned her young friends away to bed.

of Queensberry. In his old age he could clearly picture the tall, thin figure of the taciturn Duke, in high leather gaiters, short-skirted frock, and gold-laced hat; and he well remembered the Duchess, then nearly eighty, but still energetic and garrulous, in a Quaker-coloured silk and black hood. He also remembered that he was allowed (like Gay before him) to fish for carp in the Amesbury water.

When he was entering his seventeenth year, Harry Angelo was sent to Paris to learn French. He was placed *en pension* in the Rue Poupé with a M. Boileau, a half-starved *maître de langue*, who, since he is seriously likened by his pupil to the Apothecary in 'Romeo and Juliet,' must really have resembled the typical Frenchman as depicted by Smollett and Rowlandson. Boileau was a conscientious teacher, but a miserable caterer; and young Angelo, after narrowly escaping collapse from starvation and close confinement, was eventually removed from his care. He passed, in the first instance, to a M. Liviez, whose wife was English, and (notwithstanding an undeniable squint) of a shape sufficiently elegant to have served as the model for Roubillac's figure of Eloquence on the Argyll tomb at Westminster Abbey. M. Liviez had been a dancer, and ballet-master at a London theatre. At this date he was a *bon vivant*, who collected prints. He was also subject to fits of hypochondria (probably caused by over-eating), when he would imagine himself Apollo, and fiddle feverishly to the nine Muses, typified for the nonce by a hemicycle of chairs. As both he and his wife preferred to speak English, they made no pretence to teach their lodger French; but, from the point of commissariat, the change from the Rue Poupé to the Rue Battois was 'removal from Purgatory to Paradise.' While Angelo was in Paris, Garrick sent him an introduction to Préville, whom Sterne describes as 'Mercury himself,' and who was, indeed, in some respects Garrick's rival. Préville knew Foote; and when Foote came to the French capital, he invited Angelo to a supper, at which Préville was present. Foote, binding Angelo to secrecy, delighted the company by mimicking their common acquaintance, the great Roscius; and Préville in his turn imitated the leading French comedians. All this was not very favourable to proficiency in the French language, which Angelo would probably have learned better in M. Boileau's garret. On the other hand, under Motet, then the champion *pareur* of the Continent, he became an expert swordsman—able, and only too willing, to take part in the encounters which, in the Paris of the day, were as common as street rows in London. But apart from swallowing the button and some inches of a foil when fencing with Lord Massereene in the Prison of the Abbaye (where that nobleman was unhappily in durance for debt), he seems to have enjoyed an exceptional immunity from accidents of all kinds.

He returned to London in 1775. His home at this time was at Carlisle House,[1] in King's Square Court (now Carlisle Street), Soho. It was a spacious old Caroline mansion of red brick, which had belonged to the Howard family, and had been bought by Domenico Angelo from Lord Delaval, brother of Foote's patron, the Sir Francis to whom he dedicated his comedy of 'Taste.' There were lofty rooms with enriched ceilings; there was a marble-floored hall; there was a grand decorated staircase painted by Salvator's pupil, Henry Cook. In this building, at the beginning of 1763, its new owner had opened his fencing

[1] Not to be confounded with Carlisle House on the other side of Soho Square, which was occupied from 1760 to 1778 by the enterprising Mrs. Teresa Cornelys, whose ball-room was in Sutton Street, on the site of the present Roman Catholic Church of St. Patrick.

school, and subsequently, in the garden at the back, had erected stables and a *manège*, which extended to Wardour Street. Between pupils, resident and otherwise, and troops of friends, Carlisle House must always have been well filled and animated. Garrick, who was accustomed to consult the elder Angelo on matters of costume and stage machinery, was often a visitor, and presented his adviser with a magnificent silver goblet (long preserved by the Angelos as an heirloom), which held three bottles of Burgundy. Richard Brinsley Sheridan and his father were also friends, and it was from Domenico Angelo that the younger man, as a boy at Harrow, acquired that use of the small sword which was to stand him in such good stead in his later duel with Captain Mathews. Wilkes, again, resplendent in his favourite scarlet and gold, not seldom looked in on his way from his Westminster or Kensington houses; and Foote, the Chevalier D'Éon, and General Paoli were constant guests. Horne Tooke, who lived hard by in Dean Street, was another intimate; and, when he was not discussing contemporary politics with Wilkes and Tom Sheridan, would sometimes enliven the company by singing a parody on 'God save the King,' which was not entirely to the loyal taste of the elder Angelo. Bach of the harpsichord,[1] with Abel of the *viol-da-gamba*, were next-door neighbours and free of the house; Bartolozzi the engraver, and his inseparable Cipriani, were on an almost equally favoured footing. Another *habitué* was Gainsborough, whose passion for music is historical, and from whom any one could extract a sketch in return for a song or a tune. The walls of Abel's room were covered by drawings acquired in this manner, and pinned loosely to the paper-hangings,—drawings which afterwards fetched their price at Langford's in the Piazza. Besides these, came Philip de Loutherbourg, whom Domenico Angelo had introduced to Garrick as scene painter for Drury Lane; and Canaletto, whom he had known at Venice; and Zoffany; and George Stubbs, the author of the 'Anatomy of the Horse,' who carried on his studies in the Carlisle House Riding School, no doubt taking for model, among others, that famous white charger Monarch, of which the presentment survives to posterity, under King William III. of immortal memory,

[1] This was John Christian Bach, Bach's son, familiarly known as 'English Bach.' Angelo calls him Sebastian, but John Sebastian Bach died in 1750. Bach and Abel jointly conducted Mrs. Cornelys' concerts.

in West's 'Battle of the Boyne.'[1] 'All the celebrated horse painters of the last, and some of the veterans of the present age,' says the author of the 'Reminiscences,' 'were constant visitors at our table or at the *manège*.' Lastly, an enthusiastic, though scarcely artistic, amateur of the Carlisle Street stud was the corpulent 'Hero of Culloden,' William, Duke of Cumberland. If not the greatest, he was certainly the heaviest prince in Christendom, since he rode some four-and-twenty stone, and, as a boy, Harry Angelo well remembered the significant sidelong dip of the carriage when His Royal Highness poised his ponderous person on the step.

An establishment upon the scale and traditions of Carlisle House (and there was also a 'cake-house' or country-box at Acton, for which Zoffany painted decorations) could only have been maintained at considerable expense. But in this respect Domenico Angelo seems to have been unusually fortunate, even for a foreigner. Within a short period after his arrival in England his income, according to his son, was over two thousand a year; and this sum, in the height of

[1] The 'Battle of the Boyne' was engraved by John Hall, Raimbach's master. See *post*, 'An English Engraver in Paris.'

his prosperity, was nearly doubled. After Harry Angelo's account of his life in Paris, his records, always disconnected, grow looser in chronology; added to which, it is never quite easy to distinguish his personal recollections from the mere floating hearsay of a retentive but capricious memory. One of his earliest experiences, however, on returning to England, must have been his attendance, in December, 1775, at the trial, in the Old Bailey, of Mrs. Margaret Caroline Rudd, for complicity in the forgery for which the Brothers Perreau were subsequently hanged.[1] His description of this fair-haired siren suggests a humbler Becky Sharp or Valérie Marneffe, and there can be little doubt that, as he implies, she owed her undeserved acquittal to the 'irresistible power of fascination' which captivated Boswell, and interested even his 'illustrious Friend.' Another incident at which Angelo assisted shortly afterwards, and which it is also possible to place precisely, was the riot that, in February, 1776, accompanied the attempt to produce at Drury

---

[1] One wonders whether Thackeray was thinking of this *cause célèbre* in 'Denis Duval,' where there is a Miss *Rudge* and a Farmer *Perreau*. Angelo, it may be added, was present at the hanging at Tyburn of M. de la Motte, an actual character in the same book.

Lane Parson Bate's unpopular opera of 'The Blackamoor wash'd White.' Angelo was one of a boxful of the author's supporters, who were forced to retire under the furious cannonade of 'apples, oranges, and other such missiles,' to which they were exposed. But a still more important theatrical event was his presence on that historic June 10, 1776, when Garrick bade farewell to the stage. He and his mother were in Mrs. Garrick's box, and the two ladies continued sobbing so long after they had quitted the house as to prompt the ironic comment of the elder Angelo that they could not have grieved more at the great man's funeral itself. Harry Angelo was also a spectator of the progress to Tyburn, in the following February, of the unfortunate Dr. Dodd, to whom, and to the horrors of 'Execution Day' in general, he devotes some of the latter pages of his first volume. 'His [Dodd's] corpse-like appearance produced an awful picture of human woe. Tens of thousands of hats, which formed a black mass, as the coach advanced were taken off simultaneously, and so many tragic faces exhibited a spectacle the effect of which is beyond the power of words to describe. Thus the procession travelled onwards through the multitude, whose silence added to the awfulness of the scene.' Two years later Angelo witnessed the execution of another clergyman, James Hackman, who was hanged for shooting Lord Sandwich's mistress, Martha Reay. The murder—it will be remembered—took place in the Piazza at Covent Garden, as the lady was leaving the theatre, and Angelo, according to his own account, had only quitted it himself a few minutes before. He afterwards saw the body of the criminal under dissection at Surgeons' Hall, —a gruesome testimony to the truth of Hogarth's final plate in the ' Four Stages of Cruelty.'

The above, the Gordon riots of '80, and the burning in '92 of Wyatt's Pantheon, are some of the few things in Angelo's first volume which it is practicable to date with certainty. The second volume is scarcely more than a sequence of headed paragraphs, roughly parcelled into sections, and difficult to sample. Like his father (who died at Eton in 1802), he became a ' master of the sword,' and like him, again, he lived upon terms of quasi-familiarity with many titled practitioners of that art,—being, indeed, upon one occasion the guest of the Duke of Sussex at the extremely select Neapolitan Club, an honour which, as the Prince of Wales was also present, seems to have been afterwards regarded as too good to be believed. Like Domenico Angelo, also, he had an extensive acquaintance with the artists and actors of his day. He had himself learned drawing at Eton under the Prince's master, Alexander Cozens, the apostle of 'blottesque,' and had studied a little with Bartolozzi and Cipriani. He had even ventured upon a few caricatures, in particular one of Lady Queensberry's black *protégé*, Soubise; and he was intimate with Thomas Rowlandson, whom he had known from boyhood, and followed to his grave in April, 1827. When Rowlandson was on his continental travels, Angelo was living in Paris, and he possessed many of the drawings which his friend executed at this time. In London they were frequently companions at Vauxhall and other places of amusement, where Rowlandson's busy pencil found its field of activity; and together they often heard the chimes at midnight in the house at Beaufort Buildings inhabited by Rowlandson's fat Mæcenas, the banker Mitchel, one of whose favourite guests was Peter Pindar. Angelo gives a good many anecdotes which have been utilized by Rowlandson's biographers; but perhaps the least hackneyed record of their alliance is contained in the pages which describe their joint visit to Portsmouth to see the French prizes after Lord Howe's victory of the 1st June, 1794, Angelo got down first, and went on board the largest French vessel, the 'Sans Pareil' (80 guns). He gives a graphic account of the appalling devastation,—the decks ploughed up by the round shot, the masts gone by the board, the miserable boyish crew, the hogshead of spirits to keep up their courage in action, the jumble of dead and dying in the 'tween decks, and above all, the terrible, sickening stench. On Howe's vessel, the 'Queen Charlotte,' on the contrary, there was scarcely a trace of battle, though another ship, the 'Brunswick,' had suffered to a considerable extent. Rowlandson joined Angelo at Portsmouth, and they witnessed together the landing of the prisoners. Afterwards they visited Forton, where, upon leaving one of the sick wards, Rowlandson made a ghastly study of a dying 'Mounseer' sitting up in bed to write his will, a priest with a crucifix at his side. But by this time Angelo had had enough of the horrors of war, and he returned to town, leaving Rowlandson to go on to Southampton to make—so he says—sketches of Lord Moira's embarkation for La Vendée. Here, however, the writer's recollection must have failed him, for Lord Moira's fruitless expedition was nearly a year old. What Rowlandson no doubt saw, was his Lordship's departure for Ostend to join the Duke of York. Angelo speaks highly of the—for Rowlandson—unusual finish and spirit of these drawings, with their boatloads of soldiers and studies of shipping. They were purchased by Fores of Piccadilly, but do not appear to have been reproduced. There is, however, at South Kensington a sketch by Rowlandson of the French prizes coming into Portsmouth, which must have been executed at this date.

Another associate of Angelo, and also of Rowlandson, was John (or more familiarly, Jack) Bannister, the actor. Bannister and Rowlandson had been students together at the Royal Academy, and had combined in worrying, by mimicry and caricature, gruff Richard Wilson, who had succeeded Frank Hayman as librarian. In the subsequent pranks of this practical joking age, Angelo, who had known them both from boyhood, often made a third; and he was present upon an occasion which was as unfeignedly pathetic as Garrick's famous farewell,—the farewell of Bannister to the stage. Many of the anecdotes contained in the entertainment which preceded this leave-taking— namely, 'Bannister's Budget,'— were included by permission in the 'Reminiscences;'

and Angelo, who had learned elocution from Tom Sheridan, and was an excellent amateur actor, more than once played for Bannister's benefits, notably at the Italian Opera House in 1792 as Mrs. Cole in Foote's 'Minor,' and in 1800 before the Royal Family at Windsor as Papillon in 'The Liar,' also by Foote. On this latter occasion the bill records that Mr. H. Angelo, 'by particular desire,' obliged with 'A Solo Duet; or, Ballad Singers in Cranbourn Alley.' These were by no means his solitary dramatic essays. At the pretty little private theatre which, in 1788, that emphatically lively nobleman, Richard, seventh Earl of Barrymore, erected at Wargrave-on-Thames, he was a frequent performer. His first, or one of his first parts, was that of Dick in Vanbrugh's 'Confederacy,' when Barrymore played Brass; and a later and favourite impersonation was Worsdale's *rôle* of Lady Pentweazel in Foote's 'Taste.' Angelo is careful, however, to make it clear that the exigencies of his professional engagements did not permit him to go to the full length of the Wargrave Court of Comus—some of whose revels must have closely resembled the 'blind hookey' by which the footman in 'The Newcomes' described the doings of Lord Farintosh. As he seems, nevertheless, to have accompanied Barry-

more to low spouting-clubs like Jacob's Well; to
have driven with him at night through the long
straggling street of Colnbrook, while his sportive
Lordship was industriously 'fanning the daylights,'
i.e., breaking the windows to right and left with
his whip; and to have serenaded Mrs. Fitzherbert
in his company at Brighton,—he had certainly
sufficient opportunities for studying the ' caprices
and eccentricities' of this illustrious and erratic
specimen of what the late Mortimer Collins was
wont to describe as the 'strong generation.' Besides
acting at Wargrave, he had also often joined in the
private theatricals at Brandenburgh House, then
the Hammersmith home of Lord Berkeley's sister,
that Margravine of Anspach whose comedy of
' The Sleep-walker' Walpole had printed at the
Strawberry Hill Press. Lastly, he was a member
of the short-lived Pic-Nic Society inaugurated by
Lady Buckinghamshire, an association which
combined balls and private plays with suppers on
the principle of the line in Goldsmith's ' Retaliation,'—

'Each guest brought his dish, and the feast was united.'

Lady Buckinghamshire, a large personage, with
a good digestion and an unlimited appetite for
pleasure, was one of the three card-loving leaders

of fashion satirised so mercilessly by Gillray as
'Faro's Daughters,'—her fellow-sinners being
Lady Archer and Mrs. Concannon. But whatever may have happened over the green tables at
St. James's Square, 'gaming'—writes Angelo—
'formed no part of the plan of the Pic-Nics.'
Not the less, they had their element of chance.
It was the practice to draw lots for furnishing
the supper, an arrangement which, if it sometimes
permitted the drawers to escape with the trifling
contribution of a pound cake or a bag of China
oranges, more frequently imposed upon them the
enforced provision of a dozen of champagne or
a three-guinea Périgord pie.

It would take a lengthy article to exhaust the
budget of these chaotic memories, even if one
made rigid selection of those incidents only in
which the writer affirms that he was personally
concerned. Not a few of the stories, however,
are common property, and are told as well elsewhere. For instance, Angelo repeats the anecdote of Goldsmith's 'Croaker,' Shuter, who, following—for his 'Cries of London'—a particularly
musical vendor of silver eels, found to his vexation that on this particular occasion the man
was unaccountably mute. Questioning him at
length, the poor fellow explained, with a burst of

tears, that his *vife* had died that day, and that he could not 'cry.' This is related in Taylor's 'Records,' and no doubt in a dozen places besides. Similarly, the anecdote of Hayman the painter and the Marquis of Granby having a bout with the gloves previous to a sitting, is to be found in the 'Somerset House Gazette' of 'Ephraim Hardcastle' (W. H. Pyne);[1] and it has been suggested—we know not upon what authority—that Pyne had a good deal to do with Angelo's chronicles. Be this as it may, there are plenty of anecdotes which are so obviously connected with the narrator that, even if all the make-weights be discarded, a residue remains which is far too large to be dealt with here. We shall confine ourselves to the few pages which refer to Byron, whom Angelo seems to have known well. Byron, who had been one of Angelo's pupils at Harrow, had interested himself in establishing Angelo as a fencing master at Cambridge, where he entertained him and Theodore Hook at dinner, seeing them off himself afterwards by the London stage, duly fortified with stirrup cups of the famous St. John's College beer. When later Byron left Cambridge for

[1] See *post*, 'The Grub Street of the Arts.'

town, Angelo seems to have taken great pains to find a book which his noble friend wanted in order to decide a wager, and his eventual success increased the favour in which he stood. He was subsequently in the habit of giving Byron lessons at the Albany in the broadsword,—a fearsome exercise which was chosen in view of the pupil's tendency to flesh, and for which he elaborately handicapped himself with furs and flannels. Of the relations between Angelo and Byron at this date a memento is still said to survive at Mr. John Murray's in Albemarle Street. It is a screen made by Angelo for his patron. On one side are all the eminent pugilists from Broughton to Jackson; on the other the great actors from Betterton to Kean. When Byron left the country in 1816 the screen was sold with his effects, and so passed into the pious hands of its present possessor.

Reference has already been made to what Mr. Egerton Castle accurately describes as Angelo's 'graceful ease' in eluding dates, and it should be added that he gives very few particulars respecting his personal history or his professional establishments. At first, it may be assumed, he taught fencing at his father's school in Carlisle Street. Later on, the *salle d'armes* which he

mentions oftenest is that formerly belonging to
the Frenchman Redas in the Opera House buildings at the corner of the Haymarket, almost facing
the Orange Coffee House, then the chosen resort
of foreigners of all sorts.¹ When the Opera
was burned down in 1789, these rooms were
destroyed, and Angelo apparently transferred his
quarters to Bond Street. Under the heading
'My Own Boastings,' he gives a list of his titled
and aristocratic pupils to the year 1817, and it is
certainly an imposing one. 'In the year of
[Edmund] Kean's benefit' [1825?] he strained
his thigh when fencing with the actor, and was
thenceforth obliged 'to bid adieu to the practical
exertions of the science.' His last years seem to
have been passed in retirement at a village near
Bath, and from his description of his means as
'a small annuity' it must be presumed that he
was poor. He had been married, and he speaks
of two of his sons to whom the Duke of York
had given commissions in the army; but that is

¹ Also, if we may trust a sketch by Rowlandson, of the
gentlemen of the army and navy. To the Orange Coffee
House—it may be mentioned—under cover to an imaginary
'Mr. Grafton', Thomas Lowndes, the Fleet Street pub-
lisher, forwarded in 1778 the proofs of Fanny Burney's
'Evelina' ('Early Diary,' 1889, ii. 214).

all he says on the subject. Besides the volumes of 'Reminiscences,' he compiled a miscellany entitled 'Angelo's Pic-Nic,' to which George Cruikshank contributed a characteristic frontispiece. In addition to this, he issued an English version in smaller form of his father's 'École des Armes,' a magnificent subscription folio which had first appeared in 1763;[1] and was reproduced two years later, under the head *Escrime*, in the Supplement to the 'Encyclopédie' of Diderot and D'Alembert. The translation of the 'School of Fencing,' as the smaller book of 1787 was called, is attributed to Rowlandson. Rowlandson also etched twenty-four plates for Angelo on the use of the Hungarian and Highland broadsword. These were put forth in 1798-9 by T. Egerton of the 'Military Library near Whitehall', the adventurous publisher who printed the first three novels of Jane Austen.

[1] Domenico Angelo, Lord Pembroke, and the Chevalier D'Éon stood as models for the illustrations, which were designed by Gwynn the painter. They were engraved by Grignion, Ryland, and Hall.

THE LATEST LIFE OF STEELE.

ONE of the things that most pleased Lord Macaulay in connection with his famous article in the 'Edinburgh' on Miss Aikin's 'Life of Addison,' was the confirmation of a minor statement which he had risked upon internal evidence. He had asserted confidently that Addison could never have spoken of Steele in the 'Old Whig' as 'Little Dickey;' and by a stroke of good fortune, a few days after his article appeared, he found the evidence he required. At a bookstall in Holborn he happened upon Chetwood's 'History of the Stage,' and presently discovered that 'Little Dickey' was the nickname of Henry Norris, a diminutive actor who had made his first appearance as 'Dicky' in Farquhar's 'Constant Couple.' Norris—it may be added—must have been a familiar figure to both Addison and Steele, because, besides taking a female part in 'The Funeral,' he had played Mr. Tipkin in 'The Tender Husband,' which contained 'many applauded strokes' from Addison's hand; and, only three years before Addison wrote the 'Old Whig,' had also acted in Addison's own comedy of 'The Drummer.' But the anecdote, with its tardy exposure of a time-honoured blunder, aptly illustrates the main function of the modern biographer who deals with the great men of the last century. Rightly or wrongly—no doubt rightly as regards their leading characteristics—a certain conception of them has passed into currency, and it is no longer practicable to alter it materially. A 'new view,' if sufficiently ingenious or paradoxical, may appear to hold its own for a moment, but, as a rule, it lasts no longer. Swift, Addison, Pope, Steele, Fielding, Goldsmith, Johnson, remain essentially what the common consent of the past has left them, and the utmost that latter-day industry can effect lies in the rectification of minute facts, and the tracing out of neglected threads of inquiry. Especially may it concern itself with that literary *nettoyage à sec* which has for its object the attenuation, and, if possible, the entire dispersing, of doubtful or discreditable tradition.

Of this method of biography, the 'Life of Steele,'[1] by Mr. George A. Aitken, is a favour-

[1] 'The Life of Richard Steele.' By George A. Aitken, 2 vols. London: Isbister, 1889.

able, and even typical, example. That Mr. Aitken is an enthusiast is plain; but he is also an enthusiast of exceptional patience, acuteness, and tenacity of purpose. He manifestly set out determined to know all that could possibly be known about Steele, and for some five years (to judge by his first advertisements) he laboured unweariedly at his task. The mere authorities referred to in his notes constitute an ample literature of the period, while the consultation of registers, the rummaging of records, and the general disturbance of contemporary pamphlets and documents which his inquiries must obviously have entailed, are fairly enough to take one's breath away. That in these days of hasty research and hastier publication such a train of investigation should have been undertaken at all, is remarkable; that so prolonged and arduous an effort should have been selected as the diploma-work of a young and previously untried writer, is more remarkable still. It would have been discouraging in the last degree if so much industry and perseverance had been barren of result, and it is satisfactory to find that Mr. Aitken has been fortunate enough to add considerably to the existing material respecting Steele. In the pages that follow it is proposed, not so much to recapitulate

Steele's story, as to emphasise, in their order, some of the more important discoveries which are due to his latest biographer.

Richard Steele, as we know already, was born at Dublin in March, 1672 (N. S.), being thus about six weeks older than Addison, who first saw the light in the following May. Beyond some vague references in 'The Tatler,' nothing definite has hitherto been ascertained about his parents, although his father (also Richard Steele) was reported to have been a lawyer. But the fact is now established that one Richard Steele, of Mountain (Monkstown), an attorney, was married in 1670 to a widow named Elinor Symes. These were Steele's father and mother. Steele himself tells us ('Tatler,' No. 181) that the former died when he was 'not quite five years of age,' and his mother, apparently, did not long survive her husband. The boy fell into the charge of his uncle, Henry Gascoigne, secretary to the first and second Dukes of Ormond, who had married a sister of one of Steele's parents. Through Ormond's influence his nephew was placed, in November, 1684, upon the foundation at the Charterhouse. Two years later he was joined there by Addison. It was then the reign of Dr. Thomas Walker, afterwards 'the ingenious T.

W.' of the 'Spectator,' but nothing has been recovered as to Steele's school-days. In November, 1689, he was elected to Christ Church, Oxford, with the usual exhibition of a boy on the Charterhouse foundation, and he matriculated in March, 1690,—Addison, then a demy at Magdalen, having preceded him. Letters already printed by Mr. Wills and others show that Steele tried hard for a studentship at Christ Church; but eventually he became a post-master at Merton, his college-tutor being Dr. Welbore Ellis, to whom he subsequently refers in the preface to the 'Christian Hero.' Of his intercourse with Addison at Smithfield and Oxford no record has come to light, and it is therefore still open to the essayist to piece the imperfections of this period by fictitious scores with the apple-woman or imaginary musings on the Merton terraces. But, in any such excursions in search of the picturesque, the fact that Steele was older instead of younger than Addison cannot safely be disregarded.

Why Richard Steele quitted the University to become a 'gentleman of the army' still remains obscure. His University career, if not brilliant, had been respectable, and he left Merton with the love of 'the whole Society.' Perhaps, like his compatriot Goldsmith, he preferred a red coat to a black one. At all events, in 1694, his restless Irish spirit prompted him to enlist as a cadet in the second troop of Horse Guards, then commanded by his uncle's patron, James Butler, second Duke of Ormond. When he thus 'mounted a war-horse, with a great sword in his hand, and planted himself behind King William the Third against Lewis the Fourteenth' he lost (he says) 'the succession to a very good estate in the county of Wexford in Ireland;' for which, failing further particulars, we may perhaps provisionally read 'castle in Spain.' His next appearance was among the crowd of minstrels who, in black-framed *folio*, mourned Queen Mary's death. Already he had written verse, and had even burned an entire comedy at college. The chief interest, however, of 'The Procession,' which was the particular name of this particular 'melodious tear,' was its diplomatic dedication to John, Lord Cutts, himself a versifier, and what was more important, also the newly appointed colonel of the Coldstream Guards. Cutts speedily sought out his anonymous panegyrist, took him into his household, and eventually offered him a standard in his regiment. There is evidence, in the shape of transcripts from the Blenheim MSS., that Steele was acting as Cutts' secretary *circa*

1696-7 (a circumstance of which, by the way, there is confirmation in Carleton's 'Memoirs'[1]); and it has hitherto been supposed that by his employer's interest—for Cutts gave him little but patronage—he became a captain in Lucas's Fusileers. Here, however, Mr. Aitken's cautious method discloses an unsuspected error. Steele is spoken of as a captain as early as 1700, and 'Lord Lucas's Regiment of Foot' (not specifically 'Fusileers') was only raised in February, 1702. If, therefore, before this date Steele had any right to the title of captain, it must have been as captain in the Coldstream Guards. Unfortunately, all efforts to trace him in the records of that regiment have hitherto proved unsuccessful. Neither as captain nor as ensign could its historian, General Mac-Kinnon, though naturally watchful on the point, find any mention of his name.

By 1700 the former post-master of Merton had become a seasoned man about town, a recognized wit, and an habitual frequenter of Will's. 'Dick Steel is yours,' writes Congreve to a

[1] 'At the time appointed' (says Carleton, writing at the date of the Assassination Plot of 1696) 'I waited on his lordship [Lord Cutts], where I met Mr. Steel (now Sir Richard, and at that time his secretary), who immediately introduced me.' ('Memoirs,' 1728, ch. iii.)

friend early in the year. Already, too, there are indications that he had begun to feel the 'want of pence which vexes public men.' From this, however, as well as his part in the coffee-house crusade against Dryden's 'Quack Maurus,' Blackmore, we must pass to the next rectification. That Steele fought a duel is already known. That it was forced upon him, that he endeavoured in every honourable way to evade it, and that finally, by misadventure, he all but killed his man, have been often circumstantially related. But the date of the occurrence has always been a mystery. Calling Luttrell and the 'Flying-Post' to his aid, Mr. Aitken has ascertained that the place was Hyde Park, the time June 16, 1700, and the other principal an Irishman, named Kelly. Luttrell's description of Steele as 'Capt. Steele, of the Lord Cutts regiment,' is confirmatory of the assumption that he was a captain in the Guards. Whether this was his only 'affair of honour,' or whether there were others, is doubtful; but it is not improbable that the repentant spirit engendered by this event, for his adversary's life long hung trembling in the balance, is closely connected with the publication, if not the preparation, of the 'Christian Hero,' which made its appearance a few months later.

Upon the scheme of this curious and by no means uninstructive manual, once so nearly forgotten as to be described as a poem, it is not necessary to linger now. But it may be noted that it was dated from the Tower Guard, where it was written, and that the governor of the Tower was the Lord Lucas in whose regiment Steele became an officer.

The year of which the first months witnessed the publication of the 'Christian Hero' witnessed in its close the production of Steele's first play, and, inconsequently enough, the one was the cause of the other. It was an almost inevitable result of the book that many of the author's former associates were alienated from him, while others, not nicely sensitive to the distinction drawn in Boileau's *ami de la vertu plutôt que vertueux*, maliciously contrasted his precepts with his practice. Finding himself 'slighted' (he says) 'instead of being encouraged, for his declarations as to religion,' it became 'incumbent upon him to enliven his character, for which reason he writ the comedy called "The Funeral," in which (though full of incidents that move laughter) Virtue and Vice appear just as they ought to do.' In other words, Steele endeavoured to swell that tide of reformation which Collier had set flowing by his 'Short View of the Immorality and Profaneness of the English Stage,' and he followed up his first effort of 1701 by the 'Lying Lover' (1703) and the 'Tender Husband' (1705), the second of which was avowedly written 'in the severity Collier required.' His connection with the purification of the contemporary drama, however, would lead us too far from the special subject of this paper,—the revised facts of his biography. Among these, the order of the plays as given above is an important item. Owing to some traditional misconception, the 'Lying Lover,' which was a rather over-emphatic protest against duelling, was believed by all the older writers to be the last of Steele's early dramatic efforts. As a natural consequence, its being 'damned for its piety' was made responsible for the author's long abstinence from the task of theatrical regeneration. Unfortunately for logic, the facts which, in this instance, Mr. Aitken has extended rather than discovered, are diametrically opposed to any such convenient arrangement. The 'Tender Husband,' and not the 'Lying Lover,' was the last of Steele's first three plays,— that is to say, the moralized Collier mixture was succeeded by a strong infusion of Molière, while, so far from leaving off writing for the stage, there

is abundant evidence that, but for other cares and
more absorbing occupations, Steele would speedily
have proceeded to 'enliven his character' with a
fresh comedy. Indeed, in a very instructive suit
against Christopher Rich of Drury Lane, preserved among the Chancery Pleadings in the
Record Office, mention is made of what may
well have been the performance in question. It
was to have treated a subject essayed both by
Gay and Mrs. Centlivre, the 'Election of
Gotham.'

The Chancery suit above referred to, which
arose out of the profits of the 'Tender Husband,'
began in 1707. Early in 1702 Steele had become
a captain in Lucas's, and between that date and
1704 must have spent a considerable portion of
his time at Landguard Fort, doing garrison duty
with his company. He lodged, according to
report, in a farmhouse at Walton. Mr. Aitken
prints from various sources several new letters
which belong to this period, together with some
account of another in the long series of lawsuits
about money with which Steele's biography begins
to be plentifully besprinkled. In an autograph
now in the Morrison collection, we find him
certifying with Addison to the unimpeachable
character of one 'Margery Maplesden, late Sutler

at the Tilt-yard Guard,' and we get passing glances of him at the Kit Cat Club and elsewhere. Perhaps we are right, too, in placing about this date the account of his search for the 'philosopher's stone.' The details of this episode in his career rest mainly upon the narrative of Mrs. de la Rivière Manley, the author of that 'cornucopia of scandal,' the 'New Atalantis;' but there is little doubt that there was ground for the story, since Steele himself, in later life, printed, without contradiction, a reference to it in 'Town Talk,' and it is besides connected with the next of Mr. Aitken's discoveries. According to 'Rivella,' an empiric, who found the sanguine Steele 'a bubble to his mind,' engaged him in the pursuit of the *magnum arcanum*. Furnaces were built without delay, and Steele's available resources began to vanish rapidly. In these transactions Mrs. Manley's husband played an ambiguous part, and, if we are to believe her, she herself impersonated the *Dea ex machina*, and warned Steele that he was being duped. It was not too soon. He only just saved his last negotiable property, his commission, and had to go into hiding. 'Fortune,' Mrs. Manley continues, 'did more for him in his adversity than would have lain in her way in prosperity; she threw him to seek for refuge in a house where was a lady with very large possessions; he married her, she settled all upon him, and died soon after.'

This—and to some extent it is a corroboration of the story—was Steele's first wife, hitherto little more than a shifting shadow in his biography. She is now clearly proved to have been a West Indian widow called Margaret Stretch, who had inherited an estate in Barbados of £850 a year from her brother, Major Ford. Steele married her in the spring of 1705, and buried her two years later. There is some indication that her death was caused by a fright given her (when *enceinte*) by Steele's only sister, who was insane; but upon this point nothing definite can be affirmed. Looking to the circumstances in which (as narrated by Mrs. Manley) the acquaintanceship began, it is not improbable that the personal charms of the lady had less to do with the marriage than the *beaux yeux de sa cassette*. In any case Steele can scarcely escape the imputation which usually attaches to the union of a needy bachelor with a wealthy widow, and, as will be seen, he was not long inconsolable.

Whether, even at the time of the marriage, the Barbados estate was really productive of much ready money may be doubted. But in August,

1706, Steele was appointed Gentleman Waiter to Queen Anne's consort, Prince George of Denmark, and a few weeks after his wife's death, through the recommendation of Arthur Mainwaring, one of the members of the Kit Cat Club, Harley, then a Secretary of State, gave him the post of Gazetteer with an increased salary of £300 a year. 'The writer of the "Gazette" now,' says Hearne in May, 1707, 'is Captain Steele, who is the author of several romantic things, and is accounted an ingenious man.' As 'Captain Steele' he continued for many years to be known, but it is assumed that he left the army before his second marriage, which now followed. At his first wife's funeral had arrived as mourner a lady of about nine and twenty, the daughter of a deceased gentleman of Wales, and the Miss Mary Scurlock who has since become historical as the 'Prue' of the well-known Steele letters in the British Museum. That she was an heiress, and, as Mrs. Manley says, a 'cried-up beauty,' was known, though in the absence of express pictorial assurance of the latter fact, it has hitherto been difficult to see her with the admiring eyes of the enthusiastic writer who signs himself her 'most obsequious obedient husband.' But while unable to add greatly to our knowledge of her character, Mr. Aitken has succeeded in discovering and copying her portrait by Kneller, a portrait which sufficiently justifies her husband's raptures. In Sir Godfrey's 'animated canvas,' she is shown as a very beautiful brunette, in a cinnamon satin dress, with a high, almost too high, forehead, and dark, brilliant eyes. Steele's phrase 'little wife' must have been a 'dear diminutive,' for she is not especially *petite*, but rather what Fielding's Mrs. James would style 'a very fine person of a woman,' and she has an arch, humourous expression, which suggests the wit with which she is credited. From the absence of a ring it has been conjectured that the portrait was taken before marriage. But Kneller was much more likely to have painted Mrs. Steele than Miss Scurlock, and the simple explanation may be either that rings were neglected or that the hands were painted in from a model. As in the case of Mrs. Stretch, Mr. Aitken has collected a mass of information about Mrs. Steele's relations. His good luck has also helped him to one veritable find. In her letter to her mother announcing her engagement, Miss Scurlock refers scornfully to a certain 'wretched impudence, H.O.,' who had recently written to her. This was manifestly a rejected but still importunate suitor, although the precise measure of his implied iniquity remained unrevealed. It seems that his name was Henry Owen of Glassalt, Carmarthenshire, and that he was an embarrassed widower of (in the circuitous language of the law) 'thirty, thirty-five, or forty years of age at the most'—that is to say, he was over forty. Miss Scurlock had known him as a neighbour from childhood, and for four or five years past, at Bath, at London, and at other places, he, being a needy man with an entailed estate, had been bombarding her with his addresses. Only two years before her engagement to Steele, finding her obdurate, he had trumped up a suit against her for breach of contract of marriage, which apparently was not successful. The 'Libel' and 'Answer,' printed from the records of the Consistorial Court of London, are more curious than edifying, and tend to show that Owen was rather a cur. But the whole story is useful indirectly as suggesting that Miss Scurlock's constitutional prudery was not the only reason why she surrounded Steele's worship of her with so much mystery. Abhorrence of 'public doings' in 'changing the name of lover for husband' was certainly superficially justifiable in the circumstances. A gentleman who had brought a suit against her in 1704 for breach of contract, and was still pestering her in August, 1707, with his unpalatable attentions, was quite capable of putting awkward obstacles in the way of that other ardent wooer from Lord Sunderland's office in Whitehall, who, in order to pay his court to 'the beautifullest object in the world,' was confessedly neglecting the 'Gazette' and the latest news from Ostend.

According to the license the marriage was to have taken place at St. Margaret's, Westminster; but the registers of that church, as well as those of St. James's, Piccadilly, and St. Martin's-in-the-Fields, have been fruitlessly searched for the record, and it is clear that, for some days, the ceremony was kept a secret, pending the arrival from Wales of Mrs. Scurlock's consent. It probably took place on the 9th of September, 1707, the day after the license was granted. In the previous month of August, Steele had rented a house, now no longer standing, in Bury Street, close to the turning out of Jermyn Street. This was a quarter of the town described by contemporary advertisements as in close proximity 'to St. James's Church, Chapel, Park, Palace, Coffee and Chocolate Houses'—in other words, it was in the very heart of the *beau monde;* and here Steele, moreover, would be within easy distance of the Court, and the Cockpit at Whitehall. He appears to have begun his establishment upon the lavish footing of a gentleman whose expectations are larger than his means, and whose wife's dignity demands, if not 'the gilt coach and dappled Flanders mares' of Pope's Pamela, at least a chariot, a lady's-maid, and an adequate equipment of cinnamon satin. On paper his yearly income from all sources, Mrs. Scurlock's allowance not included, was about £1250. But by far the largest portion of this was derived from the Barbados property, which, besides being encumbered by legacies, seems to have made irregular returns. His salary as Gazetteer was also subject to 'deductions,' and as with the modest pay of a captain in Lucas's he had dabbled in alchemy, he was probably considerably in debt. The prospect was not a cheerful one, either for him or for 'Prue,' as he soon begins to call his more circumspect better-half, and the signs of trouble are quickly present. Always irrepressibly sanguine, and generally without ready money, he is constantly turning some pecuniary corner or other, not without anticipations and borrowings that bring their inevitable train of actions and bailiffs. All this has to be gently tempered to the apprehensive 'Prue,' who, to her other luxuries, contrives to add a confidante, described as Mrs. (probably here it means Miss) Binns. Meanwhile her husband, bustling to and fro, now detained in his passage by a friend (and a 'pint of wine'),—now, it is to be feared, attentively shadowed by the watchful 'shoulder-dabbers,'— scribbles off, from remote 'blind taverns' and other casual coigns of vantage, a string of notes and notelets designed to keep his 'Absolute Governesse' at Bury Street minutely acquainted with his doings. Through all of these the 'dusky strand' ot the 'West Indian business'—in other words, the protracted negotiation for the sale of the Barbados property—winds languidly and inextricably.

Steele's letters to his wife, accessible in the reprints by Nichols of 1787 and 1809, are, however, too well known to need description, and although Mr. Aitken has collated them with the originals, he does not profess to have made any material addition to their riches. As they progress, they record more than one of the various attempts at advancement with which their writer, egged on by his ambition and his embarrassments is perpetually preoccupied. To-day it is a gentleman-ushership that seems within his reach; to-morrow he is hoping to be Under-

Secretary, *vice* Addison promoted to Ireland.
Then the strange disquieting figure of Swift
appears upon the scene, not, as it seems, to exercise its usual power of fascination over 'Prue,' by
whom—Swift declares later—Steele is governed
'most abominably, as bad as Marlborough.' With
April, 1709, comes the establishment of the
'Tatler,' and we enter upon thrice-gleaned
ground. The period covered by 'Mr. Bickerstaff's Lucubrations' and their successor, the
'Spectator,' lighted as it is by stray side-rays
from the wonderful 'Journal to Stella,' offers few
opportunities for any fresh illumination. Beyond
printing, from the Blenheim MSS., some interesting accounts of Jacob Tonson, bearing upon the
sale of the collected editions, and, from the
British Museum, an assignment to Buckley the
bookseller of a share in the 'Spectator,' Mr.
Aitken adds nothing that is absolutely new to
what has already been collected by Drake, Percy,
Chalmers, Nichols, and other writers. With respect to the unexplained cessation of the 'Tatler,'
he apparently inclines to the view that it was in
some sort the result of an understanding with
Harley, by which Steele, having been deprived of
his Gazetteership as a caution, was allowed to
retain, *quamdiu se bene gesserit*, his recently ac-

quired appointment as Commissioner of Stamps. But it is not probable that we shall ever know much more of a transaction concerning which Addison was unconsulted, and Swift uninformed. With all his customary openness, Steele could, if he pleased, keep his own counsel, and he seems to have done so on this occasion.

Nor are we really any wiser as to the reasons for the termination of the 'Spectator' in December, 1712, except that we know it to have been premeditated, since the 'Guardian' was projected before the 'Spectator' ceased to appear. From the Berkeley letters among Lord Egmont's MSS., we learn that Steele was once more dallying with his first love, the stage; and from the same source that, either early in February or late in January, the death of his mother-in-law had put him in possession of £500 per annum. To this improvement in his affairs is doubtless traceable that increased spirit of independence which precipitated what all lovers of letters must regard as his disastrous plunge into politics. Whatever the origin of the 'Guardian,' and however sincere its opening protests of neutrality, the situation was far too strained for one who, having a journal at his command, had been from his youth a partisan of the Revolution, and had already made rash entry into party quarrels. Before May, 1713, he was involved in bitter hostilities with Swift, arising out of a Tory attack on the Nottinghams for their desertion to the Whigs. A few weeks later found him insisting upon the demolition, under the Treaty of Utrecht, of the harbour and fortifications of Dunkirk, which demolition, it was shrewdly suspected, the Ministry were intending to forego. In June he had resigned his Commissionership of Stamps, and in August he was elected member for the borough of Stockbridge. Almost concurrently he issued a pamphlet entitled 'The Importance of Dunkirk consider'd.' Swift, henceforth hanging always upon his traces, retorted with one of his cleverest pamphlets, 'The Importance of the "Guardian" considered,' and the 'under-spurleathers' of the Tory press began also to ply their pens against Steele, who by this time had dropped the 'Guardian' for a professedly political organ, the 'Englishman.' Shortly afterwards he issued 'The Crisis,' a pamphlet on the Hanoverian succession, which Swift followed by his masterly 'Publick Spirit of the Whigs.' No sooner had Steele taken his seat in the House in February than he found that in the eyes of those in power he was a marked man. He was at once impeached for seditious utterances in 'The Crisis,' and, though he seems to have made an able defence, was expelled. Then, after a few doubtful months, Queen Anne died, his party came into power, and his troubles as a politician were at an end. In his best pamphlet, his 'Apology for Himself and his Writings,' he has given an account of this part of his career.

That career, as far as literature is concerned, may be said to close with the publication of the 'Apology,' in October, 1714. Not many months afterwards, on presenting an address, he was knighted by King George. During the rest of his life, which was prolonged to September, 1729, when he died at Carmarthen, he continued to publish various periodicals and tracts, none of which is of great importance. In December, 1718, Lady Steele died, and four years later her husband produced a fourth comedy, that 'Conscious Lovers' which honest Parson Adams declared to be (in parts) 'almost solemn enough for a sermon,' but which is nevertheless, perhaps by reason of Cibber's collaboration, one of the best constructed of his plays. Part of Mr. Aitken's second volume is occupied by Steele's connection, as patentee and manager, with Drury Lane Theatre, concerning which he has brought together much curious and hitherto unpublished information. Other points upon which new light is thrown are the publication of 'The Ladies Library,' the establishment of the 'Censorium,' Steele's application for the Mastership of the Charterhouse, Mr. John Rollos and his mechanical hoop-petticoat, the failure of Steele's once famous contrivance, the Fish-Pool, his connection with the Dyers, and so forth.

As regards Steele's character, Mr. Aitken's inquiries further enforce the conclusion that, in any estimate of it, considerable allowance must be made for the influence of that miserable and malicious contemporary gossip, of which, as Fielding says, the 'only basis is lying.' For much of this, Steele's ill-starred excursion into faction is obviously responsible. 'Scandal between Whig and Tory,' said the ingenuous and experienced author of the 'New Atalantis,' 'goes for nothing,' and apart from her specific recantation in the dedication to 'Lucius,' this sentiment alone should suffice to discredit her, at all events in the absence of anything like corroborative evidence. The attacks of Dennis and the rest are as worthless. We know that Steele was not 'descended from a trooper's horse,' and we know that he was not 'born at Carrickfergus' (whatever social disqualification that particular natal accident may entail). Why should we listen to the circulators of these or other stories—those of Savage, for example? With respect to Swift, the most dangerous because the most powerful detractor, it is clear, from the way in which he speaks of Steele and Steele's abilities *before* the strife of party had estranged them, that, if they had never quarrelled, he would have ranked him only a little lower than Addison.[1] And if Steele has suffered from scandal and misrepresentation, he has also suffered from his own admissions. The perfect frankness and freedom of his letters has been accepted too literally. Charming and unique as they are, they leave upon many, who do not sufficiently bear in mind their extremely familiar character, an ill-defined impression that he was over-uxorious, over-sentimental. But a man is not necessarily this for a few extravagant *billets-doux*, or many irreproachable persons who now, in the time-honoured words of Mr. Micawber, 'walk erect before their fellow-men,' would incur the like condemnation. Again, it is, to all appearance, chiefly due to the

---

[1] Swift's extraordinary pertinacity of hatred to Steele cannot wholly be explained by his sense of Steele's ingratitude. Steele had wounded him hopelessly in his most vulnerable part—he had laughed at his pretensions to political omnipotency, and he had (as Swift thought) also challenged his Christianity.

careless candour of some half-dozen of these documents that Steele has been branded as a drunkard. The fact is that, in an age when to take too much wine was no disgrace, he was neither better nor worse than his contemporaries; and there is besides definite evidence that he was easily overcome—far more easily than Addison. As to his money difficulties, they cannot be denied. But they were the difficulties of improvidence and not of profligacy, of a man who, with Fielding's joy of life and Goldsmith's 'knack of hoping,' always rated an uncertain income at its highest and not at its average amount, and who, moreover, paid his debts before he died. For the rest, upon the question of his general personality, it will suffice to cite one unimpeachable witness, whose testimony has only of late years come to light. Berkeley, who wrote for the 'Guardian,' and visited Steele much at Bloomsbury (where he saw nothing of Savage's bailiffs in livery), speaks expressly, in a letter to Sir John Perceval, of his love and consideration for his wife, of the generosity and benevolence of his temper, of his cheerfulness, his wit, and his good sense. He should hold it, he says, a sufficient recompense for writing the 'Treatise on Human Knowledge' that it gained him 'some share in the friendship of so worthy a man.' The praise of Berkeley—Berkeley, to whom Pope gives 'every virtue under heaven,' and who is certainly one of the noblest figures of the century—outweighs whole cartloads of Grub Street scandal and skip-kennel pamphleteers.

With Steele's standing as a man of letters we are on surer ground, since his own works speak for him without the distortions of tradition. To the character of poet he made no pretence, nor could he, although—witness the Horatian lines to Marlborough—he possessed the eighteenth-century faculty of easy octosyllabics. Of his plays it has been said that they resemble essays rather than dramas, a judgment which sets one wondering what would have been the critic's opinion if Steele had never written the 'Spectator' and the 'Tatler.' It is perhaps more to the point that their perception of strongly marked humourous character is far more obvious than their stagecraft, and that their shortcomings in this latter respect are heightened by Steele's debatable endeavours not (as Cowper says) 'to let down the pulpit to the level of the stage,' but to lift the stage to a level with the pulpit. As a political writer, his honesty and enthusiasm were not sufficient to secure him permanent success in a line where they are not always thrice-armed that

have their quarrel just; and it is no discredit to
him that he was unable to contend against the
deadly irony of Swift. It is as an essayist that
he will be best remembered. In the past, it has
been too much the practice to regard him as the
colourless colleague of Addison. We now know
that he deserves a much higher place; that
Addison, in fact, was quite as much indebted to
Steele's inventive gifts as Steele could possibly
have been indebted to Addison's sublimating spirit.
It may be that he was a more negligent writer
than Addison; it may be that he was inferior as
a literary artist; but the genuineness of his feelings frequently carries him farther. Not a few
of his lay sermons on anger, pride, flattery,
magnanimity, and so forth, are unrivelled in their
kind. He rallied the follies of society with unfailing tact and good-humour; he rebuked its
vices with admirable courage and dignity; and
he wrote of women and children as, in his day,
no writer had hitherto dared to do. As the first
painter of domesticity, the modern novel owes him
much. But modern journalism owes him more,
since—to use some words of his great adversary
—he 'refined it first, and showed its use.'

Mr. Aitken's book has been described in the
title to this paper as the 'latest' Life of Steele.

It will probably be the 'last.' No one, at all events, is likely to approach the subject again with the same indefatigable energy of research. To many of us, indeed, Biography, conceived in this uncompromising fashion, would be a thing impossible. To shrink from no investigation, however tedious, to take nothing at second-hand, to verify everything, to cross-examine everything, to leave no smallest stone unturned in the establishment of the most infinitesimal fact—these are conditions which presuppose a literary constitution of iron. It is but just to note that the method has its drawbacks. So narrow an attention to minutiæ tends to impair the selective power, and the defect of Mr. Aitken's work is—almost of necessity—its superabundance. It will be said that his determination to discover has sometimes carried him too far afield; that much of these two handsome volumes might with advantage have been committed to the safe-keeping of an appendix; that the mass of detail, in short, is out of proportion to its actual relevance. To this, in all likelihood, the author would answer that his book is not designed (in Landor's phrase) to lie—

'With summer sweets, with albums gaily drest,
Where poodle snifts at flower between the leaves;'

that he does not put it forward as a study or critical monograph; but that it is a leisurely and conscientious effort, reproducing much out-of-the-way information which is the lawful prize of his individual bow and spear; and that, rather than lose again what has been so painfully acquired, he is prepared to risk the charge of surplusage, content if his labours be recognized as the fullest and most trustworthy existing contribution towards the life and achievements of a distinguished man of letters who died nearly one hundred and seventy years ago. And this recognition his labours undoubtedly deserve.

THE AUTHOR OF 'MONSIEUR TONSON.'

'NEVER have a porch to your paper.' Acting upon this excellent maxim of the late Master of Balliol, we may at once explain that 'Monsieur Tonson' is the title of a long-popular recitation. It recounts, in rhyme of the Wolcot and Colman order, how, in the heyday of hoaxes and practical joking, a wag, called King in the verses, persecutes an unhappy French refugee in St. Giles's with repeated nightly inquiries for an imaginary 'Mr. Thompson,' until at length his maddened victim flies the house. And here comes in the effective point of the story. After a protracted absence abroad, the tormentor returns to London, when the whim seizes him to knock once more at the old door with the old question. By an extraordinary coincidence the Frenchman has just resumed residence in his former dwelling.

> Without one thought of the relentless foe,
> Who, fiend-like, haunted him so long ago,
> Just in his former trim he now appears:

> The waistcoat and the nightcap seemed the same,
> With rushlight, as before, he creeping came,
> And KING's detested voice astonish'd hears,—

the result being that he takes flight again, 'and ne'er is heard of more.' The author of this *jeu d'esprit* was John Taylor, the oculist and journalist; and it originated in a current anecdote, either actually founded on fact or invented by a Governor of Jamaica. After a prosperous career in prose, Taylor versified it for Fawcett, the comedian, who was giving recitations at the Freemasons' Tavern. It had an extraordinary vogue; was turned by Moncrieff into a farce (in which Gattie, and afterwards Matthews, took the leading part of Monsieur Morbleu, the Frenchman); was illustrated by Robert Cruikshank, and still, we are told, makes furtive appearance in popular 'Reciters.' By describing himself on the title-page of his memoirs as 'Author of "Monsieur Tonson,"' its writer plainly regarded the poem as his passport to fame; and whether one agrees with him or not, it may safely be taken as a pretext for some account of the gossiping and discursive volumes which contain his recollections.

John Taylor's grandfather, also John, was a person of considerable importance in his day, being indeed none other than the notorious oculist, or 'Ophthalmiater,' known as the 'Chevalier' Taylor. Irreverent persons seem to have hinted that, as a matter of fact, this new-fangled Ophthalmiater meant no more than old Quack 'writ large;' and one William Hogarth, generally on the side of the irreverent, hitched the Chevalier into a well-known satirical etching which collectors entitle indifferently 'Consultation of Physicians' or 'Company of Undertakers.' Here the gifted recipient (as *per* advertisement) of so many distinctions 'Pontifical, Imperial, and Royal,' appears ignobly with Mrs. Sarah Mapp, the Epsom bone-setter, and that famous Dr. Joshua Ward, referred to by Fielding, whose pill (like a much-vaunted nostrum of our own day) had the property of posting at once to the part affected. Yet the Chevalier, despite inordinate vanity, and a fondness for fine clothes which made him fair game for the mocker, was undoubtedly a man of ability. 'He has a good person, is a natural orator, and has a facility of learning foreign languages'—says Dr. King, who met him at Tunbridge; and apart from the circumstance that he had been a pupil of Cheselden the anatomist, he was really a very skilful operator for cataract, and wrote a long list of works or pamphlets on the eye. He was a familiar figure in the different

Courts of Europe for his cures, real and imaginary, the story of which he relates—without showing any 'remarkable diffidence in recording his own talents and attainments,' says his grandson —in three volumes of Memoirs,[1] having a longer title-page than that of ' Pamela.' Judging from his own account (which should probably be taken with the fullest allowance of cautionary salt); his experiences must have been peculiar, and his visiting list unusually varied. He asserts, without much detail, that he knew Lord Bath and Jack Sheppard; Mary Tofts, the Godalming rabbit-breeder, and Sarah, Duchess of Marlborough. He also professed acquaintance with Marshals Saxe and Keith; with Pöllnitz of the

---

[1] 'The History of the Travels and Adventures of the Chevalier John Taylor, Ophthalmiater . . . Author of 45 works in different Languages: the Produce for upwards of Thirty years, of the greatest Practice in the Cure of distempered Eyes, of any in the Age we live [*sic*]—Who has been in every Court, Kingdom, Province, State, City, and Town of the least Consideration in all Europe, without exception. Written by Himself . . . *Qui Visum Vitam Dat.* London: J. Williams, 1761-2.' This must not be confounded with the ' Life ' in two volumes published by Cooper in 1761, a coarse catchpenny invention by Lord Chesterfield's profligate protégé, the bricklayer poet, Henry Jones.

'Virginians;' with Theodore, the bankrupt King of Corsica; with Boerhaave, Albinus, Linnæus, Pope, Voltaire, Metastasio, La Fontaine, etc. (If the fabulist be intended, there is clearly some mistake, since La Fontaine departed this life about eight years before the Chevalier was born.)[1] He was a witness, he says, of the execution at Tyburn of Counsellor Christopher Layer for high treason (May, 1723), and he affirms that he was actually present in the Old Bailey upon that memorable occasion when Blake (*alias* Blue-skin) tried to cut the throat of Jonathan Wild. Having seen many men and cities, and full of honours— chiefly of foreign manufacture — the Chevalier died in a convent at Prague in 1780. At the time of his death, it may be noted, the famous Ophthalmiater was himself blind. He can scarcely be said to have wanted a *vates sacer*, for Churchill mentions him in 'The Ghost':

> Behold the CHEVALIER—
> As well prepar'd, beyond all doubt,
> To put Eyes in, as put them out.

And Walpole gave him a not very happy epigram:

[1] On the other hand he undoubtedly ministered to the ailing and painful boyhood of Gibbon ('Autobiographies,' 1896, p. 37).

> Why Taylor the quack calls himself *Chevalier*,
> 'T is not easy a reason to render;
> Unless blinding eyes, that he thinks to make clear,
> Demonstrates he's but a *Pretender*.

His only son, John Taylor the Second, was also an oculist, but not of equal eminence, although one of his cures—that of a boy born blind—obtained the honours of a pamphlet by Oldys the antiquary, and a portrait by Worlidge the etcher. At the Chevalier's death John Taylor applied for the post, which his father had held, of oculist to the King, but the appointment was given to the Baron de Wenzel, one of the Chevalier's pupils, who had been fortunate enough to operate successfully on the old Duke of Bedford, of 'Junius' notoriety. To John Taylor the Second succeeded John Taylor the Third, the 'Author of "Monsieur Tonson."' Beginning life as an oculist, like his father and grandfather, he achieved considerable reputation in that capacity, and by good luck obtained at Wenzel's death the very appointment which his father had failed to secure. But in mid-career he relinquished his profession for journalism. For many years he was proprietor and editor of 'The Sun' newspaper, and in 1827 he also published a couple of volumes of prologues, epilogues, sonnets, and occasional verses. His chief reputation, however, was that of a *raconteur*. 'In his latter days,' says 'The Literary Gazette,' in its obituary notice of May 19, 1832, he 'was, perhaps, as entertaining in conversation, with anecdote, playfulness, and satire, as any man within the bills of mortality.' Many of his good things are preserved in the two volumes of 'Records of My Life' which appeared shortly after his death,[1] to the compilation of which he was impelled by the perfidy of a former partner and the invitation of an 'eminent publisher,' presumably Mr. Edward Bull, of Holles Street, whose imprint the volumes bear. His recollections are set down without any other method than a certain rough grouping; they have the garrulity and the repetitions of the advanced age at which they were penned; but they contain, in addition to a good deal that he had heard from others, much that had come within his own experiences. As he professes strict veracity, it is from the latter class that we shall chiefly make selection, beginning

[1] 'Records of my Life; by the late John Taylor, Esquire, Author of "Monsieur Tonson."' 2 vols. London: Bull, 1832. The copy belonging to the present writer contains, besides inserted photographs, 'Addenda' by John Stirling Taylor, the author's son.

as in duty bound, with the anecdotes of literary men.

Concerning Johnson and Goldsmith he has not much to say beyond the fact that, as a boy, he had once delivered a letter for the latter at the Temple, but without seeing him. It is, however, to the 'Author of "Monsieur Tonson"' that we owe the historic episode of the borrowed guinea slipped under the door, which recurs so prominently in all Goldsmith's biographies; while he tells one anecdote of Johnson which, as far as we can discover, has escaped the annotators of Boswell. According to Dr. Messenger Monsey, physician of Chelsea Hospital—a rough, Abernethy sort of man, whom his admirers compared with Swift — upon one occasion, when the age of George III. was under discussion, Johnson burst in with a 'Pooh! what does it signify when such an animal was born, or whether he had ever been born at all?'—an ultra-Jacobital utterance which the Whig narrator did not neglect to accentuate by reminding his hearers that to this very 'usurper' Johnson subsequently owed his pension. But as Monsey did not like the Doctor, and Taylor calls him a 'literary hippopotamus,' the incident is probably exaggerated. Then there is a story of Dr. Parr, in which is concerned an-

other of the Johnson circle, Edmund Burke.
During the Hastings trial Parr was effusive
(Taylor says 'diffusive') about the speeches of
Sheridan and Fox, but silent as to Burke's, a circumstance which led that distinguished orator to
suggest interrogatively that he presumed Parr
found it faultless. 'Not so, Edmund,' was the
reply, in Parr's best Johnsonese; 'your speech
was oppressed by epithet, dislocated by paren-
thesis, and debilitated by amplification,'—a knock-
me-down answer to which 'Edmund' made no
recorded rejoinder. There is a touch of the lexi-
cographic manner in another anecdote, this time
of Hugh Kelly, the stay-maker turned dramatist
and barrister, who was so proud of his silver
that he kept even his spurs upon the sideboard.
Examining a lady at the trial of George Barrington, the pick-pocket, Kelly inquired elaborately,
'Pray, madam, how could you, in the immensity
of the crowd determine the identity of the man?'
As he found that his question was wholly unintelligible to the witness, he reduced it to 'How
do you know he was the man?' 'Because,'
came the instant reply, 'I caught his hand in my
pocket.' Taylor apparently knew both the Bos-
wells, father and son, and, indeed, playfully
claims part-authorship in the famous 'Life' upon

the ground that he had suggested the substitution of 'comprehending' for 'containing' in the title-page; and certainly—if that be proof—'comprehending' is there, and 'containing' is not.¹ He had also relations with Wilkes, whom he praises for his wit and learning. For his learning we have the evidence of his 'Catullus,' but his wit seems, like much wit of his day, to have been largely based upon bad manners. Once a certain over-goaded Sir Watkin Lewes said angrily to him, 'I'll be your butt no longer." Wilkes at once mercilessly retorted, 'With all my heart. I never like an empty one.'

Wolcot and Caleb Whitefoord of the 'Cross Readings,' Richard Owen Cambridge and Richard Cumberland—all figure in the 'Records.' Taylor thinks that the famous Whitefoord addition to 'Retaliation' was really by Goldsmith—a supposition which is not shared by modern Goldsmith critics. Of Wolcot there is a lengthy account, the most striking part of which refers to his last hours. Taylor asked him, on his death-bed, whether anything could be done for him. 'His answer, delivered in a deep and strong tone, was, "Bring back my youth,"' after

¹ For exact title, see *post*, 'Boswell's Predecessors and Editors,' p. 149.

which futile request he fell into the sleep in which he died. Cambridge Taylor seems to have known but slightly, and apart from a long story, for the authenticity of which he does not vouch, has nothing memorable to say of him, except that he declared he had written his 'Scribleriad' while under the hands of his hairdresser,—a piece of fine-gentleman affectation which recalls Molière's poetaster. But Taylor tells a story of Cumberland which is at least well invented. Once — so it runs — Cumberland stumbled on entering a box at Drury Lane Theatre, and Sheridan sprang to his assistance. 'Ah, sir!' said the writer of the 'West Indian,' 'you are the only man to assist a *falling* author.' 'Rising,' you mean,' returned Sheridan, thus, either by malice or misadventure, employing almost the exact words which, in the 'Critic,' he had put into the mouth of 'Sir Fretful Plagiary,'—a character admittedly modelled upon Cumberland himself. Sheridan, too, supplies more than one page of these recollections, and their writer professes to have been present when he (Sheridan) spoke as follows concerning a pamphleteer who had written against him: 'I suppose that Mr. —— thinks I am angry with him, but he is mistaken, for I never harbour resentment. If his punishment depended on me, I would show him that the dignity of my mind was superior to all vindictive feelings. Far should I be from wishing to inflict a capital punishment upon him, grounded on his attack upon me; but yet on account of his general character and conduct, and as a warning to others, I would merely order him to be publicly whipped three times, to be placed in the pillory four times, to be confined in prison seven years, and then, as he would enjoy the freedom more after so long a confinement, I would have him transported for life.'

At the date of the above deliverance, the scene of which was a tavern in Portugal Street,—perhaps the now vanished Grange public house,—Sheridan was lessee of Drury Lane Theatre. In later years Taylor was to become acquainted with another Drury Lane magnate, Lord Byron, with whom he corresponded and exchanged poems. Concerning Lady Byron he reports that Mrs. Siddons, whom he regarded as an unimpeachable authority, assured him that if she had no other reason to admire his Lordship's judgment and taste, she should be fully convinced of both by his choice of a wife,—a sentiment which should certainly be set down to the credit of a lady who is by no means over-praised. Among the Portugal Street roisterers was Richard Wilson, the painter. According to Taylor he must have been vintner as well, since most of the wine came from his cellar in Lincoln's Inn Fields (Great Queen Street), the company having condemned the tavern beverages. Apart from the fact that Wilson's 'favourite fluid,' like Churchill's, was porter, this particular is more out of keeping with his traditional lack of pence than another, also related by Taylor, in which he says that, upon one occasion, having procured Wilson a commission, he was obliged to lend him the money to buy brushes and canvas. With artists, however, Taylor's acquaintance was not large. He knew Peters the academician, afterwards the Rev.; and he knew Ozias Humphry the miniaturist, who in his old age became totally blind. With West and his rival Opie (Opie, like Wilson, lived in Queen Street) he was apparently on familiar terms, and he was often the guest of the former at the dinners which the Royal Academy of that day were accustomed to have on the anniversary of Queen Charlotte's birthday. Of West he speaks warmly; does not mention his vanity, and attributes much of his baiting by Peter Pindar to that satirist's partiality for Opie. Fuseli, another resident in Great Queen Street, and Northcote, also flit through the record; and there is reference to a supper at Reynolds's, where it was idly debated whether Johnson would have written the 'Reflections on the French Revolution' better than Burke, and where—on the topic *De mortuis*—Reynolds propounded the practical dictum that 'the dead were nothing, and the living everything,'—a sentiment which shows him to have been in agreement with the *On doit des égards aux vivants* of Voltaire. But, on the whole, the annalist's memories of artists are of meagre interest, and the only compact anecdote related of a member of the profession refers to the architect known popularly as 'Capability' Brown. Once when Lord Chatham, disabled by the gout, was hobbling painfully down the stairs of St. James's Palace, Brown had the good fortune to assist him to his carriage. Lord Chatham thanked him, adding pleasantly, 'Now, sir, go and adorn your country.' To which Brown the capable retorted neatly, 'Go you, my Lord, and save it.'

Of anecdotes of actors and actresses the Author of 'Monsieur Tonson' has no lack. As already stated, he was much in request for prologues and epilogues; he was an active and

intelligent dramatic critic, and he was, moreover, intimate with most of the leading players of his day. To make any adequate summary of so large a body of theatrical gossip would be difficult; but a few stories may be selected concerning some of the older men. Of Garrick, whom Taylor's father had seen when he first came out at Goodman's Fields, and regarded as the Shakespeare of actors, he tells a number of anecdotes which, unfamiliar when the 'Records' were published, are now fairly well-known. Taylor was, however, the first, we believe, to record that effective story of Mrs. Clive, who, watching Garrick from behind the scenes, between smiles and tears, burst at last into emphatic and audible expression of her belief that he could 'act a gridiron;' and Taylor also says that once, when his father was performing an operation for cataract, Garrick, who was present, so enthralled the nervous patient by his humour, that he forgot both his fears and his pain. Of Garrick's Lady Macbeth, Mrs. Pritchard, Taylor, deriving his information from his father, speaks highly, and considers that
† Johnson degraded her memory by describing her as 'an ignorant woman, who talked of her *gownd*.' (Mrs. Pritchard had acted the heroine in the

great man's 'Irene,' and it is possible that he was prejudiced.) To Macklin, another celebrated Macbeth,—being, indeed, the first who performed that part in the old Scottish garb,—Taylor makes frequent reference. He saw him in Iago, in Sir Paul Pliant of the 'Double Dealer,' and in other characters; but held that he was 'too theoretical for nature. He had three pauses in his acting—the first, moderate; the second, twice as long; but his last, or "grand pause," as he styled it, was so long that the prompter on one occasion, thinking his memory failed, repeated the cue . . . several times, and at last so loud as to be heard by the audience.' Whereupon Macklin in a passion rushed from the stage and knocked him down, exclaiming, 'The fellow interrupted me in my grand pause!' Quin, Macklin's rival, was also given to inordinate pauses, and once, while acting Horatio in Rowe's 'Fair Penitent' (the play in which George Primrose of Wakefield was to have made his début), he delayed so long to reply to the challenge of Lothario that a man in the gallery bawled out, 'Why don't you give the gentleman an answer, whether you will or no?' Taylor cites a good many instances of Quin's *gourmandise*, and of his ready, but rather full-flavoured wit. He is perhaps best when on his dignity. Once at Allen's of Prior Park (Fielding's 'Allworthy'), the imperious Warburton attempted to degrade the guest into the actor by insidiously pressing Quin to recite something. Quin accordingly spoke a speech from Otway's 'Venice Preserved' which contained the lines,—

> '*Honest men*
> Are the soft easy cushions on which knaves
> Repose and fatten,'—

delivering them with so unmistakable an application to Allen and Warburton respectively that he was never again troubled by the divine for a specimen of his declamatory powers. Another story told by Taylor of Quin may be quoted, because it introduces Mrs. Clive. She had invited Quin to stay at Cliveden (Little Strawberry), of which the appointments were on as minute a scale as those of Petit-Trianon. When he had inspected the garden, she asked him if he had noticed a tiny piece of water which she called her pond. 'Yes, Kate,' he replied, 'I have seen your *basin*, but did not see a wash-ball.' Taylor seems surprised that Walpole should have been so much attracted to Mrs. Clive, whose personal charms were small, and whose manners, he alleges, were rough and vulgar. He quotes, with apparent approval, some unpublished lines by Peter Pindar, criticising the epitaph in which Walpole declared that Comedy had died with his friend:

> 'Horace, of Strawberry Hill I mean, not Rome,
> Lo! all thy geese are swans, I do presume;
>   Truth and thy verses seem not to agree;
> Know Comedy is hearty, all alive;
> The Comic Muse no more expired with Clive
>   Than dame Humility will die with thee.'

But one need no more swear to the truth of an epitaph than of a song. Catharine Clive had both humour and good-humour; her indefatigable needle was continually employed in the decoration of Walpole's Gothic museum, and it may be concluded that he knew perfectly what he was about. As a near neighbour, a blue stocking might have been wearisome, a beauty dangerous, and she was probably of far more use to him than either.

Except for the 'gridiron' anecdote, however, Mrs. Clive does not play any material part in Taylor's chronicle. With a later luminary, Miss Farren, he was not actually acquainted, although he had met her once with Lord Derby (whom she ultimately married), and had admired her genuine sensibility in Miss Lee's 'Chapter of Accidents.' But he seems to have been on

intimate terms with Mrs. Abington, both in her
prime and also in her decline, for he was present
when she degraded herself by acting Scrub in the
'Beaux' Stratagem;'[1] and he had dined with her
at Mrs. Jordan's, when she talked unceasingly
and enthusiastically of Garrick,—a circumstance
which, considering the trouble she had given him
in his lifetime, may perhaps be regarded in the
light of an expiatory exercise. Taylor also knew
Mrs. Siddons, of whom he speaks warmly, saying
that he had been intimate with her for years, and
had 'many of her letters, with which even her
request would not induce him to part.' He was,
as a matter of fact, connected with the Kemble
family by marriage, his first wife, Mrs. Duill,
having been a Miss Satchell, whose sister had
married Stephen Kemble, a huge Trulliber of a
man who could act Falstaff without stuffing,
and had gone through all the experiences of a
strolling player, even to lunching in a Yorkshire
turnip-field.[2] Of John Kemble, and Charles

---

[1] There is a caricature of Mrs. Abington in this part by James Sayer.

[2] Stephen George Kemble died in June, 1822. While manager of the Newcastle Theatre, he was on intimate terms with Thomas Bewick, who engraved a portrait of him as Falstaff for a benefit ticket.

Kemble and his wife there is much in the
'Records,' but most of it has grown familiar by
repetition. There is also much of other actors
and actresses, as might be expected from one who
had seen Dodd as Sir Andrew Aguecheek, Lewis
as Mercutio, 'Gentleman' Smith as Charles in
the 'School for Scandal,' and Palmer—Lamb's
Jack Palmer—as Sneer in the 'Critic.' Taylor's
portrait, in the poem called 'The Stage,' of the
last-named performer may serve as an example of
its writer's powers as a rival of Lloyd and
Churchill:

> 'Where travell'd fops, too nice for nature grown,
> Are sway'd by affectation's whims alone;
> Where the sly knave, usurping honour's guise,
> By secret villainy attempts to rise;
> Or where the footman, negligently gay,
> His master's modish airs would fain display;
> But chiefly where the rake, in higher life,
> Cajoles the husband to seduce the wife,
> And, fraught with art, but plausible to sight,
> The libertine and hypocrite unite—
> PALMER from life the faithful portrait draws,
> And calls unrivall'd for our warm applause.'

In the foregoing plunges into the Taylorian
bran-pie, we have, as promised at the outset,
depended rather upon the writer's personal experiences than upon his miscellaneous anecdotes.

The Author of 'Monsieur Tonson.'

But we have by no means exhausted the personal experiences. Not to mention political magnates like Lord Chatham and Lord Chesterfield, whom we have almost entirely neglected, there are many references to characters difficult to classify, but no less diverting to recall. As a boy, Taylor had seen Coan, the Norfolk dwarf of Churchill's *Rosciad*

('Whilst to six feet the vig'rous stripling grown,
Declares that GARRICK is another COAN'),

then lodging at a tavern in the Five Fields (now Eaton Square) kept by one of the Pinchbecks who invented the metal of that name; and he remembered the boxer Buckhorse, a debased specimen of humanity, whose humour consisted in permitting the Eton and Westminster boys to punch his battered features at the modest rate of a shilling the blow.¹ He had also visited the famous Mrs. Teresa Cornelys, when that favourite of the Nobility and Gentry had fallen upon evil days, and was subsisting precariously as a purveyor of asses' milk at Knightsbridge; he had

¹ Buckhorse can hardly have been familiar with Roman law. But twenty-five pieces of copper (about the value of a shilling) was the legal tender, or solatium, for a blow on the face (*cf.* the story of Veratius in Gibbon's 'Decline and Fall,' 1862, v. 315).

known intimately a certain Mr. Donaldson, who, like Horace Walpole, had gone in danger of his life from the 'gentleman highwayman,' James Maclean; and at Angelo's in Carlisle Street, Soho, he had frequently met the Chevalier D'Eon in his woman's dress, but old, and equally decayed in manners and means. It is singular that the Author of 'Monsieur Tonson,' with all his dramatic proclivities, should never have attempted a play. As far as can be ascertained, however, his sole contribution to stage literature, prologues and epilogues excepted, was the lines for the rhyming Butler in Mrs. Inchbald's 'Lovers' Vows,' that version of Kotzebue's 'Das Kind der Liebe' which figures so conspicuously in Miss Austen's 'Mansfield Park.' 'Lovers' Vows' would appear to be fertile in suggestion, for it was in playing this piece that Charles Kean fell in love with his future wife, Miss Ellen Tree, sister of the musical Maria (Mrs. Bradshaw), who lives for ever in Henry Luttrell's happy epigram:

> 'On this Tree when a nightingale settles and sings,
> The Tree will return her as good as she brings.'

BOSWELL'S PREDECESSORS AND EDITORS.

WRITING to Pope in July, 1728, concerning the annotation of the 'Dunciad,' Swift comments upon the prompt oblivion which overtakes the minor details of contemporary history. 'Twenty miles from London nobody understands hints, initial letters, or town facts and passages; and in a few years not even those who live in London.' A somewhat similar opinion was expressed by Johnson. 'In sixty or seventy years, or less,' he said, 'all works which describe manners, require notes.' His own biography is a striking case in point. Almost from the beginning the editorial pen was freely exercised upon it, and long before the lesser term he mentions, it was already—to use an expressive phrase of Beaumarchais—'*rongée d'extraits et couverte de critiques.*' With Mr. Croker's edition of 1831 it might have been thought that the endurable limits of illustration and interpretation had been reached, and for some time, indeed, that opinion seems to have obtained. But within a comparatively brief period three other editions of importance have made their appearance, each of which has its special features, while four and twenty years ago was published another (reissued in 1888), which had, at least, the advantage of an excellent plan. Boswell's book itself may now, in Parliamentary language, be taken for 'read.' As Johnson said of Goldsmith's 'Traveller,' 'its merit is established, and individual praise or censure can neither augment nor diminish it.' But the publication, in Colonel Grant's excellent brief memoir, of the first systematic bibliography of Johnson's works, coupled with the almost simultaneous issue by Mr. H. R. Tedder, the able and accomplished librarian to the Athenæum Club, of a bibliography of Boswell's masterpiece, affords a sufficient pretext for some review of Boswell's editors and predecessors.

Johnson died on the evening of Monday, December 13, 1784. According to a letter dated May 5, 1785, from Michael Lort to Bishop Percy, printed in Nichols' 'Literary Illustrations,' the first Life appeared on the day following the death. But this is a manifest mistake, as reference to contemporary newspapers, or even to the pamphlet itself, should have sufficed to show. At p. 120 is an account of Johnson's funeral, which did not take place until Monday, December 20. Moreover, the portrait by T. Trotter,[1] for which Johnson is said to have sat 'some time since,' is dated the 16th, and in an article in the 'Gentleman's Magazine' for December, it is expressly stated that the book 'was announced before the Doctor had been two days dead,' and appeared on the ninth morning after his death. It may even be doubtful if this is strictly accurate, as the first notification of the pamphlet in the 'Public Advertiser' appears on Thursday, the 23rd, and promises its publication that week. Its title is 'The Life of Samuel Johnson, LL.D., with Occasional Remarks on his Writings, an Authentic Copy of his Will, and a Catalogue of his Works, &c.,' 1785. It is an octavo of iv-144 pages, and its publisher was the G. Kearsley, of 46 Fleet Street, who issued so many of Goldsmith's works. Its author, too, is supposed to have been the William Cook who subsequently wrote recollections of Goldsmith in the 'European Magazine' for 1793. In Kearsley's advertisement great pains are taken

---

[1] Thomas Trotter was a friend of William Blake. Trotter's 'drawing in chalk' of Dr. Johnson 'from the life, about eighteen months before his death' [Cook says February, 1782], was exhibited at the Academy in 1785 (Gilchrist's 'Blake,' 1880, i. 57).

to avert the possible charge of catchpenny haste, by the statement that the book had been drawn up for some time, but had been withheld from motives of delicacy. This anticipatory defence, however, Sylvanus Urban promptly demolished, in the above-mentioned notice, by adducing several palpable examples of 'hurry.' The sketch professes, nevertheless, to be 'warm from the life,' and, although speedily superseded by more leisurely efforts, is certainly not without interest as the earliest of its kind, even if be not quite so early as it has hitherto been affirmed to be.

Cook's so-called Life was followed by articles in the 'European' and the 'Gentleman's Magazines' for December, 1784, which, according to the fashion of those days, appeared at the end and not at the beginning of the month. That in the 'European Magazine,' which was more critical than biographical, was continued through several numbers, and contains nothing to distinguish it from the respectable and laborious journey-work of the period. The memoir in the 'Gentleman's Magazine' is of a far more meritorious character, and was from the pen of Tom Tyers, the 'Tom Restless' of the 'Idler,' and the son of Jonathan, 'the founder of that excellent place of publick amusement, Vauxhall Gardens.' Tom Tyers had really known Johnson with a certain degree of intimacy, and even Boswell is obliged to admit that Tyers lived with his illustrious friend 'in as easy a manner as almost any of his very numerous acquaintance.' He has certainly not caught Johnson's style, as his memories are couched in abrupt shorthand sentences which are the reverse of Johnsonese. But apart from a certain vanity of classical quotation, with which he seems to have been twitted by his contemporaries, 'Tom Restless' writes like a gentleman, and is fully entitled to the praise of having produced the first animated study of Johnson, who, from a sentence towards the close, appears to have anticipated that Tyers might be one day 'called upon to assist a posthumous account of him.' Mr. Napier says that Tyers continued his work in the 'Gentleman's Magazine' for January, 1785. This is not exact, and is indeed practically contradicted by Mrs. Napier, since in the valuable volume of 'Johnsoniana' which accompanies her husband's edition, she prints no more than is to be found in the December number. What Tyers really did was to insert a number of minor corrections and additions in the annual supplement to the 'Gentleman's Magazine' for 1784, and in the number for February, 1785.

Without a close examination of contemporary advertisement sheets it would be difficult to fix precisely the date of publication of the next biography. It is a small octavo of 197 pages, entitled 'Memoirs of the Life and Writings of the Late Dr. Samuel Johnson; containing many valuable Original Letters, and several Interesting Anecdotes both of his Literary and Social Connections: the Whole authenticated by living Evidence.' The title-page is dated 1785. In the Preface mention is made of assistance rendered by Thomas Davies, the actor-bookseller of 8 Russell Street, Covent Garden, who is described as 'the late.' The book must therefore have appeared after Thursday, May 5, when Davies died. Its author is conjectured to have been the Rev. William Shaw, 'a modest and a decent man,' referred to in Boswell as the compiler of 'an Erse Grammar,' subsequently issued in 1778 as 'An Analysis of the Gaelic Language.' Colour is given to this supposition by the fact that another of the persons who supplied information was Mr James Elphinston, by whom Shaw was introduced to Johnson, and by the references made to the Ossian controversy, in which Shaw did battle on Johnson's side against Macpherson. For the book itself, it is, like most of the pre-Boswellian efforts, Tyers's sketch excepted, mainly critical, and makes no attempt to reproduce Johnson's talk or opinions, though it published, for the first time, two or three of his letters.

Chit-chat and personal characteristics are, however, somewhat more fully represented in what—neglecting for the moment Boswell's 'Journal of a Tour to the Hebrides'—may be regarded as the next effort in the biographical sequence, the famous 'Anecdotes of the Late Samuel Johnson, LL.D., during the Last Twenty Years of his Life,' by Hesther Lynch Piozzi, which was published in March, 1786. Written in Italy, where she was then living, it was printed in London. Its success, as might perhaps have been anticipated from the author's long connection with Johnson, was exceptional. The first edition, like that of Fielding's 'Amelia,' was exhausted on the day of publication, and other editions followed rapidly. Boswell, as may be guessed, was not well disposed towards the work of his fortunate rival, and in his own book is at considerable pains to expose her 'mistaken notion of Dr. Johnson's character,' while his coadjutor, Malone, who tells us that she made £500 by the 'Anecdotes,' plainly calls her both 'inaccurate and artful.' We, who are neither editors nor biographers of Boswell, need not assume so censorious an attitude. That Mrs. Piozzi, by habit of mind, and from the circumstances under which her narrative was compiled, was negligent in her facts (she even blunders as to the date when she first met Johnson) may be admitted; and it is not inconceivable that, as Mrs. Napier says in the 'Prefatory Notice' to her 'Johnsoniana,' her account would have been 'more tender and true if it had been given by Mrs. Thrale instead of Mrs. Piozzi.' But the cumulative effect of her vivacious and disconnected recollections (even Malone admits them to be 'lively') is rather corroborative of, than at variance with, that produced by Johnson's more serious biographers. Her opportunities were great,—perhaps greater than those of any of her contemporaries,—her intercourse with Johnson was most unrestrained and unconventional, and notwithstanding all its faults, her little volume remains an essential part of Johnsonian literature.

Boswell, whose *magnum opus* we are now approaching, so fills the foreground with his fame that the partial obliteration of his predecessors is almost a necessary consequence. In this way Sir John Hawkins, whose 'Life of Samuel Johnson, LL.D.,' 1787, comes next in importance to Mrs. Piozzi's 'Anecdotes,' has suffered considerably; and his book, which immediately after Johnson's death was advertised as 'forthcoming,' is, to use the words of a recent writer, 'spoken of with contempt by many who have never taken the trouble to do more than turn over its leaves.' That the author seems to have been extremely unpopular can scarcely be denied. Malone, who accumulates a page of his characteristics, says that Percy called him 'most detestable,' Reynolds, 'absolutely dishonest,' and Dyer, 'mischievous, uncharitable, and malignant,' to which chaplet of dispraise the recorder adds, as his own contribution, that he was 'rigid and sanctimonious.' Johnson, too, styled him 'an unclubable man.' But against all this censure it must be remembered that he was selected as one of the first members of 'The Club' (to whose promoters his peculiarities can scarcely have been unknown, for he had belonged to the earlier association in Ivy Lane), and that Johnson appointed him one of his executors. Boswell, whose vanity Hawkins had wounded by the slight and supercilious way in which he spoke of him in the 'Life,' could scarcely be supposed to feel kindly to him; and though he professes to have modified what he said of this particular rival on account of his death, we have no means of knowing how much he suppressed. He gives, nevertheless, what on the whole is a not unfair idea of Hawkins's volume. 'However inadequate and improper,' he says, 'as a Life of Dr. Johnson, and however discredited by unpardonable inaccuracies in other respects, [it] contains a collection of curious anecdotes and observations which few men but its authour could have brought together.' What is commendatory in this verdict is not exaggerated, and those who care enough for Johnson to travel beyond Boswell will certainly find Hawkins by no means so 'ponderous' as Boswell would have us to believe. Many of the particulars he gives are certainly not to be found elsewhere, and his knowledge of the seamy side of letters in Georgian London was 'extensive and peculiar.'

To speak of Hawkins after Mrs. Piozzi is a course more convenient than chronological, as it involves the neglect of an intermediate biographer. But the 'Essay on the Life, Character, and Writings of Dr. Samuel Johnson,' from the pen of the Rev. Joseph Towers, which comes between them in 1786, has no serious import. It treats more of the writings than the character and life, and, except as the respectable effort of an educated man, need not detain us from Boswell himself, whose first offering at the shrine of his adoration was made in September, 1785, when he published the 'Journal of a Tour to the Hebrides, with Samuel Johnson, LL.D.' The tour, of which Johnson had himself given an account in his 'Journey to the Western Islands of Scotland,' had taken place as far back as 1773, and Boswell's journal had lain by him ever since. But the manuscript had been lent to different persons,—to Mrs. Thrale among the rest. 'I am glad you read Boswell's journal,' said Johnson to her; 'you are now sufficiently informed of the whole transaction, and need not regret that you did not make the tour to the Hebrides.' A more emphatic testimony is contained in the 'Journal' itself. Johnson, we are told, perused it diligently from day to day, and declared that he took great delight in doing so. 'It might be printed,' he said, 'were the subject fit for printing,' and further on he forbade Boswell to contract it. In his dedication to Malone, whose acquaintance he made in Baldwin's printing-office while correcting the proofs, Boswell showed that he was conscious of the strong point of his work, 'the numerous conversations, which (he said) form the most valuable part.' In the third edition, dated August, 1786, the success of the book justified an ampler note of gratification: 'I will venture to predict, that this specimen of the colloquial talents and extemporaneous effusions of my illustrious fellow-traveller will become still more valuable, when, by the lapse of time, he shall have become an ANCIENT; when all those who can now bear testimony to the transcendent powers of his mind shall have passed away; and no other memorial of this great and good man shall remain but the following Journal, the other anecdotes and letters preserved by his friends, and those incomparable works, which have for many years been in the highest estimation, and will be read and admired as long as the English language shall be spoken or understood.' Whether this variation of *Exegi monumentum* is justifiable or not—and certainly some of the 'incomparable works,' have but faintly fulfilled their promise of diuturnity—Boswell's accentuation of his distinctive excellence, his admirably characteristic records of conversations, is unanswerable evidence of a settled purpose and a definite aim.

On a fly-leaf of the 'Tour to the Hebrides' (not as Mr. Napier supposed, confined to the third edition) was announced as 'preparing for the press' the greater work by which the 'Tour' was succeeded in 1791. At first it was to have been comprised in one quarto volume, but it ultimately made its appearance in two. The publisher was Charles Dilly, in the Poultry, and the title-page ran as follows :—

'The Life of Samuel Johnson, LL.D., comprehending an Account of his Studies and numerous Works, in chronological Order; a Series of his Epistolary Correspondence and Conversations with many eminent Persons; and various original Pieces of his Composition, never before published. The whole exhibiting a View of Literature and Literary Men in Great-Britain, for near half a Century, during which he flourished.'

In the dedication to Sir Joshua Reynolds, referring to the earlier book, Boswell dwells upon a difference of treatment which distinguishes the 'Life' from its predecessor. In the 'Tour' he had, it seems, been too open in his communications, freely exhibiting to the world the dexterity of Johnson's wit, even when that wit was exercised upon himself. His frankness had in some quarters been mistaken for insensibility, and he has therefore in the 'Life' been 'more reserved,' and though he tells nothing but the truth, has still kept in his mind that the whole truth is not always to be exposed. In the

Advertisement which succeeds, he enlarges upon the difficulties of his task, and the labour involved in the arrangement and collection of material; and he expresses his obligations to Malone, who had heard nearly all the work in manuscript, and had revised about half of it in type. Seventeen hundred copies of it were printed, and although the price in boards was two guineas, between May (the date of publication) and August twelve hundred of these had been sold. Boswell, who gives this information to his friend Temple, in a letter dated the 22nd of the latter month, expected that the entire impression would be disposed of before Christmas.

This hope, however, does not appear to have been realized, since the second edition in three volumes octavo, considerably revised, and including 'eight sheets of additional matter,' was not published until July, 1793. During the progress of the work through the press many additional letters and anecdotes had come to hand, which were inserted in an introduction and appendix. These numerous improvements were at the same time printed in quarto form for the benefit of the purchasers of the issue of 1791, and sold at half-a-crown, under the title of 'The Principal Corrections and Additions to the First

Edition of Mr. Boswell's Life of Dr. Johnson.' As in the 'Tour to the Hebrides,' the success of his labours inspired their author with a greater exultation of prefatory language. Referring to the death of Reynolds, which had taken place in the interval between the first and second editions, he says that Sir Joshua had read the book, and given 'the strongest testimony to its fidelity.' He has *Johnsonised* the land, he says farther on, and he trusts 'they will not only talk but think Johnson.'

He was still busily amending and retouching for a third edition when he died, on May 19, 1795, at his house, then No. 47, but now (or recently) No. 122, Great Portland Street. His task was taken up by Malone, who had been his adviser from the first, and under Malone's superintendence was issued, 'revised and augmented,' the third edition of 1799. From the fact that it contains Boswell's latest touches, this edition is held to be the most desirable by Johnson students. Boswell's friends contributed several notes, some of which were the work of the author's second son, James, then a student at Brasenose College, Oxford. Fourth, fifth, and sixth editions followed, all under the editorship of Malone. Then, shortly after the publication in 1811 of the last of these, Malone himself died. Seventh, eighth, and ninth editions, all avowedly or unavowedly reproducing Malone's last issue, subsequently appeared, the ninth having some additions by Alexander Chalmers. Then came what is known as the 'Oxford' edition, by F. P. Walesby, of Wadham College, which contained some fresh recollections of Johnson and some stray particulars as to Boswell, whose portrait, for the first time, is added. A tiny issue in one volume, small octavo, beautifully printed in double columns at the Chiswick Press, is the only one that needs mention previous to the historical edition by the Right Honourable John Wilson Croker, published in 1831.

As will be seen, the foregoing paragraphs deal more with Johnson's earlier biographers than with the main subject of this paper, Boswell's editors. But the earlier biographers are, if not the chief, at least no inconsiderable part of the material employed by those editors, and by none more conspicuously, more ably, and at the same time more unhappily, than by the one whose labours attracted the censure of Macaulay and Carlyle. What is most distinctive in Boswell is Boswell's method and Boswell's manner. Long before, Johnson had touched upon this personal quality when writing of the Corsican tour. 'Your History,' he said, 'is like other histories, but your Journal is in a very high degree curious and delightful. . . . Your History was copied from books; your Journal rose out of your own experience and observation. You express images which operated strongly upon yourself, and you have impressed them with great force upon your readers.' From less friendly critics the verdict was the same. Walpole, though caustic and flippant, speaks to like purport; and Gray, who has been 'pleased and moved strangely,' declares it proves what he has always maintained, 'that any fool may write a most valuable book by chance, if he will only tell us what he heard and saw with veracity.' This faculty of communicating his impressions accurately to his reader is Boswell's most conspicuous gift. Present in his first book, it was more present in his second, and when he began his great biography it had reached its highest point. So individual is his manner, so unique his method of collecting and arranging his information, that to disturb the native character of his narrative by interpolating foreign material, must of necessity impair its specific character and imperil its personal note. Yet, by some strange freak of fate, this was just the very treatment to which it was subjected.

From the very outset indeed, it would seem, his text was considerably 'edited.' Boswell, like many writers of his temperament, was fond of stimulating his flagging invention by miscellaneous advice, and it is plain from the comparison of his finished work with his rough notes, that in order to make his anecdotes more direct and effective he freely manipulated his reminiscences. But it is quite probable—and this is a point that we do not remember to have seen touched on — that much of the trimming which his records received is attributable to Malone. At all events, when Malone took up the editing after Boswell's death, he is known to have made many minor alterations in the process of 'settling the text,' and it is only reasonable to suppose that he had done the same thing in the author's lifetime, a supposition which would account for some at least of the variations which have been observed between Boswell's anecdotes in their earliest and their latest forms. But the admitted alterations of Malone were but trifles compared with the extraordinary readjustment which the book, as Malone left it, received at the hands of Mr. Croker. Not con-

tent with working freely upon the text itself—
compressing, omitting, transposing, as seemed
good in his eyes—by a process almost inconceivable in a critic and *littérateur* of admitted
experience, he liberally interlarded it with long
extracts and letters from Hawkins, Piozzi, Cumberland, Murphy, and others of Boswell's predecessors and successors, and so turned into an
irregular patchwork what the author had left a
continuous and methodical design. Further-
more he incorporated with it, among other
things, under its date of occurrence, the separate
volume of the 'Tour to the Hebrides,'[1] having
first polled and trimmed that work according to
his taste and fancy. Finally, he added—and
this is the least questionable of his acts—an
inordinate number of foot-notes. Many of these,
it must be conceded, are of the highest value.
Penned at a time when memories of Johnson

[1] He may have been advised to do this. Lockhart,
writing to Murray, Jan. 19, 1829, says, 'Pray ask Croker
whether Boswell's account of the Hebridean Tour ought
not to be melted into the book.' But it is clear from
Croker's first letter to Murray of Jan. 9, and his specific
words a day later, when accepting Murray's terms ('I
shall also endeavour to throw as much as I can into the
text '), that he had his own perverted ideal from the outset (Smiles's 'Memoir of John Murray,' 1891, ii. 288).

and his contemporaries were still fresh in men's minds, and collected by a writer whose industry and curiosity were as exceptional as his equipment and opportunities, they must always remain an inestimable magazine of Johnsoniana. Their worst fault is that they are more a warehouse than a treasury, and that they exhibit less of literary resource than literary incontinence.

But if the intrinsic and inherent worth of Croker's voluminous annotations has survived the verbal artillery of Macaulay and Carlyle, it has luckily been otherwise with his remodelling of Boswell's text, the principles of which were virtually abandoned in the second edition of 1835. Unfortunately, the execution of this concession to popular opinion was only partial. Although the majority of the passages added to the text were rearranged as foot-notes or distributed into appendices, the Scotch 'Tour' still upreared itself in the midst as a huge stumbling-block, while the journey to Wales and the letters of Johnson and Mrs. Thrale were retained. In 1847, when Mr. Croker prepared his definite edition, he continued impenitent to this extent, although he speaks in his 'Advertisement' of abridgment and alteration. Nay, he even acquiesced in the perpetuation of another enormity which dates from the edition of 1835 (an edition which he only partly superintended), the breaking up of the book into chapters. This was a violation of Boswell's plan which it is impossible to describe except as an act of Vandalism. 'Divisions into books and chapters,' says Mr. Napier, unanswerably (if somewhat grandiloquently), 'if they have any meaning, are, as it were, articulations in the organic whole of a literary composition; and this special form cannot be superinduced merely externally.' Yet, all these drawbacks to the contrary, Mr. Croker's edition enjoyed a long popularity, and the edition just referred to was reprinted as late as 1876.

It would be beyond our province to trace the post-Crokerian issues of Boswell's book, which, with the exception of an illustrated edition under the superintendence of Dr. Robert Carruthers, author of the life of Pope, were mainly reprints of Malone. But from what has gone before, it will be surmised that the presentation, as far as practicable, of Boswell's unsophisticated text must sooner or later become the ambition of the modern editor. In this praiseworthy enterprise the pioneer appears to have been Mr. Percy Fitzgerald. In May, 1874, acting with the encouragement and countenance of Carlyle, to whom his work was dedicated, he published with Messrs. Bickers an edition of Boswell's 'Life' in three volumes, of which the object was to exhibit Boswell's text in its first published form, and at the same time to show the alterations made or contemplated by him in the two subsequent editions with which he was concerned. Thus the reader was enabled to follow the process of revision in the author's mind, and to derive additional satisfaction from the spectacle of the *naïf* and highly ingenuous motives which prompted many of Boswell's rectifications and re-adjustments. As was inevitable in such a plan, the 'Tour to the Hebrides' was placed by itself at the end, an arrangement which had also been followed by Carruthers; the 'Diary of a Tour in Wales,' which Mr. Croker had turned into chap. xlvi. of his compilation, disappeared altogether; and the interpolated letters knew their place no more. The division into chapters also vanished with the restoration of the original text, which, together with Boswell's spelling, punctuation, paragraphs, and other special characteristics, were religiously preserved. By this arrangement, taken in connection with the foot-notes exhibiting the variations, the reader was placed in the position of a person having before him at one view the editions of 1791,

Boswell's Predecessors and Editors. 159

1793, and 1799, as well as the separate 'Corrections and Additions' issued by Boswell in 1793. Mr. Fitzgerald also appended certain notes of his own; but, wherever they occurred on the same page as Boswell's work, carefully fenced them off by a line of demarcation from what was legitimate Boswell. Upon these notes, generally brief and apposite, it is not necessary to dwell. The noticeable characteristic of Mr. Fitzgerald's edition is its loyalty to Boswell, and for that, if for that only, the lovers of Johnson owe him a deep debt of gratitude.[1]

In 1880, six years after the first appearance of the above edition of Boswell's 'Life,' Mr. Fitzgerald published, under the title of 'Croker's Boswell and Boswell,' a volume which was apparently the outcome of his earlier labours in this field. With the first part of this, which treats mainly of the feud between Macaulay and Croker, and the peculiarities and defects of the latter as an editor, we have no immediate concern. But the second part, which exhibits Boswell at his work, collects much valuable information with

[1] Mr. Fitzgerald's edition of Boswell was re-issued in 1888, with a new and interesting preface, to which was added the valuable Bibliography by Mr. Henry R. Tedder, referred to at the beginning of this paper.

respect to his method of note-making, and, with the assistance of the curious memoranda belonging to the late Lord Houghton, published in 1874 by the Grampian Club under the title of 'Boswelliana,' shows how much judicious correction and adroit compression went to produce these 'literary and characteristical anecdotes . . . told with authenticity, and in a lively manner,' which, as Boswell explained to his friend Temple, were to form the staple of his work. Other chapters of equal interest deal with Boswell's strange antipathies and second thoughts, both of which themes, and the former especially, are of no small importance to the minute student of his labours. We have mentioned this book of Mr. Fitzgerald's, because, among the many productions of his indefatigable pen, it is the one which has always interested us most, and it is obviously, as he declares in his preface, written *con amore*.

That the reproduction of Boswell neat—to use a convenient vulgarism—had attracted closer attention to the defects of Croker's concoction may be fairly assumed, and the volume just mentioned probably, and certainly among specialists, enforced this impression. Accordingly, in 1884, a new edition of the 'Life,' upon which the editor, the late Rev. Alexander Napier, vicar of Holkham,

had been engaged for several years, was issued by
Messrs. George Bell and Sons. It was illustrated
by facsimiles, steel engravings and portraits, and
was received with considerable, and even, in some
quarters, exaggerated, enthusiasm. In this edition
the arrangement of Boswell's text was strictly
followed, and the tours in Wales and Scotland
were printed separately. Many of Croker's notes
were withdrawn or abridged, and Mr. Napier, in
pursuance of a theory, which is as sound as it is
unusual, also omitted all those in which his predecessor had considered it his duty 'to act as
censor on Boswell' and even on Johnson himself.
The editor's duty, said Mr. Napier, 'is to sub-
ordinate himself to his author, and admit that
only which elucidates his author's meaning. . . .
It cannot be the duty of an editor to insult the
writer whose book he edits. I confess that the
notes of Mr. Croker which most offend are those
in which, not seldom, he delights—let me be
allowed to use a familiar colloquialism—to snub
"Mr. Boswell."' In this deliverance no reasonable reader can fail to concur. Besides the editing of Croker, however, Mr. Napier added many
useful notes of his own, as well as some very interesting appendices. One of these reproduces
the autobiographical sketch of Johnson prefixed

by Richard Wright of Lichfield, in 1805, to Miss Hill Boothby's letters; another deals with that mysterious 'History of Prince Titi' which figures in Macaulay's review of Croker's first edition; a third successfully dissipates the legendary account of a meeting between Ursa Major and Adam Smith, which represents those 'grave and reverend seignors' as engaged in competitive Billingsgate. 'Carleton's Memoirs,' Theophilus Cibber's 'Lives of the Poets,' and the daughters of Mauritius Lowe are also treated of in this, the newest part of Mr. Napier's labours.

But his edition also includes a valuable supplement in the shape of a volume of 'Johnsoniana,' collected and edited by Mrs. Napier, whose praiseworthy plan is to avoid merely fragmentary 'sayings' and 'anecdotes,' and, as far as possible, to give only complete articles. Thus Mrs. Napier opens with Mrs. Piozzi's book, and then goes on to reprint Hawkins's collection of apophthegms, the Hill Boothby correspondence, Tom Tyers' sketch from the 'Gentleman's Magazine,' the essay published by Arthur Murphy in 1792 for his edition of Johnson's works, and various recollections and so forth collected from Reynolds, Cumberland, Madame D'Arblay, Hannah More, Percy, and others. But her freshest *trouvaille* is

the diary of a certain Dr. Thomas Campbell, an Irishman who visited England in 1775, and, after the fashion of the time, recorded his impressions. This diary has a curious history. Carried to Australia by some of its writer's descendants, it was peaceably travelling towards dissolution when it was unearthed behind an old press in one of the offices of the Supreme Court of New South Wales. In 1854 it was published at Sydney by Mr. Samuel Raymond, and from that date until 1884 does not seem to have been reprinted in England. Dr. Campbell had some repute as an historian, and it was he who prepared for Percy the memoir of Goldsmith which, in 1837, was in the possession of Mr. Prior, and formed the first sketch for the straggling compilation afterwards prefixed to the well-known edition of Goldsmith's works dated 1801. Campbell's avowed object in coming to London was to 'see the lions,' and his notes are sufficiently amusing. He lodged at the Grecian Coffee House, and at the Hummums in Covent Garden, where once appeared the ghost of Johnson's dissolute relative, Parson Ford; he saw Woodward in Benjamin
† Hoadly's 'Suspicious Husband,' and Garrick as Lusignan and Lear, in which latter character Dr. Campbell, contradicting all received tradition,

considered 'he could not display himself.' He went to the auction-rooms in the Piazza; he went to the Foundling and the Temple and Dr. Dodd's Chapel; he went to Ranelagh and the Pantheon, where he watched those lapsed lovers, Lady Grosvenor and the Duke of Cumberland, carefully avoiding each other. He dined often at Thrale's, meeting Boswell and Baretti, and Murphy and Johnson. With the great man he was not impressed, and his portrait affords an example of Johnson as he struck an unsympathetic contemporary. According to Dr. Campbell this was his picture:—' He has the aspect of an Idiot, without the faintest ray of sense gleaming from any one feature—with the most awkward garb, and unpowdered grey wig, on one side only of his head—he is for ever dancing the devil's jig, and sometimes he makes the most driveling effort to whistle some thought in his absent paroxisms. He came up to me and took me by the hand, then sat down upon the sofa, and mumbled out that "he had heard two papers had appeared against him in the course of this week—one of which was—that he was to go to Ireland next summer in order to abuse the hospitality of that place also [a reference to the recently published 'Journey to the Western Islands']." His awkwardness at table is just what Chesterfield described, and his roughness of manners kept pace with that. When Mrs. Thrale quoted something from Foster's "Sermons" he flew in a passion, and said that Foster was a man of mean ability, and of no original thinking. All which tho' I took to be most true, yet I held it not meet to have it so set down.' From this it will be perceived that Dr. Campbell was of those who identified the 'respectable Hottentot' of Chesterfield's letters with the 'great Lexicographer,' an identification which Dr. Birkbeck Hill, in 'Dr. Johnson His Friends and His Critics,' and subsequent writings, has successfully shown to be untenable.

Towards the close of 1884 Mr. Napier's edition was re-issued in the 'Standard Library,' making six small volumes, in which some only of the portrait illustrations of the first issue were reproduced. The chief addition consisted of a series of seven letters from Boswell to his friend Sir David Dalrymple. Extracts from this very interesting correspondence, bearing upon Boswell's first acquaintance with his Mentor, had appeared in the volume of 'Boswelliana' already mentioned, but they had been extracts and no more. Mr. Napier gave the letters *in extenso*. Two years later the late Professor Henry Morley published, in five exceedingly handsome volumes, what, from the fact of its decoration by portraits from the brush of Sir Joshua, he christened the 'Reynolds' edition. In common with all Professor Morley's work, the editing of this issue was thoroughly straightforward and sensible. A new and noticeable feature was the prefixing to each of the prefaces of the different editors a succinct account of the writer. At the end came an essay entitled the 'Spirit of Johnson,' to which can scarcely be denied the merit claimed for it by a competent critic of being 'one of the best descriptions of Johnson's character that has ever been written.' There were also elaborate indices, of which one can only say in their dispraise that they were less elaborate than that prepared by the editor who follows Professor Morley. Like Mr. Napier, Mr. Morley was largely indebted to Croker; like Mr. Napier also he freely pruned his predecessor's luxuriance. And this brings us to the last of the three editions mentioned at the beginning of this paper, that issued in 1887 from the Clarendon Press by Dr. George Birkbeck Hill.

That Dr. Birkbeck Hill's book is '*un livre de bonne foi*,' there can indeed be little doubt. He is well known as a devoted worshipper at Johnson's shrine. He has been for years a persistent reviewer of books on this subject, and his essays (collected in 1878 from the 'Cornhill' and other periodicals under the title of 'Dr. Johnson His Friends and His Critics'), bear that unmistakable stamp which denotes the writer who has not crammed his subject for the purpose of preparing an article, but who has, so to speak, let the article write itself out of the fulness of his resources. Besides these he edited, in 1879, Boswell's 'Journal of a Tour to Corsica' and his correspondence with Andrew Erskine. But he has crowned his former labours by this sumptuous edition with its excellent typography, its handsome page, and its exhaustive index, which last, we can well believe, must have cost him, as he says, 'many months' heavy work.' That he himself executed this 'sublunary task,' as a recent writer has described it, is matter for congratulation; that he has also verified it page by page in proof almost entitles him to a Montyon prize for exceptional literary virtue. Our only regret is that his 'Preface' is touched a little too strongly with the sense of his unquestioned industry and conscientiousness. However legitimate it may be, the public is always somewhat impatient of the *superbia quæsita meritis.* Moreover, it is an extremely difficult thing to display judiciously; and, after all, as Carlyle said of Croker's attempt, the editing of Boswell is 'a praiseworthy but no miraculous procedure.'

This note of self-gratulation in Dr. Birkbeck Hill's introductory words is, nevertheless, but a trifling drawback when contrasted with the real merits of a performance which, in these days of piping-hot publication, has much of the leisurely grace of eighteenth-century scholarship. The labour—not only the labour of which the result remains on record, but that bloomless and fruitless labour with which everyone who has been engaged in editorial drudgery can sympathize—must have been unprecedented. Nothing could be more ungracious than to smear the petty blot of an occasional inaccuracy across the wide field which has been explored so observantly—certainly it could not be the desire of those who have ever experienced the multiplied chances of error involved by transcription, press-correction, revision, and re-revision. At the same time we frankly own that we think Dr. Birkbeck Hill's edition has not escaped a dangerous defect of its qualities. It unquestionably errs on the side of excess. 'I have sought,' he says, 'to follow him [Johnson] wherever a remark of his required illustration, and have read through many a book that I might trace to its source a reference or an allusion.' And he has no doubt been frequently very fortunate, notably in his identification of the quotation which Johnson made when he heard the Highland girl of Nairne singing at her spinning-wheel, in his solution of 'loplolly,' and in half a dozen similar cases. But, as regards 'remarks that require illustration,' there are manifestly two methods, the moderate and the immoderate. By the one nothing but such reference or elucidation as explains the text is admissible; by the other anything that can possibly be connected with it is drawn into its train, and the motley notes tread upon each other's heels much as, in the fairy tale, the three girls, the parson, and the sexton follow the fellow with the golden goose. To the latter of these methods rather than the former Dr. Birkbeck Hill 'seriously inclines,' and almost any portion of his book would serve to supply a case in point. Take, for instance, the note at page 269, vol. i., to the verse which Boswell quotes from Garrick's well-known 'Ode on Mr. Pelham.' Neither Malone nor Croker has anything upon this, and as Boswell himself tells us that Pelham died on the day on which Mallet's edition of Lord Bolingbroke's works came out, and as the first line of his paragraph gives the exact date of the event, it is difficult to see what ground, and certainly what pressing need, there could be for farther comment. Yet Dr. Birkbeck Hill has no less than four 'illustrations.' First he tells us, from Walpole's letters, that Pelham died of a surfeit. This suggests another quotation from Johnson himself about the death of Pope, which introduces the story of the potted lampreys. Then comes a passage from Fielding's 'Journal of a Voyage to Lisbon,' to the effect that he (Fielding) was at his worst when Pelham died. Lastly comes a second quotation from Walpole, this time from his 'George II.,' in which we are told that the king said he should now 'have no more peace,' because Pelham was dead. The recondite erudition of all this is incontestable, but its utility is more than doubtful. Dr. Birkbeck Hill's method is seen more serviceably at work in a note on Reynolds's visit to Devonshire in 1762. First we get a record how Northcote, 'with great satisfaction to his mind,' touched the skirt of Sir Joshua's coat, and this quite naturally recalls the well-known anecdote how Reynolds himself in his youth had grasped the hand of the great Mr. Pope at

Christie's. The transition to Pope's own visit as a boy of twelve to Dryden at Will's Coffee House thus becomes an easy one. 'Who touched old Northcote's hand?' says Dr. Birkbeck Hill. 'Has the apostolic succession been continued?' and then he goes on to add: 'Since writing these lines I have read with pleasure the following passage in Mr. Ruskin's 'Præterita,' chap. i. p. 16: 'When at three-and-a-half I was taken to have my portrait painted by Mr. Northcote, I had not been ten minutes alone with him before I asked him why there were holes in his carpet.' Dryden, Pope, Reynolds, Northcote, Ruskin, so runs the chain of genius, with only one weak link in it.'

This is an excellent specimen of the concatenated process at the best. We are bound to add that there are many as good. We are moreover bound to admit that the examples of its abuse are by no means obtrusive. Dr. Birkbeck Hill, in short, has done his work thoroughly. His appendices — *e.g.* those on Johnson's Debates in Parliament, and on George Psalmanazar— are practically exhaustive, and he has left no stone unturned in his labour of interpretation. If in the result of that labour there is something of what Croker himself called 'surplusage,' it must also be conceded that Boswell's famous biography has never before been annotated with equal enthusiasm, learning, and industry.[1]

[1] Since this paper was first published, Dr. Birkbeck Hill has largely supplemented his valuable Johnson labours by two volumes of letters (1892), and two more of 'Johnsonian Miscellanies' (1897). There have also been several other issues of Boswell's 'Life,' *e.g.*—a compact 'Globe' edition prefaced by Mr. Mowbray Morris, two charming six volume issues, one of which has the advantage of an Introduction by Mr. Augustine Birrell, and an edition in one volume by Mr. Percy Fitzgerald, which is a marvel of cheapness,— but that of Dr. Birkbeck Hill is still unrivalled in its kind.

AN ENGLISH ENGRAVER IN PARIS.

IT is a curious fact—and, if it has not been already recorded, must assuredly have been remarked—that Fate seems always to provide the eminent painter with his special and particular interpreter on steel or copper. Thus, around Reynolds are the great mezzotinters, McArdell, Fisher, Watson, Valentine Green. Gainsborough has his nephew Gainsborough Dupont; Constable his Lucas. For Wilson there is Woollett; for Stothard there are Heath and Finden. To come to later days, there is Turner with his Willmores and Goodalls, and Landseer with his brother and (no pun intended) his Cousens. Similarly, for Wilkie (after Burnet), the born translator into dot and line seems to have been Raimbach. It was Raimbach who engraved 'The Rent Day,' 'Blind Man's Buff,' 'The Village Politicians,' and the majority of Sir David's chief works, and it is of Raimbach that we now propose to speak. Concerning his efforts as a craftsman, these pages could scarcely be expected to treat; and his life, the life of a man occupied continuously in a sedentary pursuit, and residing, like Stothard, almost entirely in one place, affords but little incident to invite the chronicler of the picturesque. But he nevertheless left behind him a privately-printed memoir, of which a portion at least is not without its interest,—the interest attaching to every truthful record of occurrences which time has pushed backward into that perspective which transforms the trivial. In 1802 he went to Paris for a couple of months. The visits of foreigners to England have not been unattractive; and the visit of an Englishman to France, shortly after the Revolution, may also—with a few preliminary words as to the tourist—supply its *memorabilia*.

. Abraham Raimbach was born on February 16, 1776, in Cecil Court, St. Martin's Lane. His father was a naturalized Swiss; his mother a Warwickshire woman, who claimed descent from Richard Burbage, the actor of Shakespeare's day. His childhood was uneventful, save for two incidents. One of these was his falling, as a baby, out of a second-floor window, when he was miraculously 'ballooned.' by his long-clothes; the other, his being roused as a little boy of four by the roar of the Gordon rioters as they rushed through the streets, calling to the sleeping inhabitants to light up their windows. After a modest education, chiefly at the Library School of St. Martin's—where Charles Mathews the Elder was his schoolfellow, and Liston afterwards held a post as master—he was formally apprenticed to Ravenet's pupil, John Hall, historical engraver to George the Third, and popularly regarded as the legitimate successor of Woollett. Hall was a man of more than ordinary cultivation, one of whose daughters had married the composer Stephen Storace,—the Storace who wrote the music to Colman's 'Iron Chest,' and (as Raimbach recollected) superintended the rehearsals thereof from a sedan-chair, in which, arrayed in flannels, he was carried on to the stage. Hall in his day had been introduced to Garrick; and he was sometimes visited by John Kemble, who impressed the young apprentice with his solemn and sepulchral enunciation, and his manifest inability to forget, even in private life, that he was not before the footlights. Another remembered visitor was Sheridan, nervously solicitous lest Hall, who was engraving his portrait, should needlessly emphasize that facial 'efflorescence'—so familiar in Gillray's caricatures—which the too-truthful Sir Joshua had neglected to disguise.

Sheridan, however, could only have appeared occasionally in the altitudes of Hall's study. But the three flights which ascended to it were often climbed by other contemporaries. Benjamin West (whose 'Cromwell dissolving the Long Parliament' Hall engraved), Opie and Northcote, Flaxman and Westall, all came frequently on business and pleasure, while the eclectic arts were represented by George Steevens (the Shakespeare critic), John Ireland (the Hogarth commentator), and Dibdin's 'Quisquilius,' George Baker, the print-collector and laceman of St. Paul's Churchyard. These, with Storace and his theatrical circle, must have made variety enough in a wearisome craft (for Hall's larger plates were many months in hand), and their conversation and opinions no doubt conspired to fill the young apprentice with a life-long interest in art and the stage. When at length, in August, 1796, his period of servitude came to an end, the professional outlook was by no means a cheerful one. The French Revolution was engrossing all men's thoughts, and the peaceful arts—that *ars longa* of the engraver in particular—were at their lowest ebb, the only patrons of prints being the booksellers. Young Raimbach's first definite employment was on Cooke's 'Tales of the Genii,' a task which, it may be added, was even more precarious than usual, inasmuch as it was Cooke's custom, by prearrangement, not to pay for the work if he did not approve it when finished. Fortunately, in this instance he did approve, and Raimbach continued from time to time to reproduce for him in copper the designs for books of Thurston, the elder Corbould, and Madame D'Arblay's clever cousin, Edward Burney. He had long been an assiduous Royal Academy student, and he speedily 'doubled' his profession by miniature-painting, in which—'having,' as he modestly says, 'some facility of execution and the very common power [?] of making an inveterate likeness' (at three guineas a head)—he attained considerable success. Then, at the end of 1801, he procured a commission to execute three plates from Smirke's paintings for Forster's 'Arabian Nights.' He had for some time been lodging with a French modeller in Charles Street, and by this means had improved an already respectable acquaintance with the French language. With the proceeds of his three plates in his pocket, about £70, he set out in July, 1802, for a fortnight's visit to Paris.

The short-lived Peace of Amiens, patched up by the Addington ministry, had been signed in the preceding March, and the route to the Continent, closed for ten or twelve years, was again open. The result was a rush across the Channel of all sorts and conditions of Englishmen, eager to note the changes resulting from the Revolution. Among these, the number of painters was considerable,—West, Turner, Flaxman, Shee, and Opie being all included. Securing a passport from the Secretary of State's office—a preliminary precaution which, in those days, meant an outlay of £2 5*s*.—Raimbach set out *via* Brighton and Dieppe. Competition, at this time, had reduced the coach fare to the former place to half a guinea inside. On July 9 he embarked for Dieppe in a little vessel, landing in France on the following day during a glorious sunrise, but drenched to the skin. His first impressions of the French were not unlike those of Hogarth fifty years before. The filth and slovenliness of the people, the number and shameless importunity of the beggars, the dragging of loaded carts and the bearing of heavy burdens by the weaker sex—all these, with the brusque revolutionary manners and the savage sans-culottism of the men, were things for which not even the long ear-pendants and picturesque Norman caps of the women could entirely atone. From Dieppe the traveller proceeded to Rouen in a ramshackle cabriolet, drawn by two ill-matched but wiry horses which went better than they looked. At Rouen he arrived in time for a bread riot, promptly suppressed by the soldiery; and he inspected several churches, among others St. Maclou, being no doubt attracted thereto by the famous door-carvings of Jean Goujon. Then, on the *impériale* of a diligence, he made his way through the delightful landscape of Northern France, by Pontoise and St. Denis, 'cemetery of monarchs,' to Paris, which he reached on the evening of the 12th.

At Paris he took up his quarters in that 'dirtiest and noisiest of streets,' the Rue Montorgueil, where, twenty-two years before, Béranger had been born. Here he was keenly sensible of those exhalations in which the French capital competed with the 'Auld Reekie' of the eighteenth century, although, in this instance, they were blended and complicated with another odour, that of cookery. But, notwithstanding an abhorrence of 'evil smells' quite equal to that of Queen Elizabeth, he speedily became acclimatized, and pleasantly appreciative of the bright, cheerful, many-coloured life of the Parisian boulevards and the social attractions of the *table d'hôte*. In the capital, too, he found that the people were less brutal, short-spoken, and surly than in the provinces, and that the Revolution, which had disfigured their palaces and monuments,[1] had not wholly effaced their traditional politeness. On the second day after his arrival took place the annual *fêtes* of July in memory of the destruction of the Bastille. There were to be reviews and illuminations, fireworks on the Pont Neuf, dancing and *mâts de cocagne* in the Champs-Elysées and Place Vendôme, and free plays and concerts in the Tuileries gardens. But the weather was finer than the show. 'The fireworks on the bridge would not go off; the concert in the garden could not be heard, and the illuminations, though in good taste, were not sufficiently general to mark a decided national feeling.' It is consoling to our insular self-esteem that neither this celebration, nor that inaugurating Bonaparte as First Consul, which took place shortly afterwards, could be compared, in the opinion of this observer, with the Jubilee of George the Third, or the Coronation of George the Fourth, at both of which he subsequently assisted.

He was naturally anxious to get a glimpse of

[1] The Tuileries still bore the words, 'dix d'Août' painted in white letters wherever the cannon-balls had struck. Arthur Moore was looking on ('Journal,' 1793, i. 26).

the famous First Consul, but of this he had little hope, as Bonaparte seldom appeared in public except at a review or a theatre, and in the latter case always without previous announcement. After fruitless attempts to see the 'modern Attila' at the Opera and Théâtre Français, Raimbach was at length fortunate enough to effect his object at an inspection of the garrison of Paris in the Place du Carrousel, where he paid six francs for a seat at a first-floor window. After five-and-thirty years he still remembered vividly the small, thin, grave figure,—in the blue unornamented uniform, plain cocked hat, white pantaloons and jockey boots,—which, surrounded by a brilliant staff (among whom the Mameluke Roustan was conspicuous by his eastern costume), rode rapidly down the lines at a hand-canter,[1] made a brief speech to the soldiers, saluted them with military formality, and then passed back under the archway of the Tuileries. Napoleon at this date was about thirty-two. Raimbach never saw him again, and beyond a casual inspection of the ladies of the Bonaparte family at Notre Dame, enjoyed no second opportunity of study-

[1] Probably upon Marengo, the famous Arab whose skeleton is now in the Museum of the Royal United Service Institution.

ing the ruling race. But there were many things of compensating interest. At the Jardin des Plantes, for instance, there was an enormous female elephant, which had been transferred by right of conquest from the Stadtholder's collection at the Hague, and had brought its English keeper with it into captivity. Then there were the noble halls and galleries of the Louvre, crowded with the fruits of French victories ('les fruits de nos victoires!'), statues and pictures of all countries, and all exhibited free of charge to an exultant public. The Apollo Belvedere from the Vatican was already installed, and while Raimbach was still at Paris arrived the famous Venus de' Médici. Probably so splendid a 'loan collection' had never before been brought together.

It was this no doubt which attracted so many English artists to Paris, where French spoliation enabled them to study comparatively a pictorial collocation which nothing but the Grand Tour could otherwise have presented to them. Here, in all their splendour, were Rembrandt and Rubens, with the best of the Dutch and Flemish schools. Raphael's glorious 'Transfiguration;' the great rival altarpiece of Domenichino, the 'Communion of St. Jerome;' Correggio's 'Marriage of St. Catherine,'—all these, together with many of the choicest specimens of the Carracci, of Guido, of Albano, of Guercino, were at this time to be seen in the long gallery of the Louvre, which Raimbach not only visited frequently, but drew in almost daily. In the magnificent Hall of Antiques, besides, he made the acquaintance of more than one contemporary French painter. Isabey, the miniaturist; Carle Vernet; his greater son, Horace, at this time a bright boy of thirteen or fourteen—were all then residing in apartments adjoining the galleries, and in some cases at Government expense. To the illustrious leader of the new Imperio-Classical School, which had succeeded with its wide-striding and brickdust-coloured nudities to the rosy *mignardises* of Fragonard and Boucher, Raimbach was not, however, introduced. M. Jacques Louis David, whose friendship with Robespierre had not only acquainted him with the interior of a prison, but had also brought him perilously close to the guillotine itself, was for the moment living in prudent seclusion, dividing his attentions between his palette and his violoncello. Meanwhile, a good example of his manner, 'The Sabines' (which Raimbach calls 'Rape of the Sabines'), executed immediately after his release from the Luxembourg, and popularly supposed to allude to the heroic efforts which Madame David had made for her husband's safety, was at this time being exhibited to a public who were divided between enthusiasm for the subject and indignation at the door-money—door-money apparently having never before been charged for showing a picture. Of David's pupils and followers, Gérard, Girodet, Gros, Guérin, Ingres, and the rest, Raimbach also speaks, but, as in the case of the master himself, more from hearsay than personal experience. On the other hand, one of his own compatriots, Benjamin West, the favourite painter of George the Third,

> (Of modern works he makes a jest
> Except the works of Mr. West),

was very much *en évidence* in public places. He had succeeded Reynolds as President of the Royal Academy, and the diplomatic French notabilities were doing their best to flatter him into the belief that Bonaparte was not only the greatest of men but of art collectors. Indeed, the First Consul himself favoured this idea by personally commending West's own 'Death on the Pale Horse,' the finished sketch of which he had brought with him from England to exhibit at the Salon. West, whose weakness was 'more than female vanity,' was by no means backward in acknowledging these politic, if not perfidious, attentions, which he accepted without suspicion. 'Wherever I went,' he said simply, 'people looked at me, and ministers and men of influence in the State were constantly in my company. I was one day in the Louvre—all eyes were upon me, and I could not help observing to Charles Fox, *who happened to be walking with me*, how strong was the love of Art and admiration of its professors in France.' Fox, whose reputation as an orator and a patriot had preceded him, was naturally the observed of all observers, and he was besides the object of special attentions on the part of Bonaparte.

Fox's chief mission to Paris, according to his biographer, Lord Russell, was to search the archives for his 'History of the Revolution of 1688.' But transcribing the correspondence of Barillon did not so exclusively occupy him as to divert him from the charms of the Théâtre Français, or, as it was at this time called, the 'Théâtre de la République.' Fox went frequently to see that new-risen queen of tragedy Mlle. Duchesnois, of whom it was said, 'qu'elle avait des larmes dans la voix.'[1] He saw her in 'Andromaque' and 'Phèdre,' and as Roxane in 'Bajazet.' Raim-

[1] Thackeray, who applies this to Gay, quotes it of Rubini.

bach also, as might be anticipated from the schoolfellow of Charles Mathews and the admirer of Kemble, did not neglect the French theatres, which, he notes, were at this time more numerous than in all the other capitals of Europe put together. At the Grand Opéra, then rechristened 'Théâtre de la République et des Arts,' he heard the opera of 'Anacréon,' in which the principal male singer was François Lays, or Lais, and the foremost female that Mlle. Maillard to whom tradition assigned the part of the Goddess of Reason at the celebration of 1793, which celebration indeed, had been arranged by Lais with the prophet of the cult, Chaumette. Raimbach, however, thought little, as a vocalist, of the lady, then just succeeded to the place of her preceptress, the accomplished Mme. Saint-Huberty, who, as Countess d'Entraigues, was cruelly murdered with her husband at Barnes Terrace some few years later by an Italian valet.[1] But he was charmed with the vocalization of Lais, and delighted with

[1] In 1812. There is an account of this tragedy in the 'Morning's Walk from London to Kew' of Borrow's vegetarian publisher, Sir Richard Phillips, 1817, pp. 219-22. It was Mme. Saint-Huberty whose triumphant rendering of Dido, in the " Didon " of Piccinni, elicited a complimentary sonnet from Lieut. Napoleon Bonaparte.

the ballet, which included the elder Vestris ('*Diou*' *de la danse*) and Mme. Gardel. In particular the young engraver remembered an English hornpipe, executed in a jockey's dress by one Beaupré, which excelled anything of the kind he had ever seen in his own country. At the Théâtre Français,—possibly because his tastes lay rather in comedy than tragedy,—Raimbach says nothing of Racine and Mlle. Duchesnois. But he speaks of Monvel, the sole survivor of the old school of the Lekains and Prévilles and Barons, as still charming in spite of age and loss of teeth; and he also saw that practical joker and pet of the Parisians, Dugazon, who must have been almost as diminutive as Addison's 'little Dickey,' Henry Norris.[1] But after Préville he was the prince of stage valets, and despite a tendency to exaggeration (which Raimbach duly

---

[1] It was Dugazon who cajoled the original Bartholo of the 'Barbier,' Desessarts (who was enormously fat), into applying for the post of elephant to the Court. When the irate Desessarts afterwards challenged him, Dugazon, by gravely chalking a circle upon his adversary, and proposing that all punctures outside the ring should count for nothing, turned the whole affair into ridicule. (In the 'Recollections of Aubrey de Vere,' 1897, pp. 3-4, a somewhat similar story is told of two Dublin lawyers,—'one the biggest, and the other the smallest, man in Irish society.')

chronicles), almost perfect in his own line. Another stage luminary mentioned by Raimbach is Monvel's daughter, Mlle. Mars, at this time only three-and-twenty, and not yet displaying those supreme qualities which afterwards made her unrivalled in Europe. But she was already seductive as an *ingenue*; and her performance of Angélique in 'La Fausse Agnès' of Néricault Destouches (which Arthur Murphy afterwards borrowed for his farce of the 'Citizen'), is declared by Raimbach to have been 'replete with grace and good taste.' Finally, Raimbach saw the First Consul's tragedian, Talma, then in the height of his powers, and continuing successfully those reforms of costume and declamation which he was supposed to have learned in England. John Kemble, who was also visiting Paris, where he was hospitably entertained by the French actors, was now in his turn taking hints from Talma, since it was observable that when he got back to London he adopted Talma's costume for the Orestes of the 'Distressed Mother.'

The Italian Opera, of course, was not open, and of the remaining actors Raimbach says not very much. At the Vaudeville he saw Laporte, the leading harlequin of the day, and at Picart's Theatre in the Rue Feydeau witnessed what must have been the 'Tom Jones à Londres' of M. Desforges, in which Picart himself, who was a better author than actor, took the part of the so-called 'Squire Westiern.' This representation, as might be expected, was amusing for its absurdities rather than its merits. But it can hardly have been more ridiculous to an Englishman than Poinsinet's earlier Comédie Lyrique, where Western and 'l'ami Jone' pursue the flying hart to the accompaniment of *cors de chasse* and the orthodox French *hallali*. Another (unconsciously) theatrical exhibition which Raimbach occasionally attended, was the Tribunat, one of the new Legislative bodies that at this time held its sittings in the Palais Royal, then, on that account, rechristened Palais du Tribunat. Here he met with the notorious Lewis Goldsmith, not, as afterwards, the inveterate assailant of Napoleon, but for the moment actively engaged in editing a paper called 'The Argus ; or, London Reviewed in Paris,' which attacked the war and the English Government. At the Tribunat Goldsmith pointed out several of the minor men of the Revolution to Raimbach. But it was a colourless assembly, wholly in the power of the imperious First Consul, and its meetings had little instruction for a stranger. Goldsmith, however, was not the sole compatriot Raimbach met in the Palais Royal. In the *salons littéraires* he came frequently in contact with Thomas Holcroft, of the 'Road to Ruin.' Holcroft had married a French wife, had a family, and was engaged in preparing those 'Travels in France,' which Sir Richard Phillips afterwards published. Holcroft was a friend of Opie (then also in Paris), who painted the portrait of him now at St. Martin's Place; but from Raimbach's account he must have been far more petulant and irritable than befitted the austere philosopher of his writings. Of another person whom Raimbach mentions he gives a rosier account than is given generally. At the Café Jacob in the Rue Jacob, an obscure *cabaret* in an obscure street, was frequently to be seen the once redoubtable Thomas Paine, then about sixty-five. Contemporaries represent him at this date as not only fallen upon evil days, but dirty in his habits and unduly addicted to spirits. That the general appearance of the author of the 'Rights of Man' was 'mean and poverty-stricken,' and that he was 'much withered and careworn,' Raimbach admits, and he moreover adds that he had 'sunk into complete insignificance, and was quite unnoticed by the Government.' But he also describes him as 'fluent in speech, of mild and gentle de-

meanour, clear and distinct in enunciation,' and
endowed with an 'exceedingly soft and agreeable
voice'—words which, in this connection, some-
how remind one of Lord Foppington's philosophic
eulogy of Miss Hoyden. Certainly they scarcely
suggest the seedy and dilapidated personage who
drank brandy and 'declaimed upon Religion'
in his cups, with whom modern records have
acquainted us.¹

Raimbach's remaining experiences must be
rapidly summarized. He attended the Palais de
Justice, and was much impressed by the French
forensic oratory. Concerning the oratory of the
pulpit he is not equally enthusiastic, observing,
indeed, that he should think the cause of religion
derived little support from the eloquence of the
clergy. But it must be remembered that at this
period most of the priests were expatriated, and
many of the churches were still used as ware-
houses and stables. One close by him in the
Rue Montorgueil was, as a matter of fact, employed as a saddler's shop. He was much in-

¹ Some of Paine's hair, part of his brain, and a wax
mask of his face, were recently (1898) offered for sale in a
second-hand bookseller's catalogue! They had been exhibited at 'The Thomas Paine Exhibition,' held at South
Place, Finsbury, in December, 1895.

terested in the now dispersed collection brought together in the Couvent des Petits-Augustins by M. Alexandre Lenoir, the artist and antiquary who decorated Malmaison for Josephine. This consisted of such monumental efforts as had escaped the fury of the Terror—escaping, it should be added, only miserably mutilated and defaced. Lenoir, who had received a severe bayonet wound in attempting to defend the tomb of Richelieu at the church of the Sorbonne, had admirably arranged these waifs and strays, and the collection of eighteenth-century sculpture was especially notable, as were also the specimens of stained glass. Among Raimbach's personal experiences came the successful consumption at Véry's in the Palais Royal of a *fricassée* of frogs. But this was done in ignorance, and not of set purpose, as in the case of the epicure, Charles Lamb, who speaks of them as 'the nicest little delicate things.' Raimbach's return to England somewhat precipitated by the fury of the First Consul at the attacks upon him in the 'Morning Chronicle,' was made by the Picardy route. At Calais he spent a day at the historical Lion d'Argent,[1]

---

[1] Mrs. Carter ('Memoirs,' i. 253) says, in June, 1763: 'I am sorry to say it, but it is fact, that the Lion d'Argent at Calais is a much better inn than any I saw at Dover.'

where Hogarth and so many of his fellow countrymen had been before him, and he reached Dover shortly afterwards, giving, with his party, three ringing cheers at once more treading upon English soil. He had been absent two months instead of two weeks. His *impressions de voyage*, which occupy nearly half his 'Memoirs,' would have gained in permanent charm if he had described more and reflected less. All the same, his trip to Paris as a young man in 1802 was the one event of his career, for though he went abroad again on two or three occasions, received a gold medal from the Salon in 1814, for his engraving of 'The Village Politicians,' was fêted by Baron Gérard in 1825, and made a Corresponding Member of the Institute ten years later, the rest of his recollections are comparatively uninteresting, except for his intercourse with Wilkie, of whom he wrote a brief biography. He died in January, 1843, in his sixty-seventh year.[1]

[1] Since this paper was written, the newspapers have recorded the death at Harlesden, in September, 1898, of Raimbach's younger daughter, Eliza, an ancient lady of eighty-five.

OLD WHITEHALL.

NOW, when the widening of Parliament Street promises to afford an adequate approach to St. Stephen's, and another imposing range of buildings has arisen at Spring Gardens to match the Foreign and India Offices, it may be worth while to linger for a moment upon some former features of this much-changing locality. In such a retrospect, the Old Banqueting-House of Inigo Jones naturally becomes a prominent object. Its massive Northamptonshire stone and classic columns invest it with a dignity of which the towering pile of Whitehall Court can scarcely deprive it; and it seems to overlook Kent's stumpy Horse Guards opposite much as a nobleman with a pedigree might be expected to survey a neighbour of a newer creation. And yet, impressive though it is, it represents but an insignificant portion of the architect's original design, the imaginative extent of which may be studied in Campbell's 'Vitruvius Britannicus' and elsewhere. As a matter of fact, the present

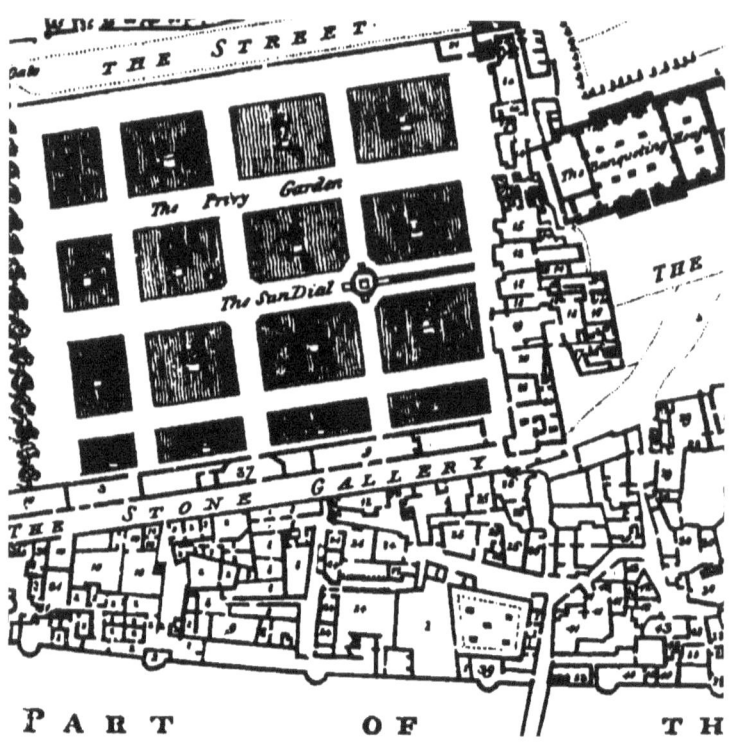

Old Whitehall. 195

Banqueting-House was only one out of four similar pavilions in a vast structure of which the ground plan would have extended from the river bank to a point far beyond the Horse Guards, and would have occupied all the space on either side of the road from Horse Guards Avenue to the Mews of Richmond Terrace. It included no fewer than seven splendid internal courts, and the façades towards the park and the Thames— the latter especially—were of great beauty. But the scheme was beyond the pocket of the first James, for whom, in 1619, it was designed; and a cheaper modification, reaching only to the roadway, and prepared twenty years later, fared no better with Charles I. The Banqueting-House, which was built in 1619-22, and is common to both projects, is consequently all that was ever executed of what, in its completed form, would have been a palace among palaces, surpassing the Louvre and the Escurial.

Apart from its existing employment as the museum of the Royal United Service Institution, the Banqueting-House to-day serves chiefly as a landmark or key by help of which its ancient environments may be mentally re-constructed. With Gibbons' fine bronze statue of James II., now erected in the enclosure at the side of

Gwydyr House,[1] it practically constitutes the sole surviving portion of Old Whitehall as it appears in Vertue's engraving of John Fisher's famous 'Survey and Ground-Plot' of 1680 (or earlier); and about it was dispersed irregularly that pell-mell of buildings dating from Henry VIII. and Elizabeth, which, in Jacobean and Caroline days, was known as 'our Palace of Westminster.' Roughly speaking, this confused aggregation[2] might be defined geographically as bounded on the north by St. James's Park; on the south by the Thames; to the east by Scotland Yard and Spring Gardens, and to the west by Richmond Terrace Mews. It was traversed throughout its entire extent by the old roadway leading to Westminster Abbey, and this divided it into two portions, the larger and more important of which lay on the side of the Thames. From Scotland Yard to the Banqueting-House the road was fairly wide and open; but at the

[1] This originally stood at the back of the Banqueting-House in Whitehall Gardens; but was moved to its present site in 1897.

[2] 'The *Seraglio*, at *Constantinople*,' says Mackay with unconscious fitness, 'is not composed of more Variety than this Palace was' ('A Journey through England,' 4th ed. 1724, i. 176). It should be added that by 'north,' 'south,' etc., the north and south of Fisher's plan are here intended.

western end of the Banqueting-House it suddenly narrowed, passing through the gate popularly known as Holbein's, and afterwards entering King Street through a second or King Street Gate. 'K[ing] Cha[rles],' the Marquis of Normanby told Evelyn, 'had a designe to buy all King Street, and build it nobly, it being the streete leading to Westm^r.' Once, too, when Evelyn had presented him with a copy of his 'book of Architecture,' he sketched a rough plan for the future building of Whitehall itself, 'together with the roomes of state, and other particulars.'[1] But His Majesty's promises were better than his performances; and he had more pressing and less worshipful ways of spending his money.

It will be convenient to speak first of that part of the palace buildings which lay to the north of the road between King Street and Charing Cross. Here was the old Cockpit, which, in the time of Fisher's Plan, was included in the apartments of Monk, Duke of Albemarle, and from which the Earl of Pembroke and Montgomery saw the first Charles walk from St. James's Palace to the scaffold. Later it

[1] 'Memoirs of John Evelyn,' etc., 1827, ii. 225, and iii. 339.

became the Privy-Council Office, where, in Anne's reign, Harley was stabbed by Guiscard. Here also was the Tennis Court; and (fronting the Banqueting-House) the Tilt-Yard, where with such 'laudable Courtesy and pardonable Insolence,' Sir Roger de Coverley's ancestor defeated his opponent.[1] On the site of the present Treasury, and looking upon the street, were the apartments of the Dukes of Monmouth and Ormond; to the west of these, the quarters of Captain Henry Cooke, 'Master of the Children [choir boys] of the Chapel Royal.' The remainder of the buildings on this side seem to have been chiefly occupied by Albemarle, though Lady Castlemaine had kitchens not far from the Tennis Court, while between the Horse Guard Yard and the Spring Garden were the rooms of one of the maids of honour, Mrs. Kirke. At the back stretched St. James's Park, where Charles II. made many improvements, and built his famous decoy for waterfowl. In Evelyn's days this must have almost attained the proportions of a menagerie. 'Here,' says he, 'was a curious sort of poultry not much exceeding the size of a tame pidgeon, with legs so short as their crops seem'd to touch ye earth; a milk-white

---

[1] 'Spectator,' No. 109.

raven ; a stork which was a rarity at this season, seeing he was loose and could flie loftily ; two Balearian [Balearic?] cranes, one of which having one of his leggs broken and cut off above the knee, had a wooden or boxen leg and thigh, with a joynt so accurately made that ye creature could walke and use it as well as if it had ben natural; it was made by a souldier. The parke was at this time stored with numerous flocks of severall sorts of ordinary and extraordinary wild fowle, breeding about the Decoy, which for being neere so greate a citty, and among such a concourse of souldiers and people, is a singular and diverting thing. There were also deere of severall countries, white ; spotted like leopards ; antelopes, an elk, red deere, roebucks, staggs, Guinea goates, Arabian sheepe, &c. There were withy-potts or nests for the wild fowle to lay their eggs in, a little above ye surface of ye water.'[1]

Thus we come to that larger and more important portion of Old Whitehall which lay to the south of the road between Westminster and Charing Cross. To the west of the Banqueting-House, and corresponding in length to the distance between the two great gates, was the

[1] 'Memoirs of John Evelyn,' etc., 1827, ii. 234.

Privy Garden, where in May, 1662, Mr. Pepys, to his great solace and content, saw my Lady Castlemaine's laced smocks and linen petticoats floating gaily to the breeze. According to Hatton, the Privy Garden occupied about three and a quarter acres, and (as our plan shows) was laid out in sixteen grass-plots with statues in the centre of each. To the north a high wall separated it from the roadway, to the west was a line of trees, and to the east a straggling range of buildings nearly at right angles to the Banqueting-House. Here lived Evelyn's friend, Sir Robert Murray; and here were the apartments of the Lord Chamberlain, where, in November, 1679, Evelyn witnessed the re-marriage of his Lordship's daughter, a child of twelve years old, to the Duke of Grafton, the king's natural son by Barbara Palmer. Here, again, were the Council Office, the Lord Keeper's Office, and the Treasury. Opposite the Treasury, in the central walk of the garden, was a famous pyramidal dial, which had been set up in 1669 by Francis Hall, a Jesuit. A much-needed 'explication' of this was printed at Liège four years later by one H. Steel, who also engraved it.[1]

[1] This pyramidal dial seems to have succeeded to an earlier one erected by the first Charles, when Prince of

Old Whitehall.

To the south of the Privy Garden, and communicating with the Bowling Green, which lay to the west of it (presumably on the site now occupied by Richmond Terrace), was the famous Stone Gallery. On its northern side were domiciled the Earl of Lauderdale, Lord Peterborough, Prince Rupert, and Mr. Hyde; and somewhere in its vicinity, although not indicated upon Fisher's plan, doubtless because granted subsequently to the date of its execution, must have been the 'luxuriously-furnished' lodgings of that 'baby-faced' (but not guileless) Breton beauty, Louise Renée de Kéroualle. This, indeed, is clear from Evelyn's diary. '4 Oct. [1683] ... Following his Majesty this morning *thro' the gallerie*, I went, with the few who attended him, into the Dutchesse of Portsmouth's [1] dressing-roome within her bedchamber, where she was in her morning loose garment, her maids combing her, newly out of her bed, his Ma^{ty} and the gallants standing about her; but that which engag'd my curiosity was the rich and splendid furniture of this woman's

Wales, and fully described, in quarto, for James I., by Edmund Gunter (1624). It 'went to ruin in King Charles II.'s time'—says Cunningham.

[1] From an autograph in the French National Archives, she signed herself ' L duchesse de Portsmout.'

apartment, now twice or thrice pull'd down and rebuilt to satisfie her prodigal and expensive pleasures, whilst her Ma⁽ᵗʸ⁾ˢ does not exceede some gentlemen's ladies in furniture and accommodation. Here I saw the new fabriq of French tapissry, for designe, tendernesse of worke, and incomparable imitation of the best paintings, beyond anything I had ever beheld. Some pieces had Versailles, St. Germain's, and other palaces of the French King, with huntings, figures, and landskips, exotiq fowls, and all to the life rarely don. Then for Japan cabinets, screenes, pendule clocks, greate vases of wrought plate, tables, stands, chimney furniture, sconces, branches, braseras, etc. all of massie silver, and out of number, besides some of her Ma⁽ᵗʸ⁾ˢ best paintings.' ' 10 April [1691]. This night a sudden and terrible fire burnt down all the buildings *over the stone gallery* at White-hall to the water-side, beginning at the apartment of the late Dutchesse of Portsmouth[1] (wᶜʰ had ben pull'd down and rebuilt no lesse than three times to please her).'[2]

---

[1] What Evelyn intends by 'late' is not clear, as the Duchess did not die until 1734. Probably he only means that she had withdrawn to France.

[2] In Bramston's 'Autobiography' (Camden Society), 1845, p. 365, this is confirmed. 'On the 9th of Aprill

Old Whitehall.

Between the Stone Gallery and the old river-line, now obliterated by the Embankment, and covering a site which extended as far as Whitehall Palace Stairs, were the apartments of the King, the Queen, the Duke of York, and the great officers of the Court. The King's rooms, in suggestive proximity to those of the Maids of Honour, and with the notorious Chiffinch conveniently at hand, were to the left of the Privy Stairs; those of Catherine of Braganza, which, on the plan, look small and unimportant, lay to the right. Neither Pepys nor Evelyn gives us much information with regard to this part of the Palace. Mention is indeed made by them and others of the Shield Gallery, the Matted Gallery, the Boarded Gallery, the Vane Room, the Robe Chamber, the Green Chamber, the Theatre, the Adam and Eve Gallery (which took its name from a picture by Mabuse), and so forth; but the indications are too vague to enable us to fix their locality with certainty. By favour, however, of 'an ancient woman who made these

[1691] a fier hapned in White Hall which burnt downe the fine lodgeings built for the Dutches of Portsmouth *at the end of the longe gallery*, and severall lodgeings, and that gallerie.' Lady Sunderland calls her 'the Lady at the end of the Gallery' (Henry Sidney's ' Diary,' i. 208).

lodgings cleane, and had all yᵉ keys,' Evelyn seems to have minutely examined the King's private library, with which, though he spent three or four days over it, he was not greatly impressed. ' I went,' he says, ' with expectation of finding some curiosities, but though there were about 1000 volumes, there were few of importance which I had not perus'd before.' He found, nevertheless, a ' folio MS. of good thicknesse' containing the school exercises of Edward VI., together with his Journal, which Burnet afterwards made use of in his ' History of the Reformation.'[1] Towards Whitehall Stairs, between the Banqueting-House and the river, were the Great Hall, and the Chapel where King of Chichester, and the witty South, and the eloquent Stillingfleet preached to an unedified congregation, and where peeping Mr. Pepys 'observed,' on a certain Sunday in October, 1660, 'how the Duke of York and Mrs. Palmer did talk to one another very wantonly through the hangings that parts the King's closet and the closet where the ladies sit.' An old view of Whitehall, from the Thames, gives a fair idea of its aspect at this time. To the right are the Chapel and Hall, with the

---

[1] 'Memoirs of John Evelyn,' etc., 1827, iii. 33-35.

loftier Banqueting-House appearing in the background, and Holbein's Gate just distinguishable at its side. To the left is the covered Privy Stairs, whence the Royal Barge with its flags and trumpeters is just putting off. Here it must have been, that, little more than two months before Charles II.'s unexpected death, Evelyn witnessed the water celebration which took place in front of the Queen's apartments:—'[Nov.] 15, [1684] Being the Queene's birthday, there were fire-works on the Thames before White-hall, with pageants of castles, forts, and other devices of gyrandolas, serpents, the King and Queene's armes and mottos, all represented in fire, such as had not ben seen here. But the most remarkable was the several fires and skirmishes in the very water, which actually mov'd a long way, burning under the water, now and then appearing above it, giving reports like muskets and cannon, with granados and innumerable other devices. It is said it cost £1,500. It was concluded with a ball, where all the young ladys and gallants daunced in the greate hall. The court had not ben seene so brave and rich in apparell since his Ma^{tys} restauration.'[1] To this

[1] 'Memoirs of John Evelyn,' etc., 1827, iii. 121-122.

may succeed that memorable and oft-cited entry, which occurs only a few pages farther on, when Charles was lying dead: 'I can never forget the inexpressible luxury and prophanenesse, gaming and all dissoluteness, and as it were total forgetfullnesse of God (it being Sunday evening) which this day se'nnight [25 January, 1685] I was witnesse of, the King sitting and toying with his concubines, Portsmouth, Cleaveland, and Mazarine, etc., a French boy [François Duperrier] singing love songs, in that glorious gallery, whilst about 20 of the greate courtiers and other dissolute persons were at basset round a large table, a bank of at least 2,000 in gold before them, upon which two gentlemen who were with me made reflexions with astonishment. Six days after was all in the dust!' The next three lines with their note of official anticlimax are not so generally reprinted: 'It was enjoyn'd that those who put on mourning should wear it as for a father, in ye most solemn manner.'

From Whitehall Palace Stairs a roadway went, past the Chapel and Great Hall, through a wide open court to the Palace Gate, close to what was the site of the old Wardrobe (afterwards Lord Carrington's). To the right of this road, and extending as far as Scotland Yard, were groups of inferior buildings and offices,—kitchens, butteries, pastries, spiceries, bakehouses, slaughter-houses, charcoal-houses, and the like,—traces of which may still be identified. The present Board of Trade, and the adjacent buildings in Horse Guards Avenue, occupy portions of the sites of the Wine-Cellar,[1] Hall, and Chapel; the Confectionary is said to have been a white house between the former Museum of the United Service Institution[2] and Lord Carrington's stables, and the old Beer Buttery long existed near the gates of Fife House, the place of which is now covered by part of Whitehall Court.

Standing in the entrance to Horse Guards Avenue (once Whitehall Yard), one may still, with the aid of an old view or two, and Fisher's indispensable plan, obtain a fair idea of the place in the time of the Stuarts. Opposite—where the Scottish Office and Horse Guards are at present—was the boundary wall of the old Tilt and Horse Guard Yards. To the left, immediately in front of the Banqueting-House, extended a row of posts, a little in advance of which—'in

[1] There is a description of some of these remains in 'Archæologia' (vol. xxv. 1832) by Sydney Smirke.

[2] The Museum of the United Service Institution was pulled down in 1898.

the open street before Whitehall '—was the spot where, after much controversy, Charles I. is now allowed to have been beheaded. From the western end a line of buildings ran out to Holbein's Gate. These, which also looked into the Privy Garden, were, as already explained, the apartments of Lord Arlington, the Lord Chamberlain. Of Holbein's Gate itself,—although, according to Mr. Wornum, we are scarcely justified in styling it Holbein's,—Pennant, who seems to have seen it, gives the following account: 'To *Holbein* was owing the most beautiful gate at *Whitehall*, built with bricks of two colours, glazed, and disposed in a tesselated fashion. The top, as well as that of an elegant tower on each side, were [*sic*] embattled. On each front were four busts in baked clay, in proper colors, which resisted to the last every attack of the weather: possibly the artificial stone revived in this century. These, I have been lately informed, are preserved in a private hand. This charming structure fell a sacrifice to conveniency within my memory: as did another in 1723, built at the same time, but of far inferior beauty. The last blocked up the road to *King-street*, and was called *King's-gate*. *Henry* built it as a passage to the park, the tennis court, bowling-green, the cock-pit, and tilting-yard ; for he was extremely fond of athletic exercises ; they suited his strength and his temper.'[1]

Both these gates were engraved by Vertue in the 'Vetusta Monumenta' published by the Society of Antiquaries. The so-called Holbein's Gate, which long survived the buildings that connected it with the Banqueting-House, was pulled down in August, 1759, to make room for Parliament Street. The Duke of Cumberland had it removed to Windsor, with the intention of re-erecting it at the end of the Long Walk, and his Deputy Ranger, Thomas Sandby (the architect), was to have made some additions at the sides, the designs for which are still to be seen in J. T. Smith's 'Westminster.' But, as seems generally the case after removals of this kind, nothing was ever done in the matter. Meanwhile the medallions of which Pennant speaks were dispersed. Three of them, according to Smith, were, when he published his book, at Hatfield Peverell in Essex ; two more got worked into keepers' lodges at Windsor. These, said Cunningham in 1849, 'are now, by Mr. Jesse's [*i.e.* the late J. Heneage Jesse's] exertions, at Hampton Court, where they are made to do

[1] 'Some Account of London,' 3rd ed., 1793, pp. 99, 100.

duty as two of the Roman Emperors, described by Hentzner, in his Travels, as then at Hampton Court.' They are of Italian workmanship, and may probably be attributed to John de Maiano.

Those who, having sufficiently examined the Palladian exterior of the Banqueting-House, and duly noted the famous weather-cock on the eastern end, which, or an earlier example thereof, James II. is said to have set up to warn him of the approach of the Dutch fleet, desire farther to inspect the interior, can easily do so, since (as already stated) the building is now a museum. Its chief feature of interest is the ceiling, which represents the Apotheosis of James I. It is painted black, partly gilded, and divided into panels by bands, ornamented with a guilloche. Of the three central compartments, that at one end represents the British Solomon on his throne, 'pointing to Prince Charles, who is being perfected by Wisdom.' The middle compartment shows him 'trampling on the globe and flying on the wings of Justice (an eagle) to heaven.' In the third he is 'embracing Minerva, and routing Rebellion and Envy.' These panels, and others at the sides, were painted by Rubens in 1635, with the assistance of his pupil, Jordaens. They were restored by Cipriani. In 1837, the whole building, which had been closed since 1829, was refitted and repaired under the direction of Sir Robert Smirke.

It would occupy too large a space to trace the history of the Banqueting-House from its first erection to its Georgian transformation into an unconsecrated chapel (1724), seductive as it might be to speak of it as the theatre of Ben Jonson's masques and the buffooneries of Cromwell. In Charles II.'s time, to which, in the foregoing remarks, we have mainly confined ourselves, it was the scene of many impressive ceremonies and state receptions. It was in the Banqueting-House that Charles begged his Honourable House of Commons to amend the ways about Whitehall, so that Catherine of Braganza might not upon her arrival find it 'surrounded by water;' it was in the Banqueting-House that he gravely went through that half solemn half ludicrous business of touching for the evil; it was in the Banqueting-House that, coming from the Tower of London with a splendid cavalcade, he created at one time six Earls and six Barons. Under its storied roof he magnificently entertained the French Ambassador, Charles Colbert, Marquis de Croissy, on which occasion he presented Mr. Evelyn, from his own royal plate, with a piece of that newly-imported Barbadian luxury, the King-pine;[1] it was here also that he received the Russian Ambassador with his presents of carpets and sables and 'sea-horse teeth;' and the swarthy envoys from Morocco, with their scymetars and white *alhagas*, and their lions and 'estridges' [ostriches]. But perhaps the brightest and most vivid page in connection with this famous old building is that in which Samuel Pepys relates what he saw from its roof on the 23rd of August, 1662:—

'. . Mr. Creed . . and I . . walked down to the Styllyard [Steel Yard] and so all along Thames-street, but could not get a boat: I offered eight shillings for a boat to attend me this afternoon, and they would not, it being the day of the Queen's coming to town from Hampton Court. So we fairly walked it to White Hall, and through my Lord's [Lord Sandwich's] lodgings we got into White Hall garden, and so to

[1] In the Breakfast Room at Strawberry Hill, Horace Walpole had a painting representing John Rose, the Royal gardener, in the act of presenting to Charles II. the first pineapple raised in England. The picture was attributed to Henry Danckers; and had belonged to a descendant of one of the firm of London and Wise, Nurserymen, mentioned in the fifth number of the 'Spectator.' It was engraved in 1823.

the Bowling-green, and up to the top of the new Banqueting-House[1] there, over the Thames, which was a most pleasant place as any I could have got; and all the show consisted chiefly in the number of boats and barges; and two pageants, one of a King, and another of a Queen, with her Maydes of Honour sitting at her feet very prettily; and they tell me the Queen is Sir Richard Ford's daughter. Anon come the King and Queen in a barge under a canopy with 10,000 [sic] barges and boats, I think, for we could see no water for them, nor discern the King nor Queen. And so they landed at White Hall Bridge and the great guns on the other side went off. But that which pleased me best was, that my Lady Castlemaine stood over against us upon a piece of White Hall, where I glutted myself with looking on her. But methought it was strange to see her Lord and her upon the same place walking up and down without taking notice one of another, only at first entry he put off his hat, and she made him a very civil salute, but afterwards took no notice one of another; but both of them now and then would take their child,

[1] No doubt still so called by habit, as it succeeded to an earlier Banqueting-House which was burnt in January, 1619.

which the nurse held in her armes, and dandle it. One thing more; there happened a scaffold below to fall, and we feared some hurt, but there was none, but she of all the great ladies only run down among the common rabble to see what hurt was done, and did take care of a child that received some little hurt, which methought was so noble. Anon there came one there booted and spurred that she talked long with. And by and by, she being in her hair, she put on his hat, which was but an ordinary one, to keep the wind off. But methinks it became her mightily, as every thing else do.'[1]

Evelyn's last curt entry respecting the old palace is as follows: '2 [4?] Jan. [1698]. . . . White-hall burnt, nothing but walls and ruins left.' Luckily there are records more specific. Writing on the 5th, the Earl of Tullibardine tells Lord Annandale, 'Yesternight about four a clock a fire broke out in one of the garrets at Whitehall, which burnt so furiously that it hath consumed all the king and queens apartments, the chappell, and all that was worth the standing at Whitehall, except the banquetting house.' And Sir James Ogilvie, Secretary of State, in a letter

---

[1] Pepys's 'Diary,' by Wheatley, ii. (1893), 316, 317.

of the same date, adds for postscript: 'Wee have had the greatest fire at Whitehal was ever seen. It al brunt doun except the bankating house and the Earl of Portlands lodgings, bot both are much damnified.'[1] Thus it comes about that Inigo Jones's stately building, besides being the sole relic of a Whitehall that never existed, is also the sole relic of the Whitehall that was.

[1] The last two quotations are from the Hope Johnstone papers ('Fifteenth Report of the Hist. MSS. Commission,' App. Pt. ix., 1897, p. 103).

LUTTRELL'S 'LETTERS TO JULIA.'

NOTHING fades with such rapidity as the reputation of the mere favourite of society. If he be a dandy his name, perhaps, lingers here and there in the circular of a fashionable tailor; if a wit, his sayings, although—like those of Praed's 'Belle'—'extremely quoted' during his lifetime, scarcely survive his contemporaries and booncompanions. It may be that he secures to himself some notice from posterity by posthumous 'Memoirs' put together by a friend—perhaps a valet; or he may leave behind him some literary legacy which now and then is disinterred from the shelves of the British Museum Library (if, indeed, it has found an asylum there) by an enquirer curious in forgotten follies, or anxious to elucidate the caricatures of Gillray and 'HB.' But, as a rule, if he does not die early, he passes 'into the line of outworn faces,' and his place knows him no more. Only from a magazine obituary, or a stray paragraph in a provincial paper, does one learn, half-a-century afterwards, that an old valetudinarian has died at Bath, or Cheltenham, or Boulogne, who, in his earlier days, was a favourite with the Prince Regent, a well-known *habitué* of Brooks's and White's, a member of the Neapolitan Club, and a frequent figure at Crockford's. These remarks, applicable, it should be observed, more exactly to the Georgian than the Victorian era, are mainly prompted by the difficulty experienced in obtaining particulars respecting the career of the once-famous wit and writer of *vers de société*, whose chief work forms the subject of this paper. Yet, if we may trust a manuscript note in our copy of the 'Letters to Julia,' the author of that book and 'Crockford House' attained the ripe age of eighty-six; and seventy years ago no one was better known in the higher classes of society as— to use a phrase which would have been employed in the days when 'Pelham' was penned—a man of the world *du meilleur crû*. The friend of Jekyll and Lord Alvanley, of Mackintosh and Sydney Smith, of Lord Holland and Jeffery, of Greville, of Moore, of Rogers; a wit with the wits, a scholar with the scholars; fairly earning a hearing, even in those days of 'Whistlecraft' burlesques and 'Twopenny Postboys,' as a writer of sparkling verse; an admirable talker and a polished gentleman—HENRY LUTTRELL must have been one of the most delightful of social companions. Secluded, however, in those inner circles to which admission was as difficult as getting on the list of 'Almack's,' he lies entirely beyond the range of the ordinary life-taker; and the few references to his character and works are only to be found sparsely scattered through the pages of contemporary, and, alas! often unindexed 'memoirs.' In Lady Holland's life of Sydney Smith, for example, there are some brief references to his lightness of hand, his willingness to be pleased, his amusing Irish stories. 'Luttrell,' says Smith, warning Lady Davy against overlooking the difficulties and embarrassments of life, 'before I taught him better, imagined muffins grew. He was wholly ignorant of all the intermediate processes of sowing, reaping, grinding, kneading, and baking.' This is not much of a contribution to a portrait, no doubt; but it affords a hint of that sublime and generally affected superiority to the homelier phenomena of life which forms an indispensable part of the equipment of the man of the world,—*du meilleur crû*. Yet, although we find Rogers regretting his attachment to, and monopoly by, 'persons of mere fashion,' Luttrell, it is only fair to infer, must have been considerably more than this. Everywhere, by happy allusion, and fine turns of expression, his work shows an intimate knowledge of classic authors; and, as might be anticipated, of Horace in particular.

In the 'Noctes Ambrosianæ,' he is called by 'Tickler' 'one of the most accomplished men in all England—a wit and a scholar.' 'Of course you know Luttrell,' said Byron to Lady Blessington; ' he is the best sayer of good things, and the most epigrammatic conversationist I ever met. There is a terseness and wit, mingled with fancy, in his observations that no one else possesses, and no one so peculiarly understands the *apropos*. Then, unlike all, or most other wits, Luttrell is never obtrusive; even the choicest *bons mots* are only brought forth when perfectly applicable, and they are given in a tone of good breeding which enhances their value.' 'None of the *talkers* whom I meet in London society,' says Rogers, ' can slide in a brilliant thing with such readiness as he does.' The impression here given is rather of a wit than a humourist; there is more in it of Chamfort or Rivarol than Thackeray or Sydney Smith; but, in default of more definite information, it enables us to form an idea of the easy, fluent *causeur*, touching all topics lightly, quick to catch the fleeting fancy and crystallize it into an epigram, to turn a dull corner with an adroit quotation from the classics (such things were possible formerly), to light up a mediocre story with a happy setting;—able and ready, in short, to give that sparkling ripple to the flow of conversation which made the gifted possessor of these rare qualities the envy of diners-out, and the delight of hostesses. The more conventional type of such a character Luttrell has himself sketched in easy octosyllabics:

> How much at home was Charles in all
> The talk aforesaid—nicknamed small!
> Never embarrassed, seldom slow,
> His maxim always, 'touch and go.'
> Chanced he to falter? A grimace
> Was ready in the proper place;
> Or a chased snuff-box, with its gems
> And gold, to mask his has and hems,
> Was offered round, and duly rapped,
> Till a fresh topic could be tapped.
> What if his envious rivals swore
> 'Twas jargon all, and he a bore?
> The surly sentence was outvoted,
> His jokes retailed, his jargon quoted;
> And while he sneered or quizzed or flirted,
> The world, half-angry, was diverted.

It would be of no service to reproduce here any of the half-dozen good things of Luttrell that linger in Moore's 'Diary.' Many of these are of that class whose prosperity lies emphatically in the ear of the listener; and we are too far removed from the speaker to be able to revive those niceties of manner and delivery which were essential to a just appreciation of them. With his verse the case is different. That, at least, was intended to be read; and although some of the allusions are necessarily obscure, we can, by a slight effort, place ourselves in the position of the audience to whom it was originally addressed. We must frankly confess, however, that, doubtless from the absence of those individual advantages of address and opportunity which gave him grace as a conversationalist, Luttrell's work, easy and polished though it be, scarcely impresses one as commensurate with the praise he received from his contemporaries. But of this the reader must judge from the specimens here reproduced.

The 'Letters to Julia,'[1] Luttrell's longest and most ambitious effort, is an amplification of that

---

[1] In the first edition of the poem, issued in 1820, it bore the title of 'Advice to Julia,' and the lady addressed corresponded more exactly with the Lydia of Horace. But we are dealing with the later edition of 1822, published under the title we quote above, and in this we are told that 'the first Julia must be forgiven and forgotten.'

pleasant little ode in the first book of Horace, in which Lydia is enjoined by the poet not to ruin Sybaris by a too exclusive attachment to her apron-strings. The reader who recalls the sixteen lines of the original, may perhaps wonder how it was possible to expand so brief a lyric into a poem of two hundred pages. And, indeed, under the digressions of the author, the primary motive almost entirely disappears. But as he himself gives us the above explanation of the origin of his work, we are bound to regard it. His first conception, he says, was 'by filling up such an outline on a wider canvass . . . to exhibit a picture, if imperfect not unfaithful, of modern habits and manners, and of the amusements and lighter occupations of the higher classes of society in England.'

Viewed in this aspect, it matters little how the idea was first suggested. In the four epistles of which the book consists, the parts of Lydia and Sybaris are taken by Charles, a man of fashion and pleasure, embarrassed, as a matter of course, but 'at the head of the *suprême bon ton*;' and Julia, a young widow of two-and-twenty, rather lower in the social scale, but rich and spoiled by flattery, who quite intends to marry her desirable admirer whenever it suits her to do so, but in the meantime subjects him to all the petty tyrannies of coquetry and caprice. The writer of the letters is a cousin of the lady, who undertakes to remonstrate with her upon her harsh treatment of her lover. In this task, thanks to numberless digressions, he manages to ramble from 'Almack's' to Newmarket, from Brighton to Paris—where you will—sketching lightly picture after picture of the fashionable life of the first quarter of the century. Now he amplifies *cur vitat olivum* into a score of lines, descriptive of his recreant hero's avoidance of Moulsey and the Fives-Court; of—

> —rubbing, racing, and raw meat;

now mourns that no longer—

> with pliant arm he stems
> The tide or current of the Thames;

now laments his abdication of his proud supremacy as a dresser, and master of the awful mysteries of the Cravat of our grandfathers. Readers will recall the anecdote of Brummell's tray-full of failures in the following:

> Yet weak, he felt, were the attacks
> Of his voluminous Cossacks;[1]

---

[1] Those trowsers named from the barbarians
Nursed in the Steppes—the Crim-Tartarians,

In vain to suffocation braced
And bandaged was his wasp-like waist;
In vain his buckram-wadded shoulders
And chest astonished all beholders;
Wear any coat he might, 'twas fruitless;
Those shoes, those very boots were bootless
Whose tops ('t was he enjoined the mixture)
Are moveable, and spurs a fixture;
All was unprofitable, flat,
And stale without a smart CRAVAT,
Muslined enough to hold its starch;
That last key-stone of Fashion's arch!

' Have you, my friend,' I've heard him say,
' Been lucky in your turns to-day?—
Think not that what I ask alludes
To Fortune's stale vicissitudes.
Or that I'm driven from *you* to learn
How cards, and dice, and women turn,
And what prodigious contributions
They levy, in their revolutions:
I ask not if, in times so critical,
You've managed well your turns political,

Who, when they scour a country, under
Those ample folds conceal their plunder.
How strange their destiny has been!
Promoted, since the year fifteen,
In honour of these fierce allies,
To grace our British legs and thighs.
But fashion's tide no barrier stems;
So the *Don* mingles with the *Thames!*

Knowing your aptitude to rat.
My question points to—your Cravat.
These are the only turns I mean.
Tell me if these have lucky been?
If round your neck, in every fold
Exact, the muslin has been rolled,
And, dexterously in front confined,
Preserved the proper set behind;
In short, by dint of hand and eye,
Have you achieved a perfect tie?

'Should yours (kind heaven, avert the omen!)
Like the cravats of vulgar, low men,
Asunder start—and, yawning wide,
Disclose a chasm on either side;
Or should it stubbornly persist,
To take some awkward tasteless twist,
Some crease indelible, and look
Just like a dunce's dog's-eared book,
How would you parry the disgrace?
In what assembly show your face?
How brook your rival's scornful glance,
Or partner's titter in the dance?
How in the morning dare to meet
The quizzers of the park or street?
Your occupation's gone,—in vain
Hope to dine out, or flirt again.
The LADIES from their lists will put you,
And even *I*, my friend, must cut you!'

This is a good sample of Luttrell's lighter manner. Here is another—a wail from 'Almack's' over the substitution of tea for supper:

> '"How niggardly" they cry, '"to stoop
> To paltry black and green from soup!
> Once, every novice could obtain
> A hearing over iced Champagne,
> And claret, ev'n of second growth,
> Gave credit to an amorous oath.
> But now, such lifeless love is made
> On cakes, orgeat, and lemonade,
> That hungry women grow unkind,
> And men too faint to speak their mind.
> Tea mars all mirth, makes evenings drag,
> And talk grow flat, and courtship flag;
> Tea, mawkish beverage, is the reason
> Why fifty flirtings in a season
> Swell with ten marriages, at most,
> The columns of the Morning-Post."'

We might easily multiply extracts of this kind. And jaunty and fluent as are the above passages, there are others which suggest that the author had a first-rate talent for natural description and quiet landscape, points which here and there seem to rise above his pictures of men and women—or rather, *belles* and *exquisites*. Here is a picture of a storm in the Park, which is close and effective, and quite as truthful in its realism as Swift's 'City Shower':

> 'How suddenly the day's obscured!
> Bless me, how dark!—Thou threatening cloud,
> Pity the *un-umbrella'd* crowd.
> The cloud rolls onward with the breeze,

> First, pattering on the distant trees
> The rain-drops fall—then quicker, denser,
> On many a parasol and spencer;
> Soon drenching, with no mercy on it,
> The straw and silk of many a bonnet.
> Think of their hapless owners fretting,
> While feathers, crape, and gauze are wetting!
> Think of the pang to well-dressed girls,
> When, pinched in vain, their hair uncurls,
> And ringlets from each lovely pate
> Hang mathematically straight!
> As off, on every side, they scour,
> Still beats the persecuting shower,
> Till, on the thirsty gravel smoking,
> It fairly earns the name of soaking.
> Breathless they scud; some helter-skelter
> To carriages, and some for shelter;
> Lisping to coachmen drunk or dumb
> In *numbers*—while no numbers come.'

And what dweller in London will not recognize the accuracy of this:

> 'Have you not seen (you must remember)
> A fog in London—time, November?
> That non-descript elsewhere, and grown
> In our congenial soil alone?
> First, at the dawn of lingering day
> It rises, of an ashey grey,
> Then, deepening with a sordid stain
> Of yellow, like a lion's mane,
> Vapour importunate and dense,
> It wars at once with every sense,

> Invades the eyes, is tasted, smelt,
> And, like Egyptian darkness, felt.
> The ears escape not. All around
> Returns a dull unwonted sound.
> Loth to stand still, afraid to stir,
> The chilled and puzzled passenger,
> Oft-blundering from the pavement, fails
> To feel his way along the rails,
> Or, at the crossings, in the roll
> Of every carriage dreads its pole.'

Here again—in a picture of the Serpentine in winter—are some lines which to us appear to be thoroughly successful in their choice and economy of epithet:

> 'What time the slanting wintry sun
> Just skirts th' horizon, and is gone;
> When from his disk a short-lived glare
> Is wasted on the clear cold air;
> When the snow sparkles, *on the sight
> Flashing intolerable white*;
> And, swept by hurried feet, the ground
> Returns a crisp and crushing sound.'

The main defect of the 'Letters to Julia' is its length. One of the poet's contemporaries (Kenney, the creator of Jeremy Diddler) complained indeed, that, besides being too long, it was 'not broad enough;' but with the absence of the latter dimension we need not quarrel. In point of even execution, and that air of reticent good breeding which Byron declared to be characteristic of the author's style in speaking, little is wanting. The *purpureus pannus* is, in truth, carefully kept out of sight; and yet, notwithstanding the strict observance of the Horatian precept, there is a certain lack of colour and variety, which begets an impatient desire for discordance of some sort. One is reminded, in turning over the pages of faultlessly rhymed couplets, of that 'Cymodocée' of Chateaubriand, in which there was not a single elision, and concerning which the irreverent said,—'*Tant pis pour Cymodocée!*' That the poem treats solely of trivial pursuits and amusements cannot justly be counted as a defect, since the author's intention was to depict the habits of the merely fashionable world. This his graver contemporaries fully recognized when they nicknamed the book, 'Letters from a Dandy to a Dolly.' A less excusable fault is, that Luttrell nowhere opposes to his picture of frivolity any hint of higher or worthier employment; nor is there, as in these days there assuredly would be if the theme were treated by a modern, any subtle indication of a graver side to the story, or any skilful suggestion as to the unreality of so-called pleasure as an object in life. But these differences are in some respects due to changed conditions of society, and altered points of view. We are sadder than our forefathers, and if we have no longer their hearty appetites, we are not so willingly grave that we do not occasionally envy them their high spirits.

Little room remains to speak of Luttrell's lesser effort of 'Crockford House,' even if it came within our scheme. The defect of tediousness is more conspicuous in it than in the former work, although the motive—denunciation of the prevailing vice of Play—is a better one. But the author seems to have had a doubt about making it public, since, according to Moore, he consulted Lord Sefton, Mr. Greville, and others, as to the expediency of a man of the town publishing such an attack upon the high priest of the gaming table—'a deference to society,' says Moore (rather unexpectedly, considering his antecedents), 'for which society will hardly thank him.' With 'Crockford House' are printed some lines on Rome and the dirtiness of that Imperial City. A rhyming *tour de force* on 'Burnham Beeches, and a few more of Luttrell's fugitive verses are included in the late Mr. Locker Lampson's 'Lyra Elegantiarum,' where is also to be found the admirable little epigram upon Miss Ellen Tree, which has already been reproduced in these pages.' Here, from the same collection, is a graver specimen :

> 'O Death, thy certainty is such,
>   The thought of thee so fearful,
> That, musing, I have wondered much
>   How men are ever cheerful.'

There is a compactness about this which makes us wish for some other brief examples of Luttrell's serious style. It is his plans that are long, not his art. If, instead of amplifying 'Lydia, dic per omnes,' he had simply translated it, or 'Vixi puellis,' or 'Vitas hinnuleo,' or any of the lighter of Horace's odes, we should have had nearly perfect versions, for no man could have done them better.

We add one more of his lesser pieces, because the first lines alone are generally quoted. They are the quatrains to Moore about his 'Lallah Rookh.' Luttrell wrote them in the name of Rogers, whose 'Human Life' Lord Lauderdale was said to have by heart :

> 'I'm told, dear Moore, your lays are sung
>   (Can it be true, you lucky man?)
> By moonlight in the Persian tongue,
>   Along the streets of Ispahan.

---

[1] See *ante*, 'The Author of "Monsieur Tonson,"' p. 136.

> ''T is hard, but one reflexion cures,
>   At once, a jealous poet's smart :
> The Persians have translated yours,
>   But Lauderdale has mine by heart.'

Not the least piquant thing connected with this little *jeu d'esprit*, so carefully transferred to his Preface and Diary by the author of the 'Irish Melodies,' is, that Luttrell's informant was none other than Thomas Moore himself.[1]

---

[1] Henry Luttrell was a natural son of Colonel Luttrell, afterwards second Earl of Carhampton. He died as late as December, 1851. Those who desire further particulars concerning this 'Old Society Wit' will do well to consult a most interesting paper with that title in 'Temple Bar' for January, 1895, by a charming writer of reminiscences, the late Mrs. Andrew Crosse.

CHANGES AT CHARING CROSS.

LOOKING from that coign of vantage, the portico of the National Gallery, upon what Peel called 'the finest site in Europe,' it is impossible not to think of its vicissitudes. With the exception of St. Martin's Church, which is comparatively modern, the only antiquity now left to link the present with the past is the statue of Charles I., riding unhasting, unresting, to his former Palace of Westminster, and dating from a day when Trafalgar Square was but an irregular range of houses surrounding a royal mews. Only a quarter of a century ago stood in its vicinity an older relic still. If the stones that formed the fine Jacobean frontage of Northumberland House could have spoken, they would have pleaded that they knew of a remoter time when, in place of the royal martyr proclaiming from his pedestal, in Waller's turncoat line, that

'Rebellion, though successful, is but vain,'

had risen the time-honoured cross which marked

the last halting-place of Queen Eleanor's body in its progress to the Abbey. The old Cross, again, had more ancient memories than Northumberland House. It could recall a falconry—not unhaunted of a certain rhyming Clerk of Works called Geoffrey Chaucer—which was long anterior to the royal mews; and it remembered how—

> 'Ere yet, in scorn of Peter's pence,
> And number'd bead, and shrift,
> Bluff Harry broke into the spence
> And turn'd the cowls adrift,'—

the hospital of St. Mary Rounceval had preceded the great palace of the Percies.

In any retrospect of Charing Cross, Queen Eleanor's monument forms a convenient starting point, and from Ralph Agas's well-known survey of 1592 we get a fair idea of its environment in the reign of Elizabeth. At this date there were, comparatively speaking, few buildings in its neighbourhood. On the river side, indeed, houses straggled from the Strand towards Whitehall; but St. Martin's was actually 'in the fields,' Spring Gardens was as open as 'S* Jemes Parke,' and where to-day stand Covent Garden and Her Majesty's Theatre, laundresses laid their clothes to dry. Along Hedge Lane, which began at the present Union Club and followed 'the line of Dorset Place and Whitcomb Street, you might, if so minded, carry your Corinna through green pastures to eat tarts at Hampstead or Highgate, passing, it may be, on the road, Master Ben Jonson from Hartshorne Lane (now Northumberland Street), unconscious for the moment of any other ' humour ' in life than the unlimited consumption of blackberries. By the windmill at St. Giles's you might find him flying his kite, or (and why not, since the child is father to the man ?) displaying prematurely his ' Roman infirmity ' of boasting to his ragged playmates of the parish school.

But to the sober antiquary the pleasures of imagination are forbidden ; and the Cross itself has yet to be described. Unfortunately, there are no really trustworthy representations of it, and even its designer's name is uncertain. It was long ascribed to Pietro Cavallini, to whom tradition also attributes the monument of Henry III. in Westminster Abbey. What is undoubted, however, is that it was one of several similar crosses erected by the executors of Eleanor of Castile ; that it was begun by one Richard de Crundale, *cementarius*, and after his death continued by another of the family ; and that its material came from Caen in Normandy, and Corfe in Dorsetshire. From Agas's map it seems to have been octagonal in shape with tiers of niches; and it was decorated with paintings and gilt metal figures modelled by Alexander Le Imaginator. It stood from 1296 until, by vote of May the 3rd, 1643, the Long Parliament, in the same iconoclastic spirit which prompted the removal of the 'Golden Cross' sign as 'superstitious and idolatrous,' decreed its demolition. 'The parliament,' says a contemporary Royalist ballad, still to be found in Percy's ' Reliques,'

> ' " The parliament to vote it down
>   Conceived it very fitting,
> For fear it should fall, and kill them all,
>   In the house as they were sitting.
> They were told, God-wot, it had a plot,[1]
>   Which made them so hard-hearted,
> To give command, it should not stand,
>   But be taken down and carted." '

Other verses bewail its disappearance as a familiar landmark :

> 'Undone, undone, the lawyers are,
>   They wander about the towne,

---

[1] This was Waller's plot of June, 1643, to disarm the London militia, etc., for which Tompkins and Chaloner were executed.

Nor can find the way to Westminster,
Now Charing-Cros is downe.'

As a matter of fact, it was not actually 'taken down and carted' till the summer of 1647. Part of its stones, says Charles's biographer, William Lilly, went to pave Whitehall, and others were fashioned into knife-hafts, 'which, being well polished, looked like marble.' *Sic transit gloria mundi!*

Its site remained unoccupied for seven-and-twenty years. But here, in the interval, the regicides met their fate. Harrison, Cromwell's chaplain Peters, John Jones, Carew, and others, all suffered 'at the railed space where Charing Cross stood.' Pepys, between an account of the wantonness of Mrs. Palmer and the episode of 'a very pretty lady' who cried out at the playhouse 'to see Desdemona smothered,' has the following entry of Harrison's death, which he witnessed: '13th [October, 1660]. I went out to Charing Cross to see Major-general Harrison hanged, drawn, and quartered; which was done there, he looking as cheerful as any man could do in that condition. He was presently cut down, and his head and heart shown to the people, at which there was great shouts of joy. It is said, that he said that he was sure to come shortly at the right hand of Christ to judge them that now had judged him; and that his wife do expect his coming again. Thus it was my chance to see the King beheaded at White Hall, and to see the first blood shed in revenge for the King at Charing Cross.'

Grave John Evelyn has also his record:—' 17 [October, 1660]. Scot, Scroope, Cook, and Jones suffered for reward of their iniquities at Charing Crosse, in sight of the place where they put to death their natural Prince, and in the presence of the King his sonn, whom they also sought to kill. I saw not their execution; but met their quarters mangl'd and cutt and reeking as they were brought from the gallows in baskets on the hurdle. Oh, the miraculous providence of God!'

For further particulars of these dismal butcheries the reader is referred to the State Trials. In the years to come, less gruesome sights succeeded. From the overseers' books of St. Martin's, Mr. Peter Cunningham discovered entries of sums paid in 1666 and 1667 by 'Punchinello, ye Italian popet-player for his Booth at Charing Cross,' and in 1668 there are similar records for the 'playhouse' of a 'Mounsr. Devone.' Then, in 1674, the present 'noble equestrian statue' as

Walpole styles it, was erected, not too promptly, by Charles II.

Its story is singular,—almost as singular as that of the statue of the Merry Monarch himself, which loyal Sir Robert Viner, 'Alderman, Knight and Baronet,' put up in the old Stocks Market. It appears to have been executed about 1633 by Hubert Le Sœur, a pupil of John of Bologna, for the Lord High Treasurer Weston, who intended it to embellish his garden at Roehampton. By the terms of the commission it was to be of brass, a foot larger than life, and the sculptor 'was to take advice of his Maj. (Charles I.) riders of greate horses, as well for the shape of the horse and action as for the graceful shape and action of his Maj. figure on the same.' Before the beginning of the Civil War, according to Walpole, the statue, cast but not erected, was sold by the Parliament to John Rivett, brazier, dwelling at the Dial near Holborn Conduit, who was strictly enjoined to break it up. Rivett, whose 'faith was large in time,' carefully buried it instead, and ingenuously exhibited some broken brass in earnest of its destruction. Report further says that, making capital out of both parties, he turned these mythic fragments into knife and fork handles, which the

Royalists bought eagerly as relics, and the Puritans as tokens of the downfall of a despot. In any case there is evidence to show that the statue was still in Rivett's possession in 1660, and it is assumed that it passed from him or his family to the second Charles. Strype says that he presented it to the King, which is not unlikely. The pedestal, finely carved with cupids, palms, armour, and so forth, is attributed to Grinling Gibbons. Somewhere near it was the Pillory where, every 10th of August, for several successive years, stood the infamous Titus Oates. Edmund Curll, too (upon that principle which makes Jack Sheppard one of the 'eminent' persons buried in St. Martin's), was once its 'distinguished' occupant, for one of his scandalous publications; and later Parsons of the Cock Lane Ghost suffered here those amenities so neatly described by Robert Lloyd in his 'Epistle to Churchill':

> 'Thus, should a wooden collar deck
> Some woefull 'squire's embarrass'd neck,
> When high above the crowd he stands
> With equidistant sprawling hands,
> And without hat, politely bare,
> Pops out his head to take the air;
> The mob his kind acceptance begs,
> Of dirt, and stones, and addle-eggs.'

Changes at Charing Cross. 241

To the right of King Charles's statue, upon a site now traversed diagonally by Northumberland Avenue, stood, until 1874, the last of the great riverside mansions, Northumberland House. Its façade extended from the statue towards Northumberland Street, and its gardens went back to Scotland Yard, into which it had a gate. Northampton House, as it was first called, was built about 1605 for Henry Howard, Earl of Northampton, by Bernard Jansen and Gerard Christmas—Christmas, it is supposed, being responsible for the florid gateway or 'frontispiece.' From the Earl of Northampton it passed to the Suffolks, and changed its name to Suffolk House, a name which it retained until 1670, when becoming the property of the Percies it was again re-christened. Londoners, except upon such special occasions as Exhibition years and the like, saw little of the place beyond the façade. Its original plan was a quadrangle, uncompleted at first on the garden-side. Algernon Percy, tenth Earl of Northumberland, added a new river-front, and a stone flight of stairs, which Mr. Evelyn regarded as clumsy and 'without any neat invention.' In the interior its chief glory was a double state-staircase with marble steps. There was also a state-gallery of magnificent proportions, a draw-

R

ing-room decorated by Angelica Kauffman, and a tapestry-chamber by Zuccarelli. The pictures which, with the wonderful stiff-tailed leaden lion so long familiar to passers by, are now transferred to Sion House at Isleworth, included Titian's famous Cornaro family (Evelyn's 'Venetian Senators'), and a number of minor masterpieces. One of the show-curiosities was a Sèvres vase nine feet high, presented to the second Duke of Northumberland by Charles X. of France.

It would be easy to accumulate anecdote around this ancient dwelling-place. From this 'house with stairs' by Charing Cross set out that merry marriage procession of Boyle and Howard, which Suckling has immortalized in the 'Ballad on a Wedding;' and hence, too, Mr. Horace Walpole, with a hackney-coach full of persons of condition fresh from the opera, started to interview the Cock Lane Ghost. Here again, in the fire of 1780, great part of the library of the Duke's chaplain and relative, Dr. Percy, was destroyed in his apartments, where, doubtless, he often received Reynolds and Johnson. Goldsmith, also, among others, made one very characteristic visit to the same spot, though not on this occasion as the guest of the Bishop of Dromore.

Let him tell the story in his own words, *apud* Washington Irving:—

'I dressed myself in the best manner I could, and, after studying some compliments I thought necessary on such an occasion, proceeded to Northumberland House, and acquainted the servants that I had particular business with the duke. They showed me into an ante-chamber, where, after waiting some time, a gentleman, very elegantly dressed, made his appearance; taking him for the duke, I delivered all the fine things I had composed in order to compliment him on the honour he had done me; when, to my great astonishment, he told me I had mistaken him for his master, who would see me immediately. At that instant the duke came into the apartment, and I was so confounded on the occasion, that I wanted words barely sufficient to express the sense I entertained of the duke's politeness, and went away exceedingly chagrined at the blunder I had committed.'[1]

Fronting Northumberland House, a little to the left, and at some distance from the site of the present hotel of the same name, stood, until the advent of railroads brought about its downfall as a

[1] 'Oliver Goldsmith: a Biography,' 1849, p. 166.

posting-house, that older Golden Cross,[1] whose idolatrous sign scandalized the Puritan House of Commons. But the sign must have been soon restored, for it is distinguishable in Canaletto's view of 1753, though the carriage at the door probably hides the long water-trough which, sixty years since, old Londoners still remembered as giving the place something of the air of a country inn. From the Golden Cross, houses extended northward to St. Martin's Church—Duncannon Street being as yet to come. Trafalgar Square and the space now occupied by the National and National Portrait Galleries was covered, as far back as Hemings' Row, by buildings surrounding the King's or Royal Mews. In the days before Agas's map this had been a falconry, dating from Richard II. or earlier; but in 1534, when Henry VIII.'s stables at Lomsbery (Bloomsbury) were fired and burned, the royal stables were transferred to the buildings at Charing Cross, which, nevertheless, retained their old name of mews (*i.e.*, a *mewing* place) which they first had

[1] In that half-authentic, half-romantic book, the 'Wine and Walnuts' of 'Ephraim Hardcastle' (W. H. Pyne), he makes Hogarth catch a cold while sketching from the inn window the pageant of the proclamation of George III. at Charing Cross.

'of the King's falcons there kept.' Here, in the Caroline days, the famous stallion 'Rowley' 'champed golden grain' like the horses in the 'Iliad,' and gave his nickname to a king. Here, too, M. St. Antoine taught the noble art of horsemanship. In 1732, William Kent rebuilt the façade. At this date, as shown in a plan in the British Museum, dated 1690, it still consisted of the 'Great Mews,' the 'Green Mews,' and the 'Back Mews.' It continued to be used for stabling until 1824, when the royal stud, gilt coach, and other paraphernalia were transferred to Pimlico. In 1830, after serving as a temporary shelter to Mr. Cross's menagerie, then ousted from Exeter Change, and to the homeless Public Records of Great Britain, it was pulled down. Not many traditions haunt its past which need a mention here. Its northeastern side, if we may trust Gay's 'Trivia,' was a chosen resort of thieves and gamblers. 'Careful Observers' (he says), 'studious of the Town,'

'Pass by the *Mewse*, nor try the Thimble's Cheats;'

and it may be observed that the ill-famed rookery, known in Ben Jonson's day as the 'Bermudas' and later, by convenient euphemism, as the 'C'ribbee Islands,' was close to St. Martin's

Church, where it survived until 1829. At the Upper Mews-Gate stood a convivial house of call, celebrated in song by 'bright broken Maginn;'[1] and hard by, from 1750 to 1790, 'Honest Tom Payne' kept the little old bookshop, 'in the shape of an L,' once so well known to book-lovers in the last century.[2]

[1] 'I miss already, with a tear,
  The Mews-Gate public house
Where many a gallant grenadier
  Did lustily carouse ;
Alas ! Macadam's droughty dust
  That honoured spot doth fill,
Where they were wont the ale robust
  In the King's name to swill.'

[2] See 'The Two Paynes' in 'Eighteenth Century Vignettes,' Second Series, pp. 192-203. Between the [Lower ?] Mews Gate and Spring Garden, was the crossing swept for many years subsequent to 1733 by the one-legged beggar, Ambrose Gwinett. Gwinett's was an extraordinary fortune. He had been hanged in chains near Deal as the murderer, on circumstantial evidence, of one Richard Collins, in reality kidnapped by privateers. Being discovered to be alive, Gwinett was taken down by his relatives, went to sea, and at Havana fell in with his supposed victim. In 1768 his story was printed from his own narrative, with a frontispiece evidently based (in part) upon the Execution plate of Hogarth's 'Apprentice' series. It is but fair to add that from a manuscript note

Towards 1829-30 the neighbourhood of Charing Cross began to assume something of its present aspect. Already, four years earlier, the College of Physicians, leaving its home in Warwick Lane, had taken up its abode in a handsome building at the bottom of Dorset Place, close by the newly-erected Union Club. Then, about 1830, the ground was cleared for Trafalgar Square, and the C'ribbee Islands and the rookeries were 'blotted from the things that be.' In 1832, the present National Gallery was begun. Nelson's Column followed, in 1840-9, and then, many years after, was finally completed by the addition of Landseer's lions. Since the National Gallery first became the laughing-stock of cockneys, it has been more than once enlarged; and even at the present moment further extensions at the back, of considerable importance to the picture-seer, are said to be in contemplation. But it is needless to dwell at any length upon the present aspect of the place. It is too modern for the uses of the antiquary; and it may be doubted if time can ever make it venerable. In justice to its unfortunate architect, Wilkins, it must, neverthe-

in a copy of the 'Life and Adventures' at the British Museum, it would seem that Bishop Percy regarded the whole thing as a concoction of Bickerstaffe the dramatist.

less, be added that his work was done under most unfavourable restrictions. He was vexatiously hampered as to space, and Carlton House having been demolished, it was an express condition that he should avail himself of its fine Corinthian portico.

The only other building near Charing Cross which merits notice is St. Martin's Church. This, however, will better be reserved for treatment on some future occasion. But Spring Garden, or Gardens, part of which has already disappeared under the new Admiralty buildings, requires and deserves a final paragraph. It lies to the southwest of the Cross, and according to old definitions had a frontage extending from the end of the Haymarket to Wallingford House (the present Admiralty). In the days of James I. and Charles I. it was a pleasure-ground attached to Whitehall Palace, taking its name from one of those *jets d'eau*, the delight of seventeenth century topiarians, which suddenly sprinkled the visitor who unwittingly pressed it with his foot. It contained butts, a bathing-pond, and apparently part of the St. James's Park menagerie, since the State papers contain an order under date of the 31st January, 1626, for payment to Philip, Earl of Montgomery, of £72 5*s.* 10*d.* for 'keeping the Spring Gardens and the beasts and fowls there.' One of the favourite amusements of the place was bowling, and it was while Charles was watching the players with his favourite Steenie, who lived at this date in Wallingford House, that an oft related incident took place:—'The Duke put on his hat; one Wilson, a Scotchman, first kissing the Duke's hand, snatched it off, saying, "Off with your hat before the King!" Buckingham, not apt to restrain his feelings, kicked the Scotchman; but the King, interfering, said, "Let him alone, George; he is either mad or a fool." "No, sir," replied the Scotchman, "I am a sober man; and if your majesty would give me leave I will tell you that of this man which many know, and none dare speak."'

Whether his majesty permitted the proffered revelation, so significant of the popular estimate of Buckingham, history has not recorded. But the garden at this time (1628) must have been private, for it was not until two years later that Charles threw it open by proclamation, appointing one Simon Osbaldeston 'keeper of the King's Garden called the Spring Garden and of His Majesty's Bowling-green there.' Four years after, it had grown so 'scandalous and insufferable' a resort that he closed it again. It must, however, have been reopened, for in June, 1649, Mr. Evelyn tells us that he 'treated divers Ladies of my relations, in Spring Garden;' and though Cromwell shut it up once more, it could not have been for long, as ten years after Evelyn's date it was still offering its sheltering thickets to lovemakers, and its neats' tongues and bad Rhenish to wandering epicures.

With the Restoration ends its history as a pleasure-ground. To the disgust of the dwellers at Charing Cross, houses began to arise upon it; and its frequenters migrated to the newer,'Spring Garden' at Vauxhall. By 1772, when Lord Berkeley was permitted to build over the so-called 'Wilderness,' its last traces had disappeared. But 'the whirligig of time brings in his revenges,' and Lord Berkeley's house in its turn has now made way for the office of the Metropolitan Board of Works, and that again for the London County Council.

As a locality Spring Gardens—the Spring Gardens of brick and mortar—has been unusually favoured with distinguished inhabitants. Here Cromwell is said to have had a house; and it was 'at one Thomson's,' next door to the Bull Head Tavern, in the thoroughfare leading to the park, that his Latin secretary, John Milton,

wrote his 'Joannis Philippi Angli Responsio,' etc.
Colley Cibber's home, for several years, was hard
by; so also was the lodging occupied by the
author of the 'Seasons,' when he first came to
London to negotiate his poem of 'Winter.' In
Buckingham Court lived and died sprightly
Mrs. Centlivre, whose husband (her third) was
yeoman of the mouth to Anne and George I.
Locket's ordinary—the 'Lackets' of my Lord
Foppington and the fine gentlemen of Vanbrugh's day—stood on the site of Drummond's
Bank. Two doors from it, towards Buckingham
Court, was the famous 'Rummer' Tavern kept
by Matthew Prior's uncle, Samuel Pryor, also
or formerly landlord of that Rhenish Wine
House in Cannon Row where Dorset first discovered the clever young student of Horace whom
he helped to turn into a statesman and ambassador.[1] The 'Rummer' appears in Hogarth's
'Night' ('Four Times of the Day,' 1738),
which gives a view of the statue with the houses
behind. Hogarth's 'Rummer,' however, is on
the left, whereas the tavern (according to
Cunningham) was, after 1710, removed to the
ight or Northumberland House side. Probably

[1] See 'Matthew Prior,' in 'Eighteenth Century Vignettes,' Third Series, 1896, p. 230.

in the plate, as in the one of Covent Garden in the same series, the view was reversed in the process of engraving.

Hogarth's name recalls another memory. It was in an auctioneer's room in Spring Gardens (now part of the offices of the London County Council) that the Society of Artists of Great Britain held their famous second exhibition of 1761, for the catalogue of which Wale and Hogarth made designs. Hogarth was also a prominent exhibitor, sending, among other oil paintings, 'The Lady's Last Stake' (Mr. Huth's), the 'Election Entertainment' (Soane Museum), and the luckless 'Sigismunda,' the last of which is now gaining, in the National Gallery, some of the reputation which was denied to it in the painter's lifetime.

JOHN GAY.

NO very material addition, in the way of supplementary information, can now be made to the frequently reprinted Life of Gay in Johnson's 'Poets,' or to the genial and kindly sketch in Thackeray's 'English Humourists.'[1] John Gay was born at Barnstaple in 1685, and baptized on the 16th September at the Old Church of that town. He came of an ancient but impoverished family, being the younger son of William Gay, who lived at the 'Red Cross,' a house in Joy Street, which, judging from the church-rate paid by its occupants, must have been

---

[1] This is still practically true. But in an excellent edition of Gay's 'Poetical Works' prepared for the 'Muses' Library' in 1893, the late John Underhill, a Barnstaple man and a Gay enthusiast, besides making certain biographical rectifications, contrived to discover a few new facts. 'Some details that have not been known to former writers' were also supplied by Mr. George A. Aitken in an interesting paper prompted by Mr. Underhill's volumes, and contributed to the 'Westminster Review' for January, 1894.

one of the best of the Barnstaple dwellings. He lost his father in 1695, his mother—whose maiden name was Hanmer—having died in the previous year. He thus became an orphan at the early age of ten, and in all probability fell into the care of a Barnstaple uncle, Thomas Gay. He was educated at the free grammar school of his native place, where his master was one Rayner, afterwards succeeded by the 'Robert Luck, A.M.,' whose 'Miscellany of New Poems' was published in April, 1736 (four years after Gay's death), by Edward Cave. One of its pieces was a Latin version of Prior's 'Female Phaeton,' and the author, in a rhymed English introduction to his work, inscribed to Gay's patron, Charles Douglas, Duke of Queensberry and Dover, sought to associate himself with his former pupil's metrical proficiency :—

> ' O *Queensberry!* cou'd happy *Gay*
> This Off'ring to thee bring,
> 'T is his, my Lord (he 'd smiling say)
> Who taught your *Gay* to sing.'

Moreover, it is asserted that Gay's dramatic turn was stimulated by the plays which the Barnstaple boys were in the habit of performing under this rhyming pedagogue. Of his schooldays, however, nothing is known with precision; but it is clear from his subsequent career that he somewhere obtained more than a bowing acquaintance with the classics. There is still preserved, in the 'Forster Library' at South Kensington, a large paper copy of Maittaire's 'Horace' (Tonson and Watts, 1715), which contains his autograph, and is copiously annotated in his beautiful handwriting. This of itself should be sufficient to refute the aspersions sometimes cast upon his scholarship; for it affords unanswerable evidence that, even at thirty, and perhaps at a much later period, he remained a diligent student of the charming lyrist and satirist, who, above all others, commends himself to the attention of idle men. In his youth, however, it must be assumed that Gay's indolence was more strongly developed than his application, for his friends could find no better opening for him than that of apprentice to a London silk mercer. With this vocation he was speedily dissatisfied. Dr. Hill Burton, in his 'History of the Reign of Queen Anne,' implies that he ran away; but there is nothing to show that he took any step of so energetic a character. His nephew, the Rev. Joseph Baller, in the little publication entitled 'Gay's Chair,' explains that, 'not being able to bear the confinement of a shop,' his uncle became depressed in spirits and health, and therefore returned to his native town, taking up his residence, not, as before, with Thomas Gay, but with his mother's brother, the Rev. John Hanmer, the Barnstaple Nonconformist minister.

That Gay should have found the littering of polished counters with taffeties and watered tabbies an uncongenial employment, is not surprising,—especially if thereto be added that thankless service of those feminine gadabouts who (as Swift says in the 'City Shower') 'pretend to cheapen Goods, but nothing buy.' Yet it is to be feared that the lack of energy which was his leading characteristic would have equally disposed him against any sustained or laborious occupation. When his health was restored, he went back to town, living for some time (according to Mr. Baller[1]) 'as a private gentleman'—a statement which is scarcely reconcilable with the modest walk in life his family had selected for him. Already he is supposed to have made some spasmodic essays in literature; and the swarming taverns and coffee-houses of the metropolis afforded easy opportunities of access to notabilities of all sorts. He had besides some friends already es-

---

[1] 'Gay's Chair,' 1820, p. 17.

tablished in London. William Fortescue, Pope's correspondent, and later Master of the Rolls, had been his schoolmate at Luck's; while another of Luck's *alumni* was Aaron Hill, the playwright. According to a time-honoured tradition, Gay acted for some time as Hill's secretary. But Hill himself was only embarking in letters when, in May, 1708, Gay published, as an eight leaf *folio*, his first poem of 'Wine,' the purport of which may be gathered from the—

> 'Nulla placere diu, nec vivere carmina possunt,
> Quæ scribuntur aquæ potoribus,'—

of its motto,—a moot theory which seems to have 'exercised' the author throughout his lifetime, since he is still discussing it in his last letters. 'I continue to drink nothing but water,' he tells Swift two years before his death, 'so that you can't require any poetry from me.'[1] The publisher of 'Wine' was William Keble, at the Black-Spread-Eagle in Westminster Hall, and it was also pirated by Henry Hills of the 'brown sheets and scurvy letter,' referred to in

---

[1] Swift, it seems, favoured this idea. 'Your master Horace,' he writes to Pope, August 30, 1716, 'was *vini somnique benignus*: and as I take it, both are *proper to your trade*.'

Gay's subsequent 'Epistle to Bernard Lintott.' 'Wine' professes to 'draw Miltonic air,' but the atmosphere inhaled is more suggestive of the 'Splendid Shilling' of John Philips. Gay did not reprint the poem in his subscription edition of 1720, perhaps because of its blank verse; but the concluding lines, which describe the breaking up of a 'midnight Modern Conversation' at the Devil Tavern by Temple Bar, already exhibit some of the more prominent characteristics of his later efforts:

> ' now all abroad
> Is hush'd and silent, nor the rumbling noise
> Of coach or cart, or smoky link-boys' call
> Is heard—but universal Silence reigns:
> When we in merry plight, airy and gay,
> Surpris'd to find the hours so swiftly fly
> With hasty knock, or twang of pendent cord,
> Alarm the drowsy youth from slumb'ring nod;
> Startled he flies, and stumbles o'er the stairs
> Erroneous, and with busy knuckles plies
> His yet clung eyelids, and with stagg'ring reel
> Enters confused, and mutt'ring asks our wills;
> When we with liberal hand the score discharge,
> And homeward each his course with steady step
> Unerring steers, of cares and coin bereft.'

As it is expressly stated that the Bordeaux—the particular vintage specified—was paid for, it is clear that, at this time, Gay must have suc-

ceeded in finding either a purse or a patron. It is
equally clear from his next ascertained production that he had already acquired some familiarity
with the world of letters. A year after the publication of 'Wine,' Steele established the 'Tatler;'
and in May, 1711, when the 'Spectator' was
two months old, Gay obliged the Town with
his impressions of 'the Histories and Characters
of all our *Periodical Papers*, whether Monthly,
Weekly or Diurnal,' in a threepenny pamphlet,
entitled 'The Present State of Wit, in a Letter
to a Friend in the Country.' This, which Mr.
Arber has reprinted in volume vi. of his 'English
Garner,' is of more than fugitive interest. It disclaims politics upon the ground that it does not
care 'one farthing either for *Whig* or *Tory*,' but
it refers to the 'Examiner' as 'a Paper which all
Men, who speak without Prejudice, allow to be
well Writ.' At this time Swift apparently knew
nothing of his critic, for he tells Stella that 'the
author seems to be a Whig' . . . 'Above all
things, he praises the "Tatlers" and "Spectators;"
and I believe Steele and Addison were privy to
the printing of it. Thus is one treated by these
impudent dogs' [with whom his relations were
strained]. Apart from his disclaimer of politics,
nevertheless, Gay, if he was anything, was a

Tory, and Swift was wrong. But Gay was evidently well informed about the secret history of Steele's ventures, and he gives an excellent account of the 'Esquire's [*i.e.* Bickerstaff's] Lucubrations.' 'He has indeed rescued it [Learning] out of the hands of Pedants, and Fools, and discover'd the true method of making it amiable and lovely to all mankind.' In the dress he gives it, 'tis a most welcome guest at Tea-tables and Assemblies, and it is relish'd and caressed by the Merchants on the Change; accordingly, there is not a Lady at Court, nor a Banker in *Lumbard-Street*, who is not verily perswaded, that *Captain Steele* is the greatest Scholar, and best Casuist, of any Man in England.' From other passages it is also manifest that the writer (like Swift) knew who was Steele's unnamed colleague, for he speaks of Addison's assistance as 'no longer a Secret,' and compares the conjunction of the two friends to that of Somers and Halifax 'in a late Reign.' It may consequently be concluded that he had at least made Steele's acquaintance, and that the set of the 'Tatlers' in four volumes on royal paper, which Tonson at this time transmitted to Gay

[1] These words read like an echo of the passage from Blackmore's Preface to 'Prince Arthur,' which Steele quotes admiringly in 'Spectator' No. 6 (March 7, 1711).

'by Mr. Steel's Orders,' is at once a confirmation of the fact and a tacit recognition of the acceptable compliments contained in 'J. G.'s' 'Present State of Wit.'

'Mr. Isaac Bickerstaff,' however, was not the only notability to whom Gay had become known. In July, 1711, we find Pope sending Henry Cromwell his 'service to all my few friends, and to Mr. Gay in particular,' and in the same year Gay wrote the already mentioned 'Epistle to Bernard Lintott,' which contained, among other things, reference to the 'harmonious Muse' of the young author of the 'Pastorals' and the recently-issued 'Essay on Criticism.'

> 'His various numbers charm our ravish'd ears,
> His steady judgment far out-shoots his years,
> And early in the youth the god appears,'—

sang this panegyrist in one of those triplets that Swift abominated. But Pope, who saw the lines in manuscript, accepted the flattering unction without reserve, and the epistle accordingly, in the following May (1712), made its appearance in Lintott's famous 'Rape of the Lock' Miscellany, to which Gay also contributed the Story of Arachne from Ovid. He was still, it seems, unknown to the general public, for the contemporary announcement of the book, while giving bold advertisement to such lesser lights as Fenton, Broome, and Henry Cromwell, refrains from including his name among the eminent hands who contributed to the collection. Nor is it probable that his reputation had been greatly served by the 'tragi-comical farce' he had issued a week or two before under the title of 'The Mohocks,'—*i.e.*, the midnight revellers whose real, or imaginary, misdeeds were at that time engaging public attention. It was dedicated to John Dennis the critic, who was informed, in his own vocabulary, that its subject was '*Horrid* and *Tremendous*,' that it was conceived 'according to the exactest Rules of Dramatick Poetry,' and that it was based upon his own 'Appius and Virginia.' Notwithstanding an intentionally ambiguous title-page,[1] it was never acted, and its interest, like others of Gay's efforts, is purely temporary.

Before 1712 had ended, Pope was able to con-

---

[1] The following is the advertisement in the 'Spectator' for 10th April, 1712:

'This Day is Published, *The Mohocks. A Tragi-Comical Farce. As it was Acted near the Watch-house in Covent-Garden. By her Majesty's Servants.* Printed for Bernard Lintott; at the Cross-Keys between the two Temple-Gates in Fleet-Street.'

gratulate his new ally upon what promised to be
a material stroke of good fortune. He was appointed 'Secretary or Domestic Steward' to the
Duchess of Monmouth,—that 'virtuous and excellent lady,' as Evelyn calls her, whose husband
had been beheaded in the year of Gay's birth.
The exact amount of dependence implied by this
office is obscure, and it is differently estimated by
different narrators. It is more material to note
that Gay must already have been engaged upon
his next poetical effort, perhaps his first serious
one, the Georgic called 'Rural Sports,' which he
inscribed to Pope. This was published by Tonson
on the 13th January, 1713. To the reader of
the post-Wordsworthian age, its merit is not
obtrusive, and Johnson anticipated the *toujours
bien, jamais mieux* of Madame Guizot, when he
described it as 'never contemptible, nor ever
excellent.' Mr. Underhill, indeed, goes so far
as to deny it any experimental knowledge of
country life; and, as a matter of fact, Gay himself admits that he had long been a town-dweller.
Still, his childhood must have been passed among
rural scenes, and it is by no means certain that if
he had written his verses at Barnstaple he would
—writing as he did under Anna Augusta—have
written them in a different way. We suspect

that the germ of the objection, as often, is to be traced, not so much to the poem itself, as to certain preconceived shortcomings in its author. Johnson's disbelief in Goldsmith's ability to distinguish between a cow and a horse no doubt coloured his appreciation of the 'Animated Nature;' and Swift (whom Mr. Underhill quotes) doubted if Gay could tell an oak from a crab tree. 'You are sensible,' Swift went on, 'that I know the full extent of your country skill is in fishing for roaches, or gudgeons at the highest.' With such a testimony before us, criticism of 'Rural Sports' easily becomes a foregone conclusion. Nevertheless, it deserves more consideration than it has received.

Apart from the production at Drury Lane, in May, 1713, of a deplorable play, 'The Wife of Bath,' and the contribution to Steele's 'Guardian' of two brightly written papers on 'Flattery' and 'Dress' (Nos. 11 and 149), Gay's next ascertained work was 'The Fan' (December). It is one of the contradictions of criticism that this poor and ineffectual poem should have been received with greater indulgence than the relatively far superior 'Rural Sports.' Gay's mythology is never very happy (Mr. Elwin roundly styles it 'stupid'), and he always writes best with his

eye on the object. Pope, however, professed to
be interested in 'The Fan,' and even touched
himself on that 'little modish machine' in parts,
—circumstances which give it a slender vitality.
A week or two later appeared Steele's 'Poetical
Miscellany,' in which Gay is represented by 'A
Contemplation on Night,' 'A Thought on
Eternity,' and by a pair of elegies ('Panthea'
and 'Araminta'). But his first individual performance, 'The Shepherd's Week,' belongs to
the early part of 1714. This again is closely
connected with his friendship with Pope. Pope,
smarting under the praise which Tickell had
given in the 'Guardian' to the Pastorals of
Ambrose Philips, and not content with per-
fidiously reviewing Philips himself in the same
periodical, now contrived to induce the author
of 'Rural Sports' to aid the cause by burlesquing
his rival in a sequence of sham eclogues, in which
he was to exhibit the Golden Age with the gilt
off, 'after the true ancient guise of *Theocritus*,'
or, in plainer words, by representing it in its
blowzed and unkempt reality, to cast merited
ridicule upon the 'mild Arcadians' of the period.
'Thou wilt not find my Shepherdesses'—says
the Author's 'Proeme'—'idly piping on oaten
Reeds, but milking the Kine, tying up the

Sheaves, or if the Hogs are astray driving them to their Styes. My Shepherd gathereth none other Nosegays but what are the growth of our own Fields, he sleepeth not under Myrtle shades, but under a Hedge, nor doth he vigilantly defend his Flocks from Wolves [this was a palpable hit at Philips!] because there are none.' Like Fielding's 'Joseph Andrews,' the execution of 'The Shepherd's Week' went far beyond its avowed purpose of mere raillery. Wheresoever and howsoever acquired, Gay's little idylls abound with interesting folk-lore and closely-studied rural scenes. Bowzybeus, the fiddler, delights his audience with 'Chevy Chace' and the 'Children of the Wood.' Bumkinet and Grubbinol sing 'Patient Grissel,' and the 'Gillian of Croydon' of the popular Mr. D'Urfey;[1] Hobnelia burns hazel-nuts to find her sweetheart; Marian, with fateful generosity, gives Colin Clout a pocket knife with a posy on it; while Buxoma, whose favourite fare is the 'White-pot thick' which was the culinary glory of Sir Roger de Coverley's

---

[1] 'I have not quoted one Latin author since I came down, but have learned without book a song of Mr. Thomas D'Urfey's, who is your only poet of tolerable reputation in this country' (Pope to Henry Cromwell, April 10, 1710).

ancestress—Buxoma plays 'Hot Cockles' with Cuddy:

> 'As at *Hot-Cockles* once I laid me down,
> And felt the weighty Hand of many a Clown;
> *Buxoma* gave a gentle Tap, and I
> Quick rose, and read soft Mischief in her Eye.'

But perhaps the most suggestive old-time touches —touches not without a kindly satire—occur in the 'Dirge' of Blouzelinda, where the parish-priest, in consideration of the ten-shilling sermon fee,

> —'Speaks the Hour-glass [1] in her praise .. quite out'—

and the lads and lasses fence her last resting-place around with wicker—

> 'Lest her new Grave the Parson's Cattle raze,
> For both his Horse and Cow the Church-yard graze.'

From a biographical point of view, however, the most interesting part of 'The Shepherd's Week' is its dedicatory prologue to Bolingbroke, a circumstance which, according to Swift, constituted that 'original sin' against the Court which afterwards interfered so much with Gay's prospects of preferment. But its allusions also show that the former mercer's apprentice had already made the acquaintance of the 'skilful

---

[1] There is a good pulpit hour-glass in Hogarth's 'Sleeping Congregation.'

Leach' Arbuthnot, and probably of some gentler critics, whose favour was of greater importance. 'No more,' says the poet,

> ' No more I'll sing *Buxoma* brown,
> Like Goldfinch in her *Sunday* Gown;
> Nor *Clumsilis*, nor *Marian* bright,
> Nor Damsel that *Hobnelia* hight.
> But *Lansdown* fresh as Flow'r of *May*,
> And *Berkly* Lady blithe and gay,
> And *Anglesey* whose Speech exceeds
> The voice of Pipe, or oaten Reeds;
> And blooming *Hide*, with Eyes so rare,
> And *Montague* beyond compare.'

" Blooming Hide, with eyes so rare,' was Lady Jane Hyde, daughter of the Earl of Clarendon, and elder sister of the Catherine who was subsequently to be Gay's firm friend.

The Scriblerus Club, to which Pope had introduced him, and for which he is said to have acted as Secretary, had also done Gay the greater service of securing him a powerful ally in Swift, and it was doubtless to his connection with this famous association, of which Lord Oxford was an occasional member, that he was indebted for his next stroke of good fortune. By June, 1714, he had resigned, or been dismissed from, his position in the household of the Duchess of Monmouth. But in that month, with the aid of his new friends, he was appointed Secretary to Lord Clarendon, then Envoy Extraordinary to the Court of Hanover, and there exists a brief rhymed appeal or 'Epigrammatical Petition' from the impecunious poet to Lord Oxford, in his capacity as Lord Treasurer, for funds to enable him to enter upon his functions.

> 'I'm no more to converse with the swains,
>   But go where fine people resort;
> One can live without money on plains,
>   But never without it at court.
>
> If, when with the swains I did gambol,
>   I array'd me in silver and blue;
> When abroad, and in courts, I shall ramble,
>   Pray, my lord, how much money will do?'[1]

He got, not without difficulty, and probably through the instrumentality of Arbuthnot, who handed in his memorial, a grant of £100, for his outfit; and he also got, from Swift in Ireland, a letter of fatherly advice exhorting him to learn to be a manager, to mind his Latin, to look up Aristotle upon Politics and Grotius 'De Jure Belli et Pacis.' For a brief space we must imagine him strutting in his fine clothes through the clipped avenues of Herrenhausen, yawning over the routine life of the petty German Court,

[1] Letter from Gay to Swift, June 8, 1714.

and perfecting himself in the diplomatic arts of
'bowing profoundly, speaking deliberately, and
wearing both sides of his long periwig before.'
Then the death of Queen Anne put an end to
all these halcyon days. What was worse, the
'Shepherd's Week,' as already stated, had been
dedicated to Bolingbroke, and Bolingbroke—ill-
luck would have it—was not in favour with Her
Most Gracious Majesty's successor. In this
juncture, as a course which 'could do no harm,'
Pope, who seems always to have treated Gay
with unfailing affection, counselled his dejected
friend 'to write something on the King, or
Prince, or Princess,' and Arbuthnot said ditto to
Pope. Gay, cheering up accordingly, set about a
formal 'Epistle to a Lady [probably Mrs. Howard,
afterwards Lady Suffolk]: Occasion'd by the
arrival of Her Royal Highness [*i.e.* the Princess
of Wales, whom he had seen at Hanover].' In
this he takes opportunity to touch plaintively
upon the forlorn hopes of needy suitors:

> 'Pensive each night, from room to room I walk'd,
> To one I bow'd, and with another talk'd;
> Enquir'd what news, or such a Lady's name,
> And did the next day, and the next, the same.
> Places, I found, were daily giv'n away
> And yet no friendly Gazette mentioned *Gay*.'

The only appreciable result of this ingenuous appeal was that Their Royal Highnesses came to Drury Lane in February, 1715, to witness Gay's next dramatic effort, the tragi-comi-pastoral farce of 'The What d' ye Call it,' a piece after the fashion of Buckingham's 'Rehearsal,' inasmuch as it parodies the popular tragedies of the day, and even roused the ire of Steele by taking liberties with Addison's 'Cato.' Without the 'Key' which was speedily prepared by Theobald and Griffin the actor, its allusions must at first have fallen rather flat upon an uninstructed audience, especially as its action was grave and its images comic. Gay's matter-of-fact friend, Cromwell, who saw the gestures but, being deaf, could not hear the words, naturally found it hopelessly unintelligible. But it brought its author a hundred pounds, and it contains one of his most musical songs, ''Twas when the seas were roaring.' A few months after its publication in book form, Lord Burlington sent the poet into Devonshire, an expedition which he commemorated in a pleasant tributary epistle published in 1715 with the title of 'A Journey to Exeter.' He had two travelling companions, no needless precaution when Bagshot Heath swarmed with 'broken gamesters' who had taken to the road, and he describes delightfully his *impressions de voyage*,—the fat and garrulous landlord at Hartley-Row, the red trout and 'rich metheglin' at Steele's borough of Stockbridge, the 'cloak'd shepherd' on Salisbury Plain, the lobsters and 'unadulterate wine' at Morecombelake,[1] and last of all, the female barber at Axminster:

> 'The weighty golden chain adorns her neck,
> And three gold rings her skilful hand bedeck:
> Smooth o'er our chin her easy fingers move,
> Soft as when *Venus* stroak'd the beard of *Jove*.'

Incidentally, we learn that Gay could draw more or less, for he sketches the 'eyeless' faces of his fellow travellers asleep in two elbow chairs at Dorchester. Also that, at thirty, he was already stout:

> 'You knew *fat* Bards might tire,
> And, mounted, sent me forth your trusty Squire.'

It must have been about this time that Gay composed another poem, somewhat akin to the Exeter epistle, inasmuch as both were probably

---

[1] A writer in the 'Athenæum' for Dec. 1, 1894, points out that this is a mistake. Gay must have 'stripped the lobster of his scarlet mail' a little farther on, at Charmouth. But these references to food at least confirm Congreve's *dictum* of Gay,—'*Edit, ergo est.*'

influenced by the verses on 'Morning' and 'A City Shower,' which Swift had contributed to Steele's 'Tatler.' Indeed, in the Preface to 'Trivia: or, the Art of Walking the Streets of London,' which appeared at the end of January, 1716, Gay specially refers to hints given to him by Dr. Swift. The theme is an unexpected one for an author whose tastes were certainly not pedestrian ('any lady with a coach and six horses would carry you to Japan,' wrote the Dean later); but it has still its attraction to the antiquary and the student of the early eighteenth century. Every one who wishes to realize the London of the first George, with its signs and its street cries (that *ramage de la ville* which candid Will. Honeycomb preferred to larks and nightingales), its link boys and its chairmen, its sweeps, small-coal men, milk-maids, Mohocks, and the rest, must give his days and nights to the study of 'Trivia.' He will obtain valuable expert advice as to the ceremony of giving or refusing the wall; learn to distinguish and divide between a Witney Roquelaure and a Kersey Wrap-Rascal; and, it may be, discover to his astonishment that there were oiled umbrellas before Jonas Hanway. And here may appropriately come in the poet's warnings of wet weather:

'But when the swinging Signs your Ears offend
With creaking Noise, then rainy Floods impend;
Soon shall the Kennels swell with rapid Streams,
And rush in muddy Torrents to the *Thames*.
The Bookseller, whose Shop's an open Square,
Foresees the Tempest, and with early Care
Of Learning strips the Rails; the rowing Crew
To tempt a Fare, cloath all their Tilts in Blue:
On Hosier's Poles depending Stockings ty'd,
Flag with the slacken'd Gale, from side to side;
Church-Monuments foretell the changing Air;
Then *Niobe* dissolves into a Tear,
And sweats with secret Grief; you'll hear the Sounds
Of whistling Winds, e'er Kennels break their Bounds;
Ungrateful Odours Common-shores diffuse,
And dropping Vaults distil unwholesom Dews,
E'er the Tiles rattle with the smoaking Show'r,
And Spouts on heedless Men their Torrents pour.'

Here also, to compare with Swift, is the 'Morning' of Gay:

'For Ease and for Despatch, the Morning's best:
No Tides of Passengers the Street molest,
You'll see a draggled Damsel, here and there,
From *Billingsgate* her fishy Traffic bear;
On Doors the sallow Milk-maid chalks her Gains;
Ah! how unlike the Milk-maid of the Plains!
Before proud Gates attending Asses bray,
Or arrogate with solemn Pace the Way;
These grave Physicians with their milky Chear,
The Love-sick Maid, and dwindling Beau repair,

Here Rows of Drummers stand in martial File,
And with their Vellom Thunder shake the Pile,
To greet the new made Bride. Are sounds like these,
The proper Prelude to a state of Peace ?
Now Industry awakes her busy Sons,
Full charg'd with News the breathless Hawker runs :
Shops open, Coaches roll, Carts shake the Ground,
And all the Streets with passing Cries resound.'

It is consoling to think that Gay made some £40 by this eighteen-penny poem, and £100 more by the subscriptions which Pope and others, always jealously watching over his interests, obtained to a large paper edition.¹ But it is impossible to commend his next production, of which, indeed, it is suspected that he did no more than bear the blame. Although he signed the advertisement of the comedy entitled 'Three Hours after Marriage,' it is pretty sure that he had Pope and Arbuthnot for active collaborators. Whether Pope libelled Dennis as 'Sir Tremendous,' or Arbuthnot Woodward, or Gay himself the Duchess of Monmouth as the very incidental 'Countess of Hippokekoana' (Ipecacuanha ?)— are questions scarcely worthy of discussion now. It is sufficient that the piece was both gross and

¹ One of these, presented by Gay to Pope, and bearing a bold 'Ex dono Authoris' in the handwriting of the latter, is in the possession of Mr. H. Buxton Forman.

silly. It failed ignominiously on the boards in January, 1717, and is not likely to be consulted in type except by such fanatics of the fugitive as George Steevens, who reprinted it in the 'Additions to Pope' of 1776.

During all this period Gay seems to have been vaguely expecting Court favour, and to have suffered most of the discouragements of hope deferred. Yet, if the Court neglected his pretensions—and it nowhere appears that they were very well grounded—he always found friends whose kindness took a practical form. Lord Burlington, as we have seen, had sent him to Exeter; in 1717, Mr. Pulteney carried him to Aix as his Secretary, a trip which furnished the occasion for a second Epistle. Then, in 1718, he went with Lord Harcourt to Cockthorpe in Oxfordshire, where befell that pretty tragedy of the two haymakers struck dead by lightning, which sentimental Mr. Pope made the subject of a fine and famous letter to Lady Mary Wortley Montagu, who, unluckily for sentiment, received it in anything but a sentimental spirit. Both the journeys to Aix and Exeter were reprinted in the grand quarto edition of Gay's poems which Tonson and Lintott published in 1720, with a frontispiece by the illustrious William Kent, and with a list of subscribers rivalling in number and exceeding in interest that prefixed to the Prior of 1718. Those munificent patrons of literature, the Earl of Burlington and the Duke of Chandos, took fifty copies each! In the second volume were included a number of epistles and miscellaneous pieces, some of which were published for the first time, as well as a new pastoral tragedy called 'Dione.' One of the ballads, 'Sweet William's Farewell to Black Ey'd Susan,' was long popular, and is still justly ranked among the best efforts of the writer's muse. Of the thousand pounds which Gay cleared over this venture his friends hoped he would make provident use, suggesting purchase of an annuity, investment in the funds, and so forth. But Craggs had given him some South Sea Stock, and to this he added his new windfall, becoming in short space master of £20,000. Again his well-wishers clustered about him with prudent counsels. At least, said easygoing Fenton, secure as much as will make you certain of ' a clean shirt, and a shoulder of mutton every day.' But the 'most refractory, honest, good-natur'd man,' as Swift calls him, was not to be so advised. He was seized by the South Sea madness, and promptly lost both principal and profits.

Among the other names on the subscription

list of the volumes of 1720 are two which have a special attraction in Gay's life, for they are those of his kindest friends, the Duke and Duchess of Queensberry. The lady was the charming and wayward Catherine Hyde,—the 'Kitty' whose first appearance at Drury Lane playhouse as a triumphant beauty of eighteen Prior had celebrated in some of his brightest and airiest verses, and whose picture, as a milkmaid of quality, painted by Charles Jervas at a later date, is to be seen at the National Portrait Gallery. As already stated, Gay had written of her sister Jane (by this time Countess of Essex) as far back as 1714; and it may be that her own acquaintance with him dated from the same period. In any case, after her marriage to the Duke of Queensberry in 1720, she appears to have taken Gay under her protection. 'He [Gay] is always with the Duchess of Queensberry'—writes Mrs. Bradshaw to Mrs. Howard in 1721;[1] and five years afterwards the poet himself tells Swift that he

[1] 'Gray [Gay] ye poet lodges in our house, so he has supt with us'—says Mrs. Osborn in a postscript to a letter from Bath, dated August 30, 1721; and a line or two higher she writes: 'Dutches of Queensborough comes tonight' ('Political and Social Letters of a Lady of the Eighteenth Century' [1890], p. 22).

has been with his patrons in Oxfordshire [Stoney Middleton] and at Petersham and 'wheresoever they would carry me.' In the interval he is helping Congreve to nurse his gout 'at the *Bath*,' or living almost altogether with Lord Burlington at Chiswick or Piccadilly or Tunbridge Wells, or acting as secretary to Pope at Twickenham ('which you know is no idle charge'), or borrowing sheets from Jervas to entertain Swift in those Whitehall lodgings which had been granted to him by the Earl of Lincoln in 1722, and were taken from him by Sir Robert Walpole in 1729. It says much for the charm of his character that he knew how to acquire and how to retain friends so constant and so diverse. But though his life sounds pleasant in the summary, it must have involved humiliations which would have been intolerable to a more independent man. According to Arbuthnot, the Burlingtons sometimes left their *protégé* in want of the necessaries of life, and neither they nor his other great friends were very active to procure him preferment. 'They wonder,' says Gay plaintively to Swift in 1722, 'at each other for not providing for me ; and I wonder at them all.' From a letter which he wrote to Pope two years later, it is nevertheless clear that somebody

had given him a lottery commissionership worth
£150 per annum, so that, for a man whose claims
were not urgent, he can hardly be said to have
been culpably neglected.

Previously to his appointment as a lottery
commissioner he had been seriously ill. The
loss of his South Sea Stock preyed upon his
spirits; and his despondency 'being attended
with the cholic'—in the unvarnished language
of the 'Biographia Britannica'—'brought his
life in danger.' Upon his recovery, and pending
the postponed advancement he was always 'lack-
ing' ('the Court keeps him at hard meat,' wrote
Swift in 1725), he produced another play, 'The
Captives,' which ran for a week in January, 1724,
the third or author's night being expressly commanded by his old patrons, the Prince and
Princess of Wales. Then, at the request of the
Princess, he set to work upon the 'Fables' by
which his reputation as a writer mainly survives.
'Gay is writing Tales for Prince William,' Pope
tells Swift. After many delays, partly in production by the press, partly owing to Gay's own
dilatory habits, the first series appeared in 1727,[1]

---

[1] A second series of sixteen fables was published in
1738, after his death, from the manuscripts in the hands
of the Duke of Queensberry.

and was well received, although, if Swift is to be believed, their 'nipping turns' upon courtiers were not best welcomed where the poet most needed encouragement. To this it is perhaps to be attributed that when George II. came at last to the throne nothing better was found for Gay than the post of gentleman-usher to the little Princess Louisa—a child under three. By this time he was more than forty, and he had self-respect enough to think himself too 'far advanced in life.' He therefore politely declined the nomination. With this, however, his long-deferred expectations definitely vanished. 'I have no prospect,' he wrote with tardy enlightenment to Swift, 'but in depending wholly upon myself, and my own conduct. As I am used to disappointments, I can bear them; but as I can have no more hopes, I can no more be disappointed, so that I am in a blessed condition.'

Strangely enough, when these words were penned in October, 1727, he had already completed what was to be his greatest dramatic success, the famous 'Beggar's Opera,' which, produced at Lincoln's Inn Fields on the 29th of January, 1728, for a season overthrew Italian song,—'that Dagon of the Nobility and Gentry, who had so long seduced them to idolatry,' as the 'Companion to the Playhouse' puts it,— and made its Author's name a household word. How it first occurred to Swift what 'an odd pretty sort of thing a Newgate Pastoral might make;' how friends hesitated, and Cibber rejected, and the public rapturously applauded; how it was sung at street corners, and painted on screens; how it procured its 'Polly' (Lavinia Fenton) a coronet, and made Rich (the manager) gay, and Gay (the author) rich—all these things are the stock in trade of literature. At Mr. John Murray's in Albemarle Street may still be seen one of the three pictures which William Hogarth painted of that all conquering company, and which, years afterwards, was engraved by another William—William Blake. The Coryphæus of the highway (Walker) appears in the centre, while 'Lucy' (Mrs. Egleton) pleads for him to the left, and 'Polly' (Miss Fenton) to the right. Rich and the Duke of Bolton, who married 'Polly,' are among the spectators. Scandal, in the person of John, Lord Hervey, adds that the opera owed a part of its popularity to something in the dilemma of Macheath 'between his twa Deborahs' which irresistibly suggested the equally equivocal position of Walpole between Catherine Shorter and Molly Skerret. This is probably exaggerated, as is also the aid which Gay is reported to have received from Pope and others,[1] but it accounts in a measure for the fate which befell Gay's next enterprise.

That some attempt to perpetuate so signal a success as the 'Beggar's Opera' should not be made was scarcely in the nature of things; and Gay set speedily about the preparation of a sequel, to which he gave the name of the popular heroine of the earlier piece. But 'Polly' was saved from the common fate of continuations by the drastic action of the Lord Chamberlain, taken, it is surmised, upon the instruction of Walpole. When it was almost ready for rehearsal, the representation was prohibited. The result of this not very far-sighted step on the part of the authorities was of course to invest its publication as a book (1729) with an unprecedented and wholly fictitious interest. Friends on all sides, and especially those opposed to the Court, strained every nerve to promote the sale. The Duchess of Marlborough (Congreve's

---

[1] Pope—'*semper ardentes acuens sagittas*'—was supposed to have pointed some of the songs. But he told Spence that neither he nor Swift gave any material aid in the work ('Anecdotes,' 1858, pp. 110, 120).

Henrietta) gave £100 for a copy; and the
Duchess of Queensberry, who had the temerity
to solicit subscriptions within the very precincts
of St. James's, was forbidden to return to them.
Thereupon the Duke, nothing loth, threw up his
appointments as Vice Admiral of Scotland and
Lord of the Bedchamber, and followed his lady,
who delivered a Parthian shaft in the shape of a
very indiscreet and saucy letter to His Majesty
King George II. In all this, it is plain that
Gay's misfortune was simply made the instru-
ment of political antagonisms: but, for the
moment, his name was on every lip. 'The
inoffensive *John Gay*'—writes Arbuthnot to
Swift under date of March 19, 1729—'is now
become one of the obstructions to the peace of
Europe, the terror of the ministers, the chief
author of the "Craftsman," and all the seditious
pamphlets, which have been published against the
Government. He has got several turned out of
their places; the greatest ornament of the court
banished from it for his sake;[1] another great
lady [Mrs. Howard] in danger of being *Chassé*
[*sic*] likewise; about seven or eight duchesses

---

[1] 'The gay Amanda let us now behold,
In thy Defence, a lovely *banish'd* Scold.'
The Female Faction, 1729.

pressing forward, like the antient *circumcelliones* in the church, who shall suffer martyrdom on his account first. He is the darling of the city . . . I can assure you, this is the very identical *John Gay*, whom you formerly knew, and lodged with in *Whitehall* two years ago.' The gross result was that Gay gained about £1200 by the publication of 'Polly' as a six shilling quarto, of which Bowyer, the printer, in one year struck off 10,500 copies; by the representation of the 'Beggar's Opera' he had made, according to his own account, 'between £700 and £800' to Rich's £4000.

During a great part of 1728 Gay resided at Bath with the Duchess of Marlborough. After the prohibition of 'Polly,' he appears, as usual, to have fallen ill, and to have been tenderly nursed by Arbuthnot. 'I may say, without vanity, his life, under God, is due to the unwearied endeavors and care of your humble servant,' writes this devoted friend to Swift. Then the Queensberrys took formal charge of John Gay and henceforth he lived either at their town house in Burlington Gardens (where now stands the Western Branch of the Bank of England), or at their pleasant country-seat of Amesbury in Wiltshire. The Duke kept the poet's money; the Duchess watched over the poet and his wardrobe.[1] 'I was a long time,' he says in 1730, 'before I could prevail with her to let me allow myself a pair of shoes with two heels; for I had lost one, and the shoes were so decayed, that they were not worth mending.' Elsewhere it is—'I am ordered by the duchess to grow rich in the manner of Sir *John Cutler*.[2] I have nothing, at this present writing, but my frock that was made at *Salisbury*, and a bob-perriwig.' In an earlier paper in these volumes [3] we have given some account of the joint letters which at this period Gay and his kind protectress wrote to Swift in Ireland, and they present a most engaging picture of the alliance between the author

---

[1] In these characteristics Gay seems to have imitated La Fontaine, who, after living twenty years with Mme. de la Sablière, passed at her death to the care of M. and Mme. d'Hervart. 'D'autres prenaient soin de lui'—says M. Taine. 'Il se donnait à ses amis, sentant bien qu'il ne pouvait pourvoir à lui-même. Mme. d'Hervart, jeune et charmante, veilla à tout, jusqu'à ses vêtements,' etc. . . . 'Ses autres amis faisaient de même' ('La Fontaine et ses Fables,' 1861, p. 37). Are all fabulists congenitally feckless?

[2] Cf. Pope's Epistle to Lord Bathurst 'Of the Use of Riches,' ll. 315-34.

[3] See 'Prior's Kitty' in 'Eighteenth Century Vignettes,' First Series, 1897, 11-23.

of 'The Hare and Many Friends' and the *grande dame de par le monde* of the last century. Most of them were written from Amesbury (where nothing but a summer house now remains of the buildings as they were in Gay's time), and their main theme is the invitation of Swift to England. The final epistle of the series is dated November 16, 1732; and in this Gay reports that he has 'come to London before the family to follow his own inventions,' which included the production of his recently written Opera of 'Achilles.' A few days later, he was attacked by a constitutional malady to which he had long been subject, and died on the 4th of December. After lying in state in Exeter Change, he was (says Arbuthnot, who had again nursed and attended him) 'interred at *Westminster*-Abbey, as if he had been a peer of the realm;' and the Queensberrys erected a handsome monument to his memory. By other friends he was mourned as sincerely, if not as sumptuously. Pope, who had always loved him, felt a genuine sorrow, and five days elapsed before Swift at Dublin could summon courage to open the boding letter which announced his death. His fortune, of which his patrons had made themselves the voluntary stewards, amounted to about £6000. It was divided between his sisters, Mrs. Baller and Mrs. Fortescue.

His last letter to Swift had ended :—' Believe me, as I am, unchangeable in the regard, love and esteem I have for you.' The words reveal the chief source of his personal charm. He was thoroughly kindly and affectionate, with just that touch of clinging in his character, and of helplessness in his nature, which, when it does not inspire contempt (and Gay's parts save him from that), makes a man the spoiled child of men and the playfellow of women. He had his faults, it is true: he was as indolent as Thomson, as fond of fine clothes as Goldsmith; as great a *gourmand* as La Fontaine. That he was easily depressed, was probably due in some measure to his inactive life and his uncertain health. But at his best, he must have been a delightfully soothing and unobtrusive companion—invaluable for fêtes and gala days, and equally well adapted for the half lights and unrestrained intercourse of familiar life. 'You will never'—writes Swift to the Duchess of Queensberry, 'be able to procure another so useful, so sincere, so virtuous, so disinterested, so entertaining, so easy, and so humble a friend, as that person whose death all good men lament.' The praise is high, but there is little doubt that it was genuine. Pope's antithetical epitaph, despite the terrible mangling it has received at the hands of Johnson, may also be quoted:

> 'Of manners gentle, of affections mild;
> In wit a man; simplicity a child;
> With native humour temp'ring virtuous rage,
> Formed to delight at once and lash the age:
> Above temptation, in a low estate,
> And uncorrupted, e'en among the great:
> A safe companion, and an easy friend,
> Unblamed through life, lamented in thy end,
> These are thy honours! not that here thy bust
> Is mixed with heroes, or with kings thy dust,
> But that the worthy and the good shall say,
> Striking their pensive bosoms—*Here* lies Gay.'

The monument in Westminster Abbey, for which the above was composed, bears, in addition, a flippant and foolish couplet of Gay's own which can only have been—as indeed it is stated to have been—the expression of a momentary mood.

To attempt any detailed examination of Gay's works is unnecessary. Those which are most likely to attract the nineteenth century reader have been mentioned in the course of the foregoing pages. Stripped of the adventitious circumstances which threw the halo of notoriety around them, his two best known plays remain of interest chiefly for their songs,[1] which have all the qualities songs possess when the writer, besides being a poet, is a musician as well. This lyric faculty is also present in all Gay's lesser pieces, and is as manifest in the ballad on Molly Mog of the 'Rose' Inn at Wokingham, as in 'Black-Ey'd Susan' or ''Twas when the Seas were roaring.' In his longer poems he is always happiest when he is most unconstrained and natural, or treads the *terra firma* of the world he knows. The 'Fan,' the miscellaneous 'Eclogues,' the 'Epistles,' are all more or less forced and conventional. But exceptions occur even in these. There is a foretaste of Fielding in 'The Birth of the Squire;' and the 'Welcome from Greece' (1720), in which he exhibits Pope's friends assembling to greet him after his successful translation of the 'Iliad,' has a brightness and vivacity of movement, which seems to be the result of an un-

---

[1] One of the couplets of the 'Beggar's Opera' bids fair to live as long as Buridan's two bundles of hay. 'How happy could I be with either, Were t' other dear Charmer away!'—was, not long since, employed by Sir William Harcourt in the House to illustrate a political dilemma. Whereupon Mr. Goschen neatly turned the laugh upon the Leader of the Opposition by continuing the quotation —'But while you thus tease me together, To neither a word will I say!'

usually fresh inspiration. It is written, moreover, in an *ottava rima* stanza far earlier than Tennant's or Frere's or Byron's.[1] The 'Tales' are mediocre, and generally indelicate; the 'Translations' have no special merit. In the 'Fables' Gay finds a more congenial vocation. The easy octosyllabic measure, not packed and idiomatic like Swift's, not light and ironical like Prior's, but ambling, colloquial, and even a little down-at-heel, after the fashion of the bard him-

---

[1] Here are two random stanzas from this clever imitation of Ariosto:

'I see two lovely sisters, hand in hand,
  The fair hair'd Martha, and Teresa brown;
Madge Bellenden, the tallest of the land;
  And smiling Mary, soft and fair as down.
Yonder I see the chearful Duchess stand,
  For friendship, zeal, and blithsome humours known;
Whence that loud shout in such a hearty strain?
Why, all the Hamiltons are in her train.

. . . .

Thee Jervas hails, robust and debonair,
  Now have [we] conquer'd Homer, friends, he cries:
Dartneuf, grave joker, joyous Ford is there,
  And wond'ring Maine, so fat with laughing eyes;
(Gay, Maine, and Cheney, boon companions dear,
  Gay fat, Maine fatter, Cheney huge of size)
Yea Dennis, Gildon, (hearing thou hast riches)
And honest, hatless Cromwell, with red breeches.'

self, suited his habits and his Muse. An uncompromising criticism might perhaps be inclined to hint that these little pieces are by no means faultless; that they are occasionally deficient in narrative art, that they lack real variety of theme, and that they are often wearisome, almost unmanly, in their querulous insistence on the vices of servility and the hollowness of Courts. On the other hand, it must be admitted that they are full of good nature and good sense; and if not characterized by the highest philosophical wisdom, show much humorous criticism of life and practical observation of mankind. They have, too, some other recommendations, which can scarcely be ignored. They have given pleasure to several generations of readers, old and young; and they have enriched the language with more than one indispensable quotation. "While there is Life, there's Hope,' 'When a Lady's in the Case,' and ' Two of a Trade can ne'er agree,'—are still part of the current coin of conversation.

THE GRUB STREET OF THE ARTS.

THAT 'fine madness' of incongruity which tempted Charles Lamb into laughter at a funeral, led him, at the top of Skiddaw, to think upon the ham-and-beef shop in St. Martin's Lane. Where was this historic ham-and-beef shop? And where, under reconstructions and renewals, is the St. Martin's Lane of Lamb?—the St. Martin's Lane of the last century? 'It butteth,' says honest John Strype in his Stow of 1720, 'on *Northumberland House* in the *Strand*, and runneth *Northwards* beyond *Long Acre*, and the new Buildings in *Cock and Pye Fields*.' In other words, it extended from the southern end of the present Little St. Andrew Street (the site of the old Cock and Pye), past Long Acre and St. Martin's Church, to a spot in the Strand then opposite Northumberland House, but now at the entrance of Northumberland Avenue. This was the St. Martin's Lane of 1720; and judging from Evans's map, it was also the St. Martin's Lane of 1799.¹ Sixty years ago, its limits had become contracted. It had been cut into at Long Acre by a continuation of Cranbourn Street, and its southern boundary was the then newly completed Trafalgar Square. Ten years later still, directories give the southern termination as Chandos Street and Hemings' Row. Hemings' Row—the 'Dirty Lane' of our grandfathers—disappeared in 1889 with the creation of Charing Cross Road, but Chandos Street still ends the eastern side of the Lane, and serves to link the old thoroughfare with Strype's description. For it was just above Chandos Street that stood an ancient turnpike, to which Steele seems to allude in his 'Ramble from Richmond to London.' In that delightful 'Voyage où il vous plaira' he relates how, out of pure idleness, he diverted himself by following in 'an Hack' the hack of a handsome young lady with a mask and a maid. The damsel's chariot was travelling 'through *Long-Acre* towards St. *James's*.' 'Thereupon,' says the vivacious essayist, 'we drove for *King-street*, to save the Pass at St. *Martin's-Lane*.' At the end of Newport Street and Long Acre the vehicles become entangled, and for a moment

¹ A facsimile of Evans's 'New and Accurate Plan' was issued with Kelly's 'London Directory' for 1899.

he gets a glimpse of his charmer 'with her Mask off.' The chase continues 'in all Parts of the Town' for an hour and a half, when the quarry is discovered to be a 'Silk-Worm,' which is your hackney-coachman's term for those profitable fares 'who ramble twice or thrice a Week from Shop to Shop, to turn over all the Goods . . without buying any thing.' So Captain Richard Steele, after a few more vagrant experiences, goes home to scribble his 'Spectator' thereon (it is No. 454, for Monday, August 11th, 1712), and, if possible, to explain his erratic proceedings to his 'Absolute Governesse' at her new residence in Bloomsbury Square.

The site of the turnpike house here referred to is supposed to have been 28, the first number on the eastern side of the Lane. But the more important buildings were on the western side, and with the western side it is convenient to begin. Just beyond Parr's Bank and the present Free Library was Peter's Court, which Strype describes as 'a very handsome and gentile Place, with good Houses, well contrived, with little Gardens to them,'—a state of things not very easy to conceive at present, as Peter's Court, which must have gone back as far as the Garrick Theatre, and the narrow entrance to which was between Nos. 111 and 110, has now given place to the establishment of Messrs. Chatto and Windus. In Peter's Court, or at its entrance, was one of the many coffee-houses known as 'Tom's,' and even, if we may believe Mr. John Ashton,[1] the best known of them, although that distinction is generally claimed for 'Tom's' in Russell Street, already referred to in the 'Tour of Covent Garden.'[2] But the most memorable building in Peter's Court must have been the dancing school which afterwards became the first studio of Monsieur Louis-François Roubillac, the sculptor, who, according to contemporary prints, there carved the statue of Handel in the character of Orpheus which so long ornamented the gardens at Vauxhall. The Handel is said to have been the first original work Roubillac executed in England, and the date of its erection, May, 1738, fixes that of his residence in Peter's Court. How much longer he remained there is unrecorded, but his old studio was subsequently, for a long period, the home of the St. Martin's Lane Academy of which we

[1] 'Social Life in the Reign of Queen Anne,' 1883, p. 174.
[2] 'Eighteenth Century Vignettes,' Third Series, 1896, p. 340.

hear so much in the middle of the last century. At the death of Sir James Thornhill the material of his drawing school in James Street, Covent Garden, came into the hands of his son-in-law, Hogarth. 'Thinking,' says Hogarth, 'that an academy conducted on proper and moderate principle had some use, [I] proposed that a number of artists should enter into a subscription for the hire of a place large enough to admit thirty or forty people to draw after a naked figure.' The former dancing school in Peter's Court exactly answered to these requirements, and Hogarth lent his coadjutors Sir James's furniture. It was in this institution, of which Michael Moser was the treasurer and manager, and of the interior of which Hogarth himself painted a picture, now at Burlington House, that the majority of the artists of the reigns of George II. and George III. received or completed their educations. Reynolds, Ramsay, Zoffany, Wilson, Hayman, Cosway, Roubillac himself, Nollekens, and a host of minor names, were all scholars in this school, whose career of usefulness only ceased with the establishment in 1769 of the Royal Academy, to which its 'anatomical figures, busts, statues, etc.,' were in course of time transferred.

After the St. Martin's Lane Academy had vacated its old quarters in Peter's Court, the great room was pulled down and rebuilt as a Friends' Meeting House. Whether it was here that—*en route* for the ham-and-beef shop—Lamb made those studies of 'uncommunicating muteness,' which he has described so vividly in his 'Essays,' his editors say not. But a Friends' Meeting House continued to occupy the site of Roubillac's old studio until far into the present century, when, with the march of renovation, it moved to the eastern side of the Lane. Beyond the site of Peter's Court is the Duke of York's (formerly the Trafalgar Square) Theatre, which extends over the ground once occupied by Nos. 107 to 103, a space with many artistic memories. Here, for instance, at or 'behind No. 104,' lived Sir James Thornhill, in a large house with a grand allegoric staircase painted by himself. One of his successors was John Van Nost, son of the Van Nost of Piccadilly, who rivalled Cheere in leaden figures, and who was credited with that egregious gilt statue of George I. which once adorned the enclosure at Leicester Fields. Another tenant of the same house was Frank Hayman, Hogarth's crony and co-decorator at Vauxhall, who filled so many eighteenth century books with noses *à la* Cyrano and spindle-shanks. (His own legs, by the way, were probably his model, if one may judge from those of Viscount Squanderfield in the 'Marriage *A-la-Mode,*' for whom he was the admitted sitter.) A jovial, careless boon-companion, he grew gouty as he grew older, and though, like Thornhill, he migrated ultimately to Dean Street, Soho, it may well have been in St. Martin's Lane that occurred the incident which Pyne relates in the 'Somerset House Gazette.' When Hayman was engaged upon one of the large canvases for Tyers' New Room next the Rotunda at Vauxhall—it would seem to have been that in which Britannia was represented distributing laurels to certain distinguished officers—the Marquis of Granby, who sat by Tyers' request to the artist, and had heard of his past prowess as a pupil of Broughton, proposed a preliminary set-to with the gloves. Hayman pleaded that he was old and infirm.. But Lord Granby maintained that he, too, was no longer young, and, moreover, that he was out of practice owing to his absence in Germany. The pair began accordingly, and, after a magnificent display of science on either side, Hayman, warming with the game, 'got home' so effectually on the 'bread basket' of the noble and gallant Marquis that they both, being heavy men, came to the ground with a terrific crash. Thereupon Mrs. Hayman (she had been the widow of Frank's friend, Fleetwood, the Drury Lane manager), rushing frantically upon the scene, discovered her husband and the illustrious hero of Minden 'rolling over each other on the carpet, like two enraged bears.'[1]

The year of Minden fight is 1759, and the date of the hand-to-hand conflict in which the popular warrior, whose bald head and blue uniform decorated half the signs in the kingdom,[2] figures so ingloriously, must consequently be placed later. But the house 'behind No. 104,' or No. 104 itself, had another resident who is more eminent than either Hayman or Thornhill. In 1753, according to Malone, Sir Joshua Reynolds, then plain 'Mr.,' took up his abode at a house in the Lane described as 'nearly opposite to May's Buildings' (on the eastern side), and 'nearly opposite to May's Buildings' must have been a pretty accurate indication of No. 104. Reynolds had not long returned from Italy, painting, as his franker friends informed him, in a manner

---

[1] 'Somerset House Gazette,' 1824, i. 78.
[2] Readers of 'Pickwick' will recall the 'Marquis of Granby' at Dorking, where Mr. Weller senior administered such condign punishment to the luckless Shepherd.

that could never succeed, since it was not in the least like the manner of Kneller. Posterity has not confirmed that sagacious prediction. Unfortunately for our paper, however, Reynolds made only a brief stay in St. Martin's Lane, and there is no existent list of his sitters at this date. But the first portrait he painted after his establishment in London was that of his assistant, Giuseppe Marchi, the Italian boy who had accompanied him from Rome, and who, eventually, after a probation in the Peter's Court Academy, became himself an indifferent painter and a capable engraver. It was, in fact, Marchi's picture in a turban and oriental dress, now at Burlington House, which prompted the unfavourable criticism quoted above. No very notable incident concerning Reynolds's residence at No. 104 has been recorded, and in the same year (1753) in which he came to it he moved higher up on the left to No. 5, Great Newport Street, the only other London dwelling he occupied until his final migration to No. 47, Leicester Fields. But it was at St. Martin's Lane that he was joined by his youngest sister, Frances, whose artistic attempts made other people laugh and her brother cry, and who figures in Boswell's pages as the 'Renny dear' of Johnson.

> 'I therefore pray thee, Renny dear,
>   That thou wilt give to me,
> With cream and sugar soften'd well,
>   Another dish of tea,'—

sang the great man, in disrespectful parody of Percy's 'Reliques.' He left her a book in his will, and loved her in spite of her fidgetty peculiarities. At this date, however, Johnson was not yet known to Reynolds, whose acquaintance he only made after Reynolds had removed to Great Newport Street.

Four doors beyond No. 104 lived the portrait-painter John Cartwright, a mediocrity whose chief claim to remembrance lies in the circumstance that he had been, while at Rome, the fellow-student of the fantastic genius Henry Fuseli, a circumstance which led the latter, when he took up his abode in town in 1778, to quarter himself upon his old associate. It must have been at No. 100 that Fuseli produced his extraordinary 'Nightmare,' of which the success may be measured by the fact that it produced some five hundred pounds to its publisher and some twenty to its inventor. In No. 100, too, he painted his 'Œdipus and his Daughters,' and planned that Cyclopean enterprise, the illustrated Shakespeare of Boydell. Thackeray thought poorly of that 'black and ghastly gallery,' whose vast atlas folios spelled ruin to the worthy alderman; and a generation accustomed to the accomplished and instructed conceptions of Mr. Edwin Abbey is hardly likely to sympathize greatly with the murky Lears and Macbeths of Fuseli, or even with his 'Titania'—for all that Allan Cunningham compares it with Hogarth's 'Strolling Actresses,' a comparison which, in this connection, has a knell of condemnation. One wonders whether it was from St. Martin's Lane that Fuseli was summoned by Horace Walpole to try his hand at Dryden's Theodore and Honoria—a task surely more in the line of Horace's friend, Lady Di Beauclerk, who did the sublime studies 'in soot water' for the 'Mysterious Mother.'[1] But in St. Martin's Lane Fuseli continued to reside until 1788, when he married his model, Miss Sophia Rawlins, of Bath, and moved to 72, Queen Anne Street, Cavendish Square.

In 1828, and, indeed, for at least a quarter of a century afterwards, No. 96 was a colour-shop, which, in Cunningham's 'Handbook' of 1849 and 1850, the attentive reader is invited to 'observe.' Its tenant previous to 1828 was

[1] Lady Di did, as a matter of fact, illustrate Dryden's 'Fables' in 1797 with Bartolozzi for her engraver.

one Powell, whose mother for many years had made 'a pipe of wine' from a vine nearly a hundred feet long which was attached to the establishment, and which must have been much more remarkable than the historical plant in Bolt Court, from which, in 1784, Dr. Johnson gathered 'three bunches of grapes.' In Powell's time No. 96 was a fine old building whose Queen Anne door-frame was deeply carved with foliage and flowers after the fashion of the doorways in Great Ormond Street; and, like Thornhill's house, it had a painted staircase. This, which represented figures viewing a procession, had been executed about 1732 by a French decorator named Clermont for the notorious empiric, Dr. John Misaubin, to whom, either ironically or in good faith, Fielding inscribed his version of Molière's 'Médecin malgré lui,' known as the 'Mock Doctor.' Misaubin was the son of a French pastor in Spitalfields, and, if we are to take Fielding seriously, a man of parts and hospitality. 'I'd send for Misaubin, and take his pill,' says Bramston's 'Man of Taste'; and, no doubt, a good many 'men of taste' knocked at the Doctor's Queen Anne portal in the Lane. The learned and platitudinous Dr. Trusler, who was briefed by Mrs. Hogarth, affirms that the 'meager figure' in Plate V. of the 'Harlot's Progress' is 'Dr. *Mizebank*, a foreigner.' If so, he cannot, as contended by other commentators, also be the bow-legged dwarf who is wiping his spectacles in the third picture of 'Marriage *A-la-Mode*.' But seeing that Misaubin died in 1734, it is quite possible that the scene of the Quack Doctor in Hogarth's masterpiece is laid at No. 96; and as he had an Irish wife, it is also possible that in the fierce virago with the hoop, 'spread out'—as Hazlitt says—'like a turkey-cock's feathers,' he was thinking of the Misaubin establishment.[1] The doctor made a considerable fortune by his nostrums, a fortune which his grandson, after the manner of Hogarth's Rake, promptly squandered, ending his days in brief space, not in Bedlam, but in St. Martin's Workhouse.

[1] Whether the furniture and accessories of M. de la Pilule's consulting room were accurate studies from those of Misaubin, it is of course difficult to affirm. But as an instance of the care with which Hogarth wrought out the details of his picture-dramas, there is now in the National Gallery a carefully finished pencil and stump study by him of a skull, which, though reversed, closely resembles that which stands on the quack's table. Hogarth has added the marks on the cranium, and apparently by an afterthought, has exaggerated the posterior part.

Close upon No. 96, and turning to the left, came Cecil Court, a somewhat different place from the reputable paved passage, flanked with tall 'mansions,' which now leads from St. Martin's Lane to Charing Cross Road. It was in Cecil Court that Hogarth's mother, a majestic old lady, lived and died, her death being thus chronicled by the 'Gentleman's Magazine': '[June] 11 [1735] Mrs. *Hogarth*, Mother of the celebrated Mr. *Hogarth*, of a Fright occasioned by the Fire.' This conflagration, which took place on the 9th, must have been an event for Cecil Court, and was alleged to have been lighted by a certain brandy-selling Mrs. Calloway, who, having been served by her landlord with a notice to quit, determined in revenge to 'warm all her rascally Neighbours,' a resolution which she carried out in a very business-like manner. No fewer than fourteen houses were burned, and one belonging to John Huggins, Esq., late Warden of The Fleet, was 'greatly damaged.' For 'John Huggins, Esq.,' co-criminal with the infamous Bambridge of an earlier paper,[1] there is little need of pity; but if it is to be inferred that his residence was in the Court itself, it seems clear

---

[1] See *ante*, 'A Paladin of Philanthropy,' pp. 6-9.

that the houses must have been of a superior class. Another resident in later years was the father of Wilkie's engraver, Abraham Raimbach; and in Cecil Court, as already stated,[1] Raimbach himself was born. History has, however, recorded no other notable dwellers in Cecil Court, while concerning the next Court, St. Martin's, it is silent altogether. By this time (1899) the north-western side of St. Martin's Court has been pulled down, and those who seek to recognize in it the 'large handsome Court' of Strype with the 'good new-built Houses' and 'open Square in the Midst' must be endowed with exceptional powers of mental reconstruction. North of St. Martin's Court there are but two sites which concern this paper. One, where the Westminster County Court now stands, is that of the tavern known as New, or Young Slaughter's; the other, which must have been at the entrance to Cranbourn Street, was occupied by the more famous Old Slaughter's. In a house between these two lodged, from 1720 to 1725, that favourite of Addison and Steele, and laughing-stock of Pope and Gay, Ambrose Philips. 'Pastoral Philips,' in spite of what Swift called

[1] See *ante*, 'An English Engraver in Paris,' p. 174.

his 'little flams on Miss Carteret,' has never ranked as a great poetical name, even among the easy eminences of the Georgian era; and certainly to have enriched the language with the epithet 'namby-pamby,' is scarcely the crown which a self-respecting bard should claim of Melpomene. Yet it is difficult not to remember that it was to see Nance Oldfield as 'Andromache' in Philips' 'borrowed play' of the 'Distrest Mother' that Sir Roger de Coverley went in state to Drury Lane Playhouse—a fictitious fact of far greater import than the unquestioned and unvarnished truth that John Kemble, long afterwards, acted its 'Orestes' in a costume borrowed from Talma. And though the sham eclogue which Gay laughed away in the 'Shepherd's Week,' is to-day only a little more forgotten than the 'Shepherd's Week' itself, the 'Persian Tales' which honest Philips did into English from Petis de La Croix were long among the popular stock of pedlars, and the delight, after M. Antoine Galland's 'Arabian Nights,' of generations of schoolboys. One cannot feel wholly ungrateful to the harmless verseman whose highest ambition went no higher—in his arch-tormentor's words—than—

'To wear red stockings, and to dine with STEELE.'

But Ambrose Philips and his red stockings have broken the logical order of our progression, an accident which may perhaps justify the farther divergence of referring to Old Slaughter's coffee-house before speaking of its rival and successor, Young Slaughter's. Previous to 1842, when it was pulled down to make room for the prolongation of Cranbourn Street, Old Slaughter's stood close to the southern corner of Great Newport Street, and its number in the Lane was 75.[1] From a sketch made by Mr. F. W. Fairholt in 1826, it must then have been a comfortable building with bow windows which looked down Long Acre. It dated as far back as 1692, when it was started by the Thomas Slaughter from

[1] In Kelly's first street Directory for 1841, No. 75 is given as 'Reid and Co., Old Slaughter's Coffee-house.' In 1842 No. 75 has disappeared altogether. Five or six years later Thackeray revived its bygone memory in 'Vanity Fair.' For it is from 'the Old Slaughter's Coffee-house,' on the 10th April, 1815, that George Osborne sets out, in a blue coat with brass buttons, and a neat buff waistcoat, to marry Amelia Sedley; and it is at the same caravanserai, ten years later, that John the waiter tells Major William Dobbin, *sans rancune*, how the late Captain Osborne had died in his debt. ' He owes me three pound at this minute,' says John of the Slaughter's, and he wonders whether George's old father would ever pay the money.

whom it derived its name, and who kept it for
more than seven-and-forty years. Dryden was
reported to have frequented it in its early days,
and Pope. But its chief customers were the
artist-folk of the Lane and its vicinity. Hither
from Leicester Fields would come Hogarth,
bragging of the new-old theories in the 'Analysis,'
and scoffing at the 'grand *contorno*' of the *vir-
tuosi*; hither Hayman, and the gold-chaser Moser,
and Isaac Ware, the chimney-sweep-turned-archi-
tect who translated 'Palladio;' and (from his
studio over the way) Roubillac, raving in broken
English of the beauties of the Chevalier Bernini.
Here, again, would be seen the shrewd Swiss
enameller Rouquet, taking notes of the state of
the Arts in England for the benefit of Marshal
Belle-Isle; and Gravelot, who held that no Englishman could draw; and 'Friar' John Pine of
the incised 'Horace,' who had a print-shop at
No. 88. Luke Sullivan, the engraver of the
'March to Finchley,' McArdell the mezzo-
tinter, and Richard Wilson from Covent Garden
were also well-known visitors; while in later
days, when evening drew on, and the last rays
of light faded from the unfinished canvas, the
tall ungainly figure of Wilkie would slip in
quietly to a remote table and a hurried meal, at

which modest repast he would sometimes be joined by a noisier and more demonstrative companion, the Benjamin Robert Haydon, whose ambitious 'Curtius leaping into the Gulf' now adorns a London restaurant. Nor was there wanting a sprinkling of authors to carry on the traditions of Pope and Dryden, for Collins of the 'Odes' is reported to have used this time-honoured hostelry, and Goldsmith refers to its Orators in the 'Essays' as if his knowledge was experimental. Here, too (as everywhere), was to be found Johnson, studying spoken French from the mouths of the French frequenters of the place, and (as always) expressing his opinions in forcible language. The 'fasting Monsieurs'— so he calls them in his 'London'—disgusted him with their hare-brained and irresponsible frivolity. 'For anything I see,' he declared, confirming the previous verdict of a friend, 'foreigners are Fools!'

As already stated, Old Slaughter's came to an end in 1842, being then one hundred and fifty years old. It had attained the mature age of sixty-seven summers before its rival at No. 82, New or Young Slaughter's, came into existence— an existence brief in comparison and relatively undistinguished. Young Slaughter's legend seems limited to the fact that, *circa* 1765, Smeaton, Solander, Banks, John Hunter, Captain Cook, and certain other scientific or literary men, used it for Club meetings. Upper St. Martin's Lane, as the part north of Long Acre is called, is barren of memories—at all events in the eighteenth century. But over-against Old Slaughter's on the east side was No. 70, where, in 1775, Nathaniel Hone, among other specimens of his skill, exhibited that irreverent picture of Sir Joshua as 'The Pictorial Conjuror displaying the whole Art of Optical Deception,' a composition which, in its first form, had the supplementary discredit of insulting Angelica Kauffmann. Below No. 70, at No. 63, was the entrance to the studio in which Roubillac took refuge after he had quitted Peter's Court, and from which, in 1762, he was buried in St. Martin's churchyard, his successor being his pupil, Nicholas Read, proficient in 'pancake clouds,' whose chief claim to remembrance lies in the tradition that he worked upon the shrouded figure of Death in Roubillac's monument to Mr. Nightingale and his wife in Westminster Abbey. After these the east side becomes uninteresting, except for the residence at No. 60 of Thomas Chippendale, 'Upholder,' whose name is probably better known now than in his own day, though we still seem to be ignorant of the dates of his birth and death. It was from his St. Martin's Lane shop, in 1754, that he put forth his 'Gentleman and Cabinet-Maker's Director,' a sumptuous series of one hundred and sixty copper-plates dedicated to the Earl of Northumberland, and even now not entirely eclipsed by the severer designs of Thomas Sheraton. Some of the courts and side streets may detain us for a moment. In New Street was the 'Golden Head,' from which in 1770, young Flaxman sent a modest 'Portrait of a Gentleman' as his first contribution to the Academy; and it was at the 'Pine Apple' in the same street that Johnson, on coming to town, was wont to seek refreshment. 'I dined (said he) very well for eight-pence, with very good company. . . Several of them had travelled. They expected to meet every day; but did not know one another's names. It used to cost the rest a shilling, for they drank wine; but I had a cut of meat for six-pence, and bread for a penny, and gave the waiter a penny; so that I was quite well served, nay, better than the rest, for they gave the waiter nothing.' At the sign of 'The Cricket Bat' in Duke's Court, was one of the toy-shops where Boydell was in the habit of exhibiting his etchings for sale, while in May's Buildings (where in later years the club called The Eccentrics held its sittings) there existed, according to Foote's 'Taste,' a manufactory of sham Rembrandts and Ostades which deceived the opulent amateur and filled the pockets of the Puffs and Carmines of the day. Probably it was the east side of the old thoroughfare which most merited the title we have borrowed from Allan Cunningham to head these desultory memoranda. If they are here brought to a close, it is by no means because the subject is exhausted, for opposite to the Church, and not far from the turnpike referred to at the beginning of this paper, stood the Watch- or Round-House, an institution which should assuredly be fruitful of anecdote. But even in topography one must draw the line somewhere, and we draw it at this favourite resort of the Georgian nobility and gentry. '*Le secret d'ennuyer est celui de tout dire.*'

MARTEILHE'S 'MEMOIRS.

THE threadbare dictum of Terentianus Maurus touching books and their destinies, was never more exactly verified than by the story of the record which gives its title to the present paper. In the year 1757 was issued at Rotterdam, by J. and D. Beman and Son of that Batavian city, a little thick octavo of 552 pages, on poor paper with worse type, of which the following is the textual title: 'Mémoires d'un Protestant, Condamné aux Galères de France pour Cause de Religion; écrits par lui même: Ouvrage, dans lequel, outre le récit, des souffrances de l'Auteur depuis 1700 jusqu'en 1713; on trouvera diverses Particularités curieuses, relatives à l'Histoire de ce Temps-là, & une Description exacte des Galères & de leur Service.' In 1774 a second edition of the book was published at the Hague, to be followed four years later by a third. In the Rotterdam impression the names of some of the personages and localities had been simply indicated by initials; in the third issue of 1778—

the author having died not many months before—these particulars were inserted at full. It then appeared that the 'Memoirs'—concerning the authenticity of which, from internal evidence, there could never have been any reasonable doubt—were those of a certain Jean Marteilhe of Bergerac on the Dordogne, in the Province of Périgord in France, and that they had been edited and prepared for the press from Marteilhe's own manuscripts by M. Daniel de Superville—probably the second of that name, since Daniel de Superville, the elder, a notable personage among the leaders of the Reformed Church, had long been dead when the work appeared in its first form.[1]

Circulating chiefly among the members of a proscribed community, and published in a foreign country, these remarkable autobiographical experiences, notwithstanding their three editions, had been practically lost sight of in France until some thirty years ago; and the account of their revival—as partly recorded in a lengthy note to the excellent 'Forçats pour la Foi' of M. A. Coquerel Fils—is sufficiently curious. About 1865, according to M. Coquerel, copies of the

[1] Daniel de Superville, senior, died in 1728. His sermons were translated in 1834 by John Allen, who prefixed to them a Memoir of his life.

volume were so rare as to be practically unobtainable. There was none in the Bibliothèque Nationale of France; and the only example known in Paris belonged to a Protestant banker, M. Félix Vernes, by whom it had been lent occasionally to historical students and connoisseurs. At Amsterdam there was a second copy in the library of M. Van Woortz, and it was believed that other copies existed in Holland. There was also, or at all events there is now, a copy at the British Museum. Meanwhile, the book had greatly impressed the fortunate few into whose hands it had come. Michelet, who makes mention of it both in his 'Louis XIV. et le Duc de Bourgogne,' and his 'Louis XIV. et la Révocation,' spoke of it in terms of the highest enthusiasm. It was written, he said, '*comme entre terre et ciel.*' Why was it not reprinted? he asked. The reply lay no doubt in the difficulty of procuring a copy to print from; and its eventual reproduction was the result of an accident. In a catalogue of German books, M. François Vidal, pastor of the Reformed Church at Bergerac, came upon the title of a work purporting to relate the history of a fugitive Camisard. Himself a native of the Cevennes, and therefore specially interested in the subject, he sent for the volume, only to discover that, instead of relating to the 'fanatics of Languedoc' (as Gibbon calls them), it was really an account of a Périgourdin Protestant who, after the Revocation, more than a century and a half earlier, of the Edict of Nantes, had fled from that very Bergerac in which he (M. Vidal) was then exercising his calling. He had seen some extracts from M. Vernes' copy of Marteilhe's 'Memoirs,' as those extracts had been made public in the Journal of an Historical Society (the 'Bulletin de la Société de l'Histoire du Protestantisme français), and he felt convinced that, notwithstanding certain (to him) transparent disguises of personages and localities, he was reading, in German, the story of Jean Marteilhe. He accordingly wrote, through the publisher of the German book, to its author, who proved to be the copious Dr. Christian Gottlob Barth, the founder of the Calwer Verlags-Verein in Wurtemburg, and a well-known writer on theological subjects. Dr. Barth informed M. Vidal that the material for the adventures of his supposititious Camisard, whom he had christened Mantal, had been derived from F. E. Rambach's 'Schicksal der Protestanten in Franckreich,' a work published at Halle in 1760, and alleged to be no longer procurable. Thereupon M. Vidal set about reconstructing the history in the light of this discovery. He translated Barth's summary into French, restored to Marteilhe the name of which Barth, with nothing but initials in his source of information, had been ignorant, and then (having by good luck chanced upon a copy of the Rotterdam edition at Le Fleix, not many miles from Bergerac), incorporated with his version some of the more striking passages of the original record. Why he did not at once substitute that original for the summary, is, in all probability, to be explained by difficulties in the way of obtaining prolonged access to the Le Fleix copy. But the revelation of Marteilhe to France, even in mangled form, was still to be deferred. A portion of M. Vidal's book had no sooner made its appearance in 'L'Eglise Réformée,' a journal issued at Nîmes, than that journal was suddenly suppressed. In 1863 he therefore printed on his own account what he had written, in the form of a small 12mo pamphlet. One result of this publication — to which he still somewhat unaccountably gave the title of 'La Fuite du Camisard'—was to stimulate search for further copies of the original 'Memoirs,' another of which was found soon after in La Vendée, and was acquired by the Bibliothèque Nationale. Finally, in 1865, the

Société des Écoles du Dimanche printed the complete text from the copy of M. Vernes with four fancy illustrations by the marine artist, Morel-Fatio,[1] and a Preface and Appendices by M. Henri Paumier. Of this, four thousand copies were sold between 1865 and 1881, in which latter year a new and revised edition, with a second Preface by M. Paumier, was put forth. In the interim, an English version was published under the auspices of the Religious Tract Society, which, in addition to a translator's Preface, gave some further particulars respecting Marteilhe himself, said to be derived from an article in the 'Quarterly Review' for July, 1866, though they are there admittedly taken from M. Coquerel. To these again, some slight supplementary contributions were made by the French editor in his new and revised edition of 1881. The translation of the Religious Tract Society was also issued in New York in 1867 by Messrs. Leypoldt and Holt under the title of 'The Huguenot Galley-Slave.'

---

[1] M. Antoine Léon Morel-Fatio, whose illustrations are not reproduced in the English and American editions, should have been well qualified for his task. He is described as the 'Horace Vernet of the sea-piece,' and was a worthy rival of Isabey and Gudin. He died of grief at the Louvre in 1871, when the Prussians entered Paris.

From what has been stated, it will be seen that, previously to the issue by the *Société des Ecoles du Dimanche*, no edition of the original 'Memoirs' had been published in France. But it will also be observed that, as early as 1760, or only three years after their first appearance in the United Provinces of the Netherlands, those 'Memoirs' had been incorporated in abridged form with Rambach's 'Schicksal der Protestanten in Frankreich.' What is perhaps even more remarkable is that—as M. Coquerel and the English translator of 1866 did not fail to point out—they had been translated earlier still in England, where, indeed, they appear to have attracted immediate attention in their first form, since the 'Monthly Review' for May, 1757, includes them in its 'Catalogue of Foreign Publications.' They must have been 'Englished' shortly afterwards, for, in February, 1758, Ralph Griffiths of the 'Dunciad' in Paternoster Row, the proprietor of the 'Monthly Review,' and Edward Dilly of the 'Rose and Crown' in the Poultry, issued conjointly, in two volumes 12mo, a version entitled 'The Memoirs of a Protestant, Condemned to the Galleys of France, for His Religion. Written by Himself.' To this followed upon the title-page a lengthy description of the contents, differing from that

Y

of the French original, in so far as it laid stress upon the fact that the 'Protestant' was 'at last set free, at the Intercession of the Court of Great Britain';—and the work was further stated to be 'Translated from the Original, just published at the Hague [Rotterdam?], by James Willington.'[1] For this enigmatical 'James Willington,' whose name as an author is otherwise entirely unknown to fame, it has long been the custom to read 'Oliver Goldsmith.' Goldsmith, in fact, was actually engaged as a writer-of-all-work upon the 'Monthly Review' when the Rotterdam edition was announced among its foreign books. To the same May number in which that announcement appeared, he supplied notices of Home's 'Douglas,' of Burke 'On the Sublime and Beautiful,' and of the new four-volume issue of Colman and Thornton's 'Connoisseur.' He continued to work for Griffiths' magazine until the September following, when, for reasons not now discoverable with certainty, he ceased his contributions to its pages.

What appears to be the earliest ascription to his pen of the English version of the 'Memoirs'

[1] Some descriptions of these volumes speak of a 'rare frontispiece by Bickham,' which we have not met with. There is no reference to it on the original title-page.

of Marteilhe is to be found in the life prefixed
by Isaac Reed to the 'Poems of Goldsmith and
Parnell,' 1795. Here he is stated to have received
twenty guineas for the work from Mr. Edward
Dilly. The next mention of it occurs in the
biographical sketch by Dr. John Aikin in the
'Goldsmith's Poetical Works' of 1805. Dr.
Aikin says (p. xvi) that Goldsmith sold the book
to Dilly for twenty guineas. Prior ('Life of
Goldsmith,' 1837, i. 252) confirms this, upon the
authority of Reed; and he further alleges, though
without giving his authority, that Griffiths 'acknowledged it [the translation] to be by Goldsmith.' Forster follows suit (1848, p. 107; and
1877, i. 129) by stating that 'the property of the
book belonged to Griffiths,' and that 'the position
of the translator appears in the subsequent assignment of the manuscript by the Paternoster Row
bookseller to bookseller Dilly of the Poultry, at
no small profit to Griffiths, for the sum of twenty
guineas.' Reed, it will be observed, says that
Goldsmith received the twenty guineas; Aikin,
that Goldsmith sold the book; Prior, as usual,
writes so loosely as to be ambiguous, and Forster,
although, in his last edition, he cites Reed and
Aikin as his authorities, affirms that Griffiths sold
it to Dilly. None of these statements would

seem to be exactly accurate. The translation of the 'Memoirs of a Protestant·' was in reality sold by the author—much as, some years since, it was ascertained that the 'Vicar of Wakefield' was sold [1]—in three separate shares. By the kindness of the late Mr. Edward Ford of Enfield, a devoted student of Goldsmith, the present writer was favoured with a transcript of Goldsmith's receipt for one of these shares from the hitherto unpublished original in Mr. Ford's possession.[2] It runs as follows:

LONDON, Jan⁷ 11ᵗʰ, 1758.

Rec'd of Mʳ Edward Dilly six pounds thirteen shillings and four pence, in full for his third share of my translation of a Book entitled *Memoirs of a Protestant condemned to the Gallies for Religion*, &c.

OLIVER GOLDSMITH.

£6 13s. 4d.

From this document—the signature only of which is in the handwriting of the poet—two things are clear,—first, that Goldsmith himself sold the book to Dilly and two others, one being Griffiths, whose name is on the title-page; and,

---

[1] See the Preface to the *facsimile* Reproduction of the First Edition, Elliot Stock, 1885.

[2] This interesting relic now [1899] belongs to his son and successor, Mr. J. W. Ford, of Enfield Old Park.

secondly, that the translation was by Goldsmith and not by James Willington.

But why, it may be asked, was the name of Willington (an old Trinity College acquaintance of Goldsmith) put forward in this connection? The question is one to which it is not easy to give an entirely satisfactory answer. Mr. Forster, it is true, does not feel any difficulty in replying. 'At this point,' he says, 'there is very manifest evidence of despair.' But it is a characteristic of Mr. Forster's sympathetic and admirable biography that it occasionally appears to be written under the influence of preconceptions, and the evidence he mentions, however manifest, is certainly not produced. Mr. Forster fills the gap with eloquent disquisition on the obstacles in the path of genius, and so conducts his hero back to Dr. Milner's door at Peckham.[1] How Goldsmith subsisted in the interval between his ceasing to write regularly for the 'Monthly Review' and

[1] 'Time's devouring hand,' it may be noted here (for the chronicler of the fugitive must make his record where he can), has now removed all trace of Dr. John Milner's Peckham Academy, which stood in Goldsmith Road (formerly Park Lane), opposite the southern end of Lower Park Road. 'Goldsmith House,' as it was called latterly, was pulled down in 1891. A sketch of it appeared in the 'Daily Graphic' for 24th February in that year.

his return to his old work as an usher, is no doubt obscure. But it is probable that there was little variation in his manner of living, although his labours were not performed under *surveillance* in the Back Parlour of the 'Dunciad.' It has been discovered that about this time he was contributing portions of a 'History of Our Own Times' to the 'Literary Magazine;' and it is also conjectured that these were not his sole contributions to that and other periodicals. Moreover, the version of Marteilhe's 'Memoirs' must have been made in the last months of 1757, since the above receipt is dated January 11, 1758, and the book was published in the following February. In addition to this, he was again, by his own account, attending patients as a doctor. 'By a very little practice as a physician, and a very little reputation as a poet'—he tells his brother-in-law, Hodson, in December, 1757, 'I make a shift to live.' He was in debt, no doubt; but he had already, says the same communication, 'discharged his most threatening and pressing demands.' Upon the whole,—Mr. Forster's 'very manifest evidence' not being forthcoming,—it must be concluded that Goldsmith's position after ceasing to write for the 'Monthly Review' (though not for Griffiths) was much what it had been before that event, perhaps even better, because he was more free; and this being so, we are driven to the commonplace and unheroic solution that, even in his Salisbury Square garret, he was too conscious of those higher things within him to care to identify himself with a mere imitation ' out of the French,' executed for bread, and not for reputation; and that he put Willington's name to the book in default of a better. He gave evidence of his genius in his most careless private letter; he could not help it; but the man who subsequently refrained from signing the 'Citizen of the World,' may be excused from signing the translated 'Memoirs of a Protestant.'

That the translation produced under these conditions might have been better if the translator had taken more pains, is but to turn Goldsmith's *bon mot* against himself. '*Verbum verbo reddere*' was scarcely his ambition, and those who wish for plain-sailing fidelity will do well, if they cannot compass the French original, to consult the rendering prepared for the Religious Tract Society.[1] The chief merits of the version of 1758

[1] This rendering, however, is incomplete, inasmuch as it omits the ' Description of the Galleys,' etc., about ninety of the final pages of the original.

are first, that it is a contemporary version, demonstrably from Goldsmith's pen; and secondly, that it is Goldsmith's earliest appearance in book-form. It is not only characterized by its writer's unique and peculiar charm, but it is as delightful to read as any of his acknowledged journey-work. Even Griffiths of the 'Dunciad,' who reviewed it himself in the 'Monthly Review' for May, 1758, cannot deny its merits in this respect. Speaking of the 'ingenious Translator,' he remarks that he 'really deserves this epithet, on account of the spirit of the performance, tho',' he adds, grudgingly, 'we have little to say in commendation of his accuracy.' Upon this latter count, it may be observed that in one instance, at least, inaccuracy is excusable. In telling, early in the book, the story of the abjuration by Marteilhe's mother of her Huguenot faith, Goldsmith makes her add to her declaration that she was 'compelled by Fear.' This is manifestly inexact, seeing that the French original runs: "*Elle ajouta ces mots :* la Force me le fait faire, *faisant sans doute allusion au nom du Duc*' (*i.e.* the Duke de la Force). All this, as we know, must have been Greek to Goldsmith, because the names in the *editio princeps* of 1757, from which he was working, were not given at full.

But it must certainly be admitted that he deals freely with his text, occasionally suppressing altogether what he regards as redundant, and now and then inserting supplementary touches of his own. Speaking of the soup prepared in the gaol at Lille he says: 'Even *Lacedæmonian* black Broth could not be more nauseous.' There is nothing in the text of this classic dietary, and what is more, Marteilhe would scarcely have used the simile. Elsewhere the decoration is in what Matthew Arnold used to call the 'Rule Britannia' vein. Of the valiant captain of the 'Nightingale' who held his own so long against the galleys in that memorable engagement which plays such a moving part in Marteilhe's record, the writer says: '*Ce capitaine, qui n'avait plus rien à faire pour mettre sa flotte en sûreté, rendit son épée.*' This Goldsmith translates: 'At last the captain gave up his Sword without further Parley, like a true Englishman, despising Ceremony, when Ceremony could be no longer useful.'

Dealing here rather with the story of the book than its contents, it would be beyond the purpose of our paper to linger longer upon the extraordinary interest and simple candour of Marteilhe's narrative. But the mention just made of the captain of the 'Nightingale' reminds us that some further particulars respecting this obscure naval hero were not long since brought to light by Professor J. K. Laughton.[1] His name (which Marteilhe had forgotten) was Seth Jermy, and he had served as a lieutenant at the battle of Barfleur. He became captain of the 'Spy' brigantine in January, 1697, and five years later was appointed to the command of the 'Nightingale,' a small 24-gun frigate, chiefly employed in convoying corn-ships and colliers between the Forth, the Tyne, the Humber, and the Thames. In this duty he was engaged up to the fight with the French galleys, which took place, not, as Marteilhe says, in 1708, but in 1707. In August, 1708, Captain Jermy returned from France on parole and was tried by court-martial for the loss of his ship. The following are the minutes of the trial from documents in the Public Record Office:

'At a court-martial held on board Her Majesty's ship the "Royal Anne" at Spithead, on Thursday, 23 Sep. 1708; Present: The Hon. Sir George Byng, Knight, Admiral of the Blue Squadron of her Majesty's fleet. . . .

'Enquiry was made by the Court into the

[1] 'English Historical Review,' January, 1889, pp. 65-80.

occasion of the loss of Her Majesty's ship the "Nightingale," of which Captain Seth Jermy was late commander, which was taken by six sail of the enemy's galleys off Harwich on 24 Aug. 1707. The court having strictly examined into the matter, it appeared by evidence upon oath that the "Nightingale" was for a considerable time engaged with a much superior force of the enemy, and did make so good a defence as thereby to give an opportunity to all the ships under his convoy to make their escape; and it is the opinion of the court that he has not been anyway wanting in his duty on that occasion; and therefore the Court does acquit the said Captain Jermy and the other officers as to the loss of Her Majesty's said ship "Nightingale."'

Beyond the fact that he was exchanged against a French prisoner a little later, served again, was superannuated, and died in 1724, nothing further seems to be known of Captain Jermy. But of the captain who succeeded him on the 'Nightingale' when that ship passed by capture into French hands—the infamous renegade whom
✻ Marteilhe calls '—— Smith,'—Professor Laughton supplies data which, since they are included only in one very limited edition of the 'Memoirs,' may here be briefly set down. After chequered

experiences in the service of Her Majesty Queen Anne, including a court-martial for irregularities while commanding the 'Bonetta' sloop, Thomas Smith, being then, according to his own account, a prisoner at Dunkirk, yielded to solicitations made to him, and entered the service of the King of France. In November, 1707, he was made commander of the captured 'Nightingale.' In the December following, being in company with another Dunkirk privateer, the 'Squirrel,' he was chased and taken by the English man-of-war 'Ludlow Castle,' Captain Haddock. Smith was brought to London, tried for high treason at the Old Bailey (2nd June, 1708), and found guilty. 'On 18th June he was put on a hurdle and conveyed to the place of execution. . . . Being dead he was cut down, his body opened and his heart shown to the people, and afterwards burnt with his bowels, and his body quartered.' And thus Marteilhe, when he came to London in 1713 to thank Queen Anne for her part in his release, may well, as he avers, have seen Smith's mangled remains 'exposed on Gibbets along the Banks of the *Thames*.'

Marteilhe's story, it may be gathered, differs in some respects from the official account disinterred from the Public Records. But the discrepancies are readily explained by the fact that much which he related must have been acquired at second hand. Speaking from his personal experience he is accurate enough. What is known of him and his book, beyond the date at which it closes, needs but few words. 'The author [of the "Memoirs"],' says Goldsmith in his Preface of 1757, 'is still alive, and known to numbers, not only in *Holland* but *London*;' and it is quite possible that in one or other of these places, Goldsmith himself may have seen and conversed with him. An *Avertissement des Libraires* prefixed to the Rotterdam edition, but not reproduced by Goldsmith or M. Paumier, is equally confirmatory of the authenticity of the book: '*Des Personnes de caractère, & dignes de toute créance, nous ont assurés, que cet Ouvrage à été véritablement composé par un de ces Protestans, condamnés aux Galères de France pour cause de Religion, & qui en furent délivrés par l'intercession de la Reine* ANNE *d'Angleterre peu après la paix* d'Utrecht. *Les mêmes Personnes nous ont dit, qu'elles ont eu des liaisons personnelles avec l'Auteur; ╪qu'elles ne doutent pas de sa bonne foi & de sa probité; & qu'elles sont persuadées, qu'autant que sa mémoire a pu lui rappeller les faits, cette Relation est exacte.*' Opposite the word '*créance*,' in the

British Museum copy, is written in an old hand, 'Mrs. Dumont & De Superville.' As Daniel de Superville Senior was dead in 1757, the De Superville here mentioned was no doubt his son of the same Christian name,—a doctor, who, as above suggested, was probably the editor of Marteilhe's manuscripts. After this come naturally the details given, from Coquerel and elsewhere, in M. Paumier's second Preface, and already referred to. Marteilhe, we learn, did not reside permanently in the Netherlands—'that Land of Liberty and Happiness,' as Goldsmith renders '*Ces heureuses Provinces*'—but for some time was in business in London. He died at Cuylenberg, in Guelderland, on the 4th November, 1777, at the age of ninety-three. Little is known about his family; but it is believed that he had a daughter who was married at Amsterdam to an English naval officer of distinction, Vice-Admiral Douglas.

APPENDIX.

THE BURNING OF WHITEHALL.

THE following extracts from the Marchmont MSS. ('Fourteenth Report of the Historical Manuscripts Commission,' Appendix, Part III. 1894, pp. 129-130, and 141) here reproduced by permission of the Controller of H.M. Stationery Office, add further detail to the quotations from the Hope Johnstone MSS. already printed at pp. 214-215 of this book.

The Earl of Argyll to the Earl of Marchmont, London, 4th January, 1697-98 : 'This minutte Whytehall is in fyre. All allmost looking to the watter syde is burnt down; how farr it will goe I know not.'

Mr. Robert Pringle, Under Secretary of State, to Lord Polwarth. Whitehall, 4th January, 1697[8] : '. . . Whilst I write to your lordship, Whythall is in flames and a verie dismal sight ; the fire broke out about 3 in the afternoon, and hes alreadie consumed all the royal lodgings both on the water and privie garden. . . .'

Sir James Ogilvie to the Earl of Marchmont, Whytehall, 5th January, 1698 : 'I cannot writt this with myne [own hand], for I find my eyes waike with the sitting up the last night and looking on the fyre. All the palace of Whytehall, at least what was built by King Charles the Second and King James, is burned downe.'

The Earl of Tullibardine, n.d., says the fire 'burnt so violently that ther is nothing left on the side of the privy garden, nor next the water till near Scotland yard, so that the King's apartment, and the Queen's, the Chappell, Councel Chamber, guard hall, . . . is burnt.'

And. Kincir to the Earl of Marchmont, Whitehall, 5th January, 1697-8 : '. . . This flying packet will bring your Lordship an account of the unlucky occasion why we sent no packet last night, for truly this Court of Whitehall was all in flames at the time. All the royall apartments with the King's chappell and gward hall, the Duke of Shrewsbury's office, the Treasury Office, Council Chamber, the late King's new chappell, the long gallerys with Devonshire's, Essex's, and Villars's, and severall other lodgings are all consumed. . . . . The best account we yet have of the occasion of it was the neglect of a lawndress in Colonel Stanley's lodgings near the river. There are five or six at least destroyed by it, but no persons of any note.'

GENERAL INDEX.

N.B.—*The titles of articles are in capitals.*

Abbey, Mr. Edwin A., 303.
Abel, 70.
Abington, Mrs., 133.
Account of the Provinces of South Carolina and Georgia, Oglethorpe's, 10.
Achilles, Gay's, 287.
Addison, Life of, Aikin's, 85.
Addison, Joseph, 85, 104, 109, 110, 112, 259, 260.
Admiralty, The, 248.
Advice to Julia, Luttrell's, 221.
Agas's Map, 234, 236.
Aitken, Mr. George A., 86-114, 253.
Aikin, Dr. John, 323.
Albemarle, Monk, Duke of, 197, 198.
Albinus, 119.

Allen, Ralph, 131.
Ally Croaker, 45.
Almack's, 225.
Alvanley, Lord, 217.
Amatis, the Piedmontese, 11.
Anacréon, 186.
Animated Nature, Goldsmith's, 47.
Angelo, Henry or Harry, 61-84, 136.
ANGELO'S 'REMINISCENCES,' 61-84.
Angelo's Pic Nic, 84.
Annandale, Lord, 214.
Apology for Himself and his Writings, Steele's, 107.
Apothegms, Hawkins's, 162.
Appius and Virginia, Dennis's, 262.
Arabian Nights, Galland's, 308.

Arabian Nights, Forster's, 177.
Arbuthnot, Dr., 268, 269, 275, 279, 284, 287.
Archæologia, 207.
Archer, Lady, 80.
Architecture, Book of, Evelyn's, 197.
Argus; or, London Reviewed in Paris, Lewis Goldsmith's, 189.
Argyll, Fort, 13.
Argyll, John, Duke of, 23.
Arlington, Lord, 208.
ARTS, GRUB STREET OF THE, THE, 293-314.
Ashton, Mr. John, 296.
Astley, Philip, 63.
Aubrey de Vere, Recollections of, 187.
Austen, Jane, 84.
Autobiography, Bramston's, 202.
AUTHOR OF 'MONSIEUR TONSON,' THE, 115-136.

Bach, John Christian, 70.
Bach, John Sebastian, 70.
Ballad on a Wedding, Suckling's, 242.
Baller, Mrs., 288.

Baller, Rev. Joseph, 256.
Bambridge, Thomas, 6, 306.
Bambridge under Examination, Hogarth's, 8.
Banks, 312.
Bannister's Budget, 77.
Bannister, Jack, 77, 78.
Banqueting House at Whitehall, 194, 195, 196, 197, 198, 199, 200, 204, 207, 210, 211, 212, 213.
Baretti, 164.
Barrington, George, 123.
Barth, Dr. C. G., 318, 319.
Barrymore, Lord, 78, 79.
Bartolozzi, Francis, 70, 75, 303.
Bate, Parson, 73.
Bath, Lord, 118.
Battle of the Boyne, West's, 71.
Beauclerk, Lady Di, 303.
Beaumarchais, Caron de, 137.
Beaupré the dancer, 187.
Beauties of English Poesy, Goldsmith's, 47.
Beautiful Youth struck dead by Lightning, Goldsmith's epitaph on, 40.

Beaux' Stratagem, Farquhar's, 48, 133.
Bee, Goldsmith's, 53.
Bedford, Duke of, 120.
Beggar's Opera, Gay's, 281-5, 290.
Betterton, Thomas, 82.
Belinda, Miss Edgeworth's, 45.
Berkeley, Dr., 4, 110, 111.
Berkeley, Lord, 250.
Béranger, Pierre de, 179.
Bermudas, The, 245.
Bernini, 310.
Bewick, Thomas, 133.
Bickerstaffe, the dramatist, 247.
Binns, Mrs., 103.
Birkbeck Hill, Dr. George, 166-172.
Birrell, Mr. Augustine, 172.
Birth of the Squire, Gay's, 290.
Blackamoor wash'd White, Bate's, 73.
Black-Ey'd Susan, Gay's, 277.
Blackmore, Sir Richard, 92.
Blake (Blue-skin), 119.
Blake, William, 139, 282.
Blessington, Lady, 219.
Board of Trade, The, 207.

Board of Works, Metropolitan, The, 250.
Boerhaave, 119.
Boileau, M., 66.
Bolingbroke, Lord, 170, 267, 270.
Bonaparte family, The, 181.
Bonaparte, Napoleon, 180, 181, 186.
Boothby, Miss Hill, 162.
Boswell, James, 27, 72, 123.
Boswell, James, Junr., 151.
Boswelliana, 160, 165.
Boswell's *Johnson*, 137-172.
BOSWELL'S PREDECESSORS AND EDITORS, 137-172.
Bowling Green at Whitehall, 201.
Boydell, John, 313.
Boydell's *Shakespeare*, 302.
Braganza, Catherine of, 203, 205, 211, 213.
Broome, William, 262.
Broughton, the prize-fighter, 82, 299.
Brown, 'Capability,' 128.
Bruce, Mr. Henry, 3.
Brummell, Beau, 223.
Buckhorse, the boxer, 135.
Buckingham Court, 251.

Buckingham, Duke of, 249.
Buckinghamshire, Lady, 79.
Bull, Edward, 121.
Bunbury, Letter to Mrs., Goldsmith's, 44.
Burbage, Richard, 174.
Burke, Edmund, 123.
Burlington, Lord, 271, 276, 279.
Burnet, John, 173.
Burney, Edward, 177.
Burney, Fanny, 83.
Burnham Beeches, Luttrell's, 230.
Buxton Forman, Mr. H., 275.
Byron, Lord, 81, 126, 219.
Byron, Lady, 126.

Calloway, Mrs., 306.
Cambridge, Richard Owen, 124, 125.
Campbell, Dr. Thomas, 163, 164.
Canaletto, 70.
Captives, Gay's, 280.
Captivity, Goldsmith's, 44.
Carhampton, Earl of, 232.
Carleton's Memoirs, 91, 162.
Carlisle House (1), 68, 69, 71.

Carlisle House (2), 68.
Carlyle, Thomas, 152, 156, 168.
Carrington, Lord, 207.
Carruthers, Dr. Robert, 157.
Carteret, Miss, 308.
Carter, Mrs., 192.
Cartwright, John, 302.
Castell, Robert, 6.
Castlemaine, Lady, 198, 204, 206, 213.
Castle, Mr. Egerton, 82.
Catherine of Braganza, 203, 205, 211, 213.
Cato, Addison's, 31.
Catullus, Wilkes's, 124.
Cavallini, Pietro, 235.
Cecil Court, 174, 306, 307.
'Censorium,' Steele's, 108.
Centlivre, Mrs., 251.
Cipriani, J. B., 70, 75, 210.
Citizen of the World, Goldsmith's, 53.
Citizen, Murphy's, 188.
City Shower, Swift's, 256, 273.
Chalmers, Alexander, 152.
Chamberlain, The Lord, 200.
Chandos Street, 294.

General Index.

CHANGES AT CHARING CROSS, 233-252.
Chapel at Whitehall, 204, 206, 207.
Chapel Royal Choir Boys, 198.
Chapter of Accidents, Lee's, 132.
Charing Cross, 234, 237.
CHARING CROSS, CHANGES AT, 233-252.
Charing Cross Road, 294, 306.
Charles I., 195, 197, 200.
Charles I., statue of, 233.
Charles II., 197, 198, 200, 203, 205, 206, 211, 213.
Chatham, Lord, 128.
Chatto and Windus, Messrs., 296.
Chaumette, P. G., 186.
Cheere, Henry, 298.
Cheselden, the anatomist, 117.
Chester, Col. J. L., 3.
Chesterfield, Lord, 165.
'Chevalier' Taylor, 116-20.
Chichester, Bishop of, 204.
Chiffinch, Mr., 203.
Chippendale, Thomas, 312.
Christie, Mr., the auctioneer, 1.
Christie's, 1, 171.
Christmas, Gerard, 241.
Churchill, Charles, 38, 119.
Clairon, Mlle., 49.
Clandestine Marriage, Garrick and Colman's, 49.
Clare, Lord, 29.
Clarendon, Lord, 269.
Cleveland, Duchess of, 206.
Clive, Catherine, 129, 131, 132.
Coan, the Norfolk dwarf, 135.
Cock and Pye Fields, 293.
Cock Lane Ghost, The, 242.
Cockpit, The, 197.
Colbert, Charles, Marquis de Croissy, 211.
Collins, William, 38, 311.
Company of Undertakers, Hogarth's, 117.
Concannon, Mrs., 80.
Conduit Street, 1.
Confederacy, Vanbrugh's, 78.
Confectionary, The, at Whitehall, 207.
Congreve, 91, 279.

Conscious Lovers, Steele's, 107.
Constant Couple, Farquhar's, 85.
Consultation of Physicians, Hogarth's, 117.
Cook, Captain, 312.
Cooke, Captain Henry, 198.
Cook, Henry, 68.
Cook, Lieut.-Col., 25.
Cook, William, 139, 140.
Coquerel, M., 316, 320, 334.
Corbould, the elder, 177.
Cornaro Family, Titian's, 242.
Cornelys, Mrs. Teresa, 68, 70, 135.
Cossack trowsers of 1820, 223.
Cosway, 297.
Council Office, The, 200.
Cousens, 173.
Coverley, Sir Roger de, 198, 266, 308.
Cowper, William, 39, 111.
Cozens, Alexander, 75.
Cradock, Joseph, 43.
Cranham Church, 3, 27.
Cranham Hall, 26, 28.
Cranbourn Street, 294, 307, 309.
Cravat of 1820, The, 223.

C'ribbee Islands, The, 245, 247.
Crisis, Steele's, 106, 107.
Crockford House, Luttrell's 217, 230.
Croker, J. W., 137, 152-157, 171,
Croker's Boswell and Boswell, Fitzgerald's, 159.
Cromwell, Henry, 261, 262, 271.
Cromwell, Oliver, 250.
Crosse, Mrs. Andrew, 232.
Cross's Menagerie, 245.
Cruikshank, George, 84.
Crundale, Richard de, 235.
Cumberland, Richard, 124, 125, 162.
Cumberland, Duke of, 71, 164, 209.
Curtius, Haydon's, 311.
Curll, Edmund, 240.
Cutts, John, Lord, 90.

Dalrymple, Sir David, 165.
Danckers, Henry, 212.
D'Arblay, Mme., 162.
Darien, 18.
David, Jacques Louis, 183.
Davies, Thomas, 142.
Death on the Pale Horse, West's, 184.

Debates in Parliament, Johnson's, 171.
Decoy in St. James's Park, The, 198.
Debtors' Prisons, Committee into, 6, 7.
Delaval, Lord, 68.
Denis Duval, Characters in Thackeray's, 72.
Dennis, John, 262.
D'Eon, Chevalier, 69, 84, 136.
Derry, Settlement of, 10.
Deserted Village, Goldsmith's, 41, 43, 44, 46, 54, 59.
Dessessarts, 187.
Devil Tavern, Temple Bar, 258.
Devone, M., 238.
Dials in the Privy Garden, 200.
Diary, Sidney's, 203.
Didon, Piccinni's, 186.
Dilly, Edward, 321, 324.
Dione, Gay's, 277.
Distressed Mother, Philips', 188, 308.
✝ *Dr. Johnson, His Friends and his Critics*, Birkbeck Hill's, 165, 167.
Dodd, Dr., 73.

Dodd's Chapel, 164.
Donaldson, Mr., 136.
Double Transformation, Goldsmith's, 39.
Douglas, Vice-Admiral, 334.
Drummond's Bank, 251.
Drummer, Addison's, 86.
Dryden, John, 38, 171, 310.
Duchesnois, Mlle., 185, 187.
Duill, Mrs., 133.
Dugazon, 187.
Duke of York's Theatre, 298.
Dumont, M., 334.
Dunciad, Pope's, 137.
Duperrier, François, 206.
Dupont, Gainsborough, 173.
D'Urfey, Thomas, 266.
Dyer, 145.

Ebenezer, 14, 18, 21.
Ecole des Armes, Angelo's, 84.
Edward VI., Journal of, 204.
Edwin and Angelina, Goldsmith's, 43.
Election Entertainment, Hogarth's, 252.

Election of Gotham, Steele's, 95.
Elegy, Gray's, 38.
Ellis, Dr. Welbore, 89.
Elphinston, James, 142.
Elwin, Rev. Whitwell, 264.
ENGLISH ENGRAVER IN PARIS, AN, 173-193.
Entraigues, Countess d', 186.
Epigrammatical Petition, Gay's, 269.
Epistle to a Lady, Gay's, 270.
Epistle to Bernard Lintott, Gay's, 258, 261.
Erskine, Boswell's Letters to, 167.
Essay on Man, Pope's, 53.
Essay on Plantations, Oglethorpe's, 10.
Evelina, Miss Burney's, 83.
Evelyn, John, 205, 211, 214, 238, 241.
Examiner, The, 259.
Fables, Dryden's, 303.
Fables, Gay's, 280, 291, 292.
Fairholt, F. W., 309.
Fair Penitent, Rowe's, 130.
False Delicacy, Kelly's, 50, 51.
Fan, Gay's, 264, 265.
Faro's Daughters, Gillray's, 80.

Farren, Miss, 132.
Fausse Agnès, La, Destouches', 188.
Fawcett, the comedian, 116.
Fenton, 262, 277.
Fenton, Lavinia, 282.
Fêtes of July, The, 180.
Fielding, 57.
Fife House, 207.
Finden, 173.
Fisher, 173.
Fisher's plan of Whitehall, 196, 201, 207.
Fitzgerald, Mr. Percy, 157, 159, 160, 172.
Fitzherbert, Mrs., 79.
Five Fields, The, 2, 135.
Flaxman, 176, 178, 313.
Fleet, Rules or Liberties of the, 6.
Foote, 67, 69.
Forçats pour la Foi, Coquerel's, 316, 320, 321.
Ford, Major, 97.
Ford, Mr. Edward, 324.
Ford, Mr. J. W., 324.
Ford, Parson, 163.
Ford, Sir Richard, 213.
Fortescue, William, 257.
Fortescue, Mrs., 288.
Forster, John, 325, 326.
Foundling Chapel, 164.

Four Stages of Cruelty, Hogarth's, 74.
Fox, C. J., 185.
Frederica, 13, 18.
Friends' Meeting House, 298.
Funeral, Steele's, 85, 93.
Fuseli, Henry, 127, 302, 303.
Fuite du Camisard, La, 319.

Gainsborough, 70, 173.
Galleries at Whitehall, 203.
Gardel, Mme., 187.
Gaelic Language, Shaw's, 142.
Garrick, 69, 129, 163, 175.
Garrick Theatre, 295.
Garrick, Mrs., 29, 65, 73.
Garrick's nephews, 65.
Gascoigne, Henry, 88.
Gattie, Henry, 116.
Gay, John, 38, 66, 185, 253-292.
Gay's Chair, Baller's, 255.
Gay, Thomas, 254, 256.
Gay, William, 253.
Gentleman and Cabinet-Maker's Director, Chippendale's, 313.
Genteel Style in Writing, Lamb's, 53.

George II., Walpole's. 170.
Georgia, charter for colonizing, 10.
Georgia, founding of, 10.
Georgia, colonization of, 11-27.
Gérard, 184.
Gibbon, Edward, 119.
Gibbons, Grinling, 195, 240.
Gillray, James, 175.
Girodet, 184.
Goddess of Reason, The, 166.
Golden Cross, The, 244.
Goldsmith and Parnell, Poems of, 323.
Goldsmith House, 325.
Goldsmith, Lewis, 189.
Goldsmith, Life of, Forster's, 323.
Goldsmith, Life of, Prior's, 323.
Goldsmith, Oliver, 28, 29, 31, 33-60, 122, 139, 163, 242, 264, 311.
GOLDSMITH'S POEMS AND PLAYS, 33-60.
Goodall, 173.
Good-Natur'd Man, Goldsmith's, 48, 50-53.
Gordon Riots, 174, 175.

Goschen, Mr., 290.
Goujon, Jean, 179.
Grafton, Duke of, 200.
Granby, Marquis of, 81, 299, 300.
Grant, Sir Archibald, 8.
Grant, Col. Francis, 138.
Gray, Thomas, 38, 153.
Gravelot, 310.
Great Hall at Whitehall, 204.
Great Newport Street, 301, 302, 309.
Grecian Coffee House, 163.
Green Chamber at Whitehall, 203.
Green, Valentine, 173.
Greville, 217.
Griffiths, Ralph, 321, 328.
Gros, 184.
Grosvenor, Lady, 164.
GRUB STREET OF THE ARTS, THE, 293-314.
Guardian, The, 105.
Guérin, 184.
Grumbler, Goldsmith's, 58.
Gwinett, Ambrose, 246.
Gwydyr House, 196.
Gwynn, the painter, 84.

Hackman, Rev. James, 74.
Hall, Francis, 200.
Hall, John, 71, 175.
Handel, Roubillac's, 296.
Hampton Court, 209, 210.
Harrison, Major-General, 237.
Handsome Housemaid, Foote's, 56.
Hanmer, Miss, 254.
Hanmer, Rev. John, 256.
Harcourt, Lord, 276.
Harcourt, Sir William, 290.
Harley, 98, 198.
Harlot's Progress, Hogarth's, 305.
Hartshorne Lane, 235.
Hastings, Lady Elizabeth, 16.
Haunch of Venison, Goldsmith's, 44.
Hawkins, Sir John, 43, 144, 145, 146.
Haydon, B. R., 311.
Hayman, 77, 81, 297, 298, 299, 300, 310.
Hayman, Mrs., 300.
Hazlitt, 305.
Heath, 173.
Hebrides, Journal of a Tour to the, Boswell's, 143, 147, 148, 155, 156.
Hedge Lane, 234.
Hemings' Row, 244, 294.

Herbert, Rev. Henry, 11.
Hermit, Goldsmith's, 43, 53.
Hervart, M. and Mme. de, 286.
Hervey, Captain Augustus, 64.
Hervey, John Lord, 282.
Hill, Aaron, 257.
Hill, Dr. G. Birkbeck, 166, 172.
Hillispilli, the Creek War Captain, 14.
Hills, Henry, 257.
History of the Reformation, Burnet's, 204.
Hogarth, Mrs., 304, 306.
Hogarth, William, 63, 178, 282, 297, 305.
Holbein's Gate, 197, 208, 209.
Holcroft, Thomas, 190.
Holland, Lord, 217.
Hone, Nathaniel, 312.
Hook, Theodore, 81.
Horace, Maittaire's, 255.
Horace, Pine's, 310.
Horse Guards, 194, 195, 207.
Horse Guards Avenue, 195, 207.
Horse Guards Yard, 198, 207.

Howard, Mrs., 284.
Howe, Lord, 76.
Huggins, John, 306.
Huguenot Galley Slave, The, 320.
Human Life, Rogers's, 231.
Hummums, The, 163.
Humphry, Ozias, 127.
Hunter, John, 312.
Hyde, Lady Catherine, 278.
Hyde, Lady Jane, 268, 278.
Hyde, Mr., 201.

Importance of Dunkirk consider'd, Steele's, 106.
Importance of the 'Guardian' considered, Swift's, 106.
Impressment for the Navy, 9.
Ingres, 184.
Ireland, John, 176.
Ireland, Samuel, 2.
Irene, Johnson's, 130.
Iris, Goldsmith's lines to, 40.
Iron Chest, Colman's, 175.
Irving, Washington, 243.
Isabey, the miniaturist, 183.

Jackson, the prizefighter, 82.
James II., 195, 210.
James Street, 297.
Jansen, Bernard, 241.
Jardin des Plantes, 182.

Jeffery, 217.
Jekyll, 217.
Jermy, Captain Seth, 330-1.
Jervas, Charles, 278, 279.
Jesse, J. Heneage, 209.
Joannis Philippi Angli Responsio, Milton's, 251.
JOHN GAY, 253-292.
Johnson, Dr., 1, 4, 28, 31, 35, 50, 56, 72, 122, 128, 289, 304, 311, 313.
Johnson, Anecdotes of, Piozzi's, 143, 144.
Johnson, Boswell's, 138, 149.
Johnson, Boswell's (Globe Edition), 172.
Johnson, Boswell's (Birkbeck Hill's Edition), 166-172.
Johnson, Boswell's (Reynolds Edition), 165.
Johnson, Elizabeth, 64.
Johnson, Life of, Cook's, 139, 140.
Johnson, Life of, Hawkins's, 144-146.
Johnson, Life of, Murphy's, 162.
Johnson, Life of, Towers's, 146.
Johnson, Memoirs of, Shaw's, 142.
Johnson, Memoir of, Tyers's, 140.
Johnsonian Miscellanies, Birkbeck Hill's, 172.
Johnsoniana, Mrs. Napier's, 162.
Jonson, Ben, 211, 235.
Jordaens, 210.
Jordan, Mrs., 133.
Journal of a Tour to Corsica, Boswell's (Birkbeck Hill's Edition), 167.
Journal of a Voyage to Lisbon, Fielding's, 170.
Journey through England, Mackay's, 196.
Journey to Exeter, Gay's, 271, 272.
Journey to the Western Islands, Johnson's, 164.
Justice, Palais de, 191.

Kauffmann, Angelica, 242, 312.
Kean, Charles, 136.
Kean, Edmund, 82, 83.
Keble, William, 257.
Keith, Marshal, 118.
Kemble, Charles, 134.
Kemble, John, 133, 175, 188, 308.
Kemble, Stephen, 133.

Kelly, Hugh, 123.
Kenney, James, 228.
Kent, William, 194.
Kéroualle, Louise Renée de, 201, 203.
Keys, Dr., 63.
Kind der Liebe, Das, Kotzebue's, 136.
King, Dr., 117.
King's Gate, 208.
King Street, 197, 208.
Kirke, Mrs., 198.
Kneller, Sir Godfrey, 99, 301.

Ladies Library, Steele's, 108.
Lady's Last Stake, Hogarth's, 252.
La Fontaine, 119, 286.
Lais, François, 186.
Lallah Rookh, Moore's, 231.
Lamb, Charles, 192, 293, 298.
La Monnoye, 40.
Landor, W. S., 113.
Laporte, 188.
LATEST LIFE OF STEELE, THE, 85-114.
Lauderdale, Earl of, 201.
Lauderdale, Earl of, 231.
Laughton, Prof. J. K., 330.

Layer, Counsellor Christopher, 119.
Lays, François, 186.
Letters, Johnson's (Birkbeck Hill's), 172.
LETTERS TO JULIA, LUTTRELL'S, 216-232.
Letters to Julia, Luttrell's, 217.
Letter to Lord Halifax, Addison's, 41.
Le Imaginator, Alexander, 236.
Lenoir, Alexandre, 192.
Le Sœur, Herbert, 239.
Liar, Foote's, 78.
Life of the Chevalier John Taylor, 118.
Lilly, William, 237.
Lincoln, Earl of, 279.
Linnæus, 119.
'Lion d'Argent' at Calais, 192.
Lisburn, Lord, 46.
Liston, 175.
Literary Illustrations, Nichols', 138.
'Little Dickey' (Henry Norris), 85.
Little St. Andrew Street, 293.
Liviez, M., 66.

Lives of the Poets, Theophilus Cibber's, 162.
Lloyd, Robert, 240.
Locker Lampson, F., 230.
Locket's Ordinary, 251.
Lockhart, 155.
Logicians Refuted, 39.
London and Wise, Nurserymen, 212.
London County Council, 250, 252.
London, Johnson's, 28, 311.
London, Pennant's, 209.
Long Acre, 293, 294, 309.
Longfellow, 39.
Lord Keeper's Office at Whitehall, 200.
Lort, Michael, 138.
Louisa, Princess, 281.
Loutherbourg, Philip de, 70.
Louvre, The, 182, 185.
Lovers' Vows, Inchbald's, 136.
Lowe, Mauritius, 162.
Lowndes, Thomas, 83.
Lucas's Foot, 91.
Lucas, Lord, 93.
Luck, Robert, 254.
Luttrell, Colonel, 232.
Luttrell, Henry, 136, 216.
LUTTRELL'S LETTERS TO JULIA, 216-232.

Lying Lover, Steele's, 94.
Lyra Elegantiarum, Locker Lampson's, 230.

Macaulay, Lord, 85, 152, 156, 159.
McArdell, 173, 310.
Mackintosh, 217.
Macklin, Charles, 130.
Maclean, James, 136.
Macpherson, James, 142.
Madame Blaize, Goldsmith's, 40.
Mad Dog, Goldsmith's, 40.
Maginn, 246.
Maillard, Mlle., 186.
Mainwaring, Arthur, 98.
Mallet, David, 169.
Malone, 143, 144, 145, 147, 150, 151, 152, 154.
Manley, Mrs., 96, 97, 98, 108.
Man of Taste, Bramston's, 304.
Mansfield Park, Austen's, 136.
Mapp, Mrs. Sarah, 117.
Marchi, Giuseppe, 301.
Marengo, Bonaparte's Arab, 181.
Marlborough, Henrietta, Duchess of, 283, 285.

'Marquis of Granby' Inn, 300.
Marriage A-la-Mode, Hogarth's, 297.
Mars, Mlle., 188.
Marteilhe, Jean, 316-334.
MARTEILHE'S MEMOIRS, 315-334.
Massareene, Lord, 68.
Matthews, the actor, 116, 175.
May's Buildings, 300, 314.
Mazarin, Duchess of, 206.
MEMOIRS, MARTEILHE'S, 315-334.
Memoirs d'un Protestant, Marteilhe's, 315-334.
Memoirs of a Protestant, Marteilhe's, 315-334.
Ménagiana, 39.
Menzel, 14.
Metastasio, 119.
Mews Gate Public House, 246.
Mews Gate, Upper and Lower, 246.
Mews, King's or Royal, 244, 245.
Michelet, 317.
Mitchel, the banker, 75.
Mildmay, Carew Harvey, 2.

Milner, Dr., 325.
Milton, John, 250.
Minor, Foote's, 78.
Misaubin, Dr. John, 304, 305.
Miscellany, Lintott's, 261.
Mock Doctor, Fielding's, 304.
Mohocks, Gay's, 262.
Moira, Lord, 76.
Monarch, Angelo's horse, 70.
Moncrieff, the dramatist, 116.
Monsey, Dr. Messenger, 122.
Monmouth, Duke of, 198.
Monmouth, Duchess of, 268.
Montorgueil, Rue, 179.
'MONSIEUR TONSON,' THE AUTHOR OF, 115-136.
Montgomery, Philip, Earl of, 248.
Monvel, 187.
Moore, Arthur, 180.
Moore, Thomas, 217, 230, 231, 232.
More, Hannah, 29, 30, 162.
Morel-Fatio, M., 320.
Morley, Prof. Henry, 166.
Morning, Swift's, 273, 274.

Morning's Walk from London to Kew, Phillips's, 186.
Morris, Mr. Mowbray, 172.
Moser, Michael, 297, 310.
Motte, M. de la, 72.
Motet, the fencer, 67.
Murray, Mr. John, 82, 282.
Murray, Sir Robert, 200.

Napier, Mrs., 141, 144.
Napier, Rev. A., 141, 157, 160, 165.
National Gallery, 244, 247.
National Portrait Gallery, 244.
Neapolitan Club, 74.
Nelson's Column, 247.
New Bath Guide, Anstey's, 44, 45.
Newport Street, 294.
New Simile, Goldsmith's, 39.
New Street, 313.
Nightingale Monument, 312.
'Nightingale,' The Captain of the, 329, 330, 331.
Night, Hogarth's, 251.
Nightmare, Fuseli's, 302.
Night Thoughts, Young's, 38.

Nivernais, Duke de, 61.
Noctes Ambrosianæ, 219.
Nollekens, 297.
Normanby, Marquis of, 197.
Norris, Henry, 85.
Northcote, 128, 170, 176.
North, Mr. Robert, 16.
Northampton House, 241.
Northumberland, Algernon Percy, Earl of, 241.
Northumberland Avenue, 293.
Northumberland, Duke of, 242.
Northumberland, Henry Howard, Earl of, 241.
Northumberland House, 233, 234, 241, 243, 293.
Northumberland Street, 235.

Oates, Titus, 240.
Œdipus and his Daughters, Fuseli's, 302.
Ogilvie, Sir James, 214, 336.
Oglethorpe, General James Edward, 1-32.
Oglethorpe, Sir Theophilus, 5.
Oglethorpe, Mrs., 26.
Oldfield, Mrs., 308.

General Index.

OLD WHITEHALL, 194-215.
Oldys, William, 120.
Opera, The Grand, 186.
Opie, 127, 176, 178, 190.
Ophthalmiater, 117.
Orange Coffee House, 83.
Ormond, Duke of, 88, 90, 198.
Osbaldeston, Simon, 249.
Osborn, Mrs., 278.
Ossian controversy, 142.
Owen of Glassalt, 99, 100.
Oxford, Lord, 268, 269.

Paine, Thomas, 190, 191.
PALADIN OF PHILANTHROPY, A, 1.
Palmer, Jack, 134.
Palmer, Mrs., 237.
Pantheon, The, 164.
Paoli, General, 69.
Parliament Street, 194, 209.
Parnell, Goldsmith's Life of, 41.
Parr's Bank, 295.
Parr, Dr., 122, 123.
Parsons of the Cock Lane Ghost, 240.
Pass at St. Martin's Lane, 294, 313.

Pasquin, Fielding's, 50.
Paumier, M. H., 320, 333, 334.
Payne, Tom, 246.
Peckham Academy, 325.
Pelham, Henry, 170.
Pelham, Ode on Mr., Garrick's, 169.
Pembroke and Montgomery, Earl of, 197.
Pembroke, Henry Herbert, Earl of, 63, 89.
Pepys, Samuel, 212, 227.
Percy, 138, 145, 162, 242, 247.
Perceval, Sir John, 110.
Persian Tales, Philips's, 208.
Peterborough, Lord, 30, 31, 201.
Peters, Rev. M. W., 127.
Petits-Augustins, Couvent des, 192.
Peters Court, 295, 296, 297, 298, 301, 312.
Petis de la Croix, 308.
PHILANTHROPY, A PALADIN OF, 1.
Philips, Ambrose, 265, 266, 307, 308, 309.
Physicians, College of, 247.
Piazza in Covent Garden, 164.

A A

Pictorial Conjurer, Hone's, 312.
Pindar, Peter, 75, 124, 125, 127, 132.
'Pine Apple' in New Street, 315.
Pine, John, 310.
Pic Nic Society, The, 79.
Piozzi, Mrs., 143, 144, 162.
'Plagiary, Sir Fretful,' 125.
POEMS AND PLAYS, GOLDSMITH'S, 33-60.
Poems (1720), Gay's, 276.
Poems for Young Ladies, Goldsmith's, 43.
Poetical Miscellany, Steele's, 265.
Poetry, Essay on, Temple's, 53.
Polite Learning, Goldsmith's, 37, 41, 49, 53.
Pöllnitz, 118.
Polly, Gay's, 283-285.
Pope, Alexander, 17, 29, 38, 39, 119, 137, 170, 261, 262, 266, 275, 276, 279, 280, 283, 287, 289, 310.
Portland, Earl of, 215.
Portsmouth, Duchess of, 201, 203, 206.
Powell, Mr., 52, 304.

Publick Spirit of the Whigs, Swift's, 106.
Pulteney, 276.
Pulchinello's booth, 238.
Purdon, Epitaph on, Goldsmith's, 40.
Practice of Christianity, Wilson's, 21.
Præterita, Ruskin's, 171.
Present State of Wit, Gay's, 259, 261.
Préville, the actor, 67.
Prince Arthur, Blackmore's, 260.
Pritchard, Mrs., 129.
Prior, Matthew, 251.
Privy Council Office, The, 198.
Privy Garden, The, 200, 201.
Privy Stairs, 205, 213.
Procession, Steele's, 90.
Pryor, Samuel, 251.
Psalmanazar, George, 171.
Pyne, W. H. (Ephraim Hardcastle), 81, 244, 299.

Queen Anne, Burton's, 255.
Queensberry, Charles, Duke of, 66, 254, 278, 284, 285.

General Index.

Queensberry, Duchess of, 66, 278, 284, 285, 288.
Quin, James, 130, 131.
'Quisquilius' (Baker), 176.

Raimbach, Abraham, 173-193, 307.
Raimbach, Eliza, 193.
Ramble from Richmond to London, Steele, 294.
Ramsay, Allan, 297.
Ranelagh, 164.
Rawlins, Sophia, 303.
Raymond, Mr. Samuel, 163.
Rayner, William, 254.
Reay, Martha, 74.
Read, Nicholas, 312.
Records of My Life, Taylor's, 121.
Redas, the fencer, 83.
Reed, Isaac, 323.
Reflections on the French Revolution, Burke's, 128.
Reliques of Ancient Poetry, Percy's, 43.
REMINISCENCES, ANGELO'S, 61-84.
Regicides, The, 237, 238.
Retaliation, Goldsmith's, 44.
Revolution of 1688, Fox's, 185.

Reynolds, Sir Joshua, 128, 145, 149, 151, 162, 170, 171, 174, 297, 300, 301.
Reynolds, Frances, 301, 302.
Rhenish Wine House, 251.
Rich, Christopher, 95.
Rich, Manager, 282, 285.
Richmond Terrace, 196, 201.
Rivals, Sheridan's, 57.
'Rivella' (Mrs. Manley), 96.
Rivett, John, 239.
Robe Chamber at Whitehall, 203.
Robespierre, 183.
Rogers, Samuel, 1, 217, 218, 219.
Rose, Dr., of Chiswick, 64.
Rose, John, 212.
Roubillac, 66, 296, 297, 298, 310, 312.
Roustan, The Mameluke, 181.
Rouquet, 310.
Rubens, P. P., 210.
Rudd, Mrs. Margaret, 72.
Rummer Tavern, 251.
Rupert, Prince, 201.

Rural Sports, Gay's, 263, 264.
Ruskin, 171.
Rowlandson, Thomas, 75, 76, 83, 84.
Rowley, 245.
Royal Academy, 297.
Royal United Service Institution, 195.

Sabines, The, David's, 183.
Sailor's Advocate, Oglethorpe's, 9.
St. Augustine, 18, 22, 23, 25.
St. Antoine, M., 245.
Saint Huberty, Mme., 186.
St. James's Park, 196.
St. James's Palace, 197.
St. Martin's Lane, 293-314.
St. Martin's Lane Academy, 296, 297.
St. Martin's Lane, Upper, 312.
St. Martin's Church, 314.
St. Martin's Court, 307.
St. Martin's Free Library, 295.
St. Simon's Island, 13, 18, 19, 22, 23, 24.

Salzburg Protestants, The, 13.
Sandby, Thomas, 209.
Sandwich, Lord, 212.
Satchell, Miss, 133.
Savage, Richard, 109, 110.
Savannah, 12, 18.
Saxe, Marshal, 118.
Schicksal der Protestanten in Franckreich, Raimbach's, 318, 321.
Scotland Yard, 196, 206.
Scottish Office, 207.
Scribleriad, Cambridge's, 125.
Scriblerus Club, 268.
Scurlock, Miss Mary (Mrs. Steele), 98, 99.
Scurlock, Mrs., 101, 102.
Senauki, wife of Tomo Chichi, 14.
Sentimental Comedy, 49, 53, 54.
Sermons, Foster's, 165.
Siddons, Mrs., 126, 133.
Sigismunda, Hogarth's, 252.
Slaughter, Thomas, 309.
Slaughter's, Old, 307, 309, 310, 311, 312.
Slaughter's, Young or New, 307, 309.

General Index.   357

Sleeping Congregation, Hogarth's, 267.
Sleep Walker, Lady Craven's, 79.
Sloane, Sir Hans, 18.
Smeaton, 312.
Smirke, 177.
Smirke, Sir Robert, 211.
Smirke, Sydney, 207.
Smith, Adam, 162.
Smith, Sydney, 217.
Smith, Captain Thomas, 331-332.
Shaw, Rev. William, 142.
Shepherd's Week, Gay's, 265-268, 308.
Sheppard, Jack, 118, 240.
She Stoops to Conquer, Goldsmith's, 55-58, 59, 60.
Sheraton, Thomas, 313.
Sheridan, R. B., 69, 125, 175, 176.
Sheridan, Tom, 69, 78.
Short View of the Immorality and Profaneness of the English Stage, Collier's, 94.
Shuter, Edward, 80.
Society of Artists, 252.
Soubise, Lady Queensberry's black, 75.
South, Robert, 204.

South American Ode, Goldsmith's, 40.
Spectator, The, 104, 105, 259, 260.
Spirit of Johnson, Morley's, 166.
Splendid Shilling, Philips's, 258.
Spring Gardens, 196, 198, 234, 248, 249.
Spunging-houses, 6.
Stage, The, Taylor's, 134.
Steevens, George, 176, 276.
Steele, 85-114, 259, 260, 294, 295, 308.
Steele, Life of, Aitken's, 86-114.
Steele, Mrs., 98, 99, 101, 102, 103, 107.
Steele, Richard, the elder, 88.
STEELE, THE LATEST LIFE OF, 85-114.
Stillingfleet, Edward, 204.
Stone Gallery at Whitehall, 201, 202.
Storace, Stephen, 175, 176.
Stothard, Thomas, 173.
Stratford Jubilee, The, 65.
Stretch, Margaret, 97.
Strolling Actresses, Hogarth's, 303.

Strype, John, 293, 294, 295.
Stubbs, George, 70.
Suffolk House, 241.
Sullivan, Luke, 310.
Sunderland, Lady, .
Superville, Daniel de, 316.
Superville, M., 334.
Sussex, Duke of, 74.
Suspicious Husband, Hoadly's, 163.
'Suspirius,' Johnson's, 52.
Swift, Jonathan, 104, 109, 137, 257, 259, 264, 273, 277, 278, 279, 280, 281, 282, 287, 288.
Sydney Smith, Lady Holland's, 218.
Symes, Elinor, 88.

Taine, H., 286.
Tales of the Genii, Cooke's, 176.
Talking Oak, Tennyson's, 44.
Talma, 188.
Taste, Foote's, 68, 314.
Tatler, The, 104, 259, 260.
Taylor, John (1), 116-20.
Taylor, John (2), 120.
Taylor, John (3), 120-1.
Taylor, John Stirling, 121.

Tedder, H. R., 138, 159.
Teillagory, 62.
Temple, , 150.
Tender Husband, Steele's, 85, 94, 95.
Tennis Court, 198.
Thackeray, 185, 309.
Theatre at Whitehall, 203.
Théâtre de la Republique, 185.
Théâtre de la Republique et des Arts, 186.
Théâtre Français, 185.
Théâtre, Picart's, 188.
Theodore of Corsica, 119.
'Thomas Paine Exhibition,' The, 191.
Thomson, James, 251.
Thornhill, Sir James, 8, 298, 299, 300, 304.
Thrale, Mrs., 144, 147.
Three Hours after Marriage, Gay's, 275.
Threnodia Augustalis, 44.
Thurston, John, 177.
Tickell, Thomas, 265.
Titania, Fuseli's, 303.
Tilt Yard, 198, 207.
Titi, History of Prince, 162.
Tofts, Mary, 118.
Tom Jones à Londres, Desforges, 189.

Tom Jones, Poinsinet's, 189.
Tomo-Chichi, King of Yamacrow, 14, 15.
Tooanahowi, 14, 15.
Tom's Coffee-house, 296.
Town Talk, Steele's, 96.
Trafalgar Square, 294.
Trafalgar Square Theatre, 298.
Traveller, Goldsmith's, 36, 41, 44, 46, 47, 59, 138.
Travels, Hentzner's, 210.
Travels and Adventures of the Chevalier John Taylor, 118.
Travels in France, Holcroft's, 190.
Treasury, The, 198, 200.
Treatise on Human Knowledge, Berkeley's, 110.
Tree, Ellen, 136, 231.
Tree, Maria (Mrs. Bradshaw), 136.
Tremamondo, D. A. M., 61-84.
Tribunat, Palais du, 189.
Trivia, Gay's, 245, 273-275.
Trotter, Thomas, 139.
Trusler, Dr., 304.
Tuileries, The, 180.
Tullibardine, Earl of, 214.

Turner, J. M. W., 173, 178.
Tyers, Jonathan, 140, 299.
Tyers, Tom, 140, 141, 162.

Underhill, John, 253, 263, 264.
Union Club, 235.

Vane Room at Whitehall, 203.
Vanity Fair, Thackeray's, 309.
Van Nost, John, 298.
Van Nost of Piccadilly, 298.
Van Woortz, M., 317.
Vauxhall Gardens, 296, 298, 299.
Vidal, François, 317, 318.
Venetian Senators, Evelyn's, 242.
Vernet, Carle, 183.
Vernet, Horace, 183.
Venice Preserved, Otway's, 131.
Verelst, William, 14.
Vernes, M. Felix, 317, 318.
Vestris, the elder, 187.
Vetusta Monumenta, 209.

Vicar of Wakefield, Goldsmith's, 43, 47, 59.
Village Politicians, Wilkie's, 193.
Viner, Sir Robert, 239.
Vitruvius Britannicus, Campbell's, 194.
Voltaire, 119.

Wake, Dr., Archbishop of Canterbury, 15.
Walesby, F. P., 152.
Wales, Diary of a Tour in, Johnson's, 158.
Walker, Dr. Thomas, 88.
Waller, Edmund, 233, 236.
Wallingford House, 248, 249.
Walpole, Horace, 8, 29, 30, 119, 131, 132, 153, 212, 242, 303.
Walpole, Sir Robert, 279, 282.
Warburton, Bishop, 131.
Ward, Dr. Joshua, 117.
Wardrobe at Whitehall, The, 206.
Ware, Isaac, 310.
Warton, Joseph, 31.
Watson, 173.
Watch-House, St. Martin's, 314.

Wesley, Charles, 17, 19.
Wesley, John, 17, 19-20.
West, Benjamin, 127, 176, 178, 184.
Westall, Richard, 176.
Welcome from Greece, Gay's, 291, 292.
Western Islands, Journey to the, Johnson's, 147.
West Indian, Cumberland's, 54.
Westminster County Court, 307.
Westminster, Smith's, 209.
Weston, Lord High Treasurer, 239.
Wenzel, Baron de, 120.
Wife of Bath, Gay's, 264.
Wild, Jonathan, 119.
Wilkes, John, 69, 124.
Wilkie, Sir David, 173, 193, 307, 310.
Wilkins, William, 247.
William, Fort, 24.
Willington, James, 322, 325, 327.
Willmore, J. T., 173.
Wills, W. H., 89.
Wilson, Dr. (the Manx bishop), 21.
Wilson, Richard, 77, 127, 173, 297, 310.

General Index.

Wine and Walnuts, Pyne's, 244.
Wine Cellar at Whitehall, 207.
What D'ye Call It, Gay's, 271.
Whitefield, George, 20, 25.
Whitefoord, Caleb, 124.
Whitehall, Burning of, 335-336.
Whitehall Court, 194, 207.
Whitehall Gardens, 196.
WHITEHALL, OLD, 194-215.
Whitehall Palace Stairs, 203, 204, 206.
Whitehall Yard, 207.

Woffington, Mrs. Margaret, 62.
Wolcot, Dr., 124.
Woodward, Henry, 163.
Wooilett, William, 173, 175.
Word to the Wise, Kelly's, 54.
Worlidge, Thomas, 120.
Wortley-Montagu, Lady Mary, 276.
Wright, Richard, of Lichfield, 162.
Wright, Mr. Robert, 3.

York, Duke of, 203, 204.

Zoffany, 70, 71, 297.

CHISWICK PRESS:—CHARLES WHITTINGHAM AND CO.
TOOKS COURT, CHANCERY LANE, LONDON.

AN ALPHABETICAL CATALOGUE
OF BOOKS IN FICTION AND GENERAL LITERATURE
PUBLISHED BY
CHATTO & WINDUS
111 ST. MARTIN'S LANE
CHARING CROSS
LONDON, W.C.
[MAR. 1899.]

About (Edmond).—The Fellah: An Egyptian Novel. Translated by Sir RANDAL ROBERTS. Post 8vo, illustrated boards, 2s.

Adams (W. Davenport), Works by.
A Dictionary of the Drama: being a comprehensive Guide to the Plays, Playwrights, Players, and Playhouses of the United Kingdom and America, from the Earliest Times to the Present Day. Crown 8vo, half-bound, 12s. 6d. [*Preparing.*
Quips and Quiddities. Selected by W. DAVENPORT ADAMS. Post 8vo, cloth limp, 2s. 6d.

Agony Column (The) of 'The Times,' from 1800 to 1870. Edited with an Introduction, by ALICE CLAY. Post 8vo, cloth limp, 2s. 6d.

Aidé (Hamilton), Novels by. Post 8vo, illustrated boards, 2s. each.
Carr of Carrlyon. | Confidences.

Alden (W. L.).—A Lost Soul: Being the Confession and Defence of Charles Lindsay. Fcap. 8vo, cloth boards, 1s. 6d.

Alexander (Mrs.), Novels by. Post 8vo, illustrated boards, 2s. each.
Maid, Wife, or Widow? | Valerie's Fate. | Blind Fate.
Crown 8vo, cloth, 3s. 6d. each; post 8vo, picture boards, 2s. each.
A Life Interest. | Mona's Choice. | By Woman's Wit.

Allen (F. M.).—Green as Grass. Crown 8vo, cloth, 3s. 6d.

Allen (Grant), Works by. Crown 8vo, cloth, 6s. each.
The Evolutionist at Large. | Moorland Idylls.
Post-Prandial Philosophy. Crown 8vo, art linen, 3s. 6d.

Crown 8vo, cloth extra, 3s. 6d. each; post 8vo, illustrated boards, 2s. each.
Babylon. 12 Illustrations. | The Devil's Die. | The Duchess of Powysland.
Strange Stories. Frontis. | This Mortal Coil. | Blood Royal.
The Beckoning Hand. | The Tents of Shem. Frontis. | Ivan Greet's Masterpiece.
For Maimie's Sake. | The Great Taboo. | The Scallywag. 24 Illusts.
Philistia. | Dumaresq's Daughter. | At Market Value.
In all Shades. | Under Sealed Orders. |

Dr. Palliser's Patient. Fcap. 8vo, cloth boards, 1s. 6d.

Anderson (Mary).—Othello's Occupation. Crown 8vo, cloth, 3s. 6d.

Antipodean (The): An Australasian Annual. Edited by A. B. PATERSON and G. ESSEX EVANS. Medium 8vo, with Illustrations, 1s.

Arnold (Edwin Lester), Stories by.
The Wonderful Adventures of Phra the Phœnician. Crown 8vo, cloth extra, with 12 Illustrations by H. M. PAGET, 3s. 6d.; post 8vo, illustrated boards, 2s.
The Constable of St. Nicholas. With Frontispiece by S. L. WOOD. Crown 8vo, cloth, 3s. 6d.

Artemus Ward's Works. With Portrait and Facsimile. Crown 8vo, cloth extra, 3s. 6d.—Also a POPULAR EDITION post 8vo, picture boards, 2s.

Ashton (John), Works by. Crown 8vo, cloth extra, 7s. 6d. each.
History of the Chap-Books of the 18th Century. With 334 Illustrations.
Humour, Wit, and Satire of the Seventeenth Century. With 82 Illustrations.
English Caricature and Satire on Napoleon the First. With 115 Illustrations.
Modern Street Ballads. With 57 Illustrations.
Social Life in the Reign of Queen Anne. With 85 Illustrations. Crown 8vo, cloth, 3s. 6d.

2 CHATTO & WINDUS, Publishers, 111 St. Martin's Lane, London, W.C.

Bacteria, Yeast Fungi, and Allied Species, A Synopsis of. By W. B. GROVE, B.A. With 87 Illustrations. Crown 8vo, cloth extra, 3s. 6d.

Bardsley (Rev. C. Wareing, M.A.), Works by.
English Surnames: Their Sources and Significations. Crown 8vo, cloth, 7s. 6d.
Curiosities of Puritan Nomenclature. Crown 8vo, cloth, 3s. 6d.

Baring Gould (Sabine, Author of 'John Herring,' &c.), Novels by.
Crown 8vo, cloth extra, 3s. 6d. each; post 8vo, illustrated boards, 2s. each.
Red Spider. | Eve.

Barr (Robert: Luke Sharp), Stories by: Cr. 8vo, cl., 3s. 6d. each.
In a Steamer Chair. With Frontispiece and Vignette by DEMAIN HAMMOND.
From Whose Bourne, &c. With 47 Illustrations by HAL HURST and others.
Revenge! With 12 Illustrations by LANCELOT SPEED and others.
A Woman Intervenes. Crown 8vo, cloth, with 8 Illustrations by HAL HURST, 3s. 6d.

Barrett (Frank), Novels by.
Post 8vo, illustrated boards, 2s. each; cloth, 2s. 6d. each.
Fettered for Life.
The Sin of Olga Zassoulich.
Between Life and Death.
Folly Morrison. | Honest Davie.
Little Lady Linton.
A Prodigal's Progress.
John Ford; and His Helpmate.
A Recoiling Vengeance.
Lieut. Barnabas. | Found Guilty.
For Love and Honour.
Crown 8vo, cloth, 3s. 6d. each; post 8vo, picture boards, 2s each; cloth limp, 2s. 6d. each.
The Woman of the Iron Bracelets. | The Harding Scandal.
A Missing Witness. With 8 Illustrations by W. H. MARGETSON.
Was She Justified? Crown 8vo, cloth, gilt top, 6s.
Under a Strange Mask. With 19 Illustrations by E. F. BREWTNALL. Crown 8vo, cloth, 3s. 6d.

Barrett (Joan).—Monte Carlo Stories. Fcap. 8vo, cloth, 1s. 6d.

Beaconsfield, Lord. By T. P. O'CONNOR, M.P. Cr. 8vo, cloth, 5s.

Beauchamp (Shelsley).—Grantley Grange. Post 8vo, boards, 2s.

Besant (Sir Walter) and James Rice, Novels by.
Crown 8vo, cloth extra, 3s. 6d. each; post 8vo, illustrated boards, 2s. each; cloth limp, 2s. 6d. each.
Ready-Money Mortiboy.
My Little Girl.
With Harp and Crown.
This Son of Vulcan.
The Golden Butterfly.
The Monks of Thelema.
By Celia's Arbour.
The Chaplain of the Fleet.
The Seamy Side.
The Case of Mr. Lucraft, &c.
'Twas in Trafalgar's Bay, &c.
The Ten Years' Tenant, &c.
*** There is also a LIBRARY EDITION of the above Twelve Volumes, handsomely set in new type on a large crown 8vo page, and bound in cloth extra, 6s. each; and a POPULAR EDITION of **The Golden Butterfly**, medium 8vo, 6d.; cloth, 1s.

Besant (Sir Walter), Novels by.
Crown 8vo, cloth extra, 3s. 6d. each; post 8vo, illustrated boards, 2s. each; cloth limp, 2s. 6d. each.
All Sorts and Conditions of Men. With 12 Illustrations by FRED. BARNARD.
The Captains' Room, &c. With Frontispiece by E. J. WHEELER.
All in a Garden Fair. With 6 Illustrations by HARRY FURNISS.
Dorothy Forster. With Frontispiece by CHARLES GREEN.
Uncle Jack, and other Stories. | Children of Gibeon.
The World Went Very Well Then. With 12 Illustrations by A. FORESTIER.
Herr Paulus: His Rise, his Greatness, and his Fall. | The Bell of St. Paul's.
For Faith and Freedom. With Illustrations by A. FORESTIER and F. WADDY.
To Call Her Mine, &c. With 9 Illustrations by A. FORESTIER.
The Holy Rose, &c. With Frontispiece by F. BARNARD.
Armorel of Lyonesse: A Romance of To-day. With 12 Illustrations by F. BARNARD.
St. Katherine's by the Tower. With 12 Illustrations by C. GREEN.
Verbena Camellia Stephanotis, &c. With a Frontispiece by GORDON BROWNE.
The Ivory Gate. | The Rebel Queen.
Beyond the Dreams of Avarice. With 12 Illustrations by W. H. HYDE.
In Deacon's Orders, &c. With Frontispiece by A. FORESTIER. | The Revolt of Man.
The Master Craftsman. | The City of Refuge.
A Fountain Sealed. With Frontispiece by H. G. BURGESS. Crown 8vo, cloth, 3s. 6d.
The Orange Girl. Crown 8vo, cloth, gilt top, 6s. [Preparing.
All Sorts and Conditions of Men. CHEAP POPULAR EDITION, medium 8vo, 6d.; cloth, 1s.; or bound with the POPULAR EDITION of **The Golden Butterfly**, cloth, 2s.

The Charm, and other Drawing-room Plays. By Sir WALTER BESANT and WALTER H. POLLOCK With 50 Illustrations by CHRIS HAMMOND and JULE GOODMAN. Crown 8vo, cloth, gilt edges, 6s.; or blue cloth, to range with the Uniform Edition of Sir WALTER BESANT'S Novels, 3s. 6d.

Fifty Years Ago. With 144 Illustrations. Crown 8vo, cloth, 3s. 6d.
The Eulogy of Richard Jefferies. With Portrait. Crown 8vo, cloth, 6s.
London. With 125 Illustrations. Demy 8vo, cloth, 7s. 6d.
Westminster. With Etched Frontispiece by F. S. WALKER, R.E., and 130 Illustrations by WILLIAM PATTEN and others. Demy 8vo, cloth, 7s. 6d.
South London. With Etched Frontispiece by F. S. WALKER, R.E., and 118 Illustrations Demy 8vo, cloth, gilt top, 18s.
Sir Richard Whittington. With Frontispiece. Crown 8vo, art linen, 3s. 6d.
Gaspard de Coligny. With a Portrait. Crown 8vo, art linen, 3s. 6d.

CHATTO & WINDUS, Publishers, 111 St. Martin's Lane, London, W.C. 3

Bechstein (Ludwig).—As Pretty as Seven, and other German Stories. With Additional Tales by the Brothers GRIMM, and 98 Illustrations by RICHTER. Square 8vo, cloth extra, 6s. 6d.; gilt edges, 7s. 6d.

Bellew (Frank).—The Art of Amusing: A Collection of Graceful Arts, Games, Tricks, Puzzles, and Charades. With 300 Illustrations. Crown 8vo, cloth extra, 4s. 6d.

Bennett (W. C., LL.D.).—Songs for Sailors. Post 8vo, cl. limp, 2s.

Bewick (Thomas) and his Pupils. By AUSTIN DOBSON. With 95 Illustrations. Square 8vo, cloth extra, 6s.

Bierce (Ambrose).—In the Midst of Life: Tales of Soldiers and Civilians. Crown 8vo, cloth extra, 3s. 6d.; post 8vo, illustrated boards, 2s.

Bill Nye's Comic History of the United States. With 146 Illustrations by F. OPPER. Crown 8vo, cloth extra, 3s. 6d.

Biré (Edmond). — Diary of a Citizen of Paris during 'The Terror.' Translated and Edited by JOHN DE VILLIERS. With 2 Photogravure Portraits. Two Vols., demy 8vo, cloth, 21s.

Blackburn's (Henry) Art Handbooks.
Academy Notes, 1898.
Academy Notes, 1875-79. Complete in One Vol., with 600 Illustrations. Cloth, 6s.
Academy Notes, 1880-84. Complete in One Vol., with 700 Illustrations. Cloth, 6s.
Academy Notes, 1890-94. Complete in One Vol., with 800 Illustrations. Cloth, 7s. 6d.
Grosvenor Notes, Vol. I., 1877-82. With 300 Illustrations. Demy 8vo, cloth, 6s.
Grosvenor Notes, Vol. II., 1883-87. With 300 Illustrations. Demy 8vo, cloth, 6s.
Grosvenor Notes, Vol. III., 1888-90. With 230 Illustrations. Demy 8vo cloth, 3s. 6d.
The New Gallery, 1888-1892. With 250 Illustrations. Demy 8vo, cloth, 6s.
English Pictures at the National Gallery. With 114 Illustrations. 1s.
Old Masters at the National Gallery. With 128 Illustrations. 1s. 6d.
Illustrated Catalogue to the National Gallery. With 242 Illusts. Demy 8vo, cloth, 3s.

The Illustrated Catalogue of the Paris Salon, 1898. With 300 Sketches, 3s.

Blind (Mathilde), Poems by.
The Ascent of Man. Crown 8vo, cloth, 5s.
Dramas in Miniature. With a Frontispiece by F. MADOX BROWN. Crown 8vo, cloth, 5s.
Songs and Sonnets. Fcap. 8vo vellum and gold, 5s.
Birds of Passage: Songs of the Orient and Occident. Second Edition. Crown 8vo, linen, 6s. net.

Bourget (Paul).—A Living Lie. Translated by JOHN DE VILLIERS. With special Preface for the English Edition. Crown 8vo, cloth, 3s. 6d.

Bourne (H. R. Fox), Books by.
English Merchants: Memoirs in Illustration of the Progress of British Commerce. With 32 Illustrations. Crown 8vo, cloth, 3s. 6d.
English Newspapers: Chapters in the History of Journalism. Two Vols., demy 8vo, cloth, 25s.
The Other Side of the Emin Pasha Relief Expedition. Crown 8vo, cloth, 6s.

Boyle (Frederick), Works by. Post 8vo, illustrated bds., 2s. each.
Chronicles of No-Man's Land. | Camp Notes. | Savage Life.

Brand (John).—Observations on Popular Antiquities; chiefly illustrating the Origin of our Vulgar Customs, Ceremonies, and Superstitions. With the Additions of Sir HENRY ELLIS, and numerous Illustrations. Crown 8vo, cloth extra, 7s. 6d.

Brayshaw (J. Dodsworth).—Slum Silhouettes: Stories of London Life. Crown 8vo, cloth, 3s. 6d.

Brewer (Rev. Dr.), Works by.
The Reader's Handbook of Famous Names in Fiction, Allusions, References, Proverbs, Plots, Stories, and Poems. Together with an ENGLISH AND AMERICAN BIBLIOGRAPHY, and a LIST OF THE AUTHORS AND DATES OF DRAMAS AND OPERAS. A New Edition, Revised and Enlarged. Crown 8vo, cloth, 7s. 6d.
A Dictionary of Miracles: Imitative, Realistic, and Dogmatic. Crown 8vo, cloth, 3s. 6d.

Brewster (Sir David), Works by. Post 8vo, cloth, 4s. 6d. each.
More Worlds than One: Creed of the Philosopher and Hope of the Christian. With Plates.
The Martyrs of Science: GALILEO, TYCHO BRAHE, and KEPLER. With Portraits.
Letters on Natural Magic. With numerous Illustrations.

Brillat-Savarin.—Gastronomy as a Fine Art. Translated by R. E. ANDERSON, M.A. Post 8vo, half-bound, 2s.

Bryden (H. A.).—An Exiled Scot: A Romance. With a Frontispiece. Crown 8vo, cloth, 6s.

Brydges (Harold).—Uncle Sam at Home. With 91 Illustrations. Post 8vo, illustrated boards, 2s.; cloth limp, 2s. 6d.

Buchanan (Robert), Novels, &c., by.
Crown 8vo, cloth extra, 3s. 6d. each; post 8vo, illustrated boards, 2s. each.
The Shadow of the Sword. | Love Me for Ever. With Frontispiece.
A Child of Nature. With Frontispiece. | Annan Water. | Foxglove Manor.
God and the Man. With 11 Illustrations by | The New Abelard. | Rachel Dene.
Lady Kilpatrick. (FRED. BARNARD). | Matt: A Story of a Caravan. With Frontispiece.
The Martyrdom of Madeline. With | The Master of the Mine. With Frontispiece.
Frontispiece by A. W. COOPER. | The Heir of Linne. | Woman and the Man.

Red and White Heather. Crown 8vo, cloth extra, 3s. 6d.

The Wandering Jew: a Christmas Carol. Crown 8vo, cloth, 6s.

The Charlatan. By ROBERT BUCHANAN and HENRY MURRAY. Crown 8vo, cloth, with a Frontispiece by T. H. ROBINSON, 3s. 6d.; post 8vo, picture boards, 2s.

Burton (Robert).—The Anatomy of Melancholy. With Translations of the Quotations. Demy 8vo, cloth extra, 7s. 6d.
Melancholy Anatomised: An Abridgment of BURTON'S ANATOMY. Post 8vo, half-bd., 2s. 6d.

Caine (Hall), Novels by. Crown 8vo, cloth extra, 3s. 6d. each.; post 8vo, illustrated boards, 2s. each; cloth limp, 2s. 6d. each.
The Shadow of a Crime. | A Son of Hagar. | The Deemster.
Also LIBRARY EDITIONS of The Deemster and The Shadow of a Crime, set in new type, crown 8vo, and bound uniform with The Christian, 6s. each; and CHEAP POPULAR EDITIONS of The Deemster and The Shadow of a Crime, medium 8vo, portrait-cover, 6d. each; cloth, 1s. each.

Cameron (Commander V. Lovett).—The Cruise of the 'Black Prince' Privateer. Post 8vo, picture boards, 2s.

Captain Coignet, Soldier of the Empire: An Autobiography. Edited by LOREDAN LARCHEY. Translated by Mrs. CAREY. With 100 Illustrations. Crown 8vo, cloth, 3s. 6d.

Carlyle (Jane Welsh), Life of. By Mrs. ALEXANDER IRELAND. With Portrait and Facsimile Letter. Small demy 8vo, cloth extra, 7s. 6d.

Carlyle (Thomas).—On the Choice of Books. Post 8vo, cl., 1s. 6d.
Correspondence of Thomas Carlyle and R. W. Emerson, 1834-1872. Edited by C. E. NORTON. With Portraits. Two Vols., crown 8vo, cloth, 24s.

Carruth (Hayden).—The Adventures of Jones. With 17 Illustrations. Fcap. 8vo, cloth, 2s.

Chambers (Robert W.), Stories of Paris Life by.
The King in Yellow. Crown 8vo, cloth, 3s. 6d.; fcap. 8vo, cloth limp, 2s. 6d.
In the Quarter. Fcap. 8vo, cloth, 2s. 6d.

Chapman's (George), Works. Vol. I., Plays Complete, including the Doubtful Ones.—Vol. II., Poems and Minor Translations, with Essay by A. C. SWINBURNE.—Vol. III., Translations of the Iliad and Odyssey. Three Vols., crown 8vo, cloth, 3s. 6d. each.

Chapple (J. Mitchell).—The Minor Chord: The Story of a Prima Donna. Crown 8vo, cloth, 3s. 6d.

Chatto (W. A.) and J. Jackson.—A Treatise on Wood Engraving, Historical and Practical. With Chapter by H. G. BOHN, and 450 fine Illusts. Large 4to, half-leather, 28s.

Chaucer for Children: A Golden Key. By Mrs. H. R. HAWEIS. With 8 Coloured Plates and 30 Woodcuts. Crown 4to, cloth extra, 3s. 6d.
Chaucer for Schools. With the Story of his Times and his Work. By Mrs. H. R. HAWEIS. A New Edition, revised. With a Frontispiece. Demy 8vo, cloth, 2s. 6d.

Chess, The Laws and Practice of. With an Analysis of the Openings. By HOWARD STAUNTON. Edited by R. B. WORMALD. Crown 8vo, cloth, 5s.
The Minor Tactics of Chess: A Treatise on the Deployment of the Forces in obedience to Strategic Principle. By F. K. YOUNG and E. C. HOWELL. Long fcap. 8vo, cloth, 2s. 6d.
The Hastings Chess Tournament. Containing the Authorised Account of the 230 Games played Aug.-Sept., 1895. With Annotations by PILLSBURY, LASKER, TARRASCH, STEINITZ, SCHIFFERS, TEICHMANN, BARDELEBEN, BLACKBURNE, GUNSBERG, TINSLEY, MASON, and ALBIN; Biographical Sketches of the Chess Masters, and 22 Portraits. Edited by H. F. CHESHIRE. Cheaper Edition. Crown 8vo, cloth, 5s.

Clare (Austin), Stories by.
For the Love of a Lass. Post 8vo, illustrated boards, 2s.; cloth, 2s. 6d.
By the Rise of the River: Tales and Sketches in South Tynedale. Crown 8vo, cloth, 3s. 6d.

Clive (Mrs. Archer), Novels by. Post 8vo, illust. boards, 2s. each.
Paul Ferroll. | Why Paul Ferroll Killed his Wife.

Clodd (Edward, F.R.A.S.).—Myths and Dreams. Cr. 8vo, 3s. 6d.

Coates (Anne).—Rie's Diary. Crown 8vo, cloth, 3s. 6d.

Cobban (J. Maclaren), Novels by.
The Cure of Souls. Post 8vo, illustrated boards, 2s.
The Red Sultan. Crown 8vo, cloth extra, 3s. 6d.; post 8vo, illustrated boards, 2s.
The Burden of Isabel. Crown 8vo, cloth extra, 3s. 6d.

Coleman (John).—Curly: An Actor's Story. With 21 Illustrations by J. C. DOLLMAN. Crown 8vo, picture cover, 1s.

Coleridge (M. E.).—The Seven Sleepers of Ephesus. Fcap 8vo, cloth, 1s. 6d.; leatherette, 1s.

Collins (C. Allston).—The Bar Sinister. Post 8vo, boards, 2s.

Collins (John Churton, M.A.), Books by.
Illustrations of Tennyson. Crown 8vo, cloth extra, 6s.
Jonathan Swift. A Biographical and Critical Study. Crown 8vo, cloth extra, 8s.

Collins (Mortimer and Frances), Novels by.
Crown 8vo, cloth extra, 3s. 6d. each; post 8vo, illustrated boards, 2s. each.
From Midnight to Midnight. | Blacksmith and Scholar.
Transmigration. | You Play me False. | The Village Comedy.
Post 8vo, illustrated boards, 2s. each.
Sweet Anne Page. | A Fight with Fortune. | Sweet and Twenty. | Frances.

Collins (Wilkie), Novels by.
Crown 8vo, cloth extra, many Illustrated, 3s. 6d. each; post 8vo, picture boards, 2s. each; cloth limp, 2s. 6d. each.

Antonina.	My Miscellanies.	Jezebel's Daughter.
Basil.	Armadale.	The Black Robe.
Hide and Seek.	Poor Miss Finch.	Heart and Science.
The Woman in White.	Miss or Mrs.?	'I Say No.'
The Moonstone.	The New Magdalen.	A Rogue's Life.
Man and Wife.	The Frozen Deep.	The Evil Genius.
After Dark.	The Law and the Lady.	Little Novels.
The Dead Secret.	The Two Destinies.	The Legacy of Cain.
The Queen of Hearts.	The Haunted Hotel.	Blind Love.
No Name.	The Fallen Leaves.	

POPULAR EDITIONS. Medium 8vo, 6d. each; cloth, 1s. each.
The Woman in White. | The Moonstone. | Antonina. | The Dead Secret.
The Woman in White and The Moonstone, POPULAR EDITION, in One Volume, medium 8vo, cloth, 2s.

Colman's (George) Humorous Works: 'Broad Grins,' 'My Nightgown and Slippers,' &c. With Life and Frontispiece. Crown 8vo, cloth extra, 3s. 6d.

Colquhoun (M. J.).—Every Inch a Soldier. Crown 8vo, cloth, 3s. 6d.; post 8vo, illustrated boards, 2s.

Colt-breaking, Hints on. By W. M. HUTCHISON. Cr. 8vo, cl., 3s. 6d.

Convalescent Cookery. By CATHERINE RYAN. Cr. 8vo, 1s.; cl., 1s. 6d.

Conway (Moncure D.).—George Washington's Rules of Civility Traced to their Sources and Restored. Fcap. 8vo, Japanese vellum, 2s. 6d.

Cook (Dutton), Novels by.
Post 8vo, illustrated boards, 2s. each.
Leo. | Paul Foster's Daughter.

Cooper (Edward H.).—Geoffory Hamilton. Cr. 8vo, cloth, 3s. 6d.

Cornwall.—Popular Romances of the West of England; or, The Drolls, Traditions, and Superstitions of Old Cornwall. Collected by ROBERT HUNT, F.R.S. With two Steel Plates by GEORGE CRUIKSHANK. Crown 8vo, cloth, 7s. 6d.

Cotes (V. Cecil).—Two Girls on a Barge. With 44 Illustrations by F. H. TOWNSEND. Crown 8vo, cloth extra, 3s. 6d.; post 8vo, cloth, 2s. 6d.

Craddock (C. Egbert), Stories by.
The Prophet of the Great Smoky Mountains. Post 8vo, illustrated boards, 2s.
His Vanished Star. Crown 8vo, cloth extra, 3s. 6d.

Cram (Ralph Adams).—Black Spirits and White. Fcap. 8vo, cloth, 1s. 6d.

6 CHATTO & WINDUS, Publishers, 111 St. Martin's Lane, London, W.C.

Crellin (H. N.), Books by.
Romances of the Old Seraglio. With 28 Illustrations by S. L. WOOD. Crown 8vo, cloth, 3s. 6d.
Tales of the Caliph. Crown 8vo, cloth, 2s.
The Nazarenes: A Drama. Crown 8vo, 1s.

Crim (Matt.).—Adventures of a Fair Rebel. Crown 8vo, cloth extra, with a Frontispiece by DAN. BEARD, 3s. 6d.; post 8vo, illustrated boards, 2s.

Crockett (S. R.) and others.—Tales of Our Coast. By S. R. CROCKETT, GILBERT PARKER, HAROLD FREDERIC, 'Q.,' and W. CLARK RUSSELL. With 2 Illustrations by FRANK BRANGWYN. Crown 8vo, cloth, 3s. 6d.

Croker (Mrs. B. M.), Novels by. Crown 8vo, cloth extra, 3s. 6d. each; post 8vo, illustrated boards, 2s. each; cloth limp, 2s. 6d. each.
Pretty Miss Neville.	Interference.	Village Tales & Jungle Tragedies.
Proper Pride.	A Family Likeness.	The Real Lady Hilda.
A Bird of Passage.	'To Let.'	Married or Single?
Diana Barrington.	A Third Person.	
Two Masters.	Mr. Jervis.	

Crown 8vo, cloth extra, 3s. 6d. each.
In the Kingdom of Kerry. | Beyond the Pale.
Miss Balmaine's Past. Crown 8vo, buckram, gilt top, 6s.
Infatuation. (A 'TIMES NOVEL.') Crown 8vo, buckram. 6s.

Cruikshank's Comic Almanack. Complete in Two SERIES: The FIRST, from 1835 to 1843; the SECOND, from 1844 to 1853. A Gathering of the Best Humour of THACKERAY, HOOD, MAYHEW, ALBERT SMITH, A'BECKETT, ROBERT BROUGH, &c. With numerous Steel Engravings and Woodcuts by GEORGE CRUIKSHANK, HINE, LANDELLS, &c. Two Vols., crown 8vo, cloth gilt, 7s. 6d. each.
The Life of George Cruikshank. By BLANCHARD JERROLD. With 84 Illustrations and a Bibliography. Crown 8vo, cloth extra, 3s. 6d.

Cumming (C. F. Gordon), Works by. Demy 8vo, cl. ex., 8s. 6d. ea.
In the Hebrides. With an Autotype Frontispiece and 23 Illustrations.
In the Himalayas and on the Indian Plains. With 42 Illustrations.
Two Happy Years in Ceylon. With 28 Illustrations.
Via Cornwall to Egypt. With a Photogravure Frontispiece. Demy 8vo, cloth, 7s. 6d.

Cussans (John E.).—A Handbook of Heraldry; with Instructions for Tracing Pedigrees and Deciphering Ancient MSS., &c. Fourth Edition, revised, with 408 Woodcuts and 2 Coloured Plates. Crown 8vo, cloth extra, 6s.

Cyples (W.).—Hearts of Gold. Cr. 8vo, cl., 3s. 6d.; post 8vo, bds., 2s.

Daudet (Alphonse).—The Evangelist; or, Port Salvation. Crown 8vo, cloth extra, 3s. 6d.; post 8vo, illustrated boards, 2s.

Davenant (Francis, M.A.).—Hints for Parents on the Choice of a Profession for their Sons when Starting in Life. Crown 8vo, cloth, 1s. 6d.

Davidson (Hugh Coleman).—Mr. Sadler's Daughters. With a Frontispiece by STANLEY WOOD. Crown 8vo, cloth extra, 3s. 6d.

Davies (Dr. N. E. Yorke-), Works by. Cr. 8vo, 1s. ea.; cl., 1s. 6d. ea.
One Thousand Medical Maxims and Surgical Hints.
Nursery Hints: A Mother's Guide in Health and Disease.
Foods for the Fat: The Dietetic Cure of Corpulency and of Gout.
Aids to Long Life. Crown 8vo, 2s.; cloth limp, 2s. 6d.

Davies' (Sir John) Complete Poetical Works. Collected and Edited, with Introduction and Notes, by Rev. A. B. GROSART, D.D. Two Vols.; crown 8vo, cloth, 3s. 6d. each.

Dawson (Erasmus, M.B.).—The Fountain of Youth. Crown 8vo, cloth extra, with Two Illustrations by HUME NISBET, 3s. 6d.; post 8vo, illustrated boards, 2s.

De Guerin (Maurice), The Journal of. Edited by G. S. TREBUTIEN. With a Memoir by SAINTE-BEUVE. Translated from the 20th French Edition by JESSIE P. FROTHINGHAM. Fcap. 8vo, half-bound, 2s. 6d.

De Maistre (Xavier).—A Journey Round my Room. Translated by HENRY ATTWELL. Post 8vo, cloth limp, 2s. 6d.

De Mille (James).—A Castle in Spain. Crown 8vo, cloth extra, with a Frontispiece, 3s. 6d.; post 8vo, illustrated boards, 2s.

Derby (The): The Blue Ribbon of the Turf. With Brief Accounts of THE OAKS. By LOUIS HENRY CURZON. Crown 8vo, cloth limp, 2s. 6d.

Derwent (Leith), Novels by. Cr. 8vo, cl., 3s. 6d. ea.; post 8vo, 2s. ea.
Our Lady of Tears. | Circe's Lovers.

Dewar (T. R.).—A Ramble Round the Globe. With 220 Illustrations. Crown 8vo, cloth extra, 7s. 6d.

CHATTO & WINDUS, Publishers, 111 St. Martin's Lane, London, W.C. 7

De Windt (Harry), Books by.
Through the Gold-Fields of Alaska to Bering Straits. With Map and 33 full-page Illustrations. Demy 8vo, cloth extra, 16s.
Stories of Travel and Adventure. Crown 8vo, cloth, 3s. 6d. [Shortly.

Dickens (Charles), About England with. By ALFRED RIMMER.
With 57 Illustrations by C. A. VANDERHOOF and the AUTHOR. Square 8vo, cloth, 3s. 6d.

Dictionaries.
The Reader's Handbook of Famous Names in Fiction, Allusions, References, Proverbs, Plots, Stories, and Poems. Together with an ENGLISH AND AMERICAN BIBLIOGRAPHY, and a LIST OF THE AUTHORS AND DATES OF DRAMAS AND OPERAS. By Rev. E. C. BREWER, LL.D. A New Edition, Revised and Enlarged. Crown 8vo, cloth, 7s. 6d.
A Dictionary of Miracles: Imitative, Realistic, and Dogmatic. By the Rev. E. C. BREWER, LL.D. Crown 8vo, cloth, 3s. 6d.
Familiar Short Sayings of Great Men. With Historical and Explanatory Notes by SAMUEL A. BENT, A.M. Crown 8vo, cloth extra, 7s. 6d.
The Slang Dictionary: Etymological, Historical, and Anecdotal. Crown 8vo, cloth, 6s. 6d.
Words, Facts, and Phrases: A Dictionary of Curious, Quaint, and Out-of-the-Way Matters. By ELIEZER EDWARDS. Crown 8vo, cloth extra, 3s. 6d.

Dilke (Rt. Hon. Sir Charles, Bart., M.P.).—The British Empire.
Crown 8vo, buckram, 3s. 6d.

Dobson (Austin), Works by.
Thomas Bewick and his Pupils. With 95 Illustrations. Square 8vo, cloth, 6s.
Four Frenchwomen. With Four Portraits. Crown 8vo, buckram, gilt top, 6s.
Eighteenth Century Vignettes. IN THREE SERIES. Crown 8vo, buckram, 6s. each.
A Paladin of Philanthropy, and other Papers. With 2 Illustrations Crown 8vo, buckram, 6s. [April.

Dobson (W. T.).—Poetical Ingenuities and Eccentricities. Post 8vo, cloth limp, 2s. 6d.

Donovan (Dick), Detective Stories by.
Post 8vo, illustrated boards, 2s. each; cloth limp, 2s. 6d. each.
The Man-Hunter. | Wanted! | A Detective's Triumphs.
Caught at Last. | In the Grip of the Law.
Tracked and Taken. | From Information Received.
Who Poisoned Hetty Duncan? | Link by Link. | Dark Deeds.
Suspicion Aroused. | Riddles Read.

Crown 8vo, cloth extra, 3s. 6d. each; post 8vo, illustrated boards, 2s. each; cloth, 2s. 6d. each.
The Man from Manchester. With 23 Illustrations.
Tracked to Doom. With Six full-page Illustrations by GORDON BROWNE.
The Mystery of Jamaica Terrace. | The Chronicles of Michael Danevitch.
The Records of Vincent Trill, of the Detective Service. Crown 8vo, cloth, 3s. 6d.

Dowling (Richard).—Old Corcoran's Money. Crown 8vo, cl., 3s. 6d.

Doyle (A. Conan).—The Firm of Girdlestone. Cr. 8vo, cl., 3s. 6d.

Dramatists, The Old. Cr. 8vo, cl. ex., with Portraits, 3s. 6d. per Vol.
Ben Jonson's Works. With Notes, Critical and Explanatory, and a Biographical Memoir by WILLIAM GIFFORD. Edited by Colonel CUNNINGHAM. Three Vols.
Chapman's Works. Three Vols. Vol. I. contains the Plays complete; Vol. II., Poems and Minor Translations, with an Essay by A. C. SWINBURNE; Vol. III., Translations of the Iliad and Odyssey.
Marlowe's Works. Edited, with Notes, by Colonel CUNNINGHAM. One Vol.
Massinger's Plays. From GIFFORD'S Text. Edited by Colonel CUNNINGHAM. One Vol.

Duncan (Sara Jeannette: Mrs. EVERARD COTES), Works by.
Crown 8vo, cloth extra, 7s. 6d. each.
A Social Departure. With 111 Illustrations by F. H. TOWNSEND.
An American Girl in London. With 80 Illustrations by F. H. TOWNSEND.
The Simple Adventures of a Memsahib. With 37 Illustrations by F. H. TOWNSEND.
Crown 8vo, cloth extra, 3s. 6d. each.
A Daughter of To-Day. | Vernon's Aunt. With 47 Illustrations by HAL HURST.

Dutt (Romesh C.).—England and India: A Record of Progress during One Hundred Years. Crown 8vo, cloth, 2s.

Dyer (T. F. Thiselton).—The Folk-Lore of Plants. Cr. 8vo, cl., 6s.

Early English Poets. Edited, with Introductions and Annotations by Rev. A. B. GROSART, D.D. Crown 8vo, cloth boards, 3s. 6d. per Volume.
Fletcher's (Giles) Complete Poems. One Vol.
Davies' (Sir John) Complete Poetical Works. Two Vols.
Herrick's (Robert) Complete Collected Poems. Three Vols.
Sidney's (Sir Philip) Complete Poetical Works. Three Vols.

Edgcumbe (Sir E. R. Pearce).—Zephyrus: A Holiday in Brazil and on the River Plate. With 41 Illustrations. Crown 8vo, cloth extra, 5s.

Edwardes (Mrs. Annie), Novels by. Post 8vo, illust. bds., 2s. each.
Archie Lovell. | A Point of Honour.
A Plaster Saint. Crown 8vo, cloth, 3s. 6d. [Shortly.

8 CHATTO & WINDUS, Publishers, 111 St. Martin's Lane, London, W.C.

Edwards (Eliezer).—Words, Facts, and Phrases: A Dictionary of Curious, Quaint, and Out-of-the-Way Matters. Cheaper Edition. Crown 8vo, cloth, 3s. 6d.

Edwards (M. Betham-), Novels by.
Kitty. Post 8vo, boards, 2s.; cloth, 2s. 6d. | Felicia. Post 8vo, illustrated boards, 2s.

Egerton (Rev. J. C., M.A.).—Sussex Folk and Sussex Ways. With Introduction by Rev. Dr. H. WACE, and Four Illustrations. Crown 8vo, cloth extra, 5s.

Eggleston (Edward).—Roxy: A Novel. Post 8vo, illust. boards, 2s.

Englishman's House, The: A Practical Guide for Selecting or Building a House. By C. J. RICHARDSON. Coloured Frontispiece and 534 Illusts. Cr. 8vo, cloth, 3s. 6d.

Ewald (Alex. Charles, F.S.A.), Works by.
The Life and Times of Prince Charles Stuart, Count of Albany (THE YOUNG PRETENDER). With a Portrait. Crown 8vo, cloth extra, 7s. 6d.
Stories from the State Papers. With Autotype Frontispiece. Crown 8vo, cloth, 6s.

Eyes, Our: How to Preserve Them. By JOHN BROWNING. Cr. 8vo, 1s.

Familiar Short Sayings of Great Men. By SAMUEL ARTHUR BENT, A.M. Fifth Edition, Revised and Enlarged. Crown 8vo, cloth extra, 7s. 6d.

Faraday (Michael), Works by. Post 8vo, cloth extra, 4s. 6d. each.
The Chemical History of a Candle: Lectures delivered before a Juvenile Audience. Edited by WILLIAM CROOKES, F.C.S. With numerous Illustrations.
On the Various Forces of Nature, and their Relations to each other. Edited by WILLIAM CROOKES, F.C.S. With Illustrations.

Farrer (J. Anson), Works by.
Military Manners and Customs. Crown 8vo, cloth extra, 6s.
War: Three Essays, reprinted from 'Military Manners and Customs.' Crown 8vo, 1s.; cloth, 1s. 6d.

Fenn (G. Manville), Novels by.
Crown 8vo, cloth extra, 3s. 6d. each; post 8vo, illustrated boards, 2s. each.
The New Mistress. | Witness to the Deed. | The Tiger Lily. | The White Virgin.
A Woman Worth Winning. Crown 8vo, cloth, gilt top, 6s.
A Crimson Crime. Crown 8vo, cloth, gilt top, 6s. [*Preparing.*

In the press. NEW EDITIONS. Crown 8vo, cloth, 3s. 6d. each.

Commodore Junk.
Black Blood.
Double Cunning.
A Bag of Diamonds; and The Dark House.
A Fluttered Dovecote.
King of the Castle.
The Master of the Ceremonies.

Eve at the Wheel; and The Chaplain's Craze.
The Man with a Shadow.
One Maid's Mischief.
The Story of Antony Grace.
This Man's Wife.
In Jeopardy.

Fin-Bec.—The Cupboard Papers: Observations on the Art of Living and Dining. Post 8vo, cloth limp, 2s. 6d.

Firework-Making, The Complete Art of; or, The Pyrotechnist's Treasury. By THOMAS KENTISH. With 267 Illustrations. Crown 8vo, cloth, 3s. 6d.

First Book, My. By WALTER BESANT, JAMES PAYN, W. CLARK RUSSELL, GRANT ALLEN, HALL CAINE, GEORGE R. SIMS, RUDYARD KIPLING, A. CONAN DOYLE, M. E. BRADDON, F. W. ROBINSON, H. RIDER HAGGARD, R. M. BALLANTYNE, I. ZANGWILL, MORLEY ROBERTS, D. CHRISTIE MURRAY, MARY CORELLI, J. K. JEROME, JOHN STRANGE WINTER, BRET HARTE, 'Q.,' ROBERT BUCHANAN, and R. L. STEVENSON. With a Prefatory Story by JEROME K. JEROME, and 185 Illustrations. A New Edition. Small demy 8vo, art linen, 3s. 6d.

Fitzgerald (Percy), Works by.
Little Essays: Passages from the Letters of CHARLES LAMB. Post 8vo, cloth, 2s. 6d.
Fatal Zero. Crown 8vo, cloth extra, 3s. 6d.; post 8vo, illustrated boards, 2s.

Post 8vo, illustrated boards, 2s. each.
Bella Donna. | The Lady of Brantome. | The Second Mrs. Tillotson.
Polly. | Never Forgotten. | Seventy-five Brooke Street.

Sir Henry Irving: Twenty Years at the Lyceum. With Portrait. Crown 8vo, 1s.; cloth, 1s. 6d.

Flammarion (Camille), Works by.
Popular Astronomy: A General Description of the Heavens. Translated by J. ELLARD GORE, F.R.A.S. With Three Plates and 288 Illustrations. Medium 8vo, cloth, 10s. 6d.
Urania: A Romance. With 87 Illustrations. Crown 8vo, cloth extra, 5s.

Fletcher's (Giles, B.D.) Complete Poems: Christ's Victorie in Heaven, Christ's Victorie on Earth, Christ's Triumph over Death, and Minor Poems. With Notes by Rev. A. B. GROSART, D.D. Crown 8vo, cloth boards, 3s. 6d.

Fonblanque (Albany).—Filthy Lucre. Post 8vo, illust. boards, 2s.

Forbes (Archibald).—The Life of Napoleon III. With Photogravure Frontispiece and Thirty-six full-page Illustrations. Demy 8vo, cloth, gilt top, 12s.

Fowler (J. Kersley).—Records of Old Times Historical, Social, Political, Sporting, and Agricultural. With Eight full-page Illustrations. Demy 8vo, cloth, 10s. 6d.

Francillon (R. E.), Novels by.
Crown 8vo, cloth extra, 3s. 6d. each; post 8vo, illustrated boards, 2s. each.
One by One. | A Real Queen. | A Dog and his Shadow.
Ropes of Sand. Illustrated

Post 8vo, Illustrated boards, 2s. each.
Queen Cophetua. | Olympia. | Romances of the Law. | King or Knave?
Jack Doyle's Daughter. Crown 8vo, cloth, 3s. 6d.

Frederic (Harold), Novels by. Post 8vo, cloth extra, 3s. 6d. each; illustrated boards 2s. each.
Seth's Brother's Wife. | The Lawton Girl.

French Literature, A History of. By HENRY VAN LAUN. Three Vols., demy 8vo, cloth boards, 7s. 6d. each.

Fry's (Herbert) Royal Guide to the London Charities. Edited by JOHN LANE. Published Annually. Crown 8vo, cloth, 1s. 6d.

Gardening Books. Post 8vo, 1s. each; cloth limp. 1s. 6d. each.
A Year's Work in Garden and Greenhouse. By GEORGE GLENNY.
Household Horticulture. By TOM and JANE JERROLD. Illustrated.
The Garden that Paid the Rent. By TOM JERROLD.
My Garden Wild. By FRANCIS G. HEATH. Crown 8vo, cloth, gilt edges, 6s.

Gardner (Mrs. Alan).—Rifle and Spear with the Rajpoots: Being the Narrative of a Winter's Travel and Sport in Northern India. With numerous Illustrations by the Author and F. H. TOWNSEND. Demy 4to, half-bound, 21s.

Garrett (Edward).—The Capel Girls: A Novel. Post 8vo, illustrated boards, 2s.

Gaulot (Paul).—The Red Shirts: A Story of the Revolution. Translated by JOHN DE VILLIERS. With a Frontispiece by STANLEY WOOD. Crown 8vo, cloth, 3s. 6d.

Gentleman's Magazine, The. 1s. Monthly. Contains Stories, Articles upon Literature, Science, Biography, and Art, and 'Table Talk' by SYLVANUS URBAN.
*** Bound Volumes for recent years kept in stock, 8s. 6d. each. Cases for binding, 2s. each.

Gentleman's Annual, The. Published Annually in November. 1s.

German Popular Stories. Collected by the Brothers GRIMM, and Translated by EDGAR TAYLOR. With Introduction by JOHN RUSKIN, and 22 Steel Plates after GEORGE CRUIKSHANK. Square 8vo, cloth, 6s. 6d.; gilt edges, 7s. 6d.

Gibbon (Chas.), Novels by. Cr. 8vo, cl., 3s. 6d. ea.; post 8vo, bds., 2s. ea.
Robin Gray. With Frontispiece. | Loving a Dream. | The Braes of Yarrow.
The Golden Shaft. With Frontispiece. | Of High Degree.

Post 8vo, illustrated boards, 2s. each.
The Flower of the Forest. | In Love and War.
The Dead Heart. | A Heart's Problem.
For Lack of Gold. | By Mead and Stream.
What Will the World Say? | Fancy Free.
For the King. | A Hard Knot. | In Honour Bound.
Queen of the Meadow. | Heart's Delight.
In Pastures Green. | Blood-Money.

Gibney (Somerville).—Sentenced! Crown 8vo, cloth, 1s. 6d.

Gilbert (W. S.), Original Plays by. In Three Series, 2s. 6d. each.
The FIRST SERIES contains: The Wicked World—Pygmalion and Galatea—Charity—The Princess—The Palace of Truth—Trial by Jury.
The SECOND SERIES: Broken Hearts—Engaged—Sweethearts—Gretchen—Dan'l Druce—Tom Cobb—H.M.S. 'Pinafore'—The Sorcerer—The Pirates of Penzance.
The THIRD SERIES: Comedy and Tragedy—Foggerty's Fairy—Rosencrantz and Guildenstern—Patience—Princess Ida—The Mikado—Ruddigore—The Yeomen of the Guard—The Gondoliers—The Mountebanks—Utopia.

Eight Original Comic Operas written by W. S. GILBERT. In Two Series. Demy 8vo, cloth, 2s. 6d. each. The FIRST containing: The Sorcerer—H.M.S. 'Pinafore'—The Pirates of Penzance—Iolanthe—Patience—Princess Ida—The Mikado—Trial by Jury.
The SECOND SERIES containing: The Gondoliers—The Grand Duke—The Yeomen of the Guard—His Excellency—Utopia, Limited—Ruddigore—The Mountebanks—Haste to the Wedding.
The Gilbert and Sullivan Birthday Book: Quotations for Every Day in the Year, selected from Plays by W. S. GILBERT set to Music by Sir A. SULLIVAN. Compiled by ALEX. WATSON. Royal 16mo, Japanese leather, 2s. 6d.

10 CHATTO & WINDUS, Publishers, 111 St. Martin's Lane, London, W.C.

Gilbert (William), Novels by. Post 8vo, illustrated bds., 2s. each.
Dr. Austin's Guests. | James Duke, Costermonger.
The Wizard of the Mountain.

Glanville (Ernest), Novels by.
Crown 8vo, cloth extra, 3s. 6d. each; post 8vo, illustrated boards, 2s. each.
The Lost Heiress: A Tale of Love, Battle, and Adventure. With Two Illustrations by H. NISBET.
The Fossicker: A Romance of Mashonaland. With Two Illustrations by HUME NISBET.
A Fair Colonist. With a Frontispiece by STANLEY WOOD.
The Golden Rock. With a Frontispiece by STANLEY WOOD. Crown 8vo, cloth extra, 3s. 6d.
Kloof Yarns. Crown 8vo, picture cover, 1s.; cloth, 1s. 6d.
Tales from the Veld. With Twelve Illustrations by M. NISBET. Crown 8vo, cloth, 3s. 6d.

Glenny (George).—A Year's Work in Garden and Greenhouse:
Practical Advice as to the Management of the Flower, Fruit, and Frame Garden. Post 8vo, 1s.; cloth, 1s. 6d.

Godwin (William).—Lives of the Necromancers. Post 8vo, cl., 2s.

Golden Treasury of Thought, The: An Encyclopædia of QUOTATIONS. Edited by THEODORE TAYLOR. Crown 8vo, cloth gilt, 7s. 6d.

Gontaut, Memoirs of the Duchesse de (Gouvernante to the Children of France), 1773-1836. With Two Photogravures. Two Vols., demy 8vo, cloth extra, 21s.

Goodman (E. J.).—The Fate of Herbert Wayne. Cr. 8vo, 3s. 6d.

Greeks and Romans, The Life of the, described from Antique Monuments. By ERNST GUHL and W. KONER. Edited by Dr. F. HUEFFER. With 545 Illustrations. Large crown 8vo, cloth extra, 7s. 6d.

Greville (Henry), Novels by.
Post 8vo, illustrated boards, 2s. each.
Nikanor. Translated by ELIZA E. CHASE.
A Noble Woman. Translated by ALBERT D. VANDAM.

Grey (Sir George).—The Romance of a Proconsul: Being the Personal Life and Memoirs of Sir GEORGE GREY, K.C.B. By JAMES MILNE. With Portrait. Crown 8vo, cloth, 5s.

Griffith (Cecil).—Corinthia Marazion: A Novel. Crown 8vo, cloth extra, 3s. 6d.; post 8vo, illustrated boards, 2s.

Grundy (Sydney).—The Days of his Vanity: A Passage in the Life of a Young Man. Crown 8vo, cloth extra, 3s. 6d.; post 8vo, illustrated boards, 2s.

Habberton (John, Author of 'Helen's Babies'), **Novels by.**
Post 8vo, illustrated boards, 2s. each; cloth limp, 2s. 6d. each.
Brueton's Bayou. | Country Luck.

Hair, The: Its Treatment in Health, Weakness, and Disease. Translated from the German of Dr. J. PINCUS. Crown 8vo, 1s.; cloth, 1s. 6d.

Hake (Dr. Thomas Gordon), Poems by. Cr. 8vo, cl. ex., 6s. each.
New Symbols. | Legends of the Morrow. | The Serpent Play.
Maiden Ecstasy. Small 4to, cloth extra, 8s.

Halifax (C.).—Dr. Rumsey's Patient. By Mrs. L. T. MEADE and CLIFFORD HALIFAX, M.D. Crown 8vo, cloth, 3s. 6d.

Hall (Mrs. S. C.).—Sketches of Irish Character. With numerous Illustrations on Steel and Wood by MACLISE, GILBERT, HARVEY, and GEORGE CRUIKSHANK. Small demy 8vo, cloth extra, 7s. 6d.

Hall (Owen), Novels by.
The Track of a Storm. Cheaper Edition. Crown 8vo, cloth, 3s. 6d.
Jetsam. Crown 8vo, cloth, 3s. 6d.

Halliday (Andrew).—Every-day Papers. Post 8vo, boards, 2s.

Hamilton (Cosmo).—The Glamour of the Impossible: An Improbability. Crown 8vo, cloth gilt, 3s. 6d.

Handwriting, The Philosophy of. With over 100 Facsimiles and Explanatory Text. By DON FELIX DE SALAMANCA. Post 8vo, cloth limp, 2s. 6d.

Hanky-Panky: Easy and Difficult Tricks, White Magic, Sleight of Hand, &c. Edited by W. H. CREMER. With 200 Illustrations. Crown 8vo, cloth extra, 4s. 6d.

Hardy (Thomas).—Under the Greenwood Tree. Crown 8vo, cloth extra, with Portrait and 15 Illustrations, 3s. 6d.; post 8vo, illustrated boards, 2s. cloth limp, 2s. 6d.

CHATTO & WINDUS, Publishers, 111 St. Martin's Lane, London, W.C. 11

Harte's (Bret) Collected Works. Revised by the Author. LIBRARY EDITION, In Nine Volumes, crown 8vo, cloth extra, 6s. each.
- Vol. I. COMPLETE POETICAL AND DRAMATIC WORKS. With Steel-plate Portrait.
- „ II. THE LUCK OF ROARING CAMP—BOHEMIAN PAPERS—AMERICAN LEGEND.
- „ III. TALES OF THE ARGONAUTS—EASTERN SKETCHES.
- „ IV. GABRIEL CONROY. | Vol. V. STORIES—CONDENSED NOVELS, &c.
- „ VI. TALES OF THE PACIFIC SLOPE.
- „ VII. TALES OF THE PACIFIC SLOPE—II. With Portrait by JOHN PETTIE, R.A.
- „ VIII. TALES OF THE PINE AND THE CYPRESS.
- „ IX. BUCKEYE AND CHAPPAREL.

Bret Harte's Choice Works, in Prose and Verse. With Portrait of the Author and 40 Illustrations. Crown 8vo, cloth, 3s. 6d.
Bret Harte's Poetical Works. Printed on hand-made paper. Crown 8vo, buckram, 4s. 6d.
Some Later Verses. Crown 8vo, lineo gilt, 5s.
The Queen of the Pirate Isle. With 28 Original Drawings by KATE GREENAWAY, reproduced in Colours by EDMUND EVANS. Small 4to, cloth, 5s.

Crown 8vo, cloth extra, 3s. 6d. each ; post 8vo, picture boards, 2s. each.
A Waif of the Plains. With 60 Illustrations by STANLEY L. WOOD.
A Ward of the Golden Gate. With 59 Illustrations by STANLEY L. WOOD.

Crown 8vo, cloth extra, 3s. 6d. each.
A Sappho of Green Springs, &c. With Two Illustrations by HUME NISBET.
Colonel Starbottle's Client, and Some Other People. With a Frontispiece.
Susy: A Novel. With Frontispiece and Vignette by J. A. CHRISTIE.
Sally Dows, &c. With 47 Illustrations by W. D. ALMOND and others.
A Protegee of Jack Hamlin's, &c. With 26 Illustrations by W. SMALL and others.
The Bell-Ringer of Angel's, &c. With 39 Illustrations by DUDLEY HARDY and others.
Clarence : A Story of the American War. With Eight Illustrations by A. JULE GOODMAN.
Barker's Luck, &c. With 39 Illustrations by A. FORESTIER, PAUL HARDY, &c.
Devil's Ford, &c. With a Frontispiece by W. H. OVEREND.
The Crusade of the "Excelsior." With a Frontispiece by J. BERNARD PARTRIDGE.
Three Partners ; or, The Big Strike on Heavy Tree Hill. With 8 Illustrations by J. GULICH.
Tales of Trail and Town. With Frontispiece by G. P. JACOMB-HOOD.

Post 8vo, Illustrated boards, 2s. each.
Gabriel Conroy. | **The Luck of Roaring Camp,** &c
An Heiress of Red Dog, &c. | **Californian Stories.**

Post 8vo, illustrated boards, 2s. each ; cloth, 2s. 6d. each.
Flip. | **Maruja.** | **A Phyllis of the Sierras.**

Haweis (Mrs. H. R.), Books by.
The Art of Beauty. With Coloured Frontispiece and 91 Illustrations. Square 8vo, cloth bds., 6s.
The Art of Decoration. With Coloured Frontispiece and 74 Illustrations. Sq. 8vo, cloth bds., 6s.
The Art of Dress. With 32 Illustrations. Post 8vo, 1s. ; cloth, 1s. 6d.
Chaucer for Schools. With the Story of his Times and his Work. A New Edition, revised. With a Frontispiece. Demy 8vo, cloth, 2s. 6d.
Chaucer for Children. With 38 Illustrations (8 Coloured). Crown 4to, cloth extra, 3s. 6d.

Haweis (Rev. H. R., M.A.), Books by.
American Humorists : WASHINGTON IRVING, OLIVER WENDELL HOLMES, JAMES RUSSELL LOWELL, ARTEMUS WARD, MARK TWAIN, and BRET HARTE. Third Edition. Crown 8vo, cloth extra, 6s.
Travel and Talk, 1885-93-95 : My Hundred Thousand Miles of Travel through America—Canada —New Zealand—Tasmania—Australia—Ceylon—The Paradises of the Pacific. With Photogravure Frontispieces. A New Edition. Two Vols., crown 8vo, cloth, 12s.

Hawthorne (Julian), Novels by.
Crown 8vo, cloth extra, 3s. 6d. each ; post 8vo, Illustrated boards, 2s. each.
Garth. | **Ellice Quentin.** | **Beatrix Randolph.** With Four Illusts.
Sebastian Strome. | | **David Poindexter's Disappearance.**
Fortune's Fool. | **Dust,** Four Illusts. | **The Spectre of the Camera.**

Post 8vo, Illustrated boards, 2s. each.
Miss Cadogna. | **Love—or a Name.**

Helps (Sir Arthur), Books by. Post 8vo, cloth limp, 2s. 6d. each.
Animals and their Masters. | **Social Pressure.**
Ivan de Biron : A Novel. Crown 8vo, cloth extra, 3s. 6d. ; post 8vo, illustrated boards, 2s.

Henderson (Isaac).—Agatha Page : A Novel. Cr. 8vo, cl., 3s. 6d.

Henty (G. A.), Novels by.
Rujub, the Juggler. With Eight Illustrations by STANLEY L. WOOD. PRESENTATION EDITION, small demy 8vo, cloth, gilt edges, 5s. ; cr. 8vo, cloth, 3s. 6d. ; post 8vo, illust. boards, 2s.

Crown 8vo, cloth, 3s. 6d. each.
The Queen's Cup. | **Dorothy's Double.**
Colonel Thorndyke's Secret. Crown 8vo, cloth, gilt top, 6s. ; PRESENTATION EDITION, with a Frontispiece by STANLEY WOOD, small demy 8vo, cloth, gilt edges, 5s.

Herman (Henry).—A Leading Lady. Post 8vo, bds., 2s. ; cl., 2s. 6d.

Herrick's (Robert) Hesperides, Noble Numbers, and Complete Collected Poems. With Memorial-Introduction and Notes by the Rev. A. B. GROSART, D.D., Steel Portrait, &c. Three Vols., crown 8vo, cloth boards, 3s. 6d. each.

12 CHATTO & WINDUS, Publishers, 141 St. Martin's Lane, London, W.C.

Hertzka (Dr. Theodor).—Freeland: A Social Anticipation. Translated by ARTHUR RANSOM. Crown 8vo, cloth extra, 6s.

Hesse-Wartegg (Chevalier Ernst von).— Tunis: The Land and the People. With 22 Illustrations. Crown 8vo, cloth extra, 3s. 6d.

Hill (Headon).—Zambra the Detective. Crown 8vo, cloth, 3s. 6d. ; post 8vo, picture boards, 2s. ; cloth, 2s. 6d.

Hill (John), Works by.
Treason-Felony. Post 8vo, boards, 2s. | The Common Ancestor. Cr. 8vo, cloth, 3s. 6d.

Hoey (Mrs. Cashel).—The Lover's Creed. Post 8vo, boards, 2s.

Holiday, Where to go for a. By E. P. SHOLL, Sir H. MAXWELL, Bart., M.P., JOHN WATSON, JANE BARLOW, MARY LOVETT CAMERON, JUSTIN H MCCARTHY, PAUL LANGE, J. W. GRAHAM, J. H. SALTER, PHŒBE ALLEN, S. J. BECKETT, L. RIVERS VINE, and C. F. GORDON CUMMING. Crown 8vo, 1s.; cloth, 1s. 6d.

Hollingshead (John).—Niagara Spray. Crown 8vo, 1s.

Holmes (Gordon, M.D.)—The Science of Voice Production and Voice Preservation. Crown 8vo, 1s.; cloth, 1s. 6d.

Holmes (Oliver Wendell), Works by.
The Autocrat of the Breakfast-Table. Illustrated by J. GORDON THOMSON. Post 8vo, cloth limp, 2s. 6d.—Another Edition, post 8vo, cloth, 2s.
The Autocrat of the Breakfast-Table and The Professor at the Breakfast-Table. In One Vol. Post 8vo, half-bound, 2s.

Hood's (Thomas) Choice Works in Prose and Verse. With Life of the Author, Portrait, and 200 Illustrations. Crown 8vo, cloth, 3s. 6d.
Hood's Whims and Oddities. With 85 Illustrations. Post 8vo, half-bound, 2s.

Hood (Tom).—From Nowhere to the North Pole: A Noah's Arkæological Narrative. With 25 Illustrations by W. BRUNTON and E. C. BARNES. Cr. 8vo, cloth, 6s.

Hook's (Theodore) Choice Humorous Works; including his Ludicrous Adventures, Bons Mots, Puns, and Hoaxes. With Life of the Author, Portraits, Facsimiles and Illustrations. Crown 8vo, cloth extra, 7s. 6d.

Hooper (Mrs. Geo.).—The House of Raby. Post 8vo, boards, 2s.

Hopkins (Tighe), Novels by.
Nell Haffenden. With 8 Illustrations by C. GREGORY. Crown 8vo, cloth, 6s.
Crown 8vo. cloth, 3s. 6d. each.
'Twixt Love and Duty. With a Frontispiece. | For Freedom.
The Nugents of Carriconna. | The Incomplete Adventurer.

Horne (R. Hengist). — Orion: An Epic Poem. With Photograph Portrait by SUMMERS. Tenth Edition. Crown 8vo, cloth extra, 7s.

Hungerford (Mrs., Author of 'Molly Bawn'), Novels by.
Post 8vo, illustrated boards, 2s. each ; cloth limp, 2s. 6d. each.
A Maiden All Forlorn. | A Modern Circe. | An Unsatisfactory Lover.
Marvel. | A Mental Struggle. | Lady Patty.
In Durance Vile.
Crown 8vo, cloth extra, 3s. 6d. each ; post 8vo, illustrated boards, 2s. each ; cloth limp, 2s. 6d. each.
April's Lady. | The Three Graces.
Peter's Wife. | The Professor's Experiment.
Lady Verner's Flight. | Nora Creina.
The Red-House Mystery.

Crown 8vo, cloth extra, 3s. 6d. each.
An Anxious Moment. | A Point of Conscience.
The Coming of Chloe. | Lovice.

Hunt's (Leigh) Essays: A Tale for a Chimney Corner, &c. Edited by EDMUND OLLIER. Post 8vo, half-bound, 2s.

Hunt (Mrs. Alfred), Novels by.
Crown 8vo, cloth extra, 3s. 6d. each ; post 8vo, illustrated boards, 2s. each.
The Leaden Casket. | Self-Condemned. | That Other Person.
Thornicroft's Model. Post 8vo, boards, 2s. | Mrs. Juliet. Crown 8vo, cloth extra, 3s. 6d.

Hutchison (W. M.).—Hints on Colt-breaking. With 25 Illustrations. Crown 8vo, cloth extra, 3s. 6d.

Hydrophobia: An Account of M. PASTEUR'S System ; The Technique of his Method, and Statistics. By RENAUD SUZOR, M.D. Crown 8vo, cloth extra, 6s.

Hyne (C. J. Cutcliffe).—Honour of Thieves. Cr. 8vo, cloth, 3s. 6d.

CHATTO & WINDUS, Publishers, 111 St. Martin's Lane, London, W.C. 13

Impressions (The) of Aureole. Cheaper Edition, with a New Preface. Post 8vo, blush-rose paper and cloth, 2s. 6d.

Indoor Paupers. By ONE OF THEM. Crown 8vo, 1s.; cloth, 1s. 6d.

Innkeeper's Handbook (The) and Licensed Victualler's Manual. By J. TREVOR-DAVIES. A New Edition. Crown 8vo, cloth, 2s. [Shortly.

Irish Wit and Humour, Songs of. Collected and Edited by A. PERCEVAL GRAVES. Post 8vo, cloth limp, 2s. 6d.

Irving (Sir Henry): A Record of over Twenty Years at the Lyceum. By PERCY FITZGERALD. With Portrait. Crown 8vo, 1s.; cloth, 1s. 6d.

James (C. T. C.).—A Romance of the Queen's Hounds. Post 8vo, cloth limp, 1s. 6d.

Jameson (William).—My Dead Self. Post 8vo, bds., 2s.; cl., 2s. 6d.

Japp (Alex. H., LL.D.).—Dramatic Pictures, &c. Cr. 8vo, cloth, 5s.

Jay (Harriett), Novels by. Post 8vo, illustrated boards. 2s. each.
The Dark Colleen. | The Queen of Connaught.

Jefferies (Richard), Books by. Post 8vo, cloth limp, 2s. 6d. each.
Nature near London. | The Life of the Fields. | The Open Air.
*** Also the HAND-MADE PAPER EDITION, crown 8vo, buckram, gilt top, 6s. each.

The Eulogy of Richard Jefferies. By Sir WALTER BESANT. With a Photograph Portrait. Crown 8vo, cloth extra, 6s.

Jennings (Henry J.), Works by.
Curiosities of Criticism. Post 8vo, cloth limp, 2s. 6d.
Lord Tennyson: A Biographical Sketch. With Portrait. Post 8vo, 1s.; cloth, 1s. 6d.

Jerome (Jerome K.), Books by.
Stageland. With 64 Illustrations by J. BERNARD PARTRIDGE. Fcap. 4to, picture cover, 1s.
John Ingerfield, &c. With 9 Illusts. by A. S. BOYD and JOHN GULICH. Fcap. 8vo, pic. cov. 1s. 6d.
The Prude's Progress: A Comedy by J. K. JEROME and EDEN PHILLPOTTS. Cr. 8vo, 1s. 6d.

Jerrold (Douglas).—The Barber's Chair; and The Hedgehog Letters. Post 8vo, printed on laid paper and half-bound, 2s.

Jerrold (Tom), Works by. Post 8vo, 1s. ea.; cloth limp, 1s. 6d. each.
The Garden that Paid the Rent.
Household Horticulture: A Gossip about Flowers. Illustrated.

Jesse (Edward).—Scenes and Occupations of a Country Life. Post 8vo, cloth limp, 2s.

Jones (William, F.S.A.), Works by. Cr. 8vo, cl. extra, 3s. 6d. each.
Finger-Ring Lore: Historical, Legendary, and Anecdotal. With Hundreds of Illustrations.
Credulities, Past and Present. Including the Sea and Seamen, Miners, Talismans, Word and Letter Divination, Exorcising and Blessing of Animals, Birds, Eggs, Luck, &c. With Frontispiece.
Crowns and Coronations: A History of Regalia. With 91 Illustrations.

Jonson's (Ben) Works. With Notes Critical and Explanatory, and a Biographical Memoir by WILLIAM GIFFORD. Edited by Colonel CUNNINGHAM. Three Vols. crown 8vo, cloth extra, 3s. 6d. each.

Josephus, The Complete Works of. Translated by WHISTON. Containing 'The Antiquities of the Jews' and 'The Wars of the Jews.' With 52 Illustrations and Maps. Two Vols., demy 8vo, half-bound, 12s. 6d.

Kempt (Robert).—Pencil and Palette: Chapters on Art and Artists. Post 8vo, cloth limp, 2s. 6d.

Kershaw (Mark). — Colonial Facts and Fictions: Humorous Sketches. Post 8vo, illustrated boards, 2s.; cloth, 2s. 6d.

King (R. Ashe), Novels by.
Post 8vo, illustrated boards, 2s. each.
'The Wearing of the Green.' | Passion's Slave. | Bell Barry.
A Drawn Game. Crown 8vo, cloth, 3s. 6d.; post 8vo, illustrated boards, 2s.

Knight (William, M.R.C.S., and Edward, L.R.C.P.). — The Patient's Vade Mecum: How to Get Most Benefit from Medical Advice. Cr. 8vo, 1s.; cl., 1s. 6d.

Knights (The) of the Lion: A Romance of the Thirteenth Century. Edited, with an Introduction, by the MARQUESS OF LORNE, K.T. Crown 8vo, cloth extra, 6s.

Lamb's (Charles) Complete Works in Prose and Verse, including 'Poetry for Children' and 'Prince Dorus.' Edited, with Notes and Introduction, by R. H. SHEPHERD. With Two Portraits and Facsimile of the 'Essay on Roast Pig.' Crown 8vo, cloth, 3s. 6d.
The Essays of Elia. Post 8vo, printed on laid paper and half-bound, 2s.
Little Essays: Sketches and Characters by CHARLES LAMB, selected from his Letters by PERCY FITZGERALD. Post 8vo, cloth limp, 2s. 6d.
The Dramatic Essays of Charles Lamb. With Introduction and Notes by BRANDER MATTHEWS, and Steel-plate Portrait. Fcap. 8vo, half-bound, 2s. 6d.

Lambert (George). — The President of Boravia. Crown 8vo, cl., 3s. 6d.

Landor (Walter Savage). — Citation and Examination of William Shakspeare, &c., before Sir Thomas Lucy, touching Deer-stealing, 19th September, 1582. To which is added, A Conference of Master Edmund Spenser with the Earl of Essex, touching the State of Ireland, 1595. Fcap. 8vo, half-Roxburghe, 2s. 6d.

Lane (Edward William). — The Thousand and One Nights, commonly called in England **The Arabian Nights' Entertainments.** Translated from the Arabic, with Notes. Illustrated with many hundred Engravings from Designs by HARVEY. Edited by EDWARD STANLEY POOLE. With Preface by STANLEY LANE-POOLE. Three Vols., demy 8vo, cloth, 7s. 6d. ea.

Larwood (Jacob), Works by.
Anecdotes of the Clergy. Post 8vo, laid paper, half-bound, 2s.
Post 8vo, cloth limp, 2s. 6d. each.
Forensic Anecdotes. | **Theatrical Anecdotes.**

Lehmann (R. C.), Works by. Post 8vo, 1s. each; cloth, 1s. 6d. each.
Harry Fludyer at Cambridge.
Conversational Hints for Young Shooters: A Guide to Polite Talk.

Leigh (Henry S.). — Carols of Cockayne. Printed on hand-made paper, bound in buckram, 5s.

Leland (C. Godfrey). — A Manual of Mending and Repairing. With Diagrams. Crown 8vo, cloth, 5s.

Lepelletier (Edmond). — Madame Sans-Gène. Translated from the French by JOHN DE VILLIERS. Crown 8vo, cloth, 3s. 6d.; post 8vo, picture boards, 2s.

Leys (John). — The Lindsays: A Romance. Post 8vo, illust. bds., 2s.

Lilburn (Adam). — A Tragedy in Marble. Crown 8vo, cloth, 3s. 6d.

Lindsay (Harry, Author of 'Methodist Idylls'), Novels by.
Rhoda Roberts. Crown 8vo, cloth, 3s. 6d.
The Jacobite: A Romance of the Conspiracy of 'The Forty.' Crown 8vo, cloth, gilt top, 6s.

Linton (E. Lynn), Works by.
Crown 8vo, cloth extra, 3s. 6d. each; post 8vo, illustrated boards, 2s. each.
Patricia Kemball. | Ione. | Under which Lord? With 12 Illustrations.
The Atonement of Leam Dundas. | 'My Love!' | Sowing the Wind.
The World Well Lost. With 12 Illusts. | Paston Carew, Millionaire and Miser.
The One Too Many. | Dulcie Everton. | With a Silken Thread.
Post 8vo, cloth limp, 2s. 6d. each.
Witch Stories. | Ourselves: Essays on Women.
Freeshooting: Extracts from the Works of Mrs. LYNN LINTON.
The Rebel of the Family. Post 8vo, illustrated boards, 2s.

Lucy (Henry W.). — Gideon Fleyce: A Novel. Crown 8vo, cloth extra, 3s. 6d.; post 8vo, illustrated boards, 2s.

Macalpine (Avery), Novels by.
Teresa Itasca. Crown 8vo, cloth extra, 1s.
Broken Wings. With Six Illustrations by W. J. HENNESSY. Crown 8vo, cloth extra, 6s.

MacColl (Hugh), Novels by.
Mr. Stranger's Sealed Packet. Post 8vo, illustrated boards, 2s.
Ednor Whitlock. Crown 8vo, cloth extra, 6s.

Macdonell (Agnes). — Quaker Cousins. Post 8vo, boards, 2s.

MacGregor (Robert). — Pastimes and Players: Notes on Popular Games. Post 8vo, cloth limp, 2s. 6d.

Mackay (Charles, LL.D.). — Interludes and Undertones; or, Music at Twilight. Crown 8vo, cloth extra, 6s.

CHATTO & WINDUS, Publishers, 111 St. Martin's Lane, London, W.C. 15.

McCarthy (Justin, M.P.), Works by.
A History of Our Own Times, from the Accession of Queen Victoria to the General Election of 1880. LIBRARY EDITION. Four Vols., demy 8vo, cloth extra, 12s. each.—Also a POPULAR EDITION, in Four Vols., crown 8vo, cloth extra, 6s. each.—And the JUBILEE EDITION, with an Appendix of Events to the end of 1886, in Two Vols., large crown 8vo, cloth extra, 7s. 6d. each.
A History of Our Own Times, from 1880 to the Diamond Jubilee. Demy 8vo, cloth extra, 12s. Uniform with the LIBRARY EDITION of the first Four Volumes.
A Short History of Our Own Times. One Vol., crown 8vo, cloth extra, 6s.—Also a CHEAP POPULAR EDITION, post 8vo, cloth limp, 2s. 6d.
A History of the Four Georges. Four Vols., demy 8vo, cl. ex., 12s. each. [Vols. I. & II. ready.
Reminiscences. Two Vols., demy 8vo, cloth, 24s. [Shortly.

Crown 8vo, cloth extra, 3s. 6d. each; post 8vo, illustrated boards, 2s. each; cloth limp, 2s. 6d. each.

The Waterdale Neighbours.	Donna Quixote. With 12 Illustrations.
My Enemy's Daughter.	The Comet of a Season.
A Fair Saxon.	Maid of Athens. With 12 Illustrations.
Linley Rochford.	Camiola: A Girl with a Fortune.
Dear Lady Disdain.	The Dictator.
Miss Misanthrope. With 12 Illustrations.	Red Diamonds. The Riddle Ring.

The Three Disgraces, and other Stories. Crown 8vo, cloth, 3s. 6d.
'The Right Honourable.' By JUSTIN MCCARTHY, M.P., and Mrs. CAMPBELL PRAED. Crown 8vo, cloth extra, 6s.

McCarthy (Justin Huntly), Works by.
The French Revolution. (Constituent Assembly, 1789-91). Four Vols., demy 8vo, cloth, 12s. each.
An Outline of the History of Ireland. Crown 8vo, 1s.; cloth, 1s. 6d.
Ireland Since the Union: Sketches of Irish History, 1798-1886. Crown 8vo, cloth, 6s.
Hafiz in London: Poems. Small 8vo, gold cloth, 3s. 6d.
Our Sensation Novel. Crown 8vo, picture cover, 1s.; cloth limp, 1s. 6d.
Doom: An Atlantic Episode. Crown 8vo, picture cover, 1s.
Dolly: A Sketch. Crown 8vo, picture cover, 1s.; cloth limp, 1s. 6d.
Lily Lass: A Romance. Crown 8vo, picture cover, 1s.; cloth limp, 1s. 6d.
The Thousand and One Days. With Two Photogravures. Two Vols., crown 8vo, half-bd., 12s.
A London Legend. Crown 8vo, cloth, 3s. 6d.
The Royal Christopher. Crown 8vo, cloth, 3s. 6d.

MacDonald (George, LL.D.), Books by.
Works of Fancy and Imagination. Ten Vols., 16mo, cloth, gilt edges, in cloth case, 21s.; or the Volumes may be had separately, in Grolier cloth, at 2s. 6d. each.
Vol. I. WITHIN AND WITHOUT.—THE HIDDEN LIFE.
" II. THE DISCIPLE.—THE GOSPEL WOMEN.—BOOK OF SONNETS.—ORGAN SONGS.
" III. VIOLIN SONGS.—SONGS OF THE DAYS AND NIGHTS.—A BOOK OF DREAMS.—ROADSIDE POEMS.—POEMS FOR CHILDREN.
" IV. PARABLES.—BALLADS.—SCOTCH SONGS.
" V. & VI. PHANTASTES: A Faerie Romance.   Vol. VII. THE PORTENT.
" VIII. THE LIGHT PRINCESS.—THE GIANT'S HEART.—SHADOWS.
" IX. CROSS PURPOSES.—THE GOLDEN KEY.—THE CARASOYN.—LITTLE DAYLIGHT.
" X. THE CRUEL PAINTER.—THE WOW O' RIVVEN.—THE CASTLE.—THE BROKEN SWORDS.—THE GRAY WOLF.—UNCLE CORNELIUS.

Poetical Works of George MacDonald. Collected and Arranged by the Author. Two Vols., crown 8vo, buckram, 12s.
A Threefold Cord. Edited by GEORGE MACDONALD. Post 8vo, cloth, 5s.
Phantastes: A Faerie Romance. With 25 Illustrations by J. BELL. Crown 8vo, cloth extra, 3s. 6d.
Heather and Snow: A Novel. Crown 8vo, cloth extra, 3s. 6d.; post 8vo, illustrated boards, 2s.
Lilith: A Romance. SECOND EDITION. Crown 8vo, cloth extra, 6s.

Maclise Portrait Gallery (The) of Illustrious Literary Characters:
85 Portraits by DANIEL MACLISE; with Memoirs—Biographical, Critical, Bibliographical, and Anecdotal—illustrative of the Literature of the former half of the Present Century, by WILLIAM BATES, B.A. Crown 8vo, cloth extra, 3s. 6d.

Macquoid (Mrs.), Works by. Square 8vo, cloth extra, 6s. each.
In the Ardennes. With 50 Illustrations by THOMAS R. MACQUOID.
Pictures and Legends from Normandy and Brittany. 34 Illusts. by T. R. MACQUOID.
Through Normandy. With 92 Illustrations by T. R. MACQUOID, and a Map.
Through Brittany. With 35 Illustrations by T. R. MACQUOID, and a Map.
About Yorkshire. With 67 Illustrations by T. R. MACQUOID.

Post 8vo, illustrated boards, 2s. each.
The Evil Eye, and other Stories.   **Lost Rose**, and other Stories.

Magician's Own Book, The: Performances with Eggs, Hats, &c.
Edited by W. H. CREMER. With 200 Illustrations. Crown 8vo, cloth extra, 4s. 6d.

Magic Lantern, The, and its Management: Including full Practical
Directions. By T. C. HEPWORTH. With 10 Illustrations. Crown 8vo, 1s.; cloth, 1s. 6d.

Magna Charta: An Exact Facsimile of the Original in the British
Museum, 3 feet by 2 feet, with Arms and Seals emblazoned in Gold and Colours, 5s.

Mallory (Sir Thomas).—Mort d'Arthur: The Stories of King
Arthur and of the Knights of the Round Table. (A Selection.) Edited by B. MONTGOMERIE RANKING.' Post 8vo, cloth limp, 2s.

16 CHATTO & WINDUS, Publishers, 111 St. Martin's Lane, London, W.C.

Mallock (W. H.), Works by.
The New Republic. Post 8vo, picture cover, 2s.; cloth limp, 2s. 6d.
The New Paul & Virginia: Positivism on an Island. Post 8vo, cloth, 2s. 6d.
A Romance of the Nineteenth Century. Crown 8vo, cloth 6s.; post 8vo, illust. boards, 2s.

Poems. Small 4to, parchment, 8s.
Is Life Worth Living? Crown 8vo, cloth extra, 6s.

Margueritte (Paul and Victor).—The Disaster. Translated by FREDERIC LEES. Crown 8vo, cloth, 3s. 6d.

Marlowe's Works. Including his Translations. Edited, with Notes and Introductions, by Colonel CUNNINGHAM. Crown 8vo, cloth extra, 3s. 6d.

Massinger's Plays. From the Text of WILLIAM GIFFORD. Edited by Col. CUNNINGHAM. Crown 8vo, cloth extra, 3s. 6d.

Masterman (J.).—Half-a-Dozen Daughters. Post 8vo, boards, 2s.

Mathams (Rev. Walter, F.R.G.S.).—Comrades All. Fcp. 8vo, cloth limp, 1s.; cloth gilt, 2s.

Matthews (Brander).—A Secret of the Sea, &c. Post 8vo, illustrated boards, 2s.; cloth limp, 2s. 6d.

Meade (L. T.), Novels by.
A Soldier of Fortune. Crown 8vo, cloth, 3s. 6d.; post 8vo, illustrated boards, 2s.
Crown 8vo, cloth, 3s. 6d. each.
The Voice of the Charmer. With 8 Illustrations.
In an Iron Grip.
Dr. Rumsey's Patient. By L. T. MEADE and CLIFFORD HALIFAX, M.D.
On the Brink of a Chasm. Crown 8vo, cloth, gilt top, 6s.

Merrick (Leonard), Novels by.
The Man who was Good. Post 8vo, picture boards, 2s.
Crown 8vo, cloth, 3s. 6d. each.
This Stage of Fools. | Cynthia: A Daughter of the Philistines.

Mexican Mustang (On a), through Texas to the Rio Grande. By A. E. SWEET and J. ARMOY KNOX. With 265 Illustrations. Crown 8vo, cloth extra, 7s. 6d.

Middlemass (Jean), Novels by. Post 8vo, illust. boards, 2s. each.
Touch and Go. | Mr. Dorillion.

Miller (Mrs. F. Fenwick).—Physiology for the Young; or, The House of Life. With numerous Illustrations. Post 8vo, cloth limp, 2s. 6d.

Milton (J. L.), Works by. Post 8vo, 1s. each; cloth, 1s. 6d. each.
The Hygiene of the Skin. With Directions for Diet, Soaps, Baths, Wines, &c.
The Bath in Diseases of the Skin.
The Laws of Life, and their Relation to Diseases of the Skin.

Minto (Wm.).—Was She Good or Bad? Cr. 8vo, 1s.; cloth, 1s. 6d.

Mitford (Bertram), Novels by. Crown 8vo, cloth extra, 3s. 6d. each.
The Gun-Runner: A Romance of Zululand. With a Frontispiece by STANLEY L. WOOD.
The Luck of Gerard Ridgeley. With a Frontispiece by STANLEY L. WOOD.
The King's Assegai. With Six full-page Illustrations by STANLEY L. WOOD.
Renshaw Fanning's Quest. With a Frontispiece by STANLEY L. WOOD.

Molesworth (Mrs.).—Hathercourt Rectory. Post 8vo, illustrated boards, 2s.

Moncrieff (W. D. Scott-).—The Abdication: An Historical Drama. With Seven Etchings by JOHN PETTIE, W. Q. ORCHARDSON, J. MACWHIRTER, COLIN HUNTER, R. MACBETH and TOM GRAHAM. Imperial 4to, buckram, 21s.

Moore (Thomas), Works by.
The Epicurean; and Alciphron. Post 8vo, half-bound, 2s.
Prose and Verse; including Suppressed Passages from the MEMOIRS OF LORD BYRON. Edited by R. H. SHEPHERD. With Portrait. Crown 8vo, cloth extra, 7s. 6d.

Muddock (J. E.) Stories by.
Crown 8vo, cloth extra, 3s. 6d. each.
Maid Marian and Robin Hood. With 12 Illustrations by STANLEY WOOD.
Basile the Jester. With Frontispiece by STANLEY WOOD.
Young Lochinvar.
Post 8vo, Illustrated boards, 2s. each.
The Dead Man's Secret. | From the Bosom of the Deep.
Stories Weird and Wonderful. Post 8vo, illustrated boards, 2s.; cloth, 2s. 6d.

Murray (D. Christie), Novels by.
Crown 8vo, cloth extra, 3s. 6d. each; post 8vo, Illustrated boards, 2s. each.

A Life's Atonement.	A Model Father.	Bob Martin's Little Girl.
Joseph's Coat. 12 Illusts.	Old Blazer's Hero.	Time's Revenges.
Coals of Fire. 3 Illusts.	Cynic Fortune. Frontisp.	A Wasted Crime.
Val Strange.	By the Gate of the Sea.	In Direst Peril.
Hearts.	A Bit of Human Nature.	Mount Despair.
The Way of the World.	First Person Singular.	A Capful o' Nails.

The Making of a Novelist: An Experiment in Autobiography. With a Collotype Portrait. Cr. 8vo, buckram, 3s. 6d.
My Contemporaries in Fiction. Crown 8vo, buckram, 3s. 6d.
Crown 8vo, cloth, 3s. 6d. each.
This Little World.
Tales in Prose and Verse. With Frontispiece by ARTHUR HOPKINS.
A Race for Millions.

Murray (D. Christie) and Henry Herman, Novels by.
Crown 8vo, cloth extra, 3s. 6d. each; post 8vo, illustrated boards, 2s. each.
One Traveller Returns. | **The Bishops' Bible.**
Paul Jones's Alias, &c. With Illustrations by A. FORESTIER and G. NICOLET.

Murray (Henry), Novels by.
Post 8vo, illustrated boards, 2s. each; cloth, 2s. 6d. each.
A Game of Bluff. | **A Song of Sixpence.**

Newbolt (Henry).—Taken from the Enemy. Fcp. 8vo, cloth, 1s. 6d.; leatherette, 1s.

Nisbet (Hume), Books by.
'Bail Up.' Crown 8vo, cloth extra, 3s. 6d.; post 8vo, Illustrated boards, 2s.
Dr. Bernard St. Vincent. Post 8vo, illustrated boards, 2s.
Lessons in Art. With 21 Illustrations. Crown 8vo, cloth extra, 2s. 6d.

Norris (W. E.), Novels by. Crown 8vo, cloth, 3s. 6d. each; post 8vo, picture boards, 2s. each.
Saint Ann's.
Billy Bellew. With a Frontispiece by F. H. TOWNSEND.
Miss Wentworth's Idea. Crown 8vo, cloth, 3s. 6d.

O'Hanlon (Alice), Novels by. Post 8vo, illustrated boards, 2s. each.
The Unforeseen. | **Chance? or Fate?**

Ohnet (Georges), Novels by. Post 8vo, illustrated boards, 2s. each.
Doctor Rameau. | **A Last Love.**
A Weird Gift. Crown 8vo, cloth, 3s. 6d.; post 8vo, picture boards, 2s.

Oliphant (Mrs.), Novels by. Post 8vo, illustrated boards, 2s. each.
The Primrose Path. | **Whiteladies.**
The Greatest Heiress in England.
The Sorceress. Crown 8vo, cloth, 3s. 6d.; post 8vo, picture boards, 2s.

O'Reilly (Mrs.).—Phœbe's Fortunes. Post 8vo, illust. boards, 2s.

O'Shaughnessy (Arthur), Poems by:
Fcap. 8vo, cloth extra, 7s. 6d. each.
Music and Moonlight. | **Songs of a Worker.**
Lays of France. Crown 8vo, cloth extra, 10s. 6d.

Ouida, Novels by. Cr. 8vo, cl., 3s. 6d. ea.; post 8vo, illust. bds., 2s. ea.

Held in Bondage.	A Dog of Flanders.	In Maremma.	Wanda.
Tricotrin.	Pascarel.	Signa.	Bimbi.	Syrlin.
Strathmore.	Chandos.	Two Wooden Shoes.	Frescoes.	Othmar.
Cecil Castlemaine's Gage	In a Winter City.	Princess Napraxine.
Under Two Flags.	Ariadne.	Friendship.	Guilderoy.	Ruffino.
Puck.	Idalia.	A Village Commune.	Two Offenders.
Folle-Farine.	Moths.	Pipistrello.	Santa Barbara.

POPULAR EDITIONS. Medium 8vo, 6d. each; cloth, 1s. each.
Under Two Flags. | **Moths.**
Under Two Flags and Moths, POPULAR EDITION, in One Volume, medium 8vo, cloth, 2s.
Wisdom, Wit, and Pathos, selected from the Works of OUIDA by F. SYDNEY MORRIS. Post 8vo, cloth extra, 5s.—CHEAP EDITION, illustrated boards, 2s.

Page (H. A.).—Thoreau: His Life and Aims. With Portrait. Post 8vo, cloth, 2s. 6d.

Pandurang Hari; or, Memoirs of a Hindoo. With Preface by Sir BARTLE FRERE. Post 8vo, illustrated boards, 2s.

Parker (Rev. Joseph, D.D.).—Might Have Been: some Life Notes. Crown 8vo, cloth, 6s.

Pascal's Provincial Letters. A New Translation, with Historical Introduction and Notes by T. M'CRIE, D.D. Post 8vo, half-cloth, 2s.

Paul (Margaret A.).—Gentle and Simple. Crown 8vo, cloth, with Frontispiece by HELEN PATERSON, 3s. 6d.; post 8vo, illustrated boards, 2s.

18 CHATTO & WINDUS, Publishers, 111 St. Martin's Lane, London, W.C.

Payn (James), Novels by.
Crown 8vo, cloth extra, 3s. 6d. each; post 8vo, illustrated boards, 2s. each.

Lost Sir Massingberd.
Walter's Word. | A County Family.
Less Black than We're Painted.
By Proxy. | For Cash Only.
High Spirits.
Under One Roof.
A Confidential Agent. With 12 Illusts.
A Grape from a Thorn. With 12 Illusts.

Holiday Tasks.
The Canon's Ward. With Portrait
The Talk of the Town. With 12 Illusts.
Glow-Worm Tales.
The Mystery of Mirbridge.
The Word and the Will.
The Burnt Million.
Sunny Stories. | A Trying Patient.

Post 8vo illustrated boards, 2s. each.

Humorous Stories. | From Exile.
The Foster Brothers.
The Family Scapegrace.
Married Beneath Him.
Bentinck's Tutor.
A Perfect Treasure.
Like Father, Like Son.
A Woman's Vengeance.
Carlyon's Year. | Cecil's Tryst.
Murphy's Master. | At Her Mercy.

The Clyffards of Clyffe.
Found Dead. | Gwendoline's Harvest.
Mirk Abbey. | A Marine Residence.
Some Private Views.
Not Wooed, But Won.
Two Hundred Pounds Reward.
The Best of Husbands.
Halves. | What He Cost Her
Fallen Fortunes. | Kit: A Memory.
A Prince of the Blood.

A Modern Dick Whittington; or, A Patron of Letters. With a Portrait of the Author. Crown 8vo, cloth, 3s. 6d.
In Peril and Privation. With 17 Illustrations. Crown 8vo, cloth, 3s. 6d.
Notes from the 'News.' Crown 8vo, portrait cover, 1s.; cloth, 1s. 6d.
By Proxy. POPULAR EDITION, medium 8vo, 6d.; cloth, 1s.

Payne (Will).—Jerry the Dreamer. Crown 8vo, cloth, 3s. 6d.

Pennell (H. Cholmondeley), Works by. Post 8vo, cloth, 2s. 6d. ea.
Puck on Pegasus. With Illustrations.
Pegasus Re-Saddled. With Ten full-page Illustrations by G. DU MAURIER.
The Muses of Mayfair: Vers de Société. Selected by H. C. PENNELL.

Phelps (E. Stuart), Works by. Post 8vo, 1s. ea.; cloth, 1s. 6d. ea.
Beyond the Gates. | An Old Maid's Paradise. | Burglars in Paradise.
Jack the Fisherman. Illustrated by C. W. REED. Crown 8vo, cloth, 1s. 6d.

Phil May's Sketch-Book. Containing 54 Humorous Cartoons. A New Edition. Crown folio, cloth, 2s. 6d.

Phipson (Dr. T. L.), Books by. Crown 8vo, art canvas, gilt top, 5s. ea.
Famous Violinists and Fine Violins.
Voice and Violin: Sketches, Anecdotes, and Reminiscences.

Planché (J. R.), Works by.
The Pursuivant of Arms. With Six Plates and 209 Illustrations. Crown 8vo, cloth, 7s. 6d.
Songs and Poems, 1819-1879. With Introduction by Mrs. MACKARNESS. Crown 8vo, cloth, 6s.

Plutarch's Lives of Illustrious Men. With Notes and a Life of Plutarch by JOHN and WM. LANGHORNE, and Portraits. Two Vols., demy 8vo, half-bound 10s. 6d.

Poe's (Edgar Allan) Choice Works in Prose and Poetry. With Introduction by CHARLES BAUDELAIRE. Portrait and Facsimiles. Crown 8vo, cloth, 7s. 6d.
The Mystery of Marie Roget, &c. Post 8vo, illustrated boards, 2s.

Pollock (W. H.).—The Charm, and other Drawing-room Plays. By Sir WALTER BESANT and WALTER H. POLLOCK. With 50 Illustrations. Crown 8vo, cloth gilt, 6s.

Pollock (Wilfred).—War and a Wheel: The Græco-Turkish War as Seen from a Bicycle. With a Map. Crown 8vo, picture cover, 1s.

Pope's Poetical Works. Post 8vo, cloth limp, 2s.

Porter (John).—Kingsclere. Edited by BYRON WEBBER. With 19 full-page and many smaller Illustrations. Cheaper Edition. Demy 8vo, cloth, 7s. 6d.

Praed (Mrs. Campbell), Novels by. Post 8vo, illust. bds., 2s. each.
The Romance of a Station. | The Soul of Countess Adrian.
Crown 8vo, cloth, 3s. 6d. each; post 8vo, boards, 2s. each.
Outlaw and Lawmaker. | Christina Chard. With Frontispiece by W. PAGET.
Mrs. Tregaskiss. With 8 Illustrations by ROBERT SAUBER.
Nulma. Crown 8vo, cloth, 3s. 6d.
Madame Izan: A Tourist Story. Crown 8vo, cloth, gilt top, 6s.

Price (E. C.), Novels by.
Crown 8vo, cloth extra, 3s. 6d. each; post 8vo, illustrated boards, 2s. each.
Valentina. | The Foreigners. | Mrs. Lancaster's Rival.
Gerald. Post 8vo, illustrated boards, 2s.

Princess Olga.—Radna: A Novel. Crown 8vo, cloth extra, 6s.

CHATTO & WINDUS, Publishers, 111 St. Martin's Lane, London, W.C. 19

Proctor (Richard A.), Works by.
Flowers of the Sky. With 55 Illustrations. Small crown 8vo, cloth extra, 3s. 6d.
Easy Star Lessons. With Star Maps for every Night in the Year. Crown 8vo, cloth, 6s.
Familiar Science Studies. Crown 8vo, cloth extra, 6s.
Saturn and its System. With 13 Steel Plates. Demy 8vo, cloth extra, 10s. 6d.
Mysteries of Time and Space. With numerous Illustrations. Crown 8vo, cloth extra, 6s.
The Universe of Suns, &c. With numerous Illustrations. Crown 8vo, cloth extra, 6s.
Wages and Wants of Science Workers. Crown 8vo, 1s. 6d.

Pryce (Richard).—Miss Maxwell's Affections. Crown 8vo, cloth, with Frontispiece by HAL LUDLOW, 3s. 6d.; post 8vo, illustrated boards, 2s.

Rambosson (J.).—Popular Astronomy. Translated by C. B. PITMAN. With 10 Coloured Plates and 63 Woodcut Illustrations. Crown 8vo, cloth, 7s. 6d.

Randolph (Col. G.).—Aunt Abigail Dykes. Crown 8vo, cloth, 7s. 6d.

Read (General Meredith).—Historic Studies in Vaud, Berne, and Savoy. With 31 full-page Illustrations. Two Vols., demy 8vo, cloth, 28s.

Reade's (Charles) Novels.
The New Collected LIBRARY EDITION, complete in Seventeen Volumes, set in new long primer type, printed on laid paper, and elegantly bound in cloth, price 3s. 6d. each.
1. Peg Woffington; and Christie Johnstone.
2. Hard Cash.
3. The Cloister and the Hearth. With a Preface by Sir WALTER BESANT.
4. 'It is Never Too Late to Mend.'
5. The Course of True Love Never Did Run Smooth; and Singleheart and Doubleface.
6. The Autobiography of a Thief; Jack of all Trades; A Hero and a Martyr; and The Wandering Heir.
7. Love Me Little, Love me Long.
8. The Double Marriage.
9. Griffith Gaunt.
10. Foul Play.
11. Put Yourself in His Place.
12. A Terrible Temptation.
13. A Simpleton.
14. A Woman-Hater.
15. The Jilt, and other Stories; and Good Stories of Man and other Animals.
16. A Perilous Secret.
17. Readiana; and Bible Characters.

In Twenty-one Volumes, post 8vo, illustrated boards, 2s. each.
Peg Woffington. | Christie Johnstone.
'It is Never Too Late to Mend.'
The Course of True Love Never Did Run Smooth.
The Autobiography of a Thief; Jack of all Trades; and James Lambert.
Love Me Little, Love Me Long.
The Double Marriage.
The Cloister and the Hearth.
Hard Cash. | Griffith Gaunt.
Foul Play. | Put Yourself in His Place.
A Terrible Temptation.
A Simpleton. | The Wandering Heir.
A Woman-Hater.
Singleheart and Doubleface.
Good Stories of Man and other Animals.
The Jilt, and other Stories.
A Perilous Secret. | Readiana.

POPULAR EDITIONS, medium 8vo, 6d. each; cloth, 1s. each.
'It is Never Too Late to Mend.' | The Cloister and the Hearth.
Peg Woffington; and Christie Johnstone. | Hard Cash.

Christie Johnstone. With Frontispiece. Choicely printed in Elzevir style. Fcap. 8vo, half-Roxb. 2s. 6d.
Peg Woffington. Choicely printed in Elzevir style. Fcap. 8vo, half-Roxburghe, 2s. 6d.
The Cloister and the Hearth. In Four Vols., post 8vo, with an Introduction by Sir WALTER BESANT, and a Frontispiece to each Vol., buckram, gilt top, 6s. the set.
Bible Characters. Fcap. 8vo, leatherette, 1s.

Selections from the Works of Charles Reade. With an Introduction by Mrs. ALEX. IRELAND. Crown 8vo, buckram, with Portrait, 6s.; CHEAP EDITION, post 8vo, cloth limp, 2s. 6d.

Riddell (Mrs. J. H.), Novels by.
Weird Stories. Crown 8vo, cloth extra, 3s. 6d.; post 8vo, illustrated boards, 2s.

Post 8vo, illustrated boards, 2s. each.
The Uninhabited House. | Fairy Water.
The Prince of Wales's Garden Party. | Her Mother's Darling.
The Mystery in Palace Gardens. | The Nun's Curse. | Idle Tales.

Rimmer (Alfred), Works by. Large crown 8vo, cloth, 3s. 6d. each.
Our Old Country Towns. With 54 Illustrations by the Author.
Rambles Round Eton and Harrow. With 52 Illustrations by the Author.
About England with Dickens. With 58 Illustrations by C. A. VANDERHOOF and A. RIMMER.

Rives (Amelie, Author of 'The Quick or the Dead?'), Works by.
Barbara Dering. Crown 8vo, cloth, 3s. 6d.; post 8vo, picture boards, 2s.
Meriel: A Love Story. Crown 8vo, cloth, 3s. 6d.

Robinson Crusoe. By DANIEL DEFOE. With 37 Illustrations by GEORGE CRUIKSHANK. Post 8vo, half-cloth, 2s.; cloth extra, gilt edges, 2s. 6d.

Robinson (F. W.), Novels by.
Women are Strange. Post 8vo, illustrated boards, 2s.
The Hands of Justice. Crown 8vo, cloth extra, 3s. 6d.; post 8vo, illustrated boards, 2s.
The Woman in the Dark. Crown 8vo, cloth, 3s. 6d.; post 8vo, illustrated boards, 2s.

CHATTO & WINDUS, Publishers, 111 St. Martin's Lane, London, W.C.

Robinson (Phil), Works by. Crown 8vo, cloth extra, 6s. each.
The Poets' Birds. | The Poets' Beasts.
The Poets and Nature: Reptiles, Fishes, and Insects.

Rochefoucauld's Maxims and Moral Reflections. With Notes and an Introductory Essay by SAINTE-BEUVE. Post 8vo, cloth limp, 2s.

Roll of Battle Abbey, The: A List of the Principal Warriors who came from Normandy with William the Conqueror, 1066. Printed in Gold and Colours, 5s.

Rosengarten (A.).—A Handbook of Architectural Styles. Translated by W. COLLETT-SANDARS. With 630 Illustrations. Crown 8vo, cloth extra, 7s. 6d.

Rowley (Hon. Hugh), Works by. Post 8vo, cloth, 2s. 6d. each.
Puniana: Riddles and Jokes. With numerous Illustrations.
More Puniana. Profusely Illustrated.

Runciman (James), Stories by. Post 8vo, bds., 2s. ea ; cl., 2s. 6d. ea.
Skippers & Shellbacks. | Grace Balmaign's Sweetheart. | Schools & Scholars.

Russell (Dora), Novels by.
A Country Sweetheart. Crown 8vo, cloth, 3s. 6d. ; post 8vo, picture boards, 2s.
The Drift of Fate. Crown 8vo, cloth, 3s. 6d.

Russell (Herbert).—True Blue; or, 'The Lass that Loved a Sailor.' Crown 8vo, cloth, 3s. 6d.

Russell (W. Clark), Novels, &c., by.
Crown 8vo, cloth extra, 3s. 6d. each ; post 8vo, illustrated boards, 2s. each ; cloth limp, 2s. 6d. each.
Round the Galley-Fire. | An Ocean Tragedy.
In the Middle Watch. | My Shipmate Louise.
On the Fo'k'sle Head. | Alone on a Wide Wide Sea.
A Voyage to the Cape. | The Good Ship 'Mohock.'
A Book for the Hammock. | The Phantom Death.
The Mystery of the 'Ocean Star.' | Is He the Man? | The Convict Ship.
The Romance of Jenny Harlowe. | Heart of Oak. | The Last Entry.
The Tale of the Ten.

The Ship: Her Story. With about 60 Illustrations by H. C. SEPPINGS WRIGHT. Small 4to, cloth, 6s. [Preparing.

Saint Aubyn (Alan), Novels by.
Crown 8vo, cloth extra, 3s. 6d. each ; post 8vo, Illustrated boards, 2s. each.
A Fellow of Trinity. With a Note by OLIVER WENDELL HOLMES and a Frontispiece.
The Junior Dean. | The Master of St. Benedict's. | To His Own Master.
Orchard Damerel. | In the Face of the World. | The Tremlett Diamonds.

Fcap. 8vo, cloth boards, 1s. 6d. each.
The Old Maid's Sweetheart. | Modest Little Sara.

Fortune's Gate. Crown 8vo, cloth, gilt top, 3s. 6d.
Mary Unwin. With 8 Illustrations by PERCY FARRANT. Crown 8vo, cloth, 6s.

Saint John (Bayle).—A Levantine Family. A New Edition. Crown 8vo, cloth, 3s. 6d.

Sala (George A.).—Gaslight and Daylight. Post 8vo, boards, 2s.

Scotland Yard, Past and Present: Experiences of Thirty-seven Years. By Ex-Chief-Inspector CAVANAGH. Post 8vo, Illustrated boards, 2s.; cloth, 2s. 6d.

Secret Out, The: One Thousand Tricks with Cards; with Entertaining Experiments in Drawing-room or 'White' Magic. By W. H. CREMER. With 300 Illustrations. Crown 8vo, cloth extra, 4s. 6d.

Seguin (L. G.), Works by.
The Country of the Passion Play (Oberammergau) and the Highlands of Bavaria. With Map and 37 Illustrations. Crown 8vo, cloth extra, 3s. 6d.
Walks in Algiers. With Two Maps and 16 Illustrations. Crown 8vo, cloth extra, 6s.

Senior (Wm.).—By Stream and Sea. Post 8vo, cloth, 2s. 6d.

Sergeant (Adeline).—Dr. Endicott's Experiment. Cr. 8vo, 3s. 6d.

Shakespeare for Children: Lamb's Tales from Shakespeare. With Illustrations, coloured and plain, by J. MOYR SMITH. Crown 4to, cloth gilt, 3s. 6d.

Shakespeare the Boy. With Sketches of the Home and School Life, the Games and Sports, the Manners, Customs, and Folk-lore of the Time. By WILLIAM J. ROLFE, Litt.D. With 42 Illustrations. Crown 8vo, cloth gilt, 2s. 6d.

Sharp (William).—Children of To-morrow. Crown 8vo, cloth, 6s.

CHATTO & WINDUS, Publishers, 111 St. Martin's Lane, London, W.C. 21

Shelley's (Percy Bysshe) Complete Works in Verse and Prose.
Edited, Prefaced, and Annotated by R. HERNE SHEPHERD. Five Vols., crown 8vo, cloth, 3s. 6d. each.
Poetical Works, in Three Vols.:
Vol. I. Introduction by the Editor; Posthumous Fragments of Margaret Nicholson; Shelley's Correspondence with Stockdale; The Wandering Jew; Queen Mab, with the Notes; Alastor, and other Poems; Rosalind and Helen; Prometheus Unbound; Adonais, &c.
,, II. Laon and Cythna; The Cenci; Julian and Maddalo; Swellfoot the Tyrant; The Witch of Atlas; Epipsychidion; Hellas.
,, III. Posthumous Poems; The Masque of Anarchy; and other Pieces.
Prose Works, in Two Vols.:
Vol. I. The Two Romances of Zastrozzi and St. Irvyne; the Dublin and Marlow Pamphlets; A Refutation of Deism; Letters to Leigh Hunt, and some Minor Writings and Fragments.
II. The Essays; Letters from Abroad; Translations and Fragments, edited by Mrs. SHELLEY. With a Biography of Shelley, and an Index of the Prose Works.
₊ Also a few copies of a LARGE-PAPER EDITION, 5 vols., cloth, £2 12s. 6d.

Sherard (R. H.).—Rogues: A Novel. Crown 8vo, cloth, 1s. 6d.

Sheridan's (Richard Brinsley) Complete Works, with Life and Anecdotes. Including his Dramatic Writings, his Works in Prose and Poetry, Translations, Speeches, and Jokes. With 10 Illustrations. Crown 8vo, cloth, 3s. 6d.
The Rivals, The School for Scandal, and other Plays. Post 8vo, half-bound, 2s.
Sheridan's Comedies: The Rivals and **The School for Scandal.** Edited, with an Introduction and Notes to each Play, and a Biographical Sketch, by BRANDER MATTHEWS. With Illustrations. Demy 8vo, half-parchment, 12s. 6d.

Sidney's (Sir Philip) Complete Poetical Works, including all those in 'Arcadia.' With Portrait, Memorial-Introduction, Notes, &c., by the Rev. A. B. GROSART, D.D. Three Vols., crown 8vo, cloth boards, 3s. 6d. each.

Signboards: Their History, including Anecdotes of Famous Taverns and Remarkable Characters. By JACOB LARWOOD and JOHN CAMDEN HOTTEN. With Coloured Frontispiece and 94 Illustrations. Crown 8vo, cloth extra, 3s. 6d.

Sims (George R.), Works by.
Post 8vo, illustrated boards, 2s. each; cloth limp, 2s. 6d. each.
The Ring o' Bells. | **Dramas of Life.** With 60 Illustrations.
Mary Jane's Memoirs. | **Memoirs of a Landlady.**
Mary Jane Married. | **My Two Wives.**
Tinkletop's Crime. | **Scenes from the Show.**
Zeph: A Circus Story, &c. | **The Ten Commandments:** Stories.
Tales of To-day.

Crown 8vo, picture cover, 1s. each; cloth, 1s. 6d. each.
The Dagonet Reciter and Reader: Being Readings and Recitations in Prose and Verse selected from his own Works by GEORGE R. SIMS.
The Case of George Candlemas. | **Dagonet Ditties.** (From *The Referee*.)
Rogues and Vagabonds. Crown 8vo, cloth, 3s. 6d.; post 8vo, picture boards, 2s.; cloth limp, 2s. 6d.
How the Poor Live; and **Horrible London.** With a Frontispiece by F. BARNARD Crown 8vo, leatherette, 1s.
Dagonet Abroad. Crown 8vo, cloth, 3s. 6d.; post 8vo, picture boards, 2s.; cloth limp, 2s. 6d.
Dagonet Dramas of the Day. Crown 8vo, 1s.
Once upon a Christmas Time. With 8 Illustrations by CHARLES GREEN, R.I. Crown 8vo, cloth gilt, 2s. 6d.

Sister Dora: A Biography. By MARGARET LONSDALE. With Four Illustrations. Demy 8vo, picture cover, 4d.; cloth, 6d.

Sketchley (Arthur).—A Match in the Dark. Post 8vo, boards, 2s.

Slang Dictionary (The): Etymological, Historical, and Anecdotal. Crown 8vo, cloth extra, 6s. 6d.

Smart (Hawley), Novels by.
Crown 8vo, cloth, 3s. 6d. each; post 8vo, picture boards, 2s. each.
Beatrice and Benedick. | **Long Odds.**
Without Love or Licence. | **The Master of Rathkelly.**
Crown 8vo, cloth, 3s. 6d. each.
The Outsider. | **A Racing Rubber.**
The Plunger. Post 8vo, picture boards, 2s.

Smith (J. Moyr), Works by.
The Prince of Argolis. With 130 Illustrations. Post 8vo, cloth extra, 3s. 6d.
The Wooing of the Water Witch. With numerous Illustrations. Post 8vo, cloth, 6s.

Snazelleparilla. Decanted by G. S. EDWARDS. With Portrait of G. H. SNAZELLE and 65 Illustrations by C. LYALL. Crown 8vo, cloth, 3s. 6d.

Society in London. Crown 8vo, 1s.; cloth, 1s. 6d.

Society in Paris: The Upper Ten Thousand. A Series of Letters from Count PAUL VASILI to a Young French Diplomat. Crown 8vo, cloth, 6s.

Somerset (Lord Henry).—Songs of Adieu. Small 4to, Jap. vel., 6s.

22 CHATTO & WINDUS, Publishers, 111 St. Martin's Lane, London, W.C.

Spalding (T. A., LL.B.).—Elizabethan Demonology: An Essay on the Belief in the Existence of Devils. Crown 8vo, cloth extra, 5s.

Speight (T. W.), Novels by.
Post 8vo, Illustrated boards, 2s. each.
The Mysteries of Heron Dyke. | The Loudwater Tragedy.
By Devious Ways, &c. | Burgo's Romance.
Hoodwinked; & Sandycroft Mystery. | Quittance in Full.
The Golden Hoop. | A Husband from the Sea.
Back to Life.

Post 8vo, cloth limp, 1s. 6d. each.
A Barren Title. | Wife or No Wife?

Crown 8vo, cloth extra, 3s. 6d. each.
A Secret of the Sea. | The Grey Monk. | The Master of Trenance.
A Minion of the Moon: A Romance of the King's Highway.
The Secret of Wyvern Towers.
The Doom of Siva. [*Shortly.*

Spenser for Children. By M. H. TOWRY. With Coloured Illustrations by WALTER J. MORGAN. Crown 4to, cloth extra, 3s. 6d.

Spettigue (H. H.).—The Heritage of Eve. Crown 8vo, cloth, 6s.

Stafford (John), Novels by.
Doris and I. Crown 8vo, cloth, 3s. 6d.
Carlton Priors. Crown 8vo, cloth, gilt top, 6s.

Starry Heavens (The): A POETICAL BIRTHDAY BOOK. Royal 16mo, cloth extra, 2s. 6d.

Stedman (E. C.), Works by. Crown 8vo, cloth extra, 9s. each.
Victorian Poets. | The Poets of America.

Stephens (Riccardo, M.B.).—The Cruciform Mark: The Strange Story of RICHARD TREGENNA, Bachelor of Medicine (Univ. Edinb.) Crown 8vo, cloth, 3s. 6d.

Sterndale (R. Armitage).—The Afghan Knife: A Novel. Post 8vo, cloth, 3s. 6d.; Illustrated boards, 2s.

Stevenson (R. Louis), Works by.
Crown 8vo, buckram, gilt top, 6s. each; post 8vo, cloth limp, 2s. 6d. each.
Travels with a Donkey. With a Frontispiece by WALTER CRANE.
An Inland Voyage. With a Frontispiece by WALTER CRANE.

Crown 8vo, buckram, gilt top, 6s. each.
Familiar Studies of Men and Books.
The Silverado Squatters. With Frontispiece by J. D. STRONG.
The Merry Men. | Underwoods: Poems.
Memories and Portraits.
Virginibus Puerisque, and other Papers. | Ballads. | Prince Otto.
Across the Plains, with other Memories and Essays.
Weir of Hermiston.
A Lowden Sabbath Morn. With 27 Illustrations by A. S. BOYD. Fcap. 8vo, cloth, 6s.
Songs of Travel. Crown 8vo, buckram, 5s.
New Arabian Nights. Crown 8vo, buckram, gilt top, 6s.; post 8vo, illustrated boards, 2s.
The Suicide Club; and The Rajah's Diamond. (From NEW ARABIAN NIGHTS.) With Eight Illustrations by W. J. HENNESSY. Crown 8vo, cloth, 3s. 6d.
The Stevenson Reader: Selections from the Writings of ROBERT LOUIS STEVENSON. Edited by LLOYD OSBOURNE. Post 8vo, cloth, 2s. 6d.; buckram, gilt top, 3s. 6d.

Storey (G. A., A.R.A.).—Sketches from Memory. With 93 Illustrations by the Author. Demy 8vo, cloth, gilt top, 12s. 6d.

Stories from Foreign Novelists. With Notices by HELEN and ALICE ZIMMERN. Crown 8vo, cloth extra, 3s. 6d.; post 8vo, illustrated boards, 2s.

Strange Manuscript (A) Found in a Copper Cylinder. Crown 8vo, cloth extra, with 19 Illustrations by GILBERT GAUL, 5s.; post 8vo, illustrated boards, 2s.

Strange Secrets. Told by PERCY FITZGERALD, CONAN DOYLE, FLORENCE MARRYAT, &c. Post 8vo, illustrated boards, 2s.

Strutt (Joseph). — The Sports and Pastimes of the People of England; including the Rural and Domestic Recreations, May Games, Mummeries, Shows, &c., from the Earliest Period to the Present Time. Edited by WILLIAM HONE. With 140 Illustrations. Crown 8vo, cloth extra, 3s. 6d.

Swift's (Dean) Choice Works, in Prose and Verse. With Memoir, Portrait, and Facsimiles of the Maps in 'Gulliver's Travels.' Crown 8vo, cloth, 3s. 6d.
Gulliver's Travels, and A Tale of a Tub. Post 8vo, half-bound, 2s.
Jonathan Swift: A Study. By J. CHURTON COLLINS. Crown 8vo, cloth extra, 8s.

CHATTO & WINDUS, Publishers, 111 St. Martin's Lane, London, W.C. 23

Swinburne (Algernon C.), Works by.
Selections from the Poetical Works of A. C. Swinburne. Fcap. 8vo 6s.
Atalanta in Calydon. Crown 8vo, 6s.
Chastelard: A Tragedy. Crown 8vo, 7s.
Poems and Ballads. FIRST SERIES. Crown 8vo, or fcap. 8vo, 9s.
Poems and Ballads. SECOND SERIES. Crown 8vo, 9s.
Poems & Ballads. THIRD SERIES. Cr. 8vo, 7s.
Songs before Sunrise. Crown 8vo, 10s. 6d.
Bothwell: A Tragedy. Crown 8vo, 12s. 6d.
Songs of Two Nations. Crown 8vo, 6s.
George Chapman. (See Vol. II. of G. CHAPMAN'S Works.) Crown 8vo, 3s. 6d.
Essays and Studies. Crown 8vo, 12s.
Erechtheus: A Tragedy. Crown 8vo, 6s.
A Note on Charlotte Bronte. Cr. 8vo, 6s.
A Study of Shakespeare. Crown 8vo, 8s.
Songs of the Springtides. Crown 8vo, 6s.
Studies in Song. Crown 8vo, 7s.
Mary Stuart: A Tragedy. Crown 8vo, 8s.
Tristram of Lyonesse. Crown 8vo, 9s.
A Century of Roundels. Small 4to, 8s.
A Midsummer Holiday. Crown 8vo, 7s.
Marino Faliero: A Tragedy. Crown 8vo, 6s.
A Study of Victor Hugo. Crown 8vo, 6s.
Miscellanies. Crown 8vo, 12s.
Locrine: A Tragedy. Crown 8vo, 6s.
A Study of Ben Jonson. Crown 8vo, 7s.
The Sisters: A Tragedy. Crown 8vo, 6s.
Astrophel, &c. Crown 8vo, 7s.
Studies in Prose and Poetry. Cr. 8vo, 9s.
The Tale of Balen. Crown 8vo, 7s.

Syntax's (Dr.) Three Tours: In Search of the Picturesque, in Search of Consolation, and in Search of a Wife. With ROWLANDSON'S Coloured Illustrations, and Life of the Author by J. C. HOTTEN. Crown 8vo, cloth extra, 7s. 6d.

Taine's History of English Literature. Translated by HENRY VAN LAUN. Four Vols., small demy 8vo, cloth boards, 30s.—POPULAR EDITION, Two Vols., large crown 8vo, cloth extra, 15s.

Taylor (Bayard). — Diversions of the Echo Club: Burlesques of Modern Writers. Post 8vo, cloth limp, 2s.

Taylor (Tom). — Historical Dramas. Containing 'Clancarty, 'Jeanne Darc,' 'Twixt Axe and Crown,' 'The Fool's Revenge,' 'Arkwright's Wife,' 'Anne Boleyn,' 'Plot and Passion.' Crown 8vo, cloth extra, 7s. 6d.
*** The Plays may also be had separately, at 1s. each.

Temple (Sir Richard, G.C.S.I.).—A Bird's-eye View of Picturesque India. With 32 Illustrations by the Author. Crown 8vo, cloth, gilt top, 6s.

Tennyson (Lord): A Biographical Sketch. By H. J. JENNINGS. Post 8vo, portrait cover, 1s.; cloth, 1s. 6d.

Thackerayana: Notes and Anecdotes. With Coloured Frontispiece and Hundreds of Sketches by WILLIAM MAKEPEACE THACKERAY. Crown 8vo, cloth extra, 3s. 6d.

Thames, A New Pictorial History of the. By A. S. KRAUSSE. With 340 Illustrations. Post 8vo, cloth, 1s. 6d.

Thiers (Adolphe). — History of the Consulate and Empire of France under Napoleon. Translated by D. FORBES CAMPBELL and JOHN STEBBING. With 36 Steel Plates. 12 Vols., demy 8vo, cloth extra, 12s. each.

Thomas (Bertha), Novels by. Cr. 8vo, cl., 3s. 6d. ea.; post 8vo, 2s. ea.
The Violin-Player. | Proud Maisie.
Cressida. Post 8vo, illustrated boards, 2s.

Thomson's Seasons, and The Castle of Indolence. With Introduction by ALLAN CUNNINGHAM, and 48 Illustrations. Post 8vo, half-bound, 2s.

Thornbury (Walter), Books by.
The Life and Correspondence of J. M. W. Turner. With Eight Illustrations in Colours and Two Woodcuts. New and Revised Edition. Crown 8vo, cloth, 3s. 6d.
Post 8vo, illustrated boards, 2s. each.
Old Stories Re-told. | Tales for the Marines.

Timbs (John), Works by. Crown 8vo, cloth, 3s. 6d. each.
Clubs and Club Life in London: Anecdotes of its Famous Coffee-houses, Hostelries, and Taverns. With 41 Illustrations.
English Eccentrics and Eccentricities: Stories of Delusions, Impostures, Sporting Scenes, Eccentric Artists, Theatrical Folk, &c. With 48 Illustrations.

Transvaal (The). By JOHN DE VILLIERS. With Map. Crown 8vo, 1s.

Trollope (Anthony), Novels by.
Crown 8vo, cloth extra, 3s. 6d. each; post 8vo, illustrated boards, 2s. each.
The Way We Live Now. | Mr. Scarborough's Family.
Frau Frohmann. | The Land-Leaguers.
Post 8vo, illustrated boards, 2s. each.
Kept in the Dark. | The American Senator.
The Golden Lion of Granpere. | John Caldigate. | Marion Fay.

Trollope (Frances E.), Novels by.
Crown 8vo, cloth extra, 3s. 6d. each; post 8vo, illustrated boards, 2s. each.
Like Ships Upon the Sea. | Mabel's Progress. | Anne Furness.

Trollope (T. A.).—Diamond Cut Diamond. Post 8vo, illust. bds., 2s.

Trowbridge (J. T.).—Farnell's Folly. Post 8vo, illust. boards, 2s.

Twain's (Mark) Books.
Crown 8vo, cloth extra, 3s. 6d. each.
The Choice Works of Mark Twain. Revised and Corrected throughout by the Author. With Life, Portrait, and numerous Illustrations.
Roughing It; and **The Innocents at Home.** With 200 Illustrations by F. A. FRASER.
The American Claimant. With 81 Illustrations by HAL HURST and others.
Tom Sawyer Abroad. With 26 Illustrations by DAN BEARD.
Tom Sawyer, Detective, &c. With Photogravure Portrait.
Pudd'nhead Wilson. With Portrait and Six Illustrations by LOUIS LOEB.
Mark Twain's Library of Humour. With 197 Illustrations by E. W. KEMBLE.

Crown 8vo, cloth extra, 3s. 6d. each; post 8vo, picture boards, 2s. each.
A Tramp Abroad. With 314 Illustrations.
The Innocents Abroad; or, The New Pilgrim's Progress. With 234 Illustrations. (The Two Shilling Edition is entitled **Mark Twain's Pleasure Trip.**)
The Gilded Age. By MARK TWAIN and C. D. WARNER. With 212 Illustrations.
The Adventures of Tom Sawyer. With 111 Illustrations.
The Prince and the Pauper. With 190 Illustrations.
Life on the Mississippi. With 300 Illustrations.
The Adventures of Huckleberry Finn. With 174 Illustrations by E. W. KEMBLE.
A Yankee at the Court of King Arthur. With 220 Illustrations by DAN BEARD.
The Stolen White Elephant.
The £1,000,000 Bank-Note.

Mark Twain's Sketches. Post 8vo, illustrated boards, 2s.
Personal Recollections of Joan of Arc. With Twelve Illustrations by F. V. DU MOND. Crown 8vo, cloth, 6s.
More Tramps Abroad. Crown 8vo, cloth, gilt top, 6s.

Tytler (C. C. Fraser-).—Mistress Judith: A Novel. Crown 8vo, cloth extra, 3s. 6d.; post 8vo, illustrated boards, 2s.

Tytler (Sarah), Novels by.
Crown 8vo, cloth extra, 3s. 6d. each; post 8vo, illustrated boards, 2s. each.
| **Lady Bell.** | **Buried Diamonds.** | **The Blackhall Ghosts.** |

Post 8vo, illustrated boards, 2s. each.
What She Came Through.	**The Huguenot Family.**
Citoyenne Jacqueline.	**Noblesse Oblige.**	**Disappeared.**
The Bride's Pass.	**Saint Mungo's City.**	**Beauty and the Beast.**

Crown 8vo, cloth, 3s. 6d. each.
| **The Macdonald Lass.** With Frontispiece. | **Mrs. Carmichael's Goddesses.** |
| **The Witch-Wife.** | **Rachel Langton.** | **Sapphira.** |

Upward (Allen), Novels by.
A Crown of Straw. Crown 8vo, cloth, 6s.

Crown 8vo, cloth, 3s. 6d. each; post 8vo, picture boards, 2s. each.
| **The Queen Against Owen.** | **The Prince of Balkistan.** |

'God Save the Queen!' a Tale of '37. Crown 8vo, decorated cover, 1s.; cloth, 2s.

Vashti and Esther. By 'Belle' of *The World*. Cr. 8vo, cloth, 3s. 6d.

Vizetelly (Ernest A.).—The Scorpion: A Romance of Spain. With a Frontispiece. Crown 8vo, cloth extra, 3s. 6d.

Wagner (Leopold).—How to Get on the Stage, and how to Succeed there. Crown 8vo, cloth, 2s. 6d.

Walford (Edward, M.A.), Works by.
Walford's County Families of the United Kingdom (1899). Containing the Descent, Birth, Marriage, Education, &c., of 12,000 Heads of Families, their Heirs, Offices, Addresses, Clubs, &c. Royal 8vo, cloth gilt, 50s.
Walford's Shilling Peerage (1899). Containing a List of the House of Lords, Scotch and Irish Peers, &c. 32mo, cloth, 1s.
Walford's Shilling Baronetage (1899). Containing a List of the Baronets of the United Kingdom, Biographical Notices, Addresses, &c. 32mo, cloth, 1s.
Walford's Shilling Knightage (1899). Containing a List of the Knights of the United Kingdom, Biographical Notices, Addresses, &c. 32mo, cloth, 1s.
Walford's Shilling House of Commons (1899). Containing a Complete List of Members of Parliament, their Addresses, Clubs, &c. 32mo, cloth, 1s.
Walford's Complete Peerage, Baronetage, Knightage, and House of Commons (1899). Royal 32mo, cloth, gilt edges, 5s.

Waller (S. E.).—Sebastiani's Secret. With 9 Illusts. Cr. 8vo, cl., 6s.

Walton and Cotton's Complete Angler; or, The Contemplative Man's Recreation, by IZAAK WALTON; and Instructions How to Angle, for a Trout or Grayling in a clear Stream, by CHARLES COTTON. With Memoirs and Notes by Sir HARRIS NICOLAS, and 61 Illustrations. Crown 8vo, cloth antique, 7s. 6d.

Walt Whitman, Poems by. Edited, with Introduction, by WILLIAM M. ROSSETTI. With Portrait. Crown 8vo, hand-made paper and buckram, 6s.

Ward (Herbert), Books by.
Five Years with the Congo Cannibals. With 92 Illustrations. Royal 8vo, cloth, 14s.
My Life with Stanley's Rear Guard. With Map. Post 8vo, 1s.; cloth, 1s. 6d.

CHATTO & WINDUS, Publishers, 111 St. Martin's Lane, London, W.C. 25

Warden (Florence).—Joan, the Curate. Crown 8vo, cloth, 3s. 6d.

Warman (Cy).—The Express Messenger, and other Tales of the Rail. Crown 8vo, cloth, 3s. 6d.

Warner (Charles Dudley).—A Roundabout Journey. Crown 8vo, cloth extra, 6s.

Warrant to Execute Charles I. A Facsimile, with the 59 Signatures and Seals. Printed on paper 22 in. by 14 in. 2s.
Warrant to Execute Mary Queen of Scots. A Facsimile, including Queen Elizabeth's Signature and the Great Seal. 2s.

Washington's (George) Rules of Civility Traced to their Sources and Restored by MONCURE D. CONWAY. Fcap. 8vo, Japanese vellum, 2s. 6d.

Wassermann (Lillias) and Aaron Watson.—The Marquis of Carabas. Post 8vo, illustrated boards, 2s.

Weather, How to Foretell the, with the Pocket Spectroscope. By F. W. CORY. With Ten Illustrations. Crown 8vo, 1s.; cloth, 1s. 6d.

Westall (William), Novels by.
Trust Money. Crown 8vo, cloth, 3s. 6d.; post 8vo, illustrated boards, 2s.; cloth limp, 2s. 6d.

Crown 8vo, cloth, 6s. each.
As a Man Sows.	A Woman Tempted Him.
With the Red Eagle.	A Red Bridal.

Crown 8vo, cloth. 3s. 6d. each.
Her Two Millions.	The Blind Musician.	The Phantom City.
Two Pinches of Snuff.	Strange Crimes.	Ralph Norbreck's Trust.
Roy of Roy's Court.	Ben Clough.	A Queer Race.
Nigel Fortescue.	The Old Factory.	Red Ryvington.
Birch Dene.	Sons of Belial.	

Westbury (Atha).—The Shadow of Hilton Fernbrook: A Romance of Maoriland. Crown 8vo, cloth, 3s. 6d.

White (Gilbert).—The Natural History of Selborne. Post 8vo, printed on laid paper and half-bound, 2s.

Williams (W. Mattieu, F.R.A.S.), Works by.
Science in Short Chapters. Crown 8vo, cloth extra, 7s. 6d.
A Simple Treatise on Heat. With Illustrations. Crown 8vo, cloth, 2s. 6d.
The Chemistry of Cookery. Crown 8vo, cloth extra, 6s.
The Chemistry of Iron and Steel Making. Crown 8vo, cloth extra, 9s.
A Vindication of Phrenology. With Portrait and 43 Illusts. Demy 8vo, cloth extra, 12s. 6d.

Williamson (Mrs. F. H.).—A Child Widow. Post 8vo, bds., 2s.

Wills (C. J.), Novels by.
An Easy-going Fellow. Crown 8vo, cloth, 3s. 6d. | His Dead Past. Crown 8vo, cloth, 6s.

Wilson (Dr. Andrew, F.R.S.E.), Works by.
Chapters on Evolution. With 259 Illustrations. Crown 8vo, cloth extra, 7s. 6d.
Leaves from a Naturalist's Note-Book. Post 8vo, cloth limp, 2s. 6d.
Leisure-Time Studies. With Illustrations. Crown 8vo, cloth extra, 6s.
Studies in Life and Sense. With 36 Illustrations. Crown 8vo, cloth. 3s. 6d.
Common Accidents: How to Treat Them. With Illustrations. Crown 8vo, 1s.; cloth, 1s. 6d.
Glimpses of Nature. With 35 Illustrations. Crown 8vo, cloth extra, 3s. 6d.

Winter (John Strange), Stories by. Post 8vo, illustrated boards, 2s. each; cloth limp, 2s. 6d. each.
Cavalry Life. | Regimental Legends.
† **Cavalry Life and Regimental Legends.** LIBRARY EDITION, set in new type and handsomely bound. Crown 8vo, cloth, 3s. 6d.
A Soldier's Children. With 34 Illustrations by E. G. THOMSON and E. STUART HARDY. Crown 8vo, cloth extra, 3s. 6d.

Wissmann (Hermann von).—My Second Journey through Equatorial Africa. With 92 Illustrations. Demy 8vo, cloth, 16s.

Wood (H. F.), Detective Stories by. Post 8vo, boards, 2s. each.
The Passenger from Scotland Yard. | The Englishman of the Rue Cain.

Woolley (Celia Parker).—Rachel Armstrong; or, Love and Theology. Post 8vo, illustrated boards, 2s.; cloth, 2s. 6d.

Wright (Thomas, F.S.A.), Works by.
Caricature History of the Georges; or, Annals of the House of Hanover. Compiled from Squibs, Broadsides, Window Pictures, Lampoons, and Pictorial Caricatures of the Time. With over 300 Illustrations. Crown 8vo, cloth, 3s. 6d.
History of Caricature and of the Grotesque in Art, Literature, Sculpture, and Painting. Illustrated by F. W. FAIRHOLT, F.S.A. Crown 8vo, cloth, 7s. 6d.

Wynman (Margaret)—My Flirtations. With 13 Illustrations by J. BERNARD PARTRIDGE. Post 8vo, cloth limp, 2s.

Yates (Edmund), Novels by. Post 8vo, illustrated boards, 2s. each.
Land at Last. | The Forlorn Hope. | Castaway.

Zangwill (I.). — Ghetto Tragedies. With Three Illustrations by A. S. BOYD. Fcap. 8vo, cloth, 2s. net.

'ZZ' (Louis Zangwill).—A Nineteenth Century Miracle. Cr. 8vo, cloth, 3s. 6d.

Zola (Emile), Novels by. Crown 8vo, cloth extra, 3s. 6d. each.
The Fortune of the Rougons. Edited by ERNEST A. VIZETELLY.
The Abbe Mouret's Transgression. Edited by ERNEST A. VIZETELLY. [Shortly.
His Excellency (Eugene Rougon). With an Introduction by ERNEST A. VIZETELLY.
The Dram-Shop (L'Assommoir). With Introduction by E. A. VIZETELLY.
The Fat and the Thin. Translated by ERNEST A. VIZETELLY.
Money. Translated by ERNEST A. VIZETELLY.
The Downfall. Translated by E. A. VIZETELLY.
The Dream. Translated by ELIZA CHASE. With Eight Illustrations by JEANNIOT.
Doctor Pascal. Translated by E. A. VIZETELLY. With Portrait of the Author.
Lourdes. Translated by ERNEST A. VIZETELLY.
Rome. Translated by ERNEST A. VIZETELLY.
Paris. Translated by ERNEST A. VIZETELLY.
Fruitfulness (La Fecondite). Translated by E. A. VIZETELLY. [Shortly.

SOME BOOKS CLASSIFIED IN SERIES.
* *For fuller cataloguing, see alphabetical arrangement, pp. 1-26.*

The Mayfair Library. Post 8vo, cloth limp, 2s. 6d. per Volume.
Quips and Quiddities. By W. D. ADAMS.
The Agony Column of 'The Times.'
Melancholy Anatomised: Abridgment of BURTON.
A Journey Round My Room. By X. DE MAISTRE. Translated by HENRY ATTWELL.
Poetical Ingenuities. By W. T. DOBSON.
The Cupboard Papers. By FIN-BEC.
W. S. Gilbert's Plays. Three Series.
Songs of Irish Wit and Humour.
Animals and their Masters. By Sir A HELPS.
Social Pressure. By Sir A. HELPS.
The Autocrat of the Breakfast-Table. By OLIVER WENDELL HOLMES.
Curiosities of Criticism. By H. J. JENNINGS.
Pencil and Palette. By R. KEMPT.
Little Essays: from LAMB'S LETTERS.
Forensic Anecdotes. By JACOB LARWOOD.
Theatrical Anecdotes. By JACOB LARWOOD.
Ourselves. By E. LYNN LINTON.
Witch Stories. By E. LYNN LINTON.
Pastimes and Players. By R. MACGREGOR.
New Paul and Virginia. By W. H. MALLOCK.
The New Republic. By W. H. MALLOCK.
Muses of Mayfair. Edited by H. C. PENNELL.
Thoreau: His Life and Aims. By H. A. PAGE.
Puck on Pegasus. By H. C. PENNELL.
Pegasus Re-saddled. By H. C. PENNELL.
Puniana. By Hon. HUGH ROWLEY.
More Puniana. By Hon. HUGH ROWLEY.
The Philosophy of Handwriting.
By Stream and Sea. By WILLIAM SENIOR.
Leaves from a Naturalist's Note-Book. By Dr. ANDREW WILSON.

The Golden Library. Post 8vo, cloth limp, 2s. per Volume.
Songs for Sailors. By W. C. BENNETT.
Lives of the Necromancers. By W. GODWIN.
The Autocrat of the Breakfast Table. By OLIVER WENDELL HOLMES.
Tale for a Chimney Corner. By LEIGH HUNT.
Scenes of Country Life. By EDWARD JESSE.
La Mort d'Arthur: Selections from MALLORY.
The Poetical Works of Alexander Pope.
Maxims and Reflections of Rochefoucauld.
Diversions of the Echo Club. BAYARD TAYLOR.

Handy Novels. Fcap. 8vo, cloth boards, 1s. 6d. each.
A Lost Soul. By W. L. ALDEN.
Dr. Palliser's Patient. By GRANT ALLEN.
Monte Carlo Stories. By JOAN BARRETT.
Black Spirits and White. By R. A. CRAM.
Seven Sleepers of Ephesus. M. E. COLERIDGE.
Taken from the Enemy. By H. NEWBOLT.
The Old Maid's Sweetheart. By A. ST. AUBYN.
Modest Little Sara. By ALAN ST. AUBYN.

My Library. Printed on laid paper, post 8vo, half-Roxburghe, 2s. 6d. each.
The Journal of Maurice de Guerin.
The Dramatic Essays of Charles Lamb.
Citation and Examination of William Shakspeare. By W. S. LANDOR.
Christie Johnstone. By CHARLES READE.
Peg Woffington. By CHARLES READE.

The Pocket Library. Post 8vo, printed on laid paper and hf.-bd., 2s. each.
Gastronomy. By BRILLAT-SAVARIN.
Robinson Crusoe. Illustrated by G. CRUIKSHANK
Autocrat of the Breakfast Table and The Professor at the Breakfast-Table. By O. W. HOLMES.
Provincial Letters of Blaise Pascal.
Whims and Oddities. By THOMAS HOOD.
Leigh Hunt's Essays. Edited by E. OLLIER.
The Barber's Chair. By DOUGLAS JERROLD.
The Essays of Elia. By CHARLES LAMB.
Anecdotes of the Clergy. By JACOB LARWOOD.
The Epicurean, &c. By THOMAS MOORE.
Plays by RICHARD BRINSLEY SHERIDAN.
Gulliver's Travels, &c. By Dean SWIFT.
Thomson's Seasons. Illustrated.
White's Natural History of Selborne.

Popular Sixpenny Novels. Medium 8vo, 6d. each; cloth, 1s. each.
All Sorts and Conditions of Men. By WALTER BESANT
The Golden Butterfly. By WALTER BESANT and JAMES RICE.
The Deemster. By HALL CAINE.
The Shadow of a Crime. By HALL CAINE.
Antonina. By WILKIE COLLINS.
The Moonstone. By WILKIE COLLINS.
The Woman in White. By WILKIE COLLINS.
The Dead Secret. By WILKIE COLLINS.
Moths. By OUIDA.
Under Two Flags. By OUIDA.
By Proxy. By JAMES PAYN.
Peg Woffington; and Christie Johnstone. By CHARLES READE.
The Cloister and the Hearth. By CHARLES READE.
It is Never Too Late to Mend. By CHARLES READE.
Hard Cash. By CHARLES READE.

CHATTO & WINDUS, Publishers, 111 St. Martin's Lane, London, W.C.

THE PICCADILLY NOVELS.

LIBRARY EDITIONS OF NOVELS, many Illustrated, crown 8vo. cloth extra, 3s. 6d. each.

By Mrs. ALEXANDER.
A Life Interest | Mona's Choice | By Woman's Wit.

By F. M. ALLEN.—Green as Grass.

By GRANT ALLEN.
Philistia. | Babylon. | The Great Taboo.
Strange Stories. | Dumaresq's Daughter.
For Maimie's Sake. | Duchess of Powysland.
In all Shades. | Blood Royal.
The Beckoning Hand. | I. Greet's Masterpiece.
The Devil's Die. | The Scallywag.
This Mortal Coil. | At Market Value.
The Tents of Shem. | Under Sealed Orders.

By M. ANDERSON.—Othello's Occupation.

By EDWIN L. ARNOLD.
Phra the Phœnician. | Constable of St. Nicholas.

By ROBERT BARR.
In a Steamer Chair. | A Woman Intervenes.
From Whose Bourne. | Revenge!

By FRANK BARRETT.
The Woman of the Iron Bracelets.
The Harding Scandal. | A Missing Witness.
Under a Strange Mask.

By 'BELLE.'—Vashti and Esther.

By Sir W. BESANT and J. RICE.
Ready-Money Mortiboy. | By Celia's Arbour.
My Little Girl. | Chaplain of the Fleet.
With Harp and Crown. | The Seamy Side.
This Son of Vulcan. | The Case of Mr. Lucraft.
The Golden Butterfly. | In Trafalgar's Bay.
The Monks of Thelema. | The Ten Years' Tenant.

By Sir WALTER BESANT.
All Sorts & Conditions. | The Holy Rose.
The Captains' Room. | Armorel of Lyonesse.
All in a Garden Fair. | S. Katherine's by Tower
Dorothy Forster. | Verbena Camellia, &c.
Uncle Jack. | The Ivory Gate.
World Went Well Then. | The Rebel Queen.
Children of Gibeon. | Beyond the Dreams of
Herr Paulus. | Avarice.
For Faith and Freedom. | The Master Craftsman.
To Call Her Mine. | The City of Refuge.
The Revolt of Man. | A Fountain Sealed.
The Bell of St. Paul's. | The Charm.

By AMBROSE BIERCE—In Midst of Life.
By PAUL BOURGET.—A Living Lie.
By J. D. BRAYSHAW.—Slum Silhouettes.

By H. A. BRYDEN.
An Exiled Scot.

By ROBERT BUCHANAN.
Shadow of the Sword. | The New Abelard.
A Child of Nature. | Matt. | Rachel Dene
God and the Man. | Master of the Mine.
Martyrdom of Madeline | The Heir of Linne.
Love Me for Ever. | Woman and the Man.
Annan Water. | Red and White Heather.
Foxglove Manor. | Lady Kilpatrick.
ROB. BUCHANAN & HY. MURRAY.
The Charlatan.

By ROBERT W. CHAMBERS.
The King in Yellow.

By J. M. CHAPPLE.—The Minor Chord.
By HALL CAINE.
Shadow of a Crime. | Deemster. | Son of Hagar.
By AUSTIN CLARE.—By Rise of River.
By ANNE COATES.—Rie's Diary.
By MACLAREN COBBAN.
The Red Sultan. | The Burden of Isabel.

By MORT. & FRANCES COLLINS.
Transmigration. | From Midnight to Midnight.
Blacksmith & Scholar. | You Play me False.
The Village Comedy.

By WILKIE COLLINS.
Armadale. | After Dark. | The Moonstone.
No Name. | Antonina | Man and Wife.
Basil. | Hide and Seek. | Poor Miss Finch.
The Dead Secret. | Miss or Mrs.?
Queen of Hearts. | The New Magdalen.
My Miscellanies. | The Frozen Deep.
The Woman in White. | The Two Destinies.

By WILKIE COLLINS—continued.
The Law and the Lady. | 'I Say No.'
The Haunted Hotel. | Little Novels.
The Fallen Leaves. | The Evil Genius.
Jezebel's Daughter. | The Legacy of Cain.
The Black Robe. | A Rogue's Life.
Heart and Science. | Blind Love.

By M. J. COLQUHOUN.
Every Inch a Soldier.

By E. H. COOPER.—Geoffory Hamilton
By V. C. COTES.—Two Girls on a Barge
By C. EGBERT CRADDOCK.
His Vanished Star.

By H. N. CRELLIN.
Romances of the Old Seraglio.

By MATT CRIM.
The Adventures of a Fair Rebel.

By S. R. CROCKETT and others.
Tales of Our Coast.

By B. M. CROKER.
Diana Barrington. | The Real Lady Hilda.
Proper Pride. | Married or Single?
A Family Likeness. | Two Masters.
Pretty Miss Neville. | In the Kingdom of Kerry
A Bird of Passage. | Interference.
'To Let.' | Mr. Jervis. | A Third Person.
Village Tales. | Beyond the Pale.

By W. CYPLES.—Hearts of Gold.
By ALPHONSE DAUDET.
The Evangelist; or, Port Salvation.

By H. COLEMAN DAVIDSON.
Mr. Sadler's Daughters.

By ERASMUS DAWSON.
The Fountain of Youth.

By J. DE MILLE.—A Castle in Spain.
By J. LEITH DERWENT.
Our Lady of Tears. | Circe's Lovers.

By DICK DONOVAN.
Tracked to Doom. | The Mystery of Jamaica.
Man from Manchester. | Terrace.
The Chronicles of Michael Danevitch.
The Records of Vincent Trill.

By RICHARD DOWLING.
Old Corcoran's Money.

By A. CONAN DOYLE
The Firm of Girdlestone.

By S. JEANNETTE DUNCAN.
A Daughter of To-day. | Vernon's Aunt.

By A. EDWARDES.—A Plaster Saint
By G. S. EDWARDS.—Snazelleparilla.

By G. MANVILLE FENN
Commodore Junk. | King of the Castle
The New Mistress. | Master of Ceremonies.
Witness to the Deed. | Eve at the Wheel. &c.
The Tiger Lily. | The Man with a Shadow
The White Virgin. | One Maid's Mischief.
Black Blood. | Story of Antony Grace.
Double Cunning. | This Man's Wife.
A Bag of Diamonds, &c. | In Jeopardy.
A Fluttered Dovecote.

By PERCY FITZGERALD.—Fatal Zero.
By R. E. FRANCILLON.
One by One. | Ropes of Sand.
A Dog and his Shadow. | Jack Doyle's Daughter.
A Real Queen.

By HAROLD FREDERIC.
Seth's Brother's Wife. | The Lawton Girl.

By PAUL GAULOT.—The Red Shirts.
By CHARLES GIBBON.
Robin Gray. | The Golden Shaft.
Loving a Dream. | The Braes of Yarrow.
Of High Degree.

THE PICCADILLY (3/6) NOVELS—continued.

By E. GLANVILLE.
The Lost Heiress. | The Golden Rock.
A Fair Colonist. | Tales from the Veld.
The Fossicker.

By E. J. GOODMAN.
The Fate of Herbert Wayne

By Rev. S. BARING GOULD.
Red Spider. | Eve.

By CECIL GRIFFITH.
Corinthia Marazion.

By SYDNEY GRUNDY.
The Days of his Vanity.

By OWEN HALL.
The Track of a Storm. | Jetsam.

By COSMO HAMILTON.
The Glamour of the Impossible.

By THOMAS HARDY.
Under the Greenwood Tree.

By BRET HARTE.
A Waif of the Plains. | A Protégée of Jack
A Ward of the Golden | Hamlin's.
Gate. | Springs. | Clarence.
A Sappho of Green | Barker's Luck.
Col. Starbottle's Client. | Devil's Ford. [celsior.'
Susy. | Sally Dows. | The Crusade of the 'Ex-
bell-Ringer of Angel's. | Three Partners.
Tales of Trail and Town.

By JULIAN HAWTHORNE.
Garth. | Dust. | Beatrix Randolph.
Ellice Quentin. | David Poindexter's Dis-
Sebastian Strome. | appearance.
Fortune's Fool. | Spectre of Camera.

By Sir A. HELPS.—Ivan de Biron.
By I. HENDERSON.—Agatha Page.

By G. A. HENTY.
Rujub the Juggler. | The Queen's Cup.
Dorothy's Double.

By JOHN HILL. The Common Ancestor.

By TIGHE HOPKINS.
'Twixt Love and Duty. | Nugents of Carriconna.
For Freedom. | The Incomplete Adventurer.
Incomplete Adventurer.

By Mrs. HUNGERFORD.
Lady Verner's Flight. | Nora Creina.
The Red-House Mystery | An Anxious Moment.
The Three Graces. | April's Lady.
Professor's Experiment. | Peter's Wife.
A Point of Conscience. | Lovice.
The Coming of Chloe.

By Mrs. ALFRED HUNT.
The Leaden Casket. | Self-Condemned.
That Other Person. | Mrs. Juliet.

By C. J. CUTCLIFFE HYNE.
Honour of Thieves.

By R. ASHE KING.
A Drawn Game.

By GEORGE LAMBERT.
The President of Boravia.

By EDMOND LEPELLETIER.
Madame Sans-Gene.

By ADAM LILBURN.
A Tragedy in Marble.

By HARRY LINDSAY.
Rhoda Roberts.

By HENRY W. LUCY.—Gideon Fleyce.

By E. LYNN LINTON.
Patricia Kemball. | The Atonement of Leam
Under which Lord? | Dundas.
'My Love!' | Ione. | The World Well Lost.
Paston Carew. | The One Too Many.
Sowing the Wind. | Dulcie Everton.
With a Silken Thread.

By JUSTIN McCARTHY.
A Fair Saxon. | Donna Quixote.
Linley Rochford. | Maid of Athens.
Dear Lady Disdain. | The Comet of a Season.
Camiola. | The Dictator.
Waterdale Neighbours. | Red Diamonds.
My Enemy's Daughter. | The Riddle Ring.
Miss Misanthrope. | The Three Disgraces.

By JUSTIN H. McCARTHY.
A London Legend. | The Royal Christopher.

By GEORGE MACDONALD.
Heather and Snow. | Phantastes.

By PAUL & VICTOR MARGUERITTE
The Disaster

By L. T. MEADE.
A Soldier of Fortune. | The Voice of the
In an Iron Grip. | Charmer.
Dr. Rumsey's Patient.

By LEONARD MERRICK.
This Stage of Fools. | Cynthia.

By BERTRAM MITFORD
The Gun-Runner. | The King's Assegai.
LuckofGerardRidgeley. | Rensh. Fanning'sQuest.

By J. E. MUDDOCK.
Maid Marian and Robin Hood.
Basile the Jester. | Young Lochinvar.

By D. CHRISTIE MURRAY.
A Life's Atonement. | The Way of the World.
Joseph's Coat. | BobMartin's Little Girl.
Coals of Fire. | Time's Revenges.
Old Blazer's Hero. | A Wasted Crime.
Val Strange. | Hearts. | In Direst Peril.
A Model Father. | Mount Despair.
By the Gate of the Sea. | A Capful o' Nails
A Bit of Human Nature. | Tales in Prose & Verse.
First Person Singular. | A Race for Millions.
Cynic Fortune. | This Little World.

By MURRAY and HERMAN.
The Bishops' Bible. | Paul Jones's Alias.
One Traveller Returns.

By HUME NISBET.
'Bail Up!'

By W. E. NORRIS.
Saint Ann's. | Billy Bellew.

By G. OHNET.
A Weird Gift.

By Mrs. OLIPHANT.
The Sorceress.

By OUIDA.
Held in Bondage. | In a Winter City.
Strathmore. | Chandos. | Friendship.
Under Two Flags. | Moths. | Ruffino.
Idalia. | (Gage. | Pipistrello. | Ariadne.
Cecil Castlemaine's | A Village Commune.
Tricotrin. | Puck. | Bimbi. | Wanda.
Folle Farine. | Frescoes. | Othmar.
A Dog of Flanders. | In Maremma.
Pascarel. | Signa. | Syrlin. | Guilderoy.
Princess Napraxine. | Santa Barbara.
Two Wooden Shoes. | Two Offenders.

By MARGARET A. PAUL.
Gentle and Simple.

By JAMES PAYN.
Lost Sir Massingberd. | Under One Roof.
Less Black than We're | Glow-worm Tales
Painted. | The Talk of the Town.
A Confidential Agent. | Holiday Tasks.
A Grape from a Thorn. | For Cash Only.
In Peril and Privation. | The Burnt Million.
The Mystery of Mir- | Sunny Stories.
By Proxy. | [bridge. | A Trying Patient.
The Canon's Ward. | A Modern Dick Whit-
Walter's Word. | tington.
High Spirits.

By WILL PAYNE.
Jerry the Dreamer.

By Mrs. CAMPBELL PRAED.
Outlaw and Lawmaker. | Mrs. Tregaskiss.
Christina Chard. | Nulma.

By E. C. PRICE.
Valentina. | Foreigners. | Mrs. Lancaster's Rival.

By RICHARD PRYCE.
Miss Maxwell's Affections.

By Mrs. J. H. RIDDELL.
Weird Stories.

By AMELIE RIVES.
Barbara Dering. | Meriel.

By F. W. ROBINSON.
The Hands of Justice. | Woman in the Dark.

By HERBERT RUSSELL.
True Blue.

CHATTO & WINDUS, Publishers, 111 St. Martin's Lane, London, W.C.

THE PICCADILLY (3/6) NOVELS—continued.

By CHARLES READE.
Peg Woffington; and Christie Johnstone.
Hard Cash.
Cloister & the Hearth.
Never Too Late to Mend.
The Course of True Love Never Did Run Smooth; and Singleheart and Doubleface.
Autobiography of a Thief; Jack of all Trades; A Hero and a Martyr; and The Wandering Heir.
Griffith Gaunt.
Love Me Little, Love Me Long.
The Double Marriage.
Foul Play.
Put Yourself in His Place.
A Terrible Temptation.
A Simpleton.
A Woman-Hater.
The Jilt, & otherStories; & Good Stories of Man and other Animals.
A Perilous Secret.
Readiana; and Bible Characters.

By W. CLARK RUSSELL.
Round the Galley-Fire.
In the Middle Watch.
On the Fo'k'sle Head.
A Voyage to the Cape.
Book for the Hammock.
Mystery of 'Ocean Star'.
The Romance of Jenny Harlowe.
An Ocean Tragedy.
My Shipmate Louise.
Alone on Wide Wide Sea.
The Phantom Death.
Is He the Man?
Good Ship 'Mohock.'
The Convict Ship.
Heart of Oak.
The Tale of the Ten.
The Last Entry.

By DORA RUSSELL.
A Country Sweetheart. | The Drift of Fate.

By BAYLE ST. JOHN.
A Levantine Family.

By ADELINE SERGEANT.
Dr. Endicott's Experiment.

By GEORGE R. SIMS.
Once Upon a Christmas Time.

By HAWLEY SMART.
Without Love or Licence.
The Master of Rathkelly.
Long Odds.
The Outsider.
Beatrice & Benedick.
A Racing Rubber.

By T. W. SPEIGHT.
A Secret of the Sea.
The Grey Monk.
The Master of Trenance.
The Doom of Siva.
A Minion of the Moon.
The Secret of Wyvern Towers.

By ALAN ST. AUBYN.
A Fellow of Trinity.
The Junior Dean.
Master of St. Benedict's.
To his Own Master.
In Face of the World.
Orchard Damerel.
The Tremlett Diamonds.
Fortune's Gate.

By JOHN STAFFORD.—Doris and I.

By RICCARDO STEPHENS.
The Cruciform Mark.

By R. A. STERNDALE.
The Afghan Knife.

By R. LOUIS STEVENSON.
The Suicide Club.

By BERTHA THOMAS.
Proud Maisie. | The Violin-Player.

By ANTHONY TROLLOPE.
The Way we Live Now.
Frau Frohmann.
Scarborough's Family.
The Land-Leaguers.

By FRANCES E. TROLLOPE.
Like Ships upon the Sea.
Anne Furness.
Mabel's Progress.

By IVAN TURGENIEFF, &c.
Stories from Foreign Novelists.

By MARK TWAIN.
Mark Twain's Choice Works.
Mark Twain's Library of Humour.
The Innocents Abroad.
Roughing It; and The Innocents at Home.
A Tramp Abroad.
The American Claimant.
Adventures Tom Sawyer
Tom Sawyer Abroad.
Tom Sawyer, Detective.
Pudd'nhead Wilson.
The Gilded Age.
Prince and the Pauper.
Life on the Mississippi.
The Adventures of Huckleberry Finn.
A Yankee at the Court of King Arthur.
Stolen White Elephant.
£1,000,000 Bank-note.

By C. C. FRASER-TYTLER.
Mistress Judith.

By SARAH TYTLER.
Buried Diamonds.
The Blackhall Ghosts.
The Macdonald Lass.
The Witch-Wife.
Mrs Carmichael's Goddesses. | Lady Bel..
Rachel Langton.
Sapphira.

By ALLEN UPWARD.
The Queen against Owen | The Prince of Balkistan.

By E. A. VIZETELLY.
The Scorpion: A Romance of Spain.

By FLORENCE WARDEN.
Joan, the Curate.

By CY WARMAN.
The Express Messenger.

By WILLIAM WESTALL.
Her Two Millions.
Two Pinches of Snuff.
Roy of Roy's Court.
Nigel Fortescue.
Birch Dene.
The Blind Musician.
Strange Crimes.
The Phantom City.
A Queer Race.
Ben Clough.
The Old Factory.
Red Ryvington.
Ralph Norbreck's Trust.
Trust-money
Sons of Belial.

By ATHA WESTBURY.
The Shadow of Hilton Fernbrook.

By C. J. WILLS.
An Easy-going Fellow.

By JOHN STRANGE WINTER.
Cavalry Life and Regimental Legends.
A Soldier's Children.

By MARGARET WYNMAN.
My Flirtations.

By E. ZOLA.
The Fortune of the Rougons.
The Abbe Mouret's Transgression.
The Downfall.
The Dream.
Dr. Pascal.
Money.
Lourdes.
The Fat and the Thin.
His Excellency.
The Dram-Shop.
Rome. | Paris.
Fruitfulness.

By 'ZZ.'
A Nineteenth Century Miracle.

CHEAP EDITIONS OF POPULAR NOVELS.

Post 8vo, Illustrated boards, 2s. each.

By ARTEMUS WARD.
Artemus Ward Complete.

By EDMOND ABOUT.
The Fellah.

By HAMILTON AÏDÉ.
Carr of Carrlyon. | Confidences.

By Mrs. ALEXANDER.
Maid, Wife, or Widow?
Blind Fate.
Valerie's Fate.
A Life Interest.
Mona's Choice.
By Woman's Wit.

By GRANT ALLEN.
Philistia. | Babylon.
Strange Stories.
For Maimie's Sake.
In all Shades.
The Beckoning Hand.
The Devil's Die.
The Tents of Shem.
The Great Taboo.
Dumaresq's Daughter.
Duchess of Powysland.
Blood Royal. [piece.
Ivan Greet's Master.
The Scallywag.
This Mortal Coil.
At Market Value.
Under Sealed Orders.

By E. LESTER ARNOLD.
Phra the Phœnician.

By FRANK BARRETT.
Fettered for Life.
Little Lady Linton.
Between Life & Death.
Sin of Olga Zassoulich.
Folly Morrison.
Lieut. Barnabas.
Honest Davie.
A Prodigal's Progress.
Found Guilty.
A Recoiling Vengeance.
For Love and Honour.
John Ford, &c.
Woman of Iron Bracelets
The Harding Scandal.
A Missing Witness.

By SHELSLEY BEAUCHAMP.
Grantley Grange.

By FREDERICK BOYLE.
Camp Notes.
Savage Life.
Chronicles of No man's Land.

CHATTO & WINDUS, Publishers, 111 St. Martin's Lane, London, W.C.

Two-Shilling Novels—continued.

By Sir W. BESANT and J. RICE.
Ready-Money Mortiboy.
My Little Girl.
With Harp and Crown.
This Son of Vulcan.
The Golden Butterfly.
The Monks of Thelema.
By Celia's Arbour.
Chaplain of the Fleet.
The Seamy Side.
The Case of Mr. Lucraft.
In Trafalgar's Bay.
The Ten Years' Tenant.

By Sir WALTER BESANT.
All Sorts and Conditions of Men.
The Captains' Room.
All in a Garden Fair.
Dorothy Forster.
Uncle Jack.
The World Went Very Well Then.
Children of Gibeon.
Herr Paulus.
For Faith and Freedom.
To Call Her Mine.
The Master Craftsman.
The Bell of St. Paul's.
The Holy Rose.
Armorel of Lyonesse.
S. Katherine's by Tower
Verbena Camellia Stephanotis.
The Ivory Gate.
The Rebel Queen.
Beyond the Dreams of Avarice.
The Revolt of Man.
In Deacon's Orders.
The City of Refuge.

By AMBROSE BIERCE.
In the Midst of Life.

BY BRET HARTE.
Californian Stories.
Gabriel Conroy.
Luck of Roaring Camp.
An Heiress of Red Dog.
Flip. | Maruja.
A Phyllis of the Sierras.
A Waif of the Plains.
Ward of Golden Gate.

By ROBERT BUCHANAN.
Shadow of the Sword.
A Child of Nature.
God and the Man.
Love Me for Ever.
Foxglove Manor.
The Master of the Mine.
Annan Water.
The Martyrdom of Madeline.
The New Abelard.
The Heir of Linne.
Woman and the Man.
Rachel Dene. | Matt.
Lady Kilpatrick.

By BUCHANAN and MURRAY.
The Charlatan.

By HALL CAINE.
The Shadow of a Crime. | The Deemster.
A Son of Hagar.

By Commander CAMERON.
The Cruise of the 'Black Prince.'

By HAYDEN CARRUTH
The Adventures of Jones.

By AUSTIN CLARE.
For the Love of a Lass.

By Mrs. ARCHER CLIVE.
Paul Ferroll.
Why Paul Ferroll Killed his Wife.

By MACLAREN COBBAN.
The Cure of Souls. | The Red Sultan.

By C. ALLSTON COLLINS.
The Bar Sinister.

By MORT. & FRANCES COLLINS.
Sweet Anne Page.
Transmigration.
From Midnight to Midnight.
A Fight with Fortune.
Sweet and Twenty.
The Village Comedy.
You Play me False.
Blacksmith and Scholar
Frances.

By WILKIE COLLINS.
Armadale. | After Dark.
No Name.
Antonina.
Basil.
Hide and Seek.
The Dead Secret.
Queen of Hearts.
Miss or Mrs.?
The New Magdalen.
The Frozen Deep.
The Law and the Lady
The Two Destinies.
The Haunted Hotel.
A Rogue's Life.
My Miscellanies.
The Woman in White.
The Moonstone.
Man and Wife.
Poor Miss Finch.
The Fallen Leaves.
Jezebel's Daughter.
The Black Robe.
Heart and Science.
'I Say No!'
The Evil Genius.
Little Novels.
Legacy of Cain.
Blind Love.

By M. J. COLQUHOUN.
Every Inch a Soldier.

By DUTTON COOK.
Leo. | Paul Foster's Daughter.

By C. EGBERT CRADDOCK.
The Prophet of the Great Smoky Mountains.

By MATT CRIM.
The Adventures of a Fair Rebel.

By B. M. CROKER.
Pretty Miss Neville.
Diana Barrington.
'To Let.'
A Bird of Passage.
Proper Pride.
A Family Likeness.
A Third Person.
Village Tales and Jungle Tragedies.
Two Masters.
Mr. Jervis.
The Real Lady Hilda.
Married or Single?
Interference.

By W. CYPLES.
Hearts of Gold.

By ALPHONSE DAUDET.
The Evangelist; or, Port Salvation.

By ERASMUS DAWSON.
The Fountain of Youth.

By JAMES DE MILLE.
A Castle in Spain.

By J. LEITH DERWENT.
Our Lady of Tears. | Circe's Lovers.

By DICK DONOVAN.
The Man-Hunter.
Tracked and Taken.
Caught at Last!
Wanted!
Who Poisoned Hetty Duncan?
Man from Manchester.
A Detective's Triumphs
The Mystery of Jamaica Terrace.
The Chronicles of Michael Danevitch.
In the Grip of the Law.
From Information Received.
Tracked to Doom.
Link by Link
Suspicion Aroused.
Dark Deeds.
Riddles Read.

By Mrs. ANNIE EDWARDES.
A Point of Honour. | Archie Lovell.

By M. BETHAM-EDWARDS.
Felicia. | Kitty.

By EDWARD EGGLESTON.
Roxy.

By G. MANVILLE FENN.
The New Mistress.
Witness to the Deed.
The Tiger Lily.
The White Virgin.

By PERCY FITZGERALD.
Bella Donna.
Never Forgotten.
Polly.
Fatal Zero.
Second Mrs. Tillotson.
Seventy-five Brooke Street.
The Lady of Brantome.

By P. FITZGERALD and others.
Strange Secrets.

By ALBANY DE FONBLANQUE.
Filthy Lucre.

By R. E. FRANCILLON.
Olympia.
One by One.
A Real Queen.
Queen Cophetua.
King or Knave?
Romances of the Law.
Ropes of Sand.
A Dog and his Shadow.

By HAROLD FREDERIC.
Seth's Brother's Wife. | The Lawton Girl.

Prefaced by Sir BARTLE FRERE.
Pandurang Hari.

By EDWARD GARRETT.
The Capel Girls.

By GILBERT GAUL.
A Strange Manuscript.

By CHARLES GIBBON.
Robin Gray.
Fancy Free.
For Lack of Gold.
What will World Say?
In Love and War.
For the King.
In Pastures Green.
Queen of the Meadow.
A Heart's Problem.
The Dead Heart.
In Honour Bound.
Flower of the Forest.
The Braes of Yarrow.
The Golden Shaft.
Of High Degree.
By Mead and Stream.
Loving a Dream.
A Hard Knot.
Heart's Delight.
Blood-Money.

By WILLIAM GILBERT.
Dr. Austin's Guests.
James Duke.
The Wizard of the Mountain

By ERNEST GLANVILLE.
The Lost Heiress. | The Fossicker.
A Fair Colonist.

CHATTO & WINDUS, Publishers, 111 St. Martin's Lane, London, W.C.

TWO-SHILLING NOVELS—continued.

By Rev. S. BARING GOULD.
Red Spider. | Eve.

By HENRY GREVILLE.
A Noble Woman. | Nikanor.

By CECIL GRIFFITH.
Corinthia Marazion.

By SYDNEY GRUNDY.
The Days of his Vanity.

By JOHN HABBERTON.
Brueton's Bayou. | Country Luck.

By ANDREW HALLIDAY.
Every-day Papers.

By THOMAS HARDY.
Under the Greenwood Tree.

By JULIAN HAWTHORNE.
Garth. | Beatrix Randolph.
Ellice Quentin. | Love—or a Name.
Fortune's Fool. | David Poindexter's Disappearance.
Miss Cadogna. |
Sebastian Strome. | The Spectre of the Camera.
Dust. |

By Sir ARTHUR HELPS.
Ivan de Biron.

By G. A. HENTY.
Rujub the Juggler.

By HENRY HERMAN.
A Leading Lady.

By HEADON HILL.
Zambra the Detective.

By JOHN HILL.
Treason Felony.

By Mrs. CASHEL HOEY.
The Lover's Creed.

By Mrs. GEORGE HOOPER.
The House of Raby.

By Mrs. HUNGERFORD.
Maiden all Forlorn. | Lady Verner's Flight.
In Durance Vile. | The Red-House Mystery.
Marvel. | The Three Graces.
A Mental Struggle. | Unsatisfactory Lover.
A Modern Circe. | Lady Patty.
April's Lady. | Nora Creina.
Peter's Wife. | Professor's Experiment.

By Mrs. ALFRED HUNT.
Thornicroft's Model. | Self-Condemned.
That Other Person. | The Leaden Casket.

By WM. JAMESON.
My Dead Self.

By HARRIETT JAY.
The Dark Colleen. | Queen of Connaught.

By MARK KERSHAW.
Colonial Facts and Fictions.

By R. ASHE KING.
A Drawn Game. | Passion's Slave.
'The Wearing of the Green.' | Bell Barry.

By EDMOND LEPELLETIER.
Madame Sans Gene.

By JOHN LEYS.
The Lindsays.

By E. LYNN LINTON.
Patricia Kemball. | The Atonement of Leam Dundas.
The World Well Lost. |
Under which Lord? | Rebel of the Family.
Paston Carew. | Sowing the Wind.
'My Love!' | The One Too Many.
Ione. | Dulcie Everton.
With a Silken Thread. |

By HENRY W. LUCY.
Gideon Fleyce.

By JUSTIN McCARTHY.
Dear Lady Disdain. | Donna Quixote.
Waterdale Neighbours. | Maid of Athens.
My Enemy's Daughter | The Comet of a Season.
A Fair Saxon. | The Dictator.
Linley Rochford. | Red Diamonds.
Miss Misanthrope | The Riddle Ring.
Camiola. |

By HUGH MACCOLL.
Mr. Stranger's Sealed Packet.

By GEORGE MACDONALD.
Heather and Snow.

By AGNES MACDONELL.
Quaker Cousins.

By KATHARINE S. MACQUOID.
The Evil Eye. | Lost Rose.

By W. H. MALLOCK.
A Romance of the Nineteenth Century. | The New Republic.

By J. MASTERMAN.
Half-a-dozen Daughters.

By BRANDER MATTHEWS.
A Secret of the Sea.

By L. T. MEADE.
A Soldier of Fortune.

By LEONARD MERRICK.
The Man who was Good.

By JEAN MIDDLEMASS.
Touch and Go. | Mr. Dorillion.

By Mrs. MOLESWORTH.
Hathercourt Rectory.

By J. E. MUDDOCK.
Stories Weird and Wonderful. | From the Bosom of the Deep.
The Dead Man's Secret. |

By D. CHRISTIE MURRAY.
A Model Father. | A Bit of Human Nature.
Joseph's Coat. | First Person Singular.
Coals of Fire. | Bob Martin's Little Girl.
Val Strange. | Hearts. | Time's Revenges.
Old Blazer's Hero. | A Wasted Crime.
The Way of the World. | In Direst Peril.
Cynic Fortune. | Mount Despair.
A Life's Atonement. | A Capful o' Nails
By the Gate of the Sea. |

By MURRAY and HERMAN.
One Traveller Returns. | The Bishops' Bible.
Paul Jones's Alias. |

By HENRY MURRAY.
A Game of Bluff. | A Song of Sixpence.

By HUME NISBET.
'Bail Up!' | Dr. Bernard St. Vincent.

By W. E. NORRIS.
Saint Ann's. | Billy Bellew

By ALICE O'HANLON.
The Unforeseen. | Chance? or Fate?

By GEORGES OHNET.
Dr. Rameau. | A Weird Gift.
A Last Love. |

By Mrs. OLIPHANT.
Whiteladies. | The Greatest Heiress in England.
The Primrose Path. |

By Mrs. ROBERT O'REILLY.
Phœbe's Fortunes.

By OUIDA.
Held in Bondage. | Two Lit. Wooden Shoes
Strathmore. | Moths.
Chandos. | Bimbi.
Idalia. | Pipistrello.
Under Two Flags. | A Village Commune.
Cecil Castlemaine's Gage | Wanda.
Tricotrin. | Othmar.
Puck. | Frescoes.
Folle Farine. | In Maremma.
A Dog of Flanders. | Guilderoy.
Pascarel. | Ruffino.
Signa. | Syrlin.
Princess Napraxine. | Santa Barbara.
In a Winter City. | Two Offenders.
Ariadne. | Ouida's Wisdom, Wit, and Pathos.
Friendship. |

By MARGARET AGNES PAUL.
Gentle and Simple.

By EDGAR A. POE.
The Mystery of Marie Roget.

By Mrs. CAMPBELL PRAED.
The Romance of a Station.
The Soul of Countess Adrian.
Outlaw and Lawmaker. | Mrs. Tregaskiss.
Christina Chard. |

CHATTO & WINDUS, Publishers, 111 St. Martin's Lane, London, W.C

TWO-SHILLING NOVELS—continued.

By E. C. PRICE.
Valentina. | Mrs. Lancaster's Rival.
The Foreigners. | Gerald.

By RICHARD PRYCE.
Miss Maxwell's Affections.

By JAMES PAYN.
Bentinck's Tutor. | The Talk of the Town.
Murphy's Master. | Holiday Tasks.
A County Family. | A Perfect Treasure.
At Her Mercy. | What He Cost Her.
Cecil's Tryst. | A Confidential Agent.
The Clyffards of Clyffe. | Glow-worm Tales.
The Foster Brothers. | The Burnt Million.
Found Dead. | Sunny Stories.
The Best of Husbands. | Lost Sir Massingberd.
Walter's Word. | A Woman's Vengeance.
Halves. | The Family Scapegrace.
Fallen Fortunes. | Gwendoline's Harvest.
Humorous Stories. | Like Father, Like Son.
£200 Reward. | Married Beneath Him.
A Marine Residence. | Not Wooed, but Won.
Mirk Abbey | Less Black than We're
By Proxy. | Painted.
Under One Roof. | Some Private Views.
High Spirits. | A Grape from a Thorn.
Carlyon's Year. | The Mystery of Mir-
From Exile. | bridge.
For Cash Only. | The Word and the Will.
Kit. | A Prince of the Blood.
The Canon's Ward. | A Trying Patient.

By CHARLES READE.
It is Never Too Late to | A Terrible Temptation.
Mend. | Foul Play.
Christie Johnstone. | The Wandering Heir.
The Double Marriage. | Hard Cash.
Put Yourself in His | Singleheart and Double-
Place | face.
Love Me Little, Love | Good Stories of Man and
Me Long. | other Animals.
The Cloister and the | Peg Woffington.
Hearth. | Griffith Gaunt.
The Course of True | A Perilous Secret.
Love. | A Simpleton.
The Jilt. | Readiana.
The Autobiography of | A Woman-Hater.
a Thief.

By Mrs. J. H. RIDDELL.
Weird Stories. | The Uninhabited House.
Fairy Water. | The Mystery in Palace
Her Mother's Darling. | Gardens.
The Prince of Wales's | The Nun's Curse.
Garden Party. | Idle Tales.

By AMELIE RIVES.
Barbara Dering.

By F. W. ROBINSON.
Women are Strange. | The Woman in the Dark
The Hands of Justice.

By JAMES RUNCIMAN.
Skippers and Shellbacks. | Schools and Scholars.
Grace Balmaign's Sweetheart.

By W. CLARK RUSSELL.
Round the Galley Fire. | An Ocean Tragedy.
On the Fo'k'sle Head. | My Shipmate Louise.
In the Middle Watch. | Alone on Wide Wide Sea.
A Voyage to the Cape. | Good Ship 'Mohock.'
A Book for the Ham- | The Phantom Death.
mock. | Is He the Man?
The Mystery of the | Heart of Oak.
'Ocean Star.' | The Convict Ship.
The Romance of Jenny | The Tale of the Ten.
Harlowe. | The Last Entry.

By DORA RUSSELL.
A Country Sweetheart.

By GEORGE AUGUSTUS SALA.
Gaslight and Daylight.

By GEORGE R. SIMS.
The Ring o' Bells. | Zeph.
Mary Jane's Memoirs. | Memoirs of a Landlady.
Mary Jane Married. | Scenes from the Show.
Tales of To-day. | The 10 Commandments.
Dramas of Life. | Dagonet Abroad.
Tinkletop's Crime. | Rogues and Vagabonds.
My Two Wives.

By ARTHUR SKETCHLEY.
A Match in the Dark.

By HAWLEY SMART.
Without Love or Licence. | The Plunger.
Beatrice and Benedick. | Long Odds.
The Master of Rathkelly.

By T. W. SPEIGHT.
The Mysteries of Heron | Back to Life.
Dyke. | The Loudwater Tragedy
The Golden Hoop. | Burgo's Romance.
Hoodwinked. | Quittance in Full.
By Devious Ways. | A Husband from the S

By ALAN ST. AUBYN.
A Fellow of Trinity. | Orchard Damerel.
The Junior Dean. | In the Face of the Wor
Master of St. Benedict's | The Tremlett Diamon
To His Own Master.

By R. A. STERNDALE.
The Afghan Knife.

By R. LOUIS STEVENSON.
New Arabian Nights.

By BERTHA THOMAS.
Cressida. | The Violin-Player.
Proud Maisie.

By WALTER THORNBURY.
Tales for the Marines. | Old Stories Retold.

By T. ADOLPHUS TROLLOPE.
Diamond Cut Diamond.

By ELEANOR TROLLOPE.
Like Ships upon the | Anne Furness.
Sea. | Mabel's Progress.

By ANTHONY TROLLOPE.
Frau Frohmann. | The Land-Leaguers.
Marion Fay. | The American Senat
Kept in the Dark. | Mr. Scarborough's
John Caldigate. | Family.
The Way We Live Now. | Golden Lion of Granp

By J. T. TROWBRIDGE.
Farnell's Folly.

By IVAN TURGENIEFF, &c.
Stories from Foreign Novelists.

By MARK TWAIN.
A Pleasure Trip on the | Life on the Mississi
Continent. | The Prince and
The Gilded Age. | Pauper.
Huckleberry Finn. | A Yankee at the Co
Mark Twain's Sketches. | of King Arthur.
Tom Sawyer. | The £1,000,000 B
A Tramp Abroad. | Note.
Stolen White Elephant.

By C. C. FRASER-TYTLER.
Mistress Judith.

By SARAH TYTLER.
The Bride's Pass. | The Huguenot Fam
Buried Diamonds. | The Blackhall Gho
St. Mungo's City. | What She Came Thr
Lady Bell. | Beauty and the B
Noblesse Oblige. | Citoyenne Jaquel
Disappeared.

By ALLEN UPWARD.
The Queen against Owen. | Prince of Bal
'God Save the Queen!'

By AARON WATSON and LI' WASSERMANN.
The Marquis of Carabas.

By WILLIAM WESTAL
Trust-Money.

By Mrs. F. H. WILLIAMS
A Child Widow.

By J. S. WINTER.
Cavalry Life. | Regimental Leg

By H. F. WOOD.
The Passenger from Scotland Yard.
The Englishman of the Rue Cain.

By CELIA PARKER WOOL
Rachel Armstrong; or, Love and The

By EDMUND YATES.
The Forlorn Hope. | Castaway.
Land at Last.

By I. ZANGWILL.
Ghetto Tragedies.

www.ingramcontent.com/pod-product-compliance
Lightning Source LLC
Chambersburg PA
CBHW050848300426
44111CB00010B/1176